Ark II

Ark II

SOCIAL RESPONSE TO
ENVIRONMENTAL IMPERATIVES

Dennis C. Pirages
Paul R. Ehrlich

THE VIKING PRESS   NEW YORK

By special arrangement, the paperbound educational
edition of this book is published and distributed by
W. H. Freeman and Company, San Francisco, California, and the
hardbound trade edition is published and distributed by
The Viking Press, Inc., New York, N.Y.

Copyright © 1974 by Dennis Pirages and Paul R. Ehrlich

First published in 1974 by The Viking Press, Inc.
625 Madison Avenue, New York, N.Y. 10022

Published simultaneously in Canada by
The Macmillan Company of Canada Limited

Printed in U.S.A. by The Colonial Press Inc.

Library of Congress Cataloguing in Publication Data
Pirages, Dennis.
    Ark II; social response to environmental imperatives.
    Bibliography: p.
    1. United States—Social conditions—1960–
    2. United States—Economic conditions—1961–
    3. Environmental policy—United States.   4. United
States—Politics and government—1969–
    I.   Ehrlich, Paul R., joint author.   II.   Title.
    HN59.P47 1974   309.1'73'092   73-10555
    ISBN 0-670-13282-9

Prologue

Noah had ample warning from a respected authority to
build his Ark, and he used his time to good advantage.
Skeptics laughed, ridiculed, and drowned—but Noah,
the original prophet of doom, survived.
We too have been warned that a flood of problems
now threatens the persistence of industrial society, but
this time the ark cannot be built out of wood and
caulking. We must ensure our survival by redesigning
the political, economic, and social institutions of
industrial society. If a new institutional ark cannot
be made watertight in time, industrial society will sink,
dragging under prophets of doom
as well as skeptics and critics.

Introduction

Something is happening to the great American dream. Even though large wage increases were won by American workers in the late sixties and early seventies, these increases have been cancelled out by rampant inflation. Wage earners who hold so-called good jobs feel that they may no longer be getting ahead in life and that American society faces a dim and uncertain future. What difference do pay increases make when the costs of housing, food, electricity, and gasoline rise just as rapidly or more rapidly than wages and salaries?

Many people realize that other, seemingly distant, occurrences are having a serious impact on their lives. They know, for example, that economic conditions had so deteriorated by 1971 that a Republican President, supposedly a stalwart defender of the free enterprise system, found it necessary to freeze wages and prices. Even though the freeze was ineffective, the President proclaimed it a success and removed most wage and price controls in 1973. Quite predictably, prices shot up astronomically. Many have also perceived that the "trickle down" theory, which holds that when times are good for business the profits trickle down to the working man, has little validity. In 1972, when the working man was told to forego wage increases in the interest of economic stability, many corporations reported record or near record earnings.

Americans fortunate enough to be able to travel abroad have also been particularly aware of unusual events. They realize, sometimes very acutely, that the once sound dollar, the currency of the world's strongest economy, has been considerably devalued. Airline fares, hotel and restaurant bills, souvenirs, and all the other things for which tourists pay now cost much more than they did in the very recent past. At home, the prices of imported items, ranging from Japanese automobiles to French wines, have been climbing out of sight.

But not all of the problems with the American dream are purely economic. Many people are rightfully confused about recent and not so recent political events. Some lost their sons in Vietnam for a cause that was not a cause against an enemy that was not really an enemy. Although very few people actively seemed to support this intervention in Asian affairs thousands of miles from home, the war ground on for more than a decade. In 1964 millions of Americans, tired of war, voted for what they thought was a peace-loving candidate. Lyndon Johnson spent four years escalating this distant war that was irrelevant to America's pressing problems, and voters—fed up with the Democrat's war—switched allegiances in droves. In 1968 they voted for a Republican candidate with a "secret peace plan." This President then spent another four years fighting the same war.

In the end, the methodical use of American airpower and advanced technology gained a cease-fire and an opportunity to escape from the lengthy embroilment. No one seemed very happy with this dubious kind of victory. The inconsistencies in Vietnam policy and the obvious propaganda that came from the White House drove a deeper wedge between elected officials and the majority of voters. People wondered why the South Vietnamese, who presumably were fighting for their freedom, were unable to beat a greatly outnumbered and outgunned enemy.

Closer to home, the Watergate scandal has shaken what little public confidence in political leaders still existed. It has been difficult for Americans to reconcile burglary, poll-rigging, illegal campaign contributions, and an Attorney General who apparently condoned various crimes, with the textbook image of the American political process. The nagging feeling lingers that this is only the tip of an iceberg that extends down through the political process at all levels.

Many Americans also have become upset and even angered by environmentalists and population experts who are predicting disaster. Much of what is said is remote from daily experience and very hard to believe, but other comments do seem to make sense. Most Americans have always thought that economic growth and improvement were synonymous, although now some of these experts claim that certain types of growth are bad. The Bible admonishes man to be fruitful and multiply, but numerous scientists claim that the planet is overpopulated, that huge famines may occur soon, and that population control is vital to a prosperous future. Scientists also say that pollution is gradually killing people, that a real energy crisis is imminent, that nuclear power plants are potentially dangerous, that pollution may alter climates and lead to crop failures, and that, in general, society is not coping with its most pressing problems.

This nagging discomfort is enhanced by evidence that the environmentalists might be right. Air and water pollution are becoming increasingly evident, as is the press of growing numbers of people. Food prices are skyrocketing, which suggests growing scarcity, and reports of food shortages appear more and more on the evening news and in the press. Furthermore, while Arab leaders threaten to withhold petroleum exports for political purposes, many Americans find their gas tanks already empty and no one able to fill them.

What cuts right to the heart of the American dream is that, because of these and similar problems, it seems likely that life will be tougher, rather than easier, for everyone's children. Most people are just beginning to learn about exponential growth, resource depletion, and environmental deterioration, and they know that these once unfamiliar phrases mean trouble for their offspring. Most Americans are willing to break their backs so that their children will have a chance to get ahead, get a higher education, and enjoy some of the good things in life. That is why it is so difficult to come to terms with prognostications that indicate these dreams may never be realized.

Americans, however, are not a passive people, and many millions have been expressing their numerous discontents at the ballot box, in letters to the editor, and in massive demonstrations that were seldom seen in the United States before the sixties. Many active and concerned citizens are willing to face these problems and want to learn more about them. More important, some have begun looking for solutions.

The environmental crises that confront twentieth-century America are not insoluble, but neither are they problems that can be swept under the rug by simply investing more billions in research and development. They are complex and interlinked problems that have hidden social roots. These roots have been ignored by most people because to admit that they are part of the problem means considering the alteration of institutions, values, and behavior. This is very difficult for most people to do because it usually means shaking cherished beliefs and perhaps completely changing the view of the world that is shared with friends and relatives.

In attempting to outline the complex of socioenvironmental problems and the type of social transformation that will be required to solve them, we are beginning a very difficult task. Ramifications of all these problems surface daily, and no two people can begin to know all the solutions. But we have become convinced that the time has come for people to start searching for comprehensive, rather than piecemeal, solutions. To continue to wait for "more complete understanding" or to commission yet another "detailed study" is to guarantee future disaster. The optimism implicit in such books as *The Greening of America* or *Where the Wasteland Ends* lulls people into a false sense of security while problems continue to mount. Such thinking discourages a rational evaluation of what is taking place in American society and leads to little in the way of concrete programs for change. There are few data to indicate that present industrial society, with all its suicidal tendencies, has begun significantly to transform itself. If anything, decisions made in the last few years have been setbacks for those programs and proposals that could lead society in new directions. Decision makers are daily committing serious errors as they attempt to hold the old system together with patchwork solutions and avoid making any major changes that would affect the nation's numerous vested interests.

We have tried to write a book that is useful on two levels. We believe it is essential to present our case in language that people can understand. Professional jargon only serves to confuse the nonspecialist and to insulate the specialist from possible criticism. We hope that we have succeeded in using language that can be easily understood, because necessary political action requires the support of an electorate that appreciates the dimensions of the crisis that must be faced. On another level, we have tried to make the book useful to those who wish to read further about particular problems by providing notes and a suggested reading list at the end of the book.

After analyzing available data we have concluded that it is time for humanity to begin risking some mistakes to move toward a more promising and viable way of life. To sit and wait, hoping that old values will see us through, is to make the biggest of all mistakes. We know that the old system will not hold together much longer, but fear may cause us to bury our heads rather than face an uncertain future. In the spirit of looking for social solutions that may help meet impending crises, we make no apologies for any of the suggestions that appear in *Ark II* that might prove to have unforeseen ramifications. We are not wed to any of them and think that they have been made in the best of all causes—initiating a debate on social alternatives. We are certainly ready to change our minds when our suppositions are shown to be wrong or when more viable alternatives to our proposals are suggested. But we feel that to hesitate to make judgments and suggest solutions in fear of error is to abdicate responsibility in the face of certain crisis. In short, we can stand the heat and have no intention of leaving the kitchen.

Contents

Ark II

1

The Rising Tide

Today nearly four billion people inhabit the Earth. Human activities currently move much larger quantities of iron, phosphorus, nitrogen, mercury, copper, zinc, and many other minerals than do the rivers of the planet, inject more sulphur into the atmosphere than do volcanoes, and add twenty times more oil to the oceans than do natural processes. *Homo sapiens*, just one of perhaps five million species of animals, has set up agricultural systems within which approximately one-twentieth of net global photosynthetic productivity occurs. By any number of measures mankind has become a truly global force.

It is tempting to say, "So what?" Why should we worry if mankind increases, multiplies, and exercises dominion over the planet? Is not the damage inflicted on the natural systems of the Earth a small price to pay for progress? Unfortunately, the larger the scale of human activities, the larger will be the consequences of human mistakes. To date there is little evidence that mankind is intellectually, emotionally, or socially prepared to assume stewardship of the Earth's ecosystems or to guarantee the continuation of their essential functions through the planning and restraint that are needed to avoid serious mistakes.*

At this very moment, mankind is escalating its attack on the life-support systems of the Earth at a rate that will double human impact every fourteen years. Thus, if the level of environmental deterioration observed at the time of the first Earth Day in 1970 was symptomatic of the stressing of ecological systems halfway to their breaking point, ecological collapse and the end of industrial civilization could occur in 1984. More optimistically, if those systems can take fifty times the level of abuse of 1970 before they disintegrate, then industrial society cannot survive past the middle of the next century, unless the rate of human attack on nature is slowed. The social, economic, and political changes required to slow that assault are the subject of *Ark II*.

Three Revolutions

There have been three "revolutions" that have profoundly changed mankind's relationship to the ecological systems of the Earth. The first, the cultural revolution, occurred more than one million years ago. It began with the development of language and a complex culture. By banding together on the hunt, dividing labor, perfecting diverse tools, and cooperating for defense, primitive man slowly gained a more secure life and the human death rate began to fall. There were no dramatic increases in numbers at this early stage. But even though the population increased very slowly at first, the trend that culminated in the extremely rapid growth rates of the twentieth century had already begun.

---

* A *population* is a group of individuals of the same *species* of organism; for instance, a flock of ducks or all the human beings on Manhattan Island. All the individuals of different populations living in a given area make up a *community*. A community, taken together with its nonliving physical environment, is known as an ecological system, or an *ecosystem*. The term ecosystem is used when it seems desirable to emphasize the physical, chemical, and biological relationships that bind communities and their physical surroundings into more or less functional units. The ecosystems of the world are linked by movements of energy, chemicals, and organisms into one global ecosystem, often called the *biosphere* or *ecosphere*. Photosynthesis is the process by which green plants convert the sun's energy into chemical energy that can be utilized by themselves and by animals. The rate of energy thus converted is the *gross productivity* of an area; primary productivity minus the energy used by the plants for their own activities is *net productivity*. Productivity may also be viewed in terms of the organic matter created in a given area over a given period.

At the beginning of the second great transformation—the agricultural revolution, which began around 8000 B.C.—there were only about five million people on the Earth. The agricultural revolution occurred when some groups gave up their nomadic hunting and food-gathering way of life, settled down, and began to farm the land. This development accelerated population growth by leading to a further decrease in the death rate. More dependable food supplies reduced the incidence of starvation and encouraged the construction of permanent settlements. There was no longer a need to travel continuously in search of food, since most nutritional needs could be met by farming. Moreover, fields and stock required constant care, effectively keeping the farmer in one place. Permanence made it possible to store food against times of shortage, further reducing the chance of starvation.

Eventually, agricultural productivity reached the point where it could support a substantial nonfarming population. Cities were thus born of the abundance created by more efficient agricultural methods. Within the newly formed cities, further divisions of labor took place, and mankind started down the path toward today's interdependent and complex industrial societies. Following the agricultural revolution, the human population increased well past the point where a return to primitive hunting and gathering was possible. Most societies quickly became dependent on agricultural technology instead of the productivity of natural ecosystems. Man had not only learned to coax greater productivity from Nature, he had also become dependent on manipulations of the ecosphere to ensure continued survival. Those manipulations began to change the character of the Earth's ecological systems, thus commencing a trend toward widespread environmental deterioration.

Approximately 10,000 years elapsed between the beginning of the agricultural revolution and the industrial revolution that succeeded it. The world population grew at a modest rate during most of this period, and by 1650 it was approximately 500 million. Then the pattern of rapidly accelerating population growth began. At first it apparently was a response to improvements in agriculture and sanitation and perhaps to the opening of the western hemisphere to colonization. Then a third great revolution in the history of humanity began to transform the world. In only 200 years the population doubled. By 1850 there were one billion human beings, and human activities began to assume global ecological importance. The population doubled again within only eighty years; by 1930 the Earth was inhabited by two billion people, and the population was growing at such a rate that it would double in only forty-five years.

The industrial revolution was made possible by the harnessing of inanimate energy and the making of further refinements in the division of labor. Production and consumption of goods accelerated at a very rapid rate. Before the industrial revolution, goods were produced on a small scale, mainly by the energy of man and beast. But the harnessing of inanimate energy—first wind and water and later fossil fuels—made available the vast quantities of energy necessary to sustain large-scale production in an increasingly complex industrial society. Factory production provided material abundance unknown to previous generations. Superficially, it appeared to render mankind less and less dependent on Nature, although the industrial revolution generated side effects that have only recently been recognized as threatening to mankind's future.

Each of the three major revolutions did much more than simply augment human numbers and make life a little easier. The new technologies that evolved in each of the major revolutionary steps increased the human impact on the natural systems that are crucial to mankind's survival. Greater numbers, *combined with* these new technologies, have led to increasing deterioration of the environment. Today, the industrial countries are entirely dependent on an industrial technology that is largely sustained by burning fossil fuels and utilizing other nonrenewable resources. Advocates of uncontrolled growth would increase this dependence even further. Yet rapidly increasing consumption of fossil fuels and minerals cannot long continue, given the Earth's limited supplies of these resources.

Perhaps most important, during each of the three revolutions, changes in material abundance, as well as changes in technology and methods of production, have been reflected in shifts in the norms, values, and institutions that shape and guide human behavior. This is why, when viewed as a whole, each of these periods of transition can properly be called a revolution. The cultural revolution led to the early development of shared values and social institutions. The agricultural revolution led to the formation of cities and urban cultures. The industrial revolution accelerated urban growth and led to a society that is increasingly dependent on technological development and oriented toward production of material goods.

During the extended course of each of these major transformations, the motivation for change came from the obvious advantages of new technologies. Those early human groups that best learned to cooperate and communicate soon surpassed other bands. Those peoples who learned to domesticate plants and animals had a higher survival rate than those still dependent on hunting and gathering for their food. Those societies that initially embraced the industrial revolution did so because of obvious material benefits. Industrial cultures have easily displaced primitive hunting and gathering tribes and subsistence agricultural societies. During each major shift, institutions, norms, and values were altered in response to new discoveries that led to obvious improvements in the standard of living.

The Assault on Nature

Humanity's first great impact on Nature resulted from the mastery of fire. By accident at first, and later by design in hunting and gathering, fire was used as a tool. As a consequence, substantial areas of the Earth were converted into "anthropogenic savannahs" (areas made nearly treeless by man) by repeated burnings. The technology of preagricultural people not only altered plant life, it also had a substantial impact on animal life. Part of this impact was an indirect result of the change in the nature of the plant life available for foraging. The rest of the impact, however, was more direct. A currently held theory is that, as primitive hunters became more skilled at the chase, numerous species of animals were hunted to extinction. This trend has continued, and today the survival of many animals is jeopardized by direct and indirect human impact on natural ecosystems.

It was, however, only with the beginning of the agricultural revolution that mankind moved along a path leading directly to today's serious threats to the ecosphere. Agriculture, by its very nature, replaces complex ecosystems with simple ones, a process that leads to ecological instability. When land is cleared for farming, woodlands and grasslands containing many types of plants and animals are removed and are replaced by crops, often with the result that only one kind of plant is grown over large areas. Thus, enormously complex tropical rain forests are replaced by patches of corn or taro, or species-rich prairies are plowed under to make way for thousands of square miles of wheat.

In the early days of agriculture, the simple ecosystems created by men were minuscule in comparison with the complex natural systems of the Earth. People made mistakes in their farming practices and caused small-scale disasters, but these were usually local in nature. A classic example is the conversion of the lush Tigris and Euphrates valleys into desert as a result of faulty irrigation practices. As the spread of agriculture permitted world population to increase, more and more land was planted in crops, and human dependence on technology and the deterioration of the environment increased apace. Interactions became more complex, and destructive activities often reinforced each other. Agriculture permitted dense urban populations, but urbanization required wood for building and fuel. Centers of civilization soon became conspicuous by their deforestation. Loss of forests changed climates, altered watersheds, and increased erosion of soil by wind and water.

Any monoculture (an extensive stand of a single kind of plant, such as a large cornfield) is highly vulnerable to plant pests and diseases. An insect pest, a fungus, or a strain of bacteria can sweep through the entire plant population. A classic example of the destruction of a monoculture is provided by one of the first "green revolutions," the introduction of the potato in Ireland in the eighteenth century. The potato provided the basis for an increase in the Irish population from three million people living in poverty to some eight million living in poverty. In such situations, expansion of the food supply does not necessarily lead to an increase in the standard of living; more frequently, it leads only to more people living at the same low standards. A major disaster occurred in Ireland between 1845 and 1848. The unstable potato ecosystem collapsed and with it the artificially augmented carrying capacity of the land. A fungal blight invaded the fields and destroyed most of the crop, producing one of history's great disasters—the Irish Potato Famine. In a four-year period, some 1.5 million people starved to death, 2.0 million emigrated, and millions of others underwent great suffering through semi-starvation.

Today much more is known about plant diseases than was known in the middle of the last century, and agricultural geneticists are continually attempting to breed new crop strains that are resistant to various plagues and pests. The organisms that attack the crops, however, are also continually evolving new strains that can attack previously resistant crops. In 1970, for example, a major portion of the corn crop in the United States was threatened by a blight that successfully attacked the most commonly planted hybrid strains.

The great productivity of twentieth-century agriculture has been based on the successes of plant breeding technology, but these genetic triumphs have not been accomplished without cost. High yields have often been bought at the price of lowered resistance to pests and diseases. Most important, the success of the new strains poses a subtle but lethal danger, stemming from the unwillingness of "economic men" to plant strains that produce less than the best crop yield. Farmers eagerly embrace new high-yielding varieties, and as a result larger and larger areas are being planted in single strains. Monocultures are thus becoming both more extensive and more uniform. Traditional strains of staple crops are rapidly being wiped out. Today only traces of the former diversity can be found where even a few decades ago numerous ancient strains of wheat and barley were commonly grown.

The loss of genetic diversity from which new strains can be developed represents the ultimate simplification of agricultural ecosystems. It is also a one-way street. Once genetic diversity is lost, there is no practical way to restore it. Genetic diversity is essential if plant breeders are to stay ahead in the "evolutionary race" that they are running with the insects and microorganisms that attack crops. Unless crop diversity is preserved, mankind might soon be plagued by sporadic destruction of sizable portions of its agricultural harvest, and the resultant famines could make the Irish Potato Famine pale by comparison. Eventually the ability to practice high-yield agriculture would be lost; and high-yield agriculture is vital to the maintenance of a human population numbering in the billions. High-yield agriculture exists and can be maintained *only* by the work of plant geneticists, and their *essential* raw material is genetic variability in plants.

Much has been made of the contemporary green revolution, a transformation of traditional agriculture in the less-developed countries (LDCs) by the introduction of high-yielding "miracle" grains. The green revolution represents just one more escalation of the destructive human impact on the life-sustaining ecological systems of the planet. Not only is it built around a limited array of miracle strains, with the attendant problems of monocultures and genetic simplification, but it is heavily dependent on irrigation, fertilizers, and pesticides for optimal production. All of these contribute to environmental deterioration.

Irrigation almost always leads to deterioration of the soil through salting, silting, or both. Phosphate and nitrogen fertilizers run off the fields to which they are applied and into streams and lakes. The streams and lakes then undergo processes of eutrophication (overfertilization). Huge blooms of algae occur and then decay. The decay process consumes oxygen, reducing the capacity of affected bodies of water to support many valuable food fish and to assimilate wastes. There is also, of necessity, a heavy investment in pesticides, since the new strains of plants often show little resistance to insects and other pest organisms. Like fertilizers, pesticides do not stay in one place. Persistent ones move into the soil and streams, are absorbed by various organisms, and become concentrated in food chains. Human beings are exposed to them directly and consume them with their food. Pesticides represent complex and as yet little understood threats both to human health and to the health of natural ecosystems on which humanity depends for its existence.

Aside from direct agricultural assaults on the ecosphere, other technological developments have been slowly chipping away at the resource base
that sustains industrial societies. Throughout history, civilization has required
an increasing amount of energy. Before industrialization, the vast majority of
energy used was derived from current solar "income." Like all other animals,
human beings were and are ultimately dependent on the life processes of green
plants to convert solar energy into the chemical energy of proteins, fats, and
carbohydrates. People then obtain this energy second hand by eating plants,
or third or fourth hand by eating animals. Thus, in a sense, all flesh is grass.

In the centuries before the industrial revolution, mankind utilized some
solar energy from sources other than food. Energy was extracted from the
wind, which was derived from the uneven heating of the Earth's surface by
the sun. Energy was also extracted from running water, a source that traces to
the evaporation and transport of water from oceans to highlands by the action
of sun and wind. And, of course, wood was burned, a process releasing as heat
solar energy that the trees had converted to chemical energy.

With the advent of industrialization, people increasingly turned from solar
income to a stock of solar "savings" for their energy. Only a small proportion
of plant life has ever been directly utilized by animals. Much early vegetation
containing stored solar energy sank into swamps where conditions prevented
decay. Over millions of years this material became highly compressed and was
converted to fossil fuels, such as peat, coal, oil, and natural gas. Eventually, the
secrets of these fossil fuels buried in the Earth were discovered. Released from
near total dependence on current solar inputs for energy, civilization began
supporting its activities by using ever larger quantities of previously stored
solar energy through the burning of fossil fuels. This fossil fuel subsidy is
essential to today's complex civilization, providing food, warmth, transportation, and conveniences for many times the number of people that could
exist within the energy constraints of naturally occurring ecosystems. But this
stored energy, which once seemed so abundant, is being rapidly depleted by
the demands of modern industry.

In contrast to yesterday's primitive farmers, today's agribusiness complex
depends on the ability of each farmer to till hundreds of times the amount of
land that could have been cleared and tilled by his predecessors. Modern
agriculture is, like the rest of industrial society, heavily dependent on an
energy subsidy from fossil fuel. Ecologist H. T. Odum expressed this idea as
follows: "Industrial man no longer eats potatoes made from solar energy;
now he eats potatoes partly made of oil." The number of calories of fossil fuel
energy needed to grow an acre of wheat in Kansas is of the same order of
magnitude as the number of food calories in an acre of wheat when harvested.

Only a small part of industrial society's consumption of stored energy, however, is directly related to agriculture. Modern industry runs on fossil fuels. World energy consumption currently increases by 5 to 6 percent each year. To keep up with its growing energy demand, the United States is planning to lay pipelines across hundreds of miles of arctic tundra to Alaska's North Slope to obtain oil. This is to be done at the risk of destroying delicate ecosystems in the process. The presently estimated yield from the field thus tapped would supply projected United States demand around the year 2000 for approximately two years. Millions of acres of land are also being strip-mined each year to obtain coal that is shipped in "unit" freight trains halfway across the United States to meet demands for electricity. Usually, deeply scarred, wasted land is all that is left behind. Huge tankers are being constructed to transport petroleum from distant wells to industrial markets. Serious petroleum pollution in the middle of the Atlantic Ocean is now well documented. In 1972 the Japanese launched a 477,000-ton ship, long enough to accommodate four football fields laid end-to-end. A collision involving a ship of this size could create an unprecedented oil pollution disaster.

Many other kinds of pollution contribute to the deterioration of the environment. They often have direct effects on human health as well as the health of ecosystems. Heat, vehicular and factory exhausts, waste chemicals, fertilizers, pesticides, and sewage from human beings and livestock are poured by industrial society into natural disposal systems, many of which are already taxed to near capacity.

One of the greatest difficulties in mobilizing public concern over environmental threats is the time lag that may occur between the release of a pollutant and the eventual damage that it does. By the time people read about something in the newspapers, the damage has already been done. Consider the case of the synthetic pesticide DDT, which was first used extensively at the end of World War II. Initially, all results seemed positive; disease-carrying insects and pests that attacked crops were killed. Then it gradually became apparent that DDT was a mixed blessing. Beneficial organisms such as honeybees and pest-eating insects were also being killed. Eventually it became clear that the entire fabric of nature was being changed by DDT.

It was not until then that books and newspapers began to publicize the problem. The most serious effects seem to have occurred in the oceans, to which DDT is transported by rivers and through the atmosphere. The pesticide becomes concentrated as it is passed along the food chains of marine ecological systems. Small fishes that eat tiny marine plants (phytoplankton) might end up with as much as ten times the concentration in their tissues as the plants. Larger fishes might have ten times the concentration found in the little fishes they eat, and the concentration in birds or sea mammals that eat the big fishes might again be ten times larger. One part per million (ppm) of DDT in phytoplankton could become 1,000 ppm in a bald eagle or seal.

High concentrations of DDT have caused massive reproductive failures in fish-eating birds, such as the brown pelican, the bald eagle, and the peregrine falcon. Populations of large fishes such as tuna may be the next to suffer. An even greater threat is that posed to the phytoplankton; DDT has been shown to reduce the rate of photosynthesis in these tiny plants. Some kinds of phytoplankton are more susceptible to DDT than others, and this might cause the relative abundance of the different species to change. Those that are more resistant to DDT would flourish at the expense of others. It is possible that, given enough DDT in the oceans, previously rare kinds of phytoplankton could become dominant. These newly dominant kinds, in turn, might not support the food chains that lead to harvestable populations of many fishes eaten by man. Thus, use of DDT on land to produce more food may well contribute to a substantial loss of food from the sea.

The critical point is that in many similar situations we do not now understand the problems that hasty acceptance of new technologies is creating for the future. It will be some time, for example, before the ultimate effect of DDT and related persistent pesticides will be known. Chemicals sprayed on inland farms require time to work their way to the sea, and it is still later that the maximum impact is felt at the top of ocean food chains. Therefore, even if use of DDT and its relatives were totally banned today, there might still be a future ecocatastrophe in the oceans that was traceable to those pesticides.

There is another important time lag connected with DDT. Every human being consumes it every day with his or her food, and Americans now average ten to twelve parts per million in their body fat. It is well known that DDT does not have a very high acute toxicity; most people can eat fairly large amounts of it without immediately becoming ill. But there is no evidence whatsoever that long-term exposure to DDT is without its hazards; indeed, there is some disturbing evidence of serious chronic effects. Carrying a load of DDT in the body for thirty years may greatly increase a person's chances of dying of cirrhosis of the liver, liver cancer, encephalomalacia (softening of the brain), or hypertension. DDT might already have cut years off the life expectancy of every American born since 1945. The facts will not be known until these young people reach middle age.

Widespread mercury pollution received a great deal of public attention in the early seventies. In many ways, this problem is similar to that of DDT pollution. Mercury can also be concentrated by ecological systems, and its most severe effects may be felt long after its initial release into the environment. Mercury can exist in many chemical forms. The form in which it is usually discharged in industrial wastes is relatively inert, and it was long thought to remain harmless on the bottoms of lakes and rivers. However, especially in polluted water, microorganisms convert this relatively inert form to methyl mercury, which is concentrated by living organisms. When consumed in food, methyl mercury may build up gradually in the brain and produce serious nervous disorders, insanity, and even death long after initial exposure. At present there is not enough information to evaluate accurately the threat of either DDT or mercury, but what *is* known about chronic mercury poisoning is hardly reassuring. Enough of the inert form now exists in many bodies of water to provide a source of methyl mercury pollution for periods ranging from a decade to a century, even if no additional mercury were released into the environment. But the American public had no advance warning; neither did the hundreds of Japanese who were killed or disabled by the mercury from industrial wastes dumped into Minimata Bay. New technologies, spurred by economic needs, can significantly alter the environment in ways deleterious to human beings before society is aware of the problem.

DDT and mercury are two of the many environmental poisons that may be concentrated by biological systems and that may produce serious disease after long exposure to low dosages, thus causing difficulties many years after their release. These difficulties may include, in addition to direct chronic or acute poisoning of people, derangements of ecosystems. Chlorinated hydrocarbons other than DDT, lead, and various radioactive substances are suspected of displaying similar behavior. Serious as direct threats to mankind may seem, however, the threats to ecosystems may well ultimately prove more lethal. Mankind is completely dependent on the stability of ecosystems for continuity in food supply, for maintenance of the quality of the atmosphere, and for biological degradation of wastes. Large disturbances in either the species composition or the size of individual populations within a local ecosystem have, in the past, often led to famine among human populations. An example is the collapse of the Irish potato monoculture, in which a dramatic decline of the once-dominant species (the potato) was brought about by the invasion of that simple ecosystem by another species (a fungus).

Over the centuries, mankind has steadily increased both the amount of land under cultivation and the amount of energy expended per acre. Today, the impact of human agriculture on natural ecosystems—already great—is amplified through the use of synthetic organic pesticides and inorganic nitrogen fertilizers. The far-flung simplifying effects of agriculture are reinforced by such additional assaults on natural complexity as urban sprawl, highway systems, and the release of industrial toxicants. In the aggregate, present human activities represent an assault on the ecosphere that is unprecedented in the history of the Earth. Every species or strain that is decimated or driven to extinction represents a step toward ecosystem instability. Mankind is now tinkering with the systems on which the carrying capacity of the planet for human life is dependent. This is being done in ignorance of the details of the operation of these systems and with utter disregard for the destabilizing consequences of random removal of their components. Aldo Leopold pointed out twenty years ago that "To keep every cog and wheel is the first precaution of intelligent tinkering."

Exponential Growth

A key to a further understanding of the growing pressures on the ecosphere lies in the meaning and manifestations of exponential growth. Most of us have grown up in a world where we perceive change occurring in a *linear* fashion. Things grow linearly when they increase by a constant amount over a constant period. A building that is being erected at the rate of one floor each week is growing linearly, as is a salary that is increasing by $200 each year, or a crop whose production is increasing by 50,000 tons annually. *Linear growth* is expressed as *amount* of increase per unit of time.

Exponential growth, on the other hand, is expressed as *percentage* of increase per unit of time. An exponentially growing quantity increases by a constant percentage of the whole during any given period. A familiar example of exponential growth is a bank savings account; interest on the money in the account is compounded. One hundred dollars might earn interest at the rate of 7 percent compounded annually. In the first year, $100 will earn interest amounting to $7.00. In the second year, the same rate of interest is paid on $107, and the interest totals $7.49. In the third year, interest is paid on $114.49, and so on. An exponentially increasing quantity grows much more rapidly than an equivalent quantity growing linearly. In exponential growth situations, each new increment produces additional increments; this is true for populations as well as for savings accounts. One hundred dollars left in a bank for 100 years to increase at the linear rate of $7.00 yearly will add $700 in value over that period. Over the same period, $100, the interest on which is growing at a rate of 7 percent continuously compounded, will have grown to more than $100,000.

As a rule of thumb, the length of time that is required for an exponentially increasing quantity to double is the percentage yearly increase divided into 70. Thus, at a rate of 7 percent a year, $100 will double in a decade. Numbers grow very large very rapidly with repeated doublings. For example, a clever child can trick friends by offering them an unbeatable deal in flipping coins. The stakes are simple. The child offers to flip the coin and give his opponent $1 for every correct call. All he wants in return is one penny for his own first correct call, two pennies for his second correct call, four pennies for his third, and so on. In the beginning it seems as if the opponent will win out. But, with his reward doubling for every victory, the smart child outgains his opponent after only eight victories. His fifteenth victory is worth $163.84. Such are the implications of exponential growth.

Looking at exponential growth from a different perspective can lead to frightening conclusions. At the beginning of this chapter, it was mentioned that the human impact on the ecosphere appears to be growing exponentially at the rate of 5 percent per annum and thus to be doubling approximately every fourteen years. This very short doubling time is legitimate cause for alarm even though the absolute magnitude of present environmental damage cannot be specified precisely. For example, if civilization should turn out to be four times further from environmental collapse than present estimates indicate, this difference would amount to only a 28-year reprieve.

The world's population is now almost 4 billion and is increasing at a rate of approximately 2 percent each year. The net rate of population growth therefore is 80 million people annually. If this rate continues, the population will double every 35 years. World industrial output has been increasing at the rate of 7 percent each year, a rate that doubles it in only 10 years. Given current rates of exponential growth, within only one lifetime 4 times as many people will be producing and consuming 128 times as much industrial output as at present. Needless to say, current exponential growth rates are unlikely to persist for even one lifetime.

Recent rapid doublings of the human population are the result of lowered death rates. A new abundance has been partly responsible for lengthening the average life span, but industrial technology has also led to biomedical advances that, by the beginning of this century, were effectively preserving lives. Early success in "death control," however, was not accompanied by similar efforts in birth control. The latest and greatest surge in population growth began immediately after World War II, and the world is still feeling its effects. Antibiotics and DDT (to control malaria-carrying mosquitos) spread from the industrial countries to the rest of the world, and death rates plummeted. Birth rates, however, have remained near the high levels appropriate to a primitive society in which a large proportion of babies and young children can be expected to die. In some areas birth rates now exceed death rates to such an extent that the population could grow sixteenfold in a single century. This situation currently prevails in tropical South America, where, in 1972, 40 persons were born for every 1,000 persons in the population, while only 10 per 1,000 were dying. The resulting 3 percent annual growth rate, if continued, would double the population every 24 years and quadruple it in only 48 years.

Many sociologists and demographers claim that a "demographic transition" (a supposedly inevitable decline in birth rates following industrialization) will take care of future population problems. It is true that in most industrially advanced countries the old norms and values that encouraged large families have lost favor. Rates of population growth in industrial countries, therefore, are much lower than those in nonindustrial countries. Population growth rates fluctuate from year to year with changing socioeconomic conditions. During the period 1963–1970, populations increased at an annual rate of 1.1 percent in the United States, 1.1 percent in the Soviet Union, 0.9 percent in France, 0.5 percent in the United Kingdom, 0.8 percent in Sweden, 1.0 percent in West Germany, and 1.1 percent in Japan. Even these relatively slow rates of increase, however, mean population doublings every 56 to 140 years. No nation since the industrial revolution has yet maintained a replacement-sized family (an average of approximately 2.1 children) for even a generation, and of course *none has reached zero population growth*. More important, in many areas of the world there can be no demographic transition sparked by industrialization for decades to come; some areas perhaps will never experience such a transition.

The birth rate in a population is a function not only of the number of children that each woman has, but also of the proportion of women of child-bearing age in the population. Even if every couple in the world decided to have only two children, there would still be an inevitable increase in population (assuming no change in death rates) because of the present superabundance of young people. If every couple in the United States miraculously limited itself to a replacement-sized family from 1975 on and if net immigration were ended, the population still would not stop growing until approximately 2040. At that time, there would be approximately 280 million Americans, some 70 million more than today.

The consequences of exponential growth in the world population are very clear in outline. The population is already too large to be comfortably supported on Earth for a long period, and population-doubling times are now alarmingly short. The present world population of approximately four billion may be much too large to be supported *permanently* at any level of affluence. If the world's available food were equitably distributed, everyone would live a life of malnutrition. Of course, there are gross inequities in distribution, and the "haves" seem little inclined to help the "have-nots." No socially acceptable program of birth control will be able to stop world population growth before the population has reached at least twice its present size. Even stopping growth when the population numbers ten to twelve billion would require something akin to a demographic miracle. In 1970 Bernard Berelson of the Population Council summarized the situation concisely: "If the replacement-sized family is realized for the world as a whole by the end of this century—itself an unlikely event—the world's population will then be sixty percent larger or about 5.8 billion, and due to the resulting age structure will not stop growing until near the end of the [twenty-first] century, at which time it will be about 8.2 billion, or about 225 percent the present size. If replacement is achieved in the developed world by 2000 and in the developing world by 2040, then the world's population will stabilize at nearly 15.5 billion about a century hence, or well over four times the present size."

Rising Expectations

This crisis of numbers is exacerbated by a worldwide revolution of rising expectations. Materialism has become a universal religion. Continued increases in production of artifacts are regarded as a necessity by almost everyone. People believe that their lives will be materially more comfortable than their parents' lives were, that humanity will continue to increase its dominion over Nature, and that technology will continue to produce solutions to the problems it helps create. Indeed, from this widely accepted point of view, it would seem that the entire sweep of evolution had as a goal the propelling of mankind toward some golden destiny characterized by conspicuous consumption. Perhaps the next in the flood of man-as-ape books should be entitled, *The Ape with Chutzpah*. A human being is a creature still very much dependent on natural ecosystems for survival, but society acts as though the human race can repeal the laws of Nature.

The result of attempting to meet these rising expectations, of course, would be an enormous intensification of human impact on the ecosphere and a correspondingly accelerated rate of environmental deterioration. Each person in an industrial society consumes many times more than his or her counterpart consumed in preindustrial settings. The average American uses twenty-two times more energy annually than does the average citizen of China and damages the environment roughly fiftyfold more than a citizen of India. The six percent of the world's population that lives in the United States now consumes approximately one-third of the world's annual production of resources, and this disproportionate consumption appears likely to *increase.*

The ideas of progress that are currently held in the industrial world, especially in the United States, are founded on the assumption that it is better to make more, bigger, and faster things. Thus, the automobile is taken to be progress over the horse or the bicycle, even though the environmental costs of its operation are much higher. In aviation there has been a steady progression of larger and faster passenger-carrying aircraft, beginning with the relatively small, propeller-driven DC-3 and culminating in the gigantic 400-passenger 747. Not content to provide travel at a speed of only 600 mph, the aircraft industry is now building supersonic transports that will cut jet travel time between the United States and Europe in half at the expense of much greater fuel consumption and the risk of possible irreparable damage to the ozone layer of the upper atmosphere, which protects life from lethal ultraviolet radiation.

The historical movement in long-distance transport from train to bus and from auto to airplane is similarly defined as progress. From an ecological point of view, however, each step has represented regression in that each is less efficient in using energy. Trains average approximately 150 passenger miles per gallon of fuel, buses approximately 115, and personal automobiles only approximately 30. These figures vary, of course, according to passenger load factors. Air travel is the most environmentally expensive method of moving from place to place, yielding an average return of only 21 passenger miles per gallon of fuel. Although it clearly would be difficult to reverse the trend toward more air transportation, it is a mistake to define increasing fuel consumption as progress. Indeed, it is doubtful that the transportation revolution has substantially increased the quality of life as measured by personal happiness. When all the social, resource, and environmental costs of autos and airplanes are accounted for, the world may realize that progress should have stopped with bicycles, trains, trams, and sailing ships.

In less-developed areas of the world, progress still is measured by the extent to which the basic human needs for food, clothing, and shelter are met, whereas in affluent nations, "needs" are manufactured by advertising in the mass media. If unfulfilled, these needs can create almost as much human misery as is created by unmet needs for food and shelter. Continued desire for progress, therefore, exerts pressure on planetary resources in two fundamentally different ways. In less-developed areas, legitimate demands arise from the basic human needs of the rapidly increasing numbers of the poor, whereas much of the demand from industrialized areas arises from the artificially created needs of the increasing numbers of the affluent.

Thus, the greatest pressure on planetary resources in the near future will come from societies in which the population is growing slowly. This is a result of exorbitant demands on the Earth's resource reserves being made by highly industrialized countries. For example, between 1957 and 1967, per capita steel consumption increased by 41 percent in India but only by 12 percent in the United States. However, the actual per capita amount of steel used yearly rose from 4.2 to 13.0 kilograms in India and from 568 to 634 kilograms in the United States. While each Indian was supported by consumption of 9 additional kilograms of steel per year at the end of that decade, each American was supported by 66 extra kilograms. The total annual steel consumption in India in 1967 was less than 7 million metric tons, whereas the much smaller population of the United States was consuming more than 126 million metric tons. Thus, even though India's population was growing twice as fast as that of the United States during that decade and the per capita *rate* of consumption was increasing much more rapidly, the impact of Indian consumption on the world's stock of iron ore remained minuscule in comparison. The same is true for other developing countries.

The total impact of the human population on the ecosphere is the product of the size of the population multiplied by the average impact of each individual. One important factor in this relationship is often overlooked, however. Individual impact also varies with population density. Two thousand people each burning one cord of wood per month from a forest ought to have twice the total impact of 1,000 people each burning one cord per month. But the calculation is not that simple. If, for instance, these people were supplied by a small forest, natural growth might easily replace 1,000 cords a month, but the cutting of 2,000 cords per month might gradually destroy the forest. Thus, the impact *per individual* might be very much greater if there were 2,000 people extracting wood from the forest than if there were only 1,000.

Initially, there can be environmental economies of scale as population density grows. A well-organized small city might have less environmental impact than a somewhat smaller population living in a series of scattered villages. In most industrial societies, however, growing numbers and increasing complexity have led to environmental diseconomies of scale. In a crowded society with an increasingly complex division of labor and many distribution problems, each additional individual adds a disproportionate burden to the environment. The population of New York City, for example, is incredibly expensive to maintain. In fact, a substantial amount of economic activity around the world is devoted simply to meeting the demand of this city for energy, raw materials, and food. Forty smaller cities with the same aggregate population might have a smaller total impact on the environment. In most of the industrialized world, increasing population now produces, at least from the environmental point of view, far more diseconomies than economies of scale. *Even without the inevitable increases in per capita consumption of food or material goods,* a simple increase in population density will cause increased *per capita* impact.

In the less-developed nations, population growth will also cause increased *per capita* impact because of the relationship between population density and demands on agriculture. Increasing pressures on available land and the resultant additional inputs of energy and fertilizers mean that each individual will have a much greater environmental impact. Moreover, the general deterioration of the agricultural land in less-developed countries has already added greatly to the haze and dust in the atmosphere and thus to the potential for significant changes in global weather patterns. Such changes in climate and weather patterns can be expected to have disastrous effects on agriculture wherever they occur.

Physical Limits to Growth

Although conventional wisdom would have us believe otherwise, there are limits to the number of people that can be sustained comfortably on Earth. Some environmentalists think that the optimal population was exceeded many years ago. Others think that it might theoretically be possible to support several times the current number. Whatever the limits, one thing is clear: Rare is the individual today who lives what he considers to be a satisfying life. Most human beings struggle to survive; obtaining food, clothing, and shelter from the elements is their primary concern. Until an adequate life can be guaranteed to the millions in the less-developed countries and to the poor in the developed countries, it seems pointless to spend time calculating what the theoretical maximum future population size might be. Given current technological achievements and environmental constraints, the human population is already too large. Furthermore, given even the most optimistic estimates about future population growth, the projected population for the Earth in the year 2000 is much too large to be sustained at any presently acceptable standard of comfort.

One of the primary constraints on continued population growth is the availability of food. Although a few industrial nations can be characterized as obese societies, beset with problems of overconsumption, they stand in sharp contrast with the rest of the world. Enough calories for many times the present population of the Earth could easily be obtained by planting larger areas with sugar cane and sugar beets (which produce a very high yield of calories per acre), but a person cannot live on calories alone. Shortage of high-quality protein—protein of optimal composition for human nutrition —is the most serious nutritional problem. High-quality protein is found mostly in animal foods—meat, fish, poultry, eggs, and dairy products. Unfortunately, high-quality protein is expensive both ecologically and economically, and there is no simple way of greatly increasing the supply. Georg Borgstrom, Professor of Food Science at Michigan State University, summarizes the nutritional situation as follows: "If all the food in the world were equally distributed and each human received identical quantities we would all be malnourished. . . . The world as a global household knows of no surpluses, merely enormous deficits. Yet, there is in the well-fed nations a great deal of nonsensical talk about abundance."

There is, of course, no global rationing or system of equitable food distribution. Starvation and severe malnutrition are a problem for a small part of the population of North America and Western Europe, and the hungry, being out of sight in ghettos and rural areas, are easily ignored. Similarly, in these rich countries, little thought is given to the plight of the starving in foreign lands. They also are out of sight and easily ignored. Members of the affluent minority of the world's population continue to appropriate high-quality protein for themselves, their farm animals, and their pets. Partly as a result of this maldistribution, today at least "one billion people suffer from overt hunger or clear-cut starvation." French agricultural experts René Dumont and Bernard Rosier estimate that 10–20 million people die annually from hunger and starvation-related diseases, that 300–500 million people get insufficient calories, and that 1.6 billion, nearly half the world's population, suffer from protein deficiency.

The amount of food that can be grown on the planet is limited by several factors, the most important being available land and available water. Population pressures have already driven mankind to farm all the world's high-quality agricultural land. Recent studies indicate that, if the most optimistic figures are accepted, there are 3.2 billion hectares (approximately 8 billion acres) of potentially farmable land. Of this land, the best, amounting to some 43 percent, is already being cultivated. The remaining untilled land is marginal. Much of it lies where the climate is either too hot or too cold much of the year, or it is too far removed from the water that is essential to agricultural production. Unfarmed land must receive a great deal of investment and attention before it can be used. Typically, it must be cleared, fertilized, and usually irrigated. In recent years, the average cost for opening land in the most promising unsettled areas has been approximately $1,150 per hectare ($460 per acre), and the cost will increase, especially as less desirable land is pressed into service. Given present rates of population growth and foreseeable agricultural technologies, all the *potentially* arable land in the world will have to be in use shortly after the year 2000 if food needs are to be met by increasing the amount of land under cultivation.

Other problems arise from using this potentially arable land aside from the initial costs of preparing it for agriculture. Much of it lies beyond the reach of present transportation networks, so further investment is needed to link this land with centers of population. In addition, vast new irrigation projects must be undertaken at very high cost; and there may not be enough fresh water to do the job. Then the newly opened areas will suffer from all of the salting and silting problems that beset heavily irrigated lands. Finally, this marginal land is not nearly as productive and dependable as land presently being cultivated. In the Soviet Union, for example, Nikita Khrushchev opened up large tracts of such land on the Eastern Frontier in the late fifties and early sixties. After some initial successes, poor weather set in and there were repeated crop failures. The land eventually deteriorated, and dust bowls, similar to those found in Oklahoma and Texas during the Depression, were created.

Throughout the world there was only a very small increase in per capita food production during the sixties, and most of this food went to people in the already well-fed nations. In the less-developed world, per capita food production remained essentially unchanged. The developed regions of the world experienced a 10 percent increase in food production per capita, led by Western Europe and the Soviet Union, where the average increases were 13 and 18 percent, respectively. In Asia and Latin America, however, production barely kept up with population growth, and the 1960 level of hunger still persisted in 1970. Food production per capita actually dropped 6 percent in Africa (Table 1.1). It is often overlooked that the "successes" in maintaining

Table 1.1 Index Numbers of Per Capita Food Production, by Regions of the World (1952–1956 = 100)

Region	1948–52	1954	1955	1956	1957	1958	1959	1960	1961	1962	1963	1964	1965	1966	1967	1968	1969	1970
Developed regions	92	98	101	104	102	107	108	110	109	112	113	114	114	119	121	124	121	121
Western Europe	86	101	101	101	104	105	107	112	111	117	118	118	117	119	126	128	127	126
Eastern Europe and U.S.S.R.	87	96	103	111	112	121	121	120	122	123	117	126	127	141	141	146	140	142
North America	100	97	99	100	93	98	98	98	96	98	102	99	99	99	101	101	99	97
Oceania	99	98	101	100	94	107	106	107	107	110	112	113	106	116	108	123	120	116
Other developed countries (Israel, Japan, and South Africa)	86	98	109	107	110	111	111	112	115	121	121	122	121	124	142	141	139	137
Developing regions	94	100	100	102	102	103	104	105	105	106	106	106	104	102	104	104	105	105
Latin America	97	100	100	102	102	105	102	101	104	104	103	102	104	100	102	99	100	100
Near East (excl. Israel)	91	98	98	104	106	106	107	106	103	109	109	109	108	108	109	111	110	107
Far East (excl. Japan)	95	100	101	103	101	102	104	106	107	106	106	106	103	101	103	105	107	108
Africa (excl. South Africa)	95	101	99	101	99	100	101	105	97	102	103	103	102	100	100	100	99	99
World	93	99	101	103	101	105	106	106	106	108	108	108	107	109	110	112	110	109

per capita levels of food production in much of the less-developed world meant that many hundreds of millions *more* people were living in misery in 1970 than in 1960, since the populations of the poor nations increased by more than half a billion people during that decade.

Even the celebrated green revolution promises little in the way of a long-term remedy to the food problem. Agricultural optimists' predictions of cornucopia have not been fulfilled. As early as 1948, *Time* magazine was reporting agriculturalists' claims that the world could be well fed by 1960. But there are hundreds of millions more hungry people in the world today than there were then. Today, the media are still filled with plans for feeding more people—from nuclear-agro-industrial complexes to whale farms. Most of these schemes for producing more food have been developed by technological optimists who have little appreciation of the social problems inherent in implementing them or of the ecological trade-offs involved. When such schemes are closely examined, they usually are found wanting, and, to date, concrete results of such projects have not even approximated predictions.

During the last few years, proponents of the green revolution have been proclaiming the great impact that miracle strains of wheat and rice were having on world hunger. For the most part, impressive results have been restricted to areas in the less-developed countries where conditions for these strains are ideal and where governments have concentrated enormous effort. The impact on *world* agricultural production as a whole has been slight. In addition, early increases in food production in the green-revolution areas of Southeast Asia were aided by unusually good weather. At the same time, the People's Republic of China had high productivity, and they had no miracle grains. Many optimistic predictions of agricultural "self-sufficiency" were made for these and other countries after several record harvests during good years in the late sixties. By 1973, difficulties with the green revolution and a return of poor weather again produced increasing hunger and food riots in India. The Soviet Union, Indonesia, the Philippines, China, and sub-Saharan Africa also experienced severe agricultural difficulties, and the outlook for human nutrition in the mid-seventies is bleak indeed.

Although the social and ecological problems accompanying the green revolution are legion, there must be a continued substantial investment in increasing crop yields. Every human being has a great stake in the development of new, *ecologically sound* technologies for increasing agricultural production. This must be done merely to keep pace with population growth. Until population growth subsides, any foreseeable green revolution is unlikely to have a significant effect on the important task of improving nutrition throughout the world.

Both opening new land and the green revolution are heavily dependent on large quantities of water. Production of a pound of grain requires from 60 to 225 gallons of water, and production of a pound of meat can require anywhere from 2,500 to 6,000 gallons. Industry also requires water; approximately 100,000 gallons are needed to manufacture one automobile. It has been estimated that the United States will consume 247 billion gallons of water per day by the year 2000 and will require another 447 billion gallons of water per day to carry off and dilute wastes. The present dependable flow of surface water in the United States is between 100 and 125 billion gallons per day, and this flow can only be maintained by impressive engineering feats. As the shortage of water grows, urban water imperialists can be expected to spread their water-catching nets into previously untouched natural reserves to sustain overly dense concentrations of population. Towing icebergs from the Antarctic to bring water to Los Angeles has been suggested, but even such (literally) far-fetched schemes will not provide permanent relief from the unpleasant consequences of continued growth in demand.

Water shortages are also being felt in the less-developed areas of the world, which lack the technology and capital necessary to carry out elaborate technological schemes. These countries are destined to be forever drilling new wells as the old ones are pumped dry to satisfy the demand for irrigation water for the green revolution. Underground water, like fossil fuels, often represents the accumulation of hundreds of thousands of years of rainfall. In many areas water is being removed from the ground faster than it can be replaced. This water must be considered a nonrenewable resource. Just as with minerals and petroleum, it will be necessary to go farther and deeper to find enough water, and eventually expensive large-scale desalinization will have to be undertaken. Economic and environmental costs of obtaining and processing this water, however, may eventually become prohibitive.

There are other barriers to maintaining an adequate food supply for the expanding human population. Looking to the apparently boundless reaches of the ocean, some optimists claim that food from the sea will solve the problem of world hunger. Unfortunately, this food-from-the-sea myth has long been known to be a "red herring"—a comforting distraction that keeps people from facing the grim realities of the world food problem.

Only a small percentage of the world's total food calories are obtained from the sea, but a substantial fraction of the world's high-quality protein is marine in origin. Almost 15 percent of all animal protein used for human consumption comes from the sea, and fish are an especially critical part of the diet of people in many less-developed countries. Fish are also important to the nutrition of resource-poor Japan and some other industrial countries.

Obviously, it is essential to maintain and even to increase protein yields from the sea if mankind is to weather the crucial decades ahead. From 1950 to 1968, the production of world fisheries increased enough every year to stay well ahead of population growth and to maintain a steady increase in per capita yields. In 1969, however, this trend was reversed. The reported yield dropped from 57.5 million metric tons to 56.0 million metric tons. In 1970 there was another increase to 62 million metric tons, but preliminary figures for 1971 indicated another drop. The Peruvian anchoveta fishery, which alone has yielded as much as 12 million metric tons annually, was in deep trouble in 1972–1973. In 1973 the catch was less than 3 million metric tons. Declines in fish catches have occured even though Peru, the Soviet Union, Japan, and the Scandinavian countries have been using ever more sophisticated fishing equipment to locate and harvest the crop, including fine-meshed nets that do not permit young fish to escape and perpetuate the stock.

It is interesting to consider what would happen if the world's population were to continue to double every thirty-five years. Marine biologists have spent a great deal of time and effort measuring the supposedly immeasurable fishery resources of the sea. Most estimate that, under optimal conditions, a maximum of 100 million metric tons of fish can be extracted from the ocean annually. Other, more optimistic biologists consider this estimate a bit low and claim that it might be possible to harvest 200 million metric tons annually. If each person's share of the yield of fisheries in the year 2005 is to be maintained at the 1970 level, some 140 million metric tons of fish will have to be harvested—twice the 1970 total harvest. Note that this figure is considerably higher than the 100 million metric ton maximum sustainable yield that many experts predict. Even if the more optimistic marine biologists are correct and the ultimate yield can be stretched to 200 million metric tons, the *per capita* yield will begin to drop around the year 2025. The Earth's population will have doubled again by 2040, so that by then twice the yield obtained in the year 2005 will be needed. If population growth continues at its present rate, mankind can count on a reduced per capita yield from the sea within 50 years, even if the most optimistic projections are correct. Obviously, this will put pressure on already overextended terrestrial agricultural resources.

In fact, humanity will need sound planning and a great deal of luck if *any* significant proportion of protein is to continue to come from the sea, even over the next few decades. The theoretical maximums can only be reached under optimal conditions. One immediate priority is to restrict "overfishing" and to ensure that only surplus fish are harvested, thus leaving appropriate breeding stocks to maintain an adequate supply for future years. To date, governments have been notoriously lax in regulating the ocean commons, and all fishing nations are currently locked in a fiercely competitive race to harvest the most fish, regardless of the long-term consequences.

Moreover, if the maximum sustainable yield is to be extracted from the seas, the quality of the oceanic environment must be maintained. The present trend, however, is in the opposite direction. Oceanic ecosystems are in grave jeopardy from an enormous influx of pollutants and from widespread destruction of estuaries that are critical to the production of many kinds of fish. More than 95 percent of the yield of fisheries comes from waters close to shore, precisely those waters that are most polluted. In 1973, for example, the United States National Oceanic and Atmospheric Administration (NOAA) reported that oceanic pollution was far more widespread than previously expected. They estimated that contamination by oil and bits of plastic covered 50 percent of a survey area off the east coast of the United States, 80 percent of the Caribbean, and 90 percent of the area around the Bahama Islands. Both deterioration of the marine environment and overfishing have certainly influenced the recent fluctuations in harvests. It is quite reasonable to expect a decline or even a collapse of the yield of fisheries in the near future, rather than a continued climb toward theoretical maximums.

Food is not the only factor that can potentially limit growth. Industrial societies need energy and essential mineral resources such as iron, copper, and phosphate rock. Factories, offices, and apartment buildings cannot now be built without steel or aluminum for the structure, copper for electrical wiring, and copper, lead, or petroleum-based plastic tubing for plumbing. Automobiles, trains, trucks, and planes cannot now run without petroleum. Power plants cannot produce electricity without coal, petroleum, natural gas, or, in some cases, uranium. High-yield agricultural systems require fertilizers. Demand for all these resources is increasing exponentially along with growth of population and industry. Unfortunately, readily accessible supplies of some of them are very limited.

Although the annual rate of increase in demand for each mineral varies, projections indicate an average increase of 4 to 5 percent for the foreseeable future. If this rate of growth continues, by the first years of the twenty-first century, total mineral demand will be more than four times that now being met. Petroleum consumption is projected to double every eighteen years, with an average annual increase in consumption of approximately 3.9 percent.

The seriousness of the depletion of nonrenewable resources and the present prospects for some key resources are shown in Table 1.2, which is based on recent evaluations of future needs and estimates of available supplies. The

Table 1.2   *Estimates of Year of Depletion for Key Minerals*

Mineral	(1) Constant Consumption Levels	(2) Exponentially Increasing Consumption	(3) With 5X Known Reserves
Aluminum	2070 A.D.	2001 A.D.	2025 A.D.
Copper	2006 A.D.	1991 A.D.	2018 A.D.
Iron	2210 A.D.	2063 A.D.	2143 A.D.
Lead	1996 A.D.	1991 A.D.	2034 A.D.
Manganese	2067 A.D.	2016 A.D.	2064 A.D.
Mercury	1983 A.D.	1983 A.D.	2011 A.D.
Nickel	2120 A.D.	2023 A.D.	2066 A.D.
Tungsten	2010 A.D.	1998 A.D.	2042 A.D.
Zinc	1993 A.D.	1988 A.D.	2020 A.D.
Petroleum	2001 A.D.	1990 A.D.	2020 A.D.
Natural gas	2008 A.D.	1992 A.D.	2019 A.D.

"constant consumption levels" column (1) estimates the year that these resources will become critically scarce if current levels of consumption continue and no new reserves are discovered. The estimates in the "exponentially increasing consumption" column (2) assume that there will be no increase in known reserves and are predicated on exponential growth in consumption at the average rate projected by the United States Bureau of Mines.

It seems likely, however, that at least some additional rich reserves of each mineral will be found. Therefore, the most important dates are those found in column (3) because they make generous allowance for the discovery of new resources. These estimates of stock depletion assume that exponential growth in resource consumption will continue as in column (2) and that five times the present known resource reserves will be discovered in the near future. Even under these optimistic assumptions, aluminum supplies will be placed under stress by the year 2025, mercury by the year 2011, and petroleum by the year 2020.

It is important to emphasize that, even though figures are frequently projected suggesting that resources will "run out," this, in fact, will never happen. Our grandchildren will not pick up their morning papers on July 30, 2020, and read a headline that the last drop of petroleum was sucked from the ground the day before. Market mechanisms will drive up the prices of scarce resources before supplies are exhausted, although not necessarily a long time before a serious situation develops. The use of more expensive substitutes will then become economically feasible.

Prices of those resources for which no adequate substitutes can be found may become astronomical, and most people will then have to do without. In the absence of new social policies ensuring equitable distribution, only the very wealthy will be able to afford luxuries dependent on such materials. Commodities such as petroleum will certainly be rationed by direct or indirect methods as scarcities develop. The price of electricity is already rising rapidly, and it is questionable whether future spiraling demands can be met at any price. Already, many sections of the United States have been plagued by summer and winter "brown-outs" caused by poor planning and excessive demand. Steel, aluminum, copper, lead, and lumber will become more expensive or even unavailable, thus driving up the cost of constructing new buildings.

The problem, then, is one of increasing costs. As readily accessible and rich deposits of nonrenewable resources are pumped or mined out, mankind will be forced to turn to less desirable and less accessible sources. It will be necessary to transport fuels and minerals further and to dig deeper to get them. Oil wells in the United States are currently being drilled to depths of 25,000 to 30,000 feet at a unit cost of $4 million, and only one-third of those drilled actually produce petroleum. Extensive research and development efforts will be necessary to provide new technologies for extracting and transporting minerals and fuels. For example, techniques must be developed for processing oil high in sulphur content so that it may be used without creating additional pollution. Using oil shales as a source of petroleum presents another agenda of problems because present methods of extraction, production, and waste disposal entail unacceptable environmental costs.

Scarcity of some nonrenewable resources is already having an impact. The price of lead has risen 300 percent in the last thirty years. The cost of mercury has risen 500 percent in the last twenty years. In late 1972, the Federal Power Commission approved a 25 percent increase in the field of natural gas. Experts predict the price of fuels will increase between 33 and 100 percent, depending on the type of fuel, by 1980. These higher prices will inevitably be translated into higher consumer costs and have an important and inequitable impact on society.

The most frightening aspect of these data is that there is no hope of avoiding serious economic and technological crises if population and industry continue to grow at present rates into the twenty-first century. This is especially true if large-scale preparations are not begun immediately. It is sobering to consider the tremendous effort that will be necessary to locate reserves of resources amounting to more than five times those presently known. Much of the land surface of the planet has already been scoured in a search for profit, and most of the readily accessible resources are already in the process of being extracted.

The natural gas negotiations between the United States and the Soviet Union that were conducted in the early seventies demonstrate the economic and political costs that must be paid in an effort to meet escalating demand for energy resources. The United States apparently would be willing to go all the way to Siberia to find enough natural gas to meet projected needs. As a result of the proposed gas deal, the United States would eventually pay the Soviet Union at least $53 billion for natural gas. Little matter that only a few years ago there was a virtual embargo on dealings with the Soviet Union. Demands for energy make strange bedfellows!

Aside from the problem of increased costs, such massive projects bring up the consideration of maintaining a continuous supply. The United States could become heavily dependent on this source of natural gas as well as other, equally risky sources of energy materials. It is poor politics to put the nation's energy future in the hands of a country that is *in theory* bent on destroying the capitalist system. In 1973, for example, even a friendly nation, Canada, moved to control exports of petroleum to the United States. The longer the lines of supply are stretched, the more likely it is that a serious natural or political disaster will interrupt the flow of resources. Suppose that the pipelines are destroyed, or that gas tankers, containing liquid gas cooled to $-253°$ Fahrenheit, prove to be unreliable and explode at sea. What would be the likely impact of such disasters on a nation that has become heavily dependent on this gas for heating and industrial uses? Even more important, what would be the probable result of political action taken by the Organization of Petroleum Exporting Countries (OPEC) in denying oil to selected customers?

The Search for Solutions

Technological optimists hope that the energy crisis can be met by lessening dependence on oil and coal and by developing fission and then fusion reactors. Fission reactors depend on splitting nuclei of certain forms (isotopes) of uranium and plutonium in "chain reactions" to produce heat that is converted to electricity. A few such reactors are already on line. But these "burner" reactors do not provide an ultimate answer, as rich deposits of suitable uranium are also in limited supply. Scientists have been attempting to perfect second-generation nuclear reactors called breeders, which will produce more usable fuel than they consume by converting presently unusable, but fairly abundant forms of uranium and thorium into forms of uranium and plutonium that will support chain reactions. Unfortunately, the breeder reactors are very complicated and potentially more accident-prone than the first-generation burners.

Part of the answer to the energy crisis would seem to be the development of fusion reactors that will produce heat, and then electricity, by the fusing of nuclei of light atoms (certain isotopes of hydrogen and helium). This is the same process that fuels the fires of the sun and creates the explosion of a hydrogen bomb. Fusion technology is still in the developmental stage, however, and sober assessments concede that, barring an incredibly expensive crash program, it will be at least fifty years before fusion reactors can meet a significant percentage of the power demand in the United States. The rest of the world, particularly the less-developed countries, cannot expect to develop fusion reactors and will have to buy this technology from the industrial nations.

Increased utilization of solar power is another new technology that can help fill the energy gap. At present, electricity derived from solar energy is much more expensive than electricity obtained by conventional means; but solar energy for home and water heating and air conditioning could become economically competitive with other energy sources used in many parts of the world. Existing technology for harnessing solar energy will take time to deploy, and development of new technologies for harnessing the sun in other ways will take time and a great deal of money. These tasks should be begun at once, however, as the sun is environmentally by far the best energy source available to mankind.

Several caveats should be made about the potential of fission and fusion technologies to solve future environmental problems. First, developing them is certain to be very costly. Even though the fuel required for fusion is abundant and very cheap, the capital costs of the power plants will be very high. Second, fission technologies are presently very dangerous and are likely to remain so for some time. There will always be significant risk attending the use of radioactive materials. We still have little experience with nuclear power, and as many plants are brought on line, a great deal of luck will be needed to avoid a major disaster. The common idea that a runaway fission reactor will create an explosion on the scale of an A-bomb is incorrect, but there is a very real danger of smaller explosions caused by various types of failure. Such explosions could rupture containment vessels and release far more radioactivity than would an atomic bomb. Millions of people could be killed and as much as 10 percent of the United States could be rendered uninhabitable by such a mishap. No disaster of this scale has yet occurred, but some have been narrowly averted.

An accident in the transportation of radioactive materials is even more likely. Fuel for reactor cores must be shipped to the reactor site, and waste materials must be carried away and stored. When only a few reactors are functioning, appropriate security procedures can make a major accident unlikely. If a large number of such facilities exist, however, the chances of accidents increase. If the great number of reactors needed to fill projected electricity demand in the year 2000 are built, trains and trucks loaded with deadly radioactive materials will constantly be crisscrossing the United States. It should be kept in mind that our experience with such dangerous cargoes has not been very satisfactory. Trains carrying powerful bombs destined for Southeast Asia blew up twice in 1973, causing great damage for miles around. Had these trains been passing through populated areas, a major disaster would have taken place. When asked about security precautions for such dangerous loads, railroad officials claimed that no special procedures are taken with weapons trains. That being so, possibly the radioactive cargoes of the future will also receive no special safety attention. Under those circumstances, it would be only a matter of time until an accident released deadly radioactivity and caused a disaster of gigantic proportions.

Storage of radioactive materials also presents a serious problem. Waste products must be isolated from the environment for thousands of years to allow their deadly qualities to diminish. Thus far, however, no solution has been found for the storage problem, although many wild schemes, such as shooting wastes into the sun in rockets or burying them in ice in the Antarctic, have been proposed. The safety record of the Atomic Energy Commission has been far from good in this respect, as highly radioactive wastes stored in Hanford, Washington, have repeatedly escaped from the storage tanks and seeped into the ground beneath them.

In addition, there is an ever-present possibility that plutonium needed to fuel reactors could fall into the hands of some demented individuals. Possessing this basic component of nuclear weapons, they would need little more than a college-level knowledge of physics and a good machine shop to construct a weapon adequate to devastate a major American city. This may sound implausible, but it is not in an era when hijackers have threatened lives for millions of dollars in ransom and have even threatened to crash a jet airliner into the Atomic Energy Commission facility at Oak Ridge, Tennessee. An entire reactor has been seized by guerrillas in Argentina, although, fortunately, it was still under construction at the time. A junior high school student recently presented a nuclear bomb threat to a Florida city. The threat was made credible by a working diagram of the weapon, although it was intended as a prank. Today the Atomic Energy Commission can account for only 99 percent of the plutonium supposedly under its control. If control is no better by the year 2000, this missing 1 percent could provide enough plutonium to make 1,000 Nagasaki-size nuclear weapons.

Finally, nuclear technologies are designed to produce electricity. Although the United States is moving toward an electrified society, three-quarters of the nation's energy consumption today is still used for purposes other than generating electricity. If present forms of energy utilization are to be supplanted by nuclear power, another major investment in new technologies will be needed so that electricity can do most of the work now done by other forms of energy. For instance, electric vehicles will have to be developed to replace those with internal combustion engines. This process is likely to be difficult, expensive, and in some cases less efficient. In addition, such a changeover would place great stress on nonrenewable resources such as copper, lead, nickel, and cadmium. Substitution of electricity for fossil fuels will doubtless prove impossible in some situations (aircraft, for example). Electrical energy will then have to be used to produce fuels such as hydrogen, and this will require additional expense and technological effort.

It is human nature to emphasize the positive and de-emphasize the negative aspects of new technologies. Certainly, research and development in these areas must be pushed forward as rapidly as society's resources permit and not be halted because of fear. We must always bear in mind, however, that capital investment and intellectual resources are not unlimited, and a large investment here means a smaller investment in meeting other important social needs. A very sober assessment of national priorities, social policies, and the dangers inherent in new technologies will be required if society is to allocate its resources optimally in solving pressing problems.

Whatever technological short-run solutions to the energy problem are adopted, however, there is no way around the ultimate problem: the heat barrier. All human activities, from digestion to driving (and stopping) an automobile, result in the degradation of useful energy into relatively useless heat. In a power plant, for example, the heat transferred to the ecosphere ultimately includes not only the unused heat at the site, but all the useful output as well. The electricity itself is transformed into heat through resistance in wires, filaments in lights, bearings in electric motors, and so on. That all the energy we use, electrical and otherwise, is eventually degraded to heat is a consequence of the second law of thermodynamics. No technological gimmickry or scientific breakthrough can overcome this natural constraint. The heat load imposed on the environment by energy consumption can be moderated only by limiting the number of consumers or by reducing per capita consumption.

The possibility that mankind will soon become an important climatic force over large areas (coastlines, river basins, megalopolises) cannot be dismissed lightly. According to one recent estimate, in the year 2000 the Boston-Washington megalopolis will include 56 million people in an area of 11,500 square miles. The dissipation of heat caused by human activities will be equal to 50 percent of the sun's energy arriving at the surface in that area in winter and 15 percent of solar energy in summer. Nor can it be safely assumed that serious effects will not occur even before man's energy contribution reaches a large fraction of the sun's over appreciable areas. Regional climates are often the result of numerous powerful forces operating in a rather delicate balance. Major climatic changes can result from small differences in very large numbers.

The understanding that scientists have of the detailed operation of the climatic system is as yet inadequate to predict the exact consequences of such human impact, but the onset of instabilities seems a distinct possibility. Local perturbations of sufficient size could trigger disproportionate fluctuations or semipermanent changes on a continental or perhaps even hemispheric scale. Unhappily for an undernourished world, the first casualty of sudden climatic change of any sort is likely to be agricultural productivity.

Large-scale thermal pollution is, *in principle* and in the long term, less manageable than any other global environmental problem. Even if mankind should be clever enough and lucky enough to ameliorate or evade every other threat accompanying continued population growth and increasing consumption, the laws of thermodynamics will finally force a halt. For instance, if the present global rate of increase in energy consumption—approximately 5 percent annually—should persist for another century and a half, man's energy dissipation then would be equal to 10 percent of the solar energy absorbed over the entire surface of the globe, or one-third of the solar energy absorbed on land. A rough heat balance calculation by physicist John Holdren suggests a corresponding *mean global temperature increase of approximately 1.3° Fahrenheit.* The actual mean increase might be somewhat greater or smaller, but it is fair to say that the associated climatological and ecological disruption would be enormous.

In conclusion, there are three critical points to be made about limits to growth. The first is that the most serious limitations on the amount of nonrenewable resources mankind can use are economic and environmental. Increased demand for resources inevitably means increased environmental impact. How much land can we afford to strip-mine for coal? How much energy can we afford to spend in extracting, transporting, and recycling resources? After all, metals are not "used up" after they are mined; they are simply dispersed and/or combined with other elements. In theory, if enough energy could be used, they could be reconcentrated and purified. But such a strategy is only of limited value because of the "heat barrier" problem discussed previously.

The second point is that various substitutions will not solve all resource problems. It has been proposed, for example, that plastics can serve as substitutes for many metals as these metals become scarce. Plastics, however, are manufactured from petroleum, which is in shorter supply than many metals. Moreover, plastic production contributes to important ecological problems (such as mercury pollution). If the resource picture is viewed as a whole (rather than one resource at a time), substitution is clearly a limited strategy at best. In addition, although rich countries may be able to afford to develop expensive substitutions after the world's high-grade resources have been depleted, the poor countries will not, and this fact becomes obvious to their citizens as they watch the rich drain them of their high-grade resources.

The third point is that for the next half century, *rate of change* problems and many temporary shortages and dislocations rather than absolute depletion will dominate the resource picture. We can envision a transformation of the United States' energy economy from heavy dependence on fossil fuels to dependence primarily on solar and fusion-generated electric power. However, long time lags must be dealt with in developing new power-generating technologies, deploying them, and converting to an electrically powered economy. There are also tremendous economic problems in financing the required research and development. Whether an orderly conversion can or will be made at the required rate is debatable. Even if we unrealistically assume prompt recognition of the problem by decision makers, large invest-ments in the changeover, and good luck, massive disruptions will undoubt-edly occur. Indeed, in 1973 a relatively mild and temporary shortage of petroleum and natural gas led to an all-out effort to expand supply at the cost of relaxing already inadequate measures to protect the environment. Few organized attempts were made to reduce demand. "Voluntary compliance" is a contradiction in terms, and when essential commodities are at stake, "good will" is not likely to produce concrete results. But as President Nixon's energy adviser stated in 1973, "It is not the philosophy of this Administration to control demand by government fiat. We believe the free market should operate. . . . We are not going to ask everybody to heat their homes at 68 degrees."

Although dangers and uncertainties are inherent in the development of new technologies, it is clear that society must plan very carefully and then make these efforts. A tremendous investment in new technologies will be needed merely to *stay even* with the population growth that is now projected. Substitutes for scarce resources must be developed wherever possible. Recycling should be subsidized *wherever it is energetically or ecologically desirable*. Research must be carried out to find new methods of processing low-grade ores as well as new sources of energy. These developments and many more will be necessary to preserve anything resembling current living standards over the next few decades.

It should be recognized, however, that these programs will require a very heavy public investment. People often forget that many social trade-offs will be needed to finance the necessary research and development. Pouring billions of dollars into fusion research and additional billions or trillions into a global search for resources means that other programs will suffer. A report by the Chase Manhattan Bank estimates that an investment of $1 trillion will be needed to meet world oil needs alone by 1985. The American people must clearly establish their priorities as the costs of continued growth begin to tax the public treasury. The decision to put men on the moon, for example, meant an initial investment of many billions of dollars that came out of taxpayers' pockets. This money could have been used to support fusion research, improve education, renew decaying cities, or to provide adequate incomes for all citizens. All the new technologies that are required to meet impending problems will require much greater public expenditures, because these problems are so massive in scale that private enterprise alone cannot possibly provide the necessary funds.

In the long run, however, the real solutions to present dilemmas do not lie only in physical science. Physical technology can indirectly create as many problems as it solves, and each round of new solutions can leave mankind even more dependent on an artificially created world for survival. The green revolution is a case in point. By increasing food supplies, it has permitted politicians in some areas to ignore the dangers of population growth, while at the same time it is creating ever more unstable ecosystems and equally unstable social conditions. Subtle ecological costs of the green revolution may have to be paid in such vital currency as a reduction in fisheries production resulting from pesticide and fertilizer pollution in rivers, lakes, and oceans. The green revolution has also exacted social costs that were not anticipated by many of the plan's proponents. New seeds and fertilizers have been purchased by the wealthier farmers who can afford them, and their yields have risen accordingly. The rich are getting richer and the poor are getting poorer. Tenants are being forced off their land by landlords eager to profit from new high-yielding varieties and introduction of modern machinery. Modernization of agriculture thus threatens, in countries like India, to worsen already critical problems of urbanization and unemployment by forcing more people off the land.

Technological innovation, of course, is in itself neither objectively good nor bad, and carefully managed new technologies will be essential for a prosperous future. We must recognize, however, that new technologies must be effectively assessed and directed if they are to have the desired impact. It is clear that the United States should invest heavily in ways to increase the efficiency of resource use. Making a given quantity of fossil fuel or a ton of iron ore go further is as important as developing fusion power. Investments in such potentially rewarding enterprises as the use of solar energy for the generation of electricity and solar heating and the perfection of a new generation of soft technologies (technologies requiring little capital investment) for less-developed countries are likely to be among the most profitable investments.

But even with the best of luck, continued dependence on one-dimensional thinking that relies heavily on technological fixes will be inadequate to meet future needs. Exponential growth is leading to a worsening resource situation and there is no hope that supply can keep up with an ever-increasing demand in the long run. Unless demand in the overdeveloped countries* is stabilized or even reduced, there is little hope that energy and resource flows sufficient to support an industrialized world can be maintained.

Almost every country in the world emulates the United States and is striving to "industrialize" and "catch up." An ideology that encourages exponential growth in consumption has been exported by industrial countries

---

*Overdeveloped countries are those in which population levels and per capita resource demands are so high as to make it impossible to maintain present living standards without making exorbitant demands on global resources and ecosystems.

to the rest of the world. Unless the United States curbs its increasing appetite, however, the gap between the rich and the poor will continue to widen, and there will be little possibility for the less-developed countries to realize any of their goals. Technologies to exploit successfully less accessible or lower-grade deposits of resources and substitutes for fossil fuels will be developed and used by the rich nations, not the poor nations. The poor cannot begin to catch up without cooperation from the rich.

It is ironic that those who plead for stabilizing consumption and putting the brakes on exponentially increasing demands are considered "nuts" and "extremists," while the proponents of continued rapid growth are considered sane, sensible, and even conservative. When a loaded passenger ship approaches a fog bank, the sensible strategy is to slow down and make certain that the course is safe. But precisely the opposite strategy is advocated for the Earth with its dwindling supply of resources and its future befogged by environmental unknowns. When a deepening crisis of hidden dimensions is approached, the demand is for acceleration rather than easing back on society's throttle.

It seems that very few people consider the welfare of their children and grandchildren when evaluating present environmental problems. Although it is expected that, in the long run, present behavior might well lead to lower standards of living, mankind continues to assault the natural systems that are vital to survival. No one can predict exactly how much punishment these ecosystems can endure before they begin to collapse, but the level of assault is escalating daily. The time has come to slow down and evaluate carefully what price future generations will pay for today's excesses. By slowing down now and planning carefully, much greater freedom of choice can be preserved for our descendants.

When demand exceeds available supply, there are two basic strategies for coping with the problem. The first depends on investing heavily in research and development and gambling that future innovations will meet the growing demand. This is the path that industrial society has taken in the past. B. F. Skinner calls it our "strong suit," as it requires no modification of old norms and behavior. Obviously, mankind cannot afford to stop playing this suit, in spite of the gambles that are required, but the odds on success could be enhanced by adding a second suit. The second suit is social in nature and involves dampening rapidly rising expectations by using social policies to complement physical technology in reducing consumption of nonrenewable resources. This is an alternative that has not yet been attempted, but in the long run it must be an essential part of any rational survival strategy, even if adding it runs against the current of industrial society.

2

An Ark Needs
More than
Wood and Nails

Historically, environmental problems and ecocatastrophes (events resulting in large-scale deterioration of the environment) were blamed on bad weather, bad luck, fate, or the will of God. Conception, pregnancy, and birth were considered to be religious matters and not amenable to human choice or planning. Resources were thought to be in infinite supply, and little attention was given to the ultimate level of consumption that existing stocks could support. Environmental deterioration was gradual, little noticed, and infrequently associated with its causes. With the notable exception of Thomas Malthus and his followers, people seldom considered these to be factors that would limit future growth.

Widespread recognition that problems of population, resources, and environment are interrelated has developed very recently. As late as 1960 only a few people were speaking or writing about the total problem, but in the middle of the twentieth century, industrial society seemingly crossed a threshold in recognizing its own impact on the ecosphere, and public attention turned to consideration of mankind's assault on Nature. By 1970 environmental awareness had led to a wave of new books on environmental problems and to the first and much celebrated "Earth Day" with an attendant public expression of sympathy for nature's plight.

Now that interrelationships among population, resource, and environmental problems have been "publicly" discovered, the social roots and effects of these problems are at least being "privately" discussed. Nevertheless, public attention too often focuses on symptoms, while causes are ignored. Famines, floods, riots, and wars are front-page news, but few newscasters or newspapers systematically analyze their social and demographic roots. Without an understanding of these roots, industrial mankind is destined to continue relying on technological fixes and avoid coming to terms with the causes of these problems.

Perceiving the Crisis

The specter of overpopulation was first publicized by Thomas Malthus at the end of the eighteenth century. He illuminated the relationship between the size of the human population and the size of its resource base. It was he who pointed out that the "power of population is indefinitely greater than the power in the earth to produce subsistence. . . ." His views were challenged as advances in industrial and agricultural methods and the abundance of the New World expanded the resource base, permitting the support of many more people. Since Malthus' time the population has more than quadrupled, and the Earth still seems to produce enough food for subsistence. Unfortunately, this apparent disproof of his basically correct ideas has led to a prevailing notion that technology can provide for unlimited population growth and unlimited increase in per capita consumption.

Birth control emerged as an acceptable practice in industrial countries more than a century after Malthus, but its use was justified mainly as a benefit to mothers with very large families, not as a way to ease population pressures. After World War I, especially during the Depression, there was even widespread concern that birth rates in industrialized countries were too low to facilitate economic recovery and provide manpower for armies. Population growth became an issue again after World War II; but for the following two decades the dialogue was largely confined to scientific circles. Public education in the United States was limited to discussing population problems in other areas, creating an awareness of too-rapid population growth in less-developed countries. Accordingly, systematic attempts to introduce family planning programs began in less-developed countries in the hope of slowing population growth and thus facilitating industrial development and higher standards of living. The social and economic conditions that led to lowered birth rates as the industrial revolution proceeded in the West, however, were absent in the less-developed nations of the fifties and sixties, and as a result, the introduction of family planning had very little effect on birth rates. The social milieu was not conducive to its ready acceptance and continued use.

Public awareness of environmental deterioration in the United States seemed to begin when the air in the Los Angeles area became noticeably polluted soon after World War II. The position of Los Angeles as an entertainment center meant that the entire United States quickly found out about smog. Then came the discovery that other cities had the same ailment. The Donora, Pennsylvania, smog disaster in 1948, in which a number of people died because of a persistent thermal inversion that kept factory exhausts trapped in the air near the ground, brought the realization that the problem was not limited to large cities and that industrial sources of pollution were as dangerous as automobile exhausts.

Throughout the fifties and sixties, as population, technology, and the economy grew, pollution problems intensified and proliferated. Education and research brought previously unnoticed forms of pollution to public attention. The publication of Rachel Carson's book *Silent Spring* alerted the public to the misuse of pesticides, and the sixties witnessed a growing trend toward legislation for pollution abatement, beginning at state and local levels. The courts began to recognize claims for pollution damage, and, because of public pressure, more stringent federal regulations were passed to protect the quality of the air and water.

The three linked elements of mankind's twentieth-century crisis—population growth, resource depletion, and environmental deterioration—are now familiar to many Americans. Yet the physical, biological, and particularly the social roots of the problems, as well as the hazards of failure to solve them, are not yet fully understood. Stronger and stronger measures have been taken to control various kinds of noticeable pollution. Air pollution from automobile exhausts and factory chimneys and industrial pollution of many streams have been reduced, while some steps have been taken to eliminate other sources of future environmental deterioration. These include the requirement of environmental impact statements for major construction efforts and the establishment of seed banks to preserve genetic diversity in crop strains. Even if such measures are fully implemented, however, they will not be enough unless the social and technological forces that generate *increases* in environmental pressure are also controlled.

American attitudes toward resources and the environment have their roots in the enormous abundance of the Great Frontier. The nation's early history was marked by a rapid population and geographic expansion, which was followed by economic and industrial growth. All this was supported by apparently limitless resources. Today the news that the United States depends increasingly on imported resources and is a net importer of energy comes as a shock to most people. The sudden onset of power failures and fuel shortages is blamed on poor planning or faulty price structures or on environmentalists who delay new power plant construction. All three are elements in the national energy crisis, but increasing resource costs and skyrocketing consumption also have played important roles. Even though the public has been repeatedly warned of impending resource problems, present minor crises have apparently caught many by surprise. Such shortages are completely foreign to American peacetime experience.

Similar histories could be written for other industrial nations with a time lag of a few years. Recognition of environmental problems in the Soviet Union has progressed to the point that programs for exchange of information and technology with the United States have been initiated. United States Environmental Quality Council member Russell Train, as well as scholars in Soviet studies, have pointed out that Soviet understanding of environmental problems is certainly no more sophisticated than that of the United States. But the Soviet Union has not yet approached the levels of environmental pressure found in the United States. Western Europe, on the other hand, is not very far behind in environmental impact, and some cooperative efforts have been made to limit pollution within the Common Market countries. Much discussion has centered on cleaning up the Rhine River, which is one of the world's most polluted streams because of the industrial and human waste emanating from cities along its banks and tributaries.

Japan's environmental problems have erupted explosively along with her rapid industrial growth. Public concern has also begun to develop in that country, and there will certainly be many clashes between advocates of more Japanese growth and those who realize that such growth is undesirable. In 1973 a court decision against Chisso Corporation, which polluted Minamata Bay with mercury waste, ordered the company to pay damages of $3.6 million to 138 plaintiffs who were either injured or killed by mercury poisoning. This was the fourth and most significant of such cases that began in 1971. In 1973 the Japanese also began discussing a major program to make Japan liveable again. The 1972 United Nations Conference on the Environment in

Stockholm marked at least a beginning of worldwide awareness of environmental problems. It also called attention to the erroneous belief of the less-developed countries that pollution is mainly a problem for industrialized countries.

Not until the late sixties was it widely recognized that population growth, resource shortages, and environmental deterioration are dangerous in *all* nations of the world. The notion that, because of enormous per capita impact, growth of populations in overdeveloped countries was a more serious problem for the world than growth of populations of the poor countries was even slower in penetrating public consciousness in the industrial countries. In the seventies this point has been successfully made, and the relationship between population size, industrial growth, and environmental deterioration is becoming widely recognized. But people still ignore the close link between social values and these phenomena, preferring instead to concentrate on physical manifestations of problems and technological solutions.

As the idea that population growth might not be altogether beneficial has taken hold in the United States, a concomitant change in behavior has occurred. This has been reinforced by other changes, such as the women's movement for human rights and equality, deteriorating economic conditions, pressure to liberalize abortion laws and remove restrictions on access to contraceptives, and a general disenchantment with large families. The result has been an unprecedentedly low national birth rate in the early seventies. In 1972 the size of completed families had dropped to approximately the replacement level, a level that, if maintained, would mean an end to American population growth (that is, zero population growth or ZPG) before the middle of the twenty-first century. If the American birthrate remains very low, it is unlikely that any significant public policies will be adopted to discourage population growth. This could be unfortunate because resource and environmental pressures make it imperative to shorten the time needed to end population growth by lowering fertility to slightly *below* replacement level, a procedure that would also have the effect of reducing the ultimate maximum population size. There is no guarantee, moreover, that the present degree of concern about overpopulation will be sufficient even to keep fertility at the replacement level. Other factors that influence reproductive attitudes could easily reverse the present trend. Attitudes toward childbearing have favored large families for thousands of years, and many subtle reproductive pressures that have been built into our culture still persist, although at present they might be sublimated.

Cultural Evolution

Mankind is constantly undergoing two kinds of evolution: biological and cultural. Biological evolution takes place within the pool of genetic information that is physically transferred from generation to generation through reproduction. Virtually all important changes in biological evolution result from differential reproductive rates of those with different genetic endowments. This differential reproduction is called natural selection. Human biological evolution is not now amenable to rational direction, in part because the genetic mechanism is incompletely understood, in part because the process operates over many generations, and in part because of social constraints against the selective breeding of human beings.

Cultural evolution, on the other hand, is change in the nongenetic information that humanity passes from generation to generation. Cultural evolution, unlike biological evolution, is amenable to rational control. Human beings can culturally "evolve" without waiting for natural selection. To a small degree, cultural evolution is already directed and controlled in that transmitted information is sometimes altered in anticipation of future problems. Human societies can alter both values and behavior, through planning, to create future conditions that will be more conducive to human health and welfare.

Culture is passed from one generation to the next through learning and socialization processes. The use of spoken and then written language has immensely expanded the amount of information that can be passed from generation to generation. Human beings are unique in the complexity of the information thus transmitted. It is this nongenetic mode of inheritance that has permitted mankind to achieve a dominant position on Earth. Today, however, in view of the rapid rate of environmental change, it is debatable whether cultural evolution can take place rapidly enough to be an ally in the struggle for societal survival.

Institutions are the vehicles through which cultural norms, values, and beliefs are transmitted. Children learn many of their values within the framework of the family, the church, the peer group, or the school. These influences act as a social mold or template for each generation, much as DNA and RNA carry messages in genetic evolution. In industrial societies, both the content of culture and the institutions responsible for passing it on have largely been shaped by the successes of the industrial revolution. The affluence that has come with industrialization and the resultant materialism have significantly contributed to the habits, norms, and values that are now transmitted as a part of a secular industrial culture.

The collection of norms, beliefs, values, habits, and so on that form the world view most commonly held within a culture and transmitted from generation to generation by social institutions may be called a dominant social paradigm (DSP). Paradigm is a useful shorthand term for describing the prominent world view, model, or frame of reference through which individuals or, collectively, a society, interpret the meaning of the external world. In other words, a DSP is a mental image of social reality that guides expectations in a society. A DSP is the socially relevant part of a total culture. Different societies have different DSPs. A social paradigm is important to society because it helps make sense of an otherwise incomprehensible universe and to make organized activity possible. It is an essential part of the cultural information that is passed from generation to generation as it guides the behavior and expectations of those born into it.

The world view of each individual is somewhat different from that of every other, as are the shared world views of members of different families, classes, and so forth. Thus a DSP, even within a single industrial nation, must be considered as the common content of the paradigms shared by most individuals, although it does not, of course, encompass all views of all citizens.

There are even greater differences among nations in the composite content of the DSP. In many industrial societies, for example, it is taken for granted that essential social services will be provided by the government. In Great Britain, the Soviet Union, and Scandinavia, everyone *expects* the government to provide free or very inexpensive health care. Citizens of these countries would be shocked if they were suddenly forced to pay for this essential service. In the United States, however, even a suggestion of federally subsidized health care evokes a shudder from most people and elicits a new burst of denunciations from the A.M.A. and certain sectors of the insurance industry.

Similarly, in Great Britain few people would consider attacking a policeman. Social pressures there are strong enough to keep all but the most hardened criminals from attacking an officer of the law, whereas in Japan students think nothing of fighting pitched battles with police during frequent demonstrations, and in the United States policemen have become frequent targets of criminal attacks. Attitudes toward authority clearly differ. In Great Britain there is a tradition of deference to authority and trust that political decisions will be made in the common interest. In the United States and much of the rest of the industrial world, authority is treated with less respect, and it is expected that political figures may frequently act like criminals in pursuing their own interest.

Despite many such differences, citizens in most industrial countries share with Americans a belief in progress, faith in the steady increase of material affluence (which unfortunately is often equated with progress), and belief in the necessity and goodness of growth. Other central features of the industrial DSP seemingly include high values placed on work, the nuclear family, and career-oriented formal education; a strong faith in the efficacy of science and technology (as opposed to religion) to solve problems; and a view of Nature as something to be subdued by mankind.

In all societies, DSPs are constantly altered by experience. But in the United States today the DSP is not changing fast enough or in the right direction to keep society abreast of the dazzling changes in mankind's technological and biological environments.

No DSP can persist unaltered unless its content corresponds to or gives valid guidance for dealing with reality. Twenty years ago it would have been unusual for anyone in the United States to question the "fundamental truths" of what was then the orthodox view of the world, but today countless citizens *are* questioning many basic beliefs inherent in the present DSP, for these beliefs are no longer useful in successfully interpreting social reality. The system no longer seems to be working, and millions of Americans are uneasy, if not disillusioned.

It must be understood that deliberately changing fundamental assumptions and attitudes inherent in the industrial DSP means nothing less than designing a new culture. This would represent a revolutionary step that has rarely been attempted, although it would be akin to the cultural revolution that has recently shaken China. Designing a new culture means adopting an activist attitude toward cultural evolution rather than passive acquiescence to the results of technology; but most important of all, it means actively intervening to modify norms, values, and institutions to bring them into line with the physical and biological constraints within which mankind must operate. *The entire world society must soon reach a consensus on what is meant by a livable world and must cooperate in using science, technology, and social institutions to construct that world, rather than forcing human beings to conform to a world shaped by these forces out of control.*

To direct cultural evolution is to make culture an effective weapon in the battle for human survival. In the past, culture has represented the accumulated wisdom of the ages; cultural change tends to follow events, rather than helping to shape them. Today much of the old wisdom is no longer relevant to the survival of a society faced with changes of unprecedented speed and magnitude. Cultural evolution should be so directed that societies can anticipate and effectively deal with problems or, better yet, avoid them altogether. This will require the rational development of a *social technology* to meet mankind's psychosocial needs that is as effective as the *material technology* that was developed within industrial culture to meet mankind's physical needs.

The Industrial Trap

The industrial paradigm, molded by three centuries of cultural evolution, offers twentieth-century man a conventional understanding of the complexities of society, a set of common wisdoms with supposed survival value, a framework for collecting and storing relevant information and a definition of problems in need of solution. People sharing this paradigm live in a world much different from that of their ancestors who lived in predominantly agricultural societies. Industrial man sees a world that is "developing" and "progressing." Into exactly what it is developing and toward what it is progressing remain conveniently obscure, but presumably desirable. Higher material consumption standards have been ordained as a great social good; this is not surprising since they are the main offering of a technologically advanced society.

The industrial paradigm also performs another very important function for members of industrial society. It offers an elaborate supporting ethical theory for the inequities and seeming inconsistencies that beset the industrial system. Most people want to do the "right" thing in their relations with others. Therefore, complex ethical theories have developed that permit people to think they are doing the right thing while living luxuriously in the presence of poverty, starvation, and huge economic gaps between rich and poor. According to popular myth, the wealthy got that way through cleverness or hard work. They deserve to live a life of opulence; the poor deserve no charity because their failures condemn them. A world without such supporting ethical theories would be a psychologically grim place, because each person would be forced to face the full range of social consequences of his own actions. Although the industrial DSP, with its supporting ethical theories spawned by the industrial revolution, offers sophisticated justifications for various inequities, it is currently proving to be a less than adequate mechanism for sustaining an enduring social peace. Consider the following examples of inconsistencies that have begun to bother some Americans:

> In a society in which more than 25 million Americans are defined as living below the "official" poverty line, supporting ethical theories permit the very rich to engage in fantastic orgies of consumption. Cadillac limousines, three-car families, huge mansions with unoccupied rooms, and families with large numbers of servants coexist with pockets of severe poverty, often in the same geographic area. Those who can afford to engage in this behavior spend incredible sums on yachts, wines, and the good life but often are unwilling to support even minimal government programs to help the poor. It is not unknown for an individual to pay as much as $10,000 for one bottle of wine—to consume at one meal an item that is worth two to three times the annual income of many American families. If these individuals were forced to pay similar amounts in extra taxes, the shouts of protest would be deafening.
>
> Conservative politicians are reelected to office after decrying as socialism even limited aid to destitute women and children. They oppose measures designed to create child-care centers for working mothers on the grounds that such centers have "family-weakening implications" or that they will "create federalized kindergartens." While adding "workfare" clauses to welfare schemes, they hand out tax monies to keep incompetent corporations in business. Welfare for the poor is ethically dismissed as a social evil, whereas subsidies for the rich are often considered necessary parts of intelligent economic policy.
>
> Officials of publicly regulated utilities argue that it is necessary to accept the dangers of building nuclear power plants to meet "increasing demands for power," while many have, over the last few years, been spending millions of dollars for advertising to create even more demand. Simultaneously, they attack those who suggest that the problem be solved by reducing consumption as fanatics who do not understand the true nature of the power problem. These utilities have previously given little consideration to ideas for moderating demand, such as requiring better insulation of homes and offices so that use of electricity for heating and cooling can be decreased. Now, of course, inability to supply power has changed the utilities' approach, but increasing consumption of energy is still considered a social necessity, even though it may destroy society's resource base and the environment within which all of us must live.

From a different perspective, it could be said that the ethical theories that supported the early stages of the industrial revolution have been transcended by new ideas about equity and morality. Unfortunately, there is little or no agreement as to how to go about redesigning institutions to take account of this change. Now that the largest portions of industrial society are well fed and affluent, the poor have been reduced to a minority. It used to be acceptable to say that the poor will always be with us, but today such a statement is likely to be met with a rather sharp retort.

Even more important, the *successes* of the industrial revolution have created a culture filled with enigmas, dilemmas, and inconsistencies. For example, automation has reduced the length of the work week while rendering each worker much more productive than before. Now industrial societies have great difficulty in dividing up this automation dividend, and substantial numbers are left unemployed. Similarly, the factory system of production has created untold material abundance, although the products of this system are depleting stocks of resources and leading to large-scale environmental deterioration. Most importantly, however, affluence in industrial society has not led to enduring domestic social peace or stability in the international system. In fact, many would argue that the coming decades will be filled with tension because industrial nations must spread their tentacles in search of more mineral resources to sustain their high levels of living.

The persistence of any society is threatened when its DSP no longer offers valid guidance for survival. History is littered with the ruins of societies in which the cultural information passed from generation to generation became inadequate or irrelevant in coping with changes in their environments. The Mayas could not deal with population pressures that overstressed their slash-and-burn agricultural system. The Mesopotamians were unable to maintain the quality of their agricultural production when their elaborate irrigation system resulted in the accumulation of salts in the soil. Although conquest may have been the immediate cause for the collapse of many great societies of the past, social rigidity in the face of ecological changes and technological challenges has played a major role. Today industrial society is threatened, not by external enemies, but by the uncritical acceptance of an outmoded DSP that cannot be sustained in the environment of the future.

It is ironic that the problems that threaten to destroy industrial society have their origin in the successes of the industrial revolution. For instance, advances in public health, and especially the development of miracle drugs, have combined to cut infant and child mortality and to increase the average life span, thus leading to problems of overpopulation. Thanks to technology, perhaps one-half billion people now lead lives of health and affluence un-paralleled in human history; but at least 1.5 billion exist in a state of unprecedented misery—unprecedented not only because their numbers are so much greater, but because never before have the hungry and the poor been so aware of the affluence that might be theirs.

The industrial reaction to the problems fostered by the industrial revolution has been to rely on more science and more technology. Proponents of the "quick fix" argue that solutions to problems resulting from industrial technology must lie in greater doses of the same technology. This is symptomatic of the "one-dimensional" thinking that Herbert Marcuse contends prevents industrial man from seeing beyond the narrow bounds of the present DSP. Overpopulation will be technologically cured by showering contraceptives from helicopters. Starvation will be countered by a green revolution based on fertilizers and new miracle crops. The energy crisis will be overcome with nuclear power. Crime and discontent will be handled by more effective riot control equipment, by drugs, or by behavioral modification. Technological optimists see the tip of a problem "iceberg," the obvious symptoms, and come up with technological treatments for those symptoms. These treatments may hold the system together for a while longer, although they almost always create new problems. But technological optimists pay little attention to a huge, unseen part of the iceberg—to the *social, political, and economic roots* of these problems embedded in the norms and expectations developed during the heyday of industrial expansion.

Cultures and DSPs that developed in hunting and gathering societies were destroyed by a new way of life introduced by the agricultural revolution. Similarly, the world view produced by the development of industrialism overwhelmed the previous cultures. In both instances a shift in outlook took place as old norms, values, and institutions were replaced by new ones reflecting new social conditions. In both, a "paradigm shift" was facilitated by obvious economic benefits received by, and higher survival rates among, those who moved to a new way of life. Today there are no obvious economic incentives to encourage acceptance of a new DSP. In fact, quite the opposite is true. Nevertheless, the inadequacy of the present paradigm to cope with new, simultaneously developing problems is becoming increasingly evident to people who are prepared to recognize it. But time is too short to await the evolution of an alternative viable paradigm. The main problem for industrial society in the last quarter of the twentieth century will be to design new and feasible alternatives and to move toward the best of them. Mankind must begin to turn this *new awareness of planetary danger into meaningful social action.* Development of alternatives, however, requires understanding in greater detail many of the dangerous trends in industrial society.

Technological Momentum

The problem of survival is accentuated by the rapid pace at which un-directed, technology-inspired change takes place. The accumulated wisdom of generations passed on within a culture is useful only insofar as it gives guidance in solving current problems. The environment of a hunting and gathering society remained much the same from generation to generation. The game stalked by grandfather was the same game pursued by the grandchildren. Information transmitted from one generation to another was altered very little over time because the problems to be dealt with were much the same century after century. The changeover from hunting and gathering to farming occurred incrementally over many generations, and even the industrial paradigm of today certainly did not appear full-blown the day the spinning jenny was invented.

The nature of society and human consumption patterns have been changing in exponential fashion over the past 150 years. Growth and rapid change, fed by new technologies and tremendous amounts of investment capital, have become an essential part of the DSP. Development and progress require continuous change, and industrial society cannot stand still. To slow down and plan is to risk exposing questions that have been buried by the affluence already achieved. In times of large-scale economic growth, everyone can receive an additional increment of wealth without obviously affecting the interests of others. When growth slows, however, social and economic life become a "zero sum game," a contest in which one person's gain must be another person's loss.

Science and technology quicken the pace of change because innovation begets more innovation and because the effects of innovation feed back to accelerate change in social life. We have yet to develop methods of assessing technology or of managing social change to obtain collective welfare. Those changes that are planned are most often changes in physical technology; social changes usually are but inadvertent fallout from new technology. Thus in the United States the creation and distribution of television required a great deal of technical research and development, but there was little or no anticipation of the inevitable impact that television was to have on political life, the level of violence in society, or even patterns of social behavior in general.

Today society, through its collective decision-making processes, rarely rejects any innovation, not only because of one-dimensional thinking, but also because advertising and propaganda campaigns assure acceptance of what technology has to offer. An innovation that can cause serious social turmoil almost never becomes an overt political issue *before* it does serious damage. Galloping technology "plans" the social future for everyone. No collective decisions were made to create a society of three-car families living a long-distance drive on crowded freeways from their place of work, or a society filled with air conditioners to cleanse the air of heat and effluents produced by other machines. Society did not collectively decide to develop drive-in restaurants selling non-nutritious food, aluminum beer cans that clutter the landscape, or supercharged V-8 automobiles that pollute entire cities with noise and effluents. Decisions were made on an *ad hoc* basis by the profit motive backed up by advertising. These "innovations" have often been offered by entrepreneurs who created the demands that they then claim to fill. Most of the time people adjust to such "progress" and even learn to like it, although rarely is consideration given to other paths that could have been taken. We tread a road chosen by an advertising anarchy that shapes public opinion. Most important of all, those who are disenchanted with the laissez-faire drift of society have no way to express their displeasure directly. Breaking machines went out of fashion with the Luddites, and punching extra holes in IBM cards cannot really shake the system.

Leaders of industrial societies, those who might be able to guide the evolution of culture, tend not to be "protean men" who understand the implications of change. It seems as if politicians often represent society's lowest common denominators, a sort of perverse selection of the morally least fit. Religious leaders still appeal to codes developed among agricultural peoples and desert nomads to regulate their rather simple societies and fail to bring religious doctrines up to date. Political leaders attempt to mitigate the effects of change through laws that seem enlightened only by the standards of twenty years ago. Teachers prepare students for life in a society that will no longer exist by the time they reach maturity. Economists beat the drums for rapid economic growth despite evidence that the costs of such growth will be more than the benefits received; indeed, such costs will be more than mankind can afford to pay. Leaders seem unable to deal with the present, let alone the future, and behave as if they were living in their own prime, sometime between two and five decades in the past.

Because the pace of change has been accelerating, agencies that should be planning for the future are increasingly left to correct the problems created by previously unmanaged technology. These agencies cannot put their efforts into anticipating problems and producing plans to avert future difficulties. The Environmental Protection Agency, for instance, spends a great deal of time trying to "clean up" automobiles. A social planning agency, had it existed, might decades ago have foreseen the horrors of an automobile-centered society and encouraged the United States to develop a balanced transportation network. Even though society is capable of altering the DSP, no institutional provisions have ever been made for doing so. Industrial society has some methods of forecasting future problems and can develop others. For instance, the energy and meat crises of 1973 were foreseeable and to a degree foreseen, as were the consequences of unrestricted use of pesticides such as DDT. But so far no heavy investment in planning and technological forecasting has been made. Planning and control are now anathema to a society that has learned to fight for "limited" government and laissez-faire development, both of which have been associated with the successes of the industrial revolution. While the pace of change accelerates, people demand less bureaucracy, less planning, less governmental control, and fewer public expenditures. Limited government is a worthy goal, but such demands are often misdirected. People attack the regulation and planning that are necessary for the common good, while supporting outmoded and useless bureaucracies that devote their time to overregulating individual lives and ferreting out crimes where no victims exist.

Increasing Interdependence

On the day in 1971 on which public employees of New York City raised the drawbridges leading into Manhattan, they demonstrated the dependence of one person on others in a complex industrial society more clearly than could any theoretical treatise. To emphasize their wage demands, New York City employees attempted to jam drawbridges at twenty-nine critical points leading into the city. They succeeded in jamming twenty-five. The results of this destructive action were never adequately quantified. It created the worst traffic jam in the city's history. Traffic was backed up bumper to bumper for fifteen miles. Tens of thousands of commuters never arrived at work, countless cars were stalled on the freeways, and many cars were simply abandoned. In other incidents, public employees reduced water pressure to a dangerously low level by refusing to service fire hydrants opened by overheated children. Other employees caused raw sewage to be discharged into the East and Hudson Rivers when they walked off the job at treatment plants.

These actions and similar stoppages in other large-scale labor disputes not only illustrate the power that small segments of the population can exercise over the welfare of countless others; they also dramatize the paradox that exists in a complex interdependent society living by social rules developed under frontier conditions. Industrial society is now so interdependent that any dedicated group can throw a wrench into the delicate social machinery. Simultaneously, accepted social values encourage intense competition, social conflict, and labor strife, rather than a spirit of cooperation, responsibility, and concern for the welfare of others.

The price for sustaining dense populations is the weaving of an increasingly complex and fragile web of interdependence among people. Today everything must be done right lest millions be inconvenienced or harmed. There are no empty frontiers left to absorb social deviants, and no rich, open lands for people to occupy after areas now occupied have been befouled and exhausted. Without an open frontier, industrial society no longer has a wide margin of error and cannot ignore developing problems. All of us must now live in close proximity with each other and with the complex situations that we have jointly created.

This interdependence is not caused solely by increasing numbers. Industrialization has brought an increasingly complex division of labor, and its mass-production techniques depend on cooperation among many groups often located some distance apart. Factories and factorylike farms require raw materials and equipment that must be transported from afar. Farm and manufactured products, in turn, must also be transported to widely dispersed markets. Industrial nations have become dependent on the material abundance that emerges from the factory system, and it would be psychologically difficult or even impossible for most individuals to get along without it. Moreover, there is very little prospect of turning back to some simple earlier system; population size alone militates against it. Without a major revolution, the dimensions and results of which are virtually unimaginable, societies are destined to become even more interdependent in the future.

Industrialization has created a related situation in which individuals, often complete strangers, have life-and-death power over others. It is not necessary to cite the melodramatic, still relatively isolated, incidents in which an individual goes berserk and decides to take as many others with him as possible. Fortunately, random sniper slayings or politically motivated killings are still rare events in the United States. But as conflict-based social tension increases, such occurrences may become more likely. Mass murders, police riots, assassinations, and criminal behavior by paranoid government officials are symptomatic of a deeply troubled people living in an armed camp. The surge of radical bombing attempts and threats to lace water supplies with dangerous chemicals during the late sixties and early seventies is likewise symptomatic of severe social stress. Internationally, the activities of such organizations as the Palestinian guerrillas and the Irish Republican Army give some clue to the level of disruption and destruction that can be created by a few with strong motives and goals. In the near future, with hundreds of nuclear power plants producing plutonium, such dedicated radical groups will be able to multiply many times the havoc they can wreak today.

The power held over the lives of others by small groups and individuals in industrial society is passive as well as active. Destruction can be wrought through acts of omission as well as by planned assaults. Everyone depends on the highway engineer, the assembly-line worker, the airline pilot, and the auto mechanic for his or her life. One unnoticed slip, and dozens or even hundreds of people may be dead. Again, this situation is not likely to change for the better as unproven and potentially hazardous technologies, such as those of nuclear power plants and supersonic transports, are rushed into service. The chances for serious accidents will steadily increase, and each person's life will depend on the fallible performance of many more individuals. Carelessness by welders constructing a reactor or by a reactor operator could kill millions of people and render hundreds of thousands of square miles uninhabitable. Similarly, a truck driver or railroad engineer could wreak havoc through carelessness while transporting waste products from a nuclear reactor. One mistake in scientific calculations about the atmospheric effects of SSTs could mortgage mankind's future.

A driving force behind the industrial revolution has been the organization of large numbers of workers in a cooperative division of labor, resulting in dense populations crowded into urban areas. Increasing concentrations of population mean less living space for each person. But Americans strenuously object to any restrictions on personal liberties, even as social insulating space shrinks. Individual "rights and freedoms," particularly economic freedoms, are vigorously defended in the face of the mounting collective problems they are causing. The increasing "oneness" of mankind is widely recognized in word, but old values and habits block its recognition in deed.

Social Lag

Modern industrial society can be described as technologically overdeveloped, while remaining institutionally and socially underdeveloped. Science and technology have eliminated many of the problems of physical survival that have always confronted man, but as yet science has offered little advice germane to the settlement of the social problems that it has been instrumental in creating. The industrial revolution has been unbalanced; mankind has forged ahead in the manipulation of nature but has lagged in attempts to understand and modify the social environment.

A paradox inherent in social lag is that the United States is able to run the most complex of technological circuses but seems paralyzed when called on to reach goals related to social change. Billions of dollars and vast amounts of technical expertise were poured into the effort to put men on the moon, whereas policies intended to give jobs and a decent income to all Americans apparently cannot be successfully designed and enacted. Although almost everyone agrees that America's blighted urban areas need drastic action to make them liveable, even the billions already spent have resulted in largely unsuccessful efforts to resurrect them. Similarly, it has so far been socially impossible to equalize educational and economic opportunity in spite of apparent agreement that equality of opportunity is a desirable social goal.

This problem is caused largely by taboos that have become part of today's supporting ethical theories. In preindustrial society it was considered immoral for human beings to work actively to modify what God had created. Industrialization changed that, but active attempts to alter social behavior, norms, and values are still considered by many to be improper and immoral. Behavioral psychologist B. F. Skinner refers to this attitude as a "cult of freedom and dignity"—the misplaced belief that the norms and values by which men live should not be studied and certainly not modified since the essence of being human is to be free. According to Skinner, freedom means freedom to act in conformity with the dictates of one's society.

Social lag does not trace to any unfortunate "nature of man"; for human nature is demonstrably subject to extreme modifications in different cultural and environmental circumstances. People are good, noble, and responsible, as well as evil, base, and irresponsible. Social institutions are the core of the problem. Political scientist Thomas Schelling has pointed out that American society is characterized by an institutional inability to generate more individual feelings of responsibility for others and a similar inability to translate existing individual tendencies toward cooperation into collective action. Individuals acting in their own self-interest, even only weak self-interest, frequently produce long-range societal effects that are to no one's benefit. Biophysicist John Platt uses the term "social traps" to characterize existing institutional arrangements that actually work against individuals cooperating to solve common problems.

Garrett Hardin has outlined the crux of the problem in his now classic essay, "The Tragedy of the Commons." According to Hardin, mankind is caught in a situation akin to a classic tragedy. Although each individual apparently has no ill will toward others, all men acting in self-interest move inexorably toward self-destruction. Hardin uses the example of animals being kept on a commons, an area open to all villagers for pasturing their stock. There are no problems on the commons as long as the number of animals is small in relation to the size of the pasture. From the point of view of each herder, however, the optimal strategy is to enlarge his herd as much as possible. If his animals do not eat the grass, someone else's will. Thus, the size of each herd grows, and the density of stock increases until it exceeds the carrying capacity of the commons. The result is that everyone eventually loses as the animals die of starvation. The sum of a set of apparently rational individual strategies equals social irresponsibility leading to disaster. The tragedy is that, even though the eventual result should be perfectly clear, no one acts to avert disaster. In a democratic society there are few remedies to keep the size of herds in line.

The ecosphere is one big commons stocked with air, water, and irreplaceable mineral resources—a "people's pasture," but a pasture with limited carrying capacity. Each nation attempts to extract as much from the commons as possible while enough remains to sustain the herd. Thus, the United States and other industrial nations consume far more than their share of the total world resource harvest each year, much of it imported from less-developed nations. The nations of the world compete frantically for all the fish that can be taken from the sea before the fisheries are destroyed. Each nation freely uses the commons to dispose of its wastes, ignoring the dangers inherent in overtaxing the waste-absorbing capacity of rivers, oceans, and the atmosphere. It is wastes of industrial nations that make up the largest and most dangerous part of the ecosphere's burden.

This tragedy also exists in the United States. Many states are willing to maintain lower antipollution standards than others to retain current industries and to attract new ones. Thus, for two consecutive summers in the early seventies, air pollution, largely originating in the steel industry, which was not forced to curb atmospheric pollution, reached such severe levels in Alabama that the health of the local people was seriously endangered. The damage was not limited to Alabama; the polluted air spread over adjacent states. Similarly, cities along the Mississippi River treat it as a commons for dumping sewage. Often the filth is dumped just above the "freshwater" intakes for other cities. In every situation, whether among cities or states, an effort is made to utilize as much as possible of the commons with little thought of collective welfare.

The tragedy of the commons also operates on an individual level. Most people are aware of air pollution, but they continue to drive their unnecessarily powerful automobiles. Many families claim to need a second or even a third car. It is not that these people are antisocial; most would be willing to drive smaller or fewer cars if everyone else did, and they could get along with only one small car if public transport were adequate. But people frequently get "locked into" harmful situations, waiting for others to take the first step, and many unwittingly contribute to tragedies of the commons. After all, what harm can be done by the birth of one more child, the careless disposal of one more beer can, or the installation of one more air conditioner?

Social Diseconomies of Scale

The industrial revolution fostered sizable organizations of workers in combination with increasingly complex machines in large factories and resulted in levels of production unimaginable for an individual artisan. The larger the factory, the longer the assembly lines, the bigger the machines, and the larger the total market, generally the more efficiently and profitably an industry could operate. With such large-scale production, the unit price of a product could be kept much lower than if one individual performed all the necessary operations. This is known as economy of scale.

Obviously, not everything can be mass produced successfully, but during the course of the industrial revolution mass production has at least been tried for almost everything. Economies of scale are best illustrated by the automobile industry. A skilled mechanic working by himself, with ready access to needed materials and machinery, might be able to build a few automobiles from rough parts each year, if he were very efficient. By contrast, 500 workers in an assembly plant can do the major part of the work required to produce tens of thousands of automobiles each year. Obviously, labor productivity in the factory is much higher than that of a skilled craftsman working alone.

There have always been some social disadvantages to mass production, but they have previously been overshadowed by economic efficiencies. One of these disadvantages is the psychological separation of the worker from his product. No one can receive much satisfaction from putting identical bolts through identical pieces of iron moving down an assembly line, especially in comparison with the satisfaction an artisan receives from making a complete product. The assembly line often leads to production of shoddy merchandise, because each worker feels little responsibility for the finished product. Numerous reports indicate that workers in many industries have even deliberately sabotaged finished products. Moreover, the so-called efficiencies behind economies of scale have often caused the extinction of many competitors, leaving only a very few large companies within an industry. Millions of American-made automobiles are sold in the United States every year, but most of them are manufactured by only three large companies. The social disadvantages of such oligopolies are obvious. Consumers and the public can do little to command industry responsiveness since competition is much reduced and there are few possibilities for new competitors to establish themselves. Thus, when it came to forcing automobile manufacturers to meet new antipollution standards, the Big Three stood together and claimed it could not be done—even though the producers of two Japanese imports found that they could meet the standards.

Growth in scale has now led to a trend in which *production economies* of scale are outweighed by *social diseconomies* of scale—increased social costs associated with large size. We live in an extremely complex society dominated by the activities of industrial giants. Huge conglomerates produce a bewildering variety of products that have no common connection; increasing size seems to produce no benefits for society. *It seems that no one really understands the complex socioeconomic system and that the scale on which things are being done is so large that people have lost control of economic activities.*

Macroconstraints and Microfreedoms

As industrial societies have become more complex and their destructive impact on the ecosphere has become global, the social and environmental consequences of individual behavior have greatly increased. The interdependence of people and the large amount of power available to each individual require that increasingly heavy constraints be placed on many activities. Without such constraints, the integrity of both social and environmental systems is in jeopardy.

Societies have always limited the behavior of their members by a variety of mechanisms ranging from subtle social disapproval to outright force. In the

United States the need for constraint has been growing rapidly, and therefore new forms of social restriction must be developed. As with all types of constraints, these should first be openly discussed. Because individual freedom and initiative are highly cherished, changes should be devised to minimize the perceived impact of regulation on individual day-to-day decision making.

In the long term, of course, the ideal way for any society to regulate the behavior of individuals without seeming to restrict individual freedom is through socialization of the young. Few Americans feel that their freedoms have been restricted because they may not rob banks, torture kittens, or murder their parents. Although these activities are against the law, the necessary social constraints provided by early training, not the threat of jail or execution, keep the vast majority of individuals from engaging in such acts. There is every reason to believe that more cooperative and environmentally sound behavior than is observed today could be elicited through changes in patterns of child-rearing and grade-school education.

In the short term, however, society is faced with framing new legislation to protect individuals from the consequences of other people's behavior and to guard the environment from further deterioration. More laws and bigger bureaucracies to administer and enforce them seem, at first glance, to be the answer. Unfortunately, regulatory bureaucracies rarely accomplish their goals, and "big government" all too often fails either to plan for the future or to administer the present. This is one of the major paradoxes in advanced industrial societies. People perceive the need for more government, while at the same time realizing that more government will not work. For example, almost everyone would like the government to guarantee that their food be wholesome, that their water be fit to drink, that the drugs they use be safe, that appliances and automobiles be durable, and that all consumer goods and services be fairly priced; but almost everyone also realizes that the costs in the form of taxes and bureaucratic red tape would be prohibitive.

There are no easy answers to this dilemma, but this section describes one approach to its solution: a combination of *macroconstraints* (*macro* meaning large scale) and *microfreedoms* (*micro* meaning small scale, or individual). The essence of this approach is to concentrate governmental regulatory activities at critical pressure points as far "upstream" from the individual as possible, thus minimizing the perceived restrictions on an individual's freedoms. Perhaps the best example is economist Herman Daly's suggestion, discussed in the next chapter, of the use of resource depletion quotas as a macroconstraint to solve many problems of pollution and resource depletion. According to this plan, the amount of each key resource to be used annually would be determined by the government, although distribution of finished products among consumers would still be decided by the free market. This limitation on resource depletion would raise prices of certain raw materials, thus encouraging development of substitutes, maximum recycling, and reclamation of pollutants. Such a system would be far less complicated to administer and less unfair than taxing resource users and polluters after the fact.

An example of introducing microfreedoms would be to remove all criminal sanctions for "crimes without victims." The repeal of laws against marijuana use, prostitution, gambling, and homosexuality would be an example. Great savings of time and effort could be made by the police and the courts by permitting individuals to behave as they see fit in private, as long as others are not hurt. Criminal sanctions against such behavior as public drunkenness and private sexual conduct among adults are pointless, and they take up large amounts of public time and resources that are badly needed elsewhere.

It seems likely that, in the long term, advanced industrial societies can be successfully run with much less big government than is found in the United States today. But the present partitioning of the economic system into public and private sectors, a result of laissez-faire development, will have to be drastically modified. Governmental and nongovernmental institutions, corporations, and individuals must play roles in the future that are quite different from the roles they play at present. But even in the short term, careful attention to the macroconstraints/microfreedoms principle should help see us through the transition with no great growth of governmental bureaucracy.

Transforming Society

A very fundamental question must be answered before considering ideas for a cultural transformation. If many people are seemingly dissatisfied with the system and are discontent with the present society, what prevents a transformation from taking place? The problem is not that people are always opposed to change. They will support new ideas that appear to work in their favor. Most of the required changes, however, will not be perceived as being to anyone's advantage. Limiting consumption sounds distasteful, and giving up old ways of life could be difficult. People also reject the idea that a superior alternative society can be developed; indeed, most cannot even imagine one. That is why there are so many complaints about the present system and so few novel ideas for changing it. In a sense, almost every individual and organized group represents a "vested interest," afraid of change because of the chance that there will be a net loss of privilege. Those who strongly defend the present society include not only the wealthy, who are profiting handsomely from this system, but quite surprisingly the poor, who many times perceive that they possess just a small amount of privilege more than someone else and will defend this increment to the last. A private poll commissioned by Senator George McGovern during the 1972 election campaign revealed that it was the poor who were most opposed to a fundamental reform of inheritance taxes aimed at heavily taxing large estates. The poor fear changing a system that nourishes even a little hope of advancement, although objectively it would hardly seem in their interest to support the concentration of wealth from generation to generation.

In general, however, it is those people who feel that they have "made it" within the present system who represent the strongest vested interests. The greater the perceived stake in the old society, the more stubborn the support for the system. Human beings are social animals and depend in large part on the approval and praise of others who share the same world view for their satisfaction. It would be odd behavior, indeed, to turn against a system within which social success has come. As the industrial DSP continues to erode, however, an important impetus to paradigm shift could well come from new supporting ethical theories that stress environmentally sound and socially aware behavior.

Dominant social paradigms are not easily overthrown, and in the past their destruction has often been the result of events external to a society, such as enemy attack or natural disasters. For the most part, however, world views shift very slowly as values and norms are modified in keeping with new realities after considerable time lags required for learning. For example, massed cavalry and infantry charges, once accepted methods of conducting warfare, persisted suicidally into the age of the machine gun. In the early sixties, the Communist Party of Czechoslovakia rigidly followed economic practices that nearly destroyed the economy. In the seventies the United States seems to be following suit and sticking to outmoded free market concepts. Societies today still support the war system for settling international disputes, although it threatens the very existence of mankind.

Human beings conform and expect conformity from others. Leaders do not like to challenge accepted norms and values because to do so means loss of support from a silent conforming majority. Dominant social paradigms are solidly anchored in socially shared perceptions of the surrounding world. It is uncomfortable to hold or espouse beliefs that differ from those held by friends, relatives, or others with whom we normally interact. This is one reason that people feel a need to reduce differences of opinion among members of committees, political parties, clubs or church groups, or even among friends. Men and women seek out individuals with compatible belief systems and shun those who hold "far out" views.

Psychologist Leon Festinger has outlined psychological mechanisms used in coping with anomalies found in DSPs. When two or more strongly held beliefs come into conflict, an individual experiences "cognitive dissonance." Festinger observes that people cannot easily tolerate inconsistent beliefs and that when inconsistencies occur there is a powerful force working to reduce this dissonance. Under conditions in which DSPs are widely accepted, the social support of those sharing the paradigm keeps inconsistencies and anomalies from occurring. But when DSPs begin to break down, needed social support is not always forthcoming, and people feel very uncomfortable trying to reconcile paradigm values with real-world information that seems at variance. One response, of course, is selective perception and manipulation of information. Another response is to shake faith in beliefs underlying the DSP. Both seem to be occurring in contemporary industrial society.

Even when its shortcomings become obvious, there is powerful social pressure to cling to the belief that a paradigm is basically sound. Until a shift to a new paradigm occurs, most people continue to believe in old common wisdoms and virtues and to condemn those who challenge the system. When a paradigm shift does take place, however, the faults of the old paradigm suddenly become very clear to all, people flock to support new ideas, and a new DSP slowly becomes established.

The task before us, then, is one of accelerating this movement toward a new DSP to replace the one that has been shaped by the industrial revolution and that is now leading inexorably toward the destruction of industrial society. Industrial mankind must remake its culture and direct future cultural evolution. A rationally controlled technology does give us a means of survival for ourselves and many generations to come, although it must be supplemented by a social technology that encourages people to value and reward ecologically sound behavior. *Mankind must respond to survival imperatives with meaningful social action.* Culture must again become an ally, rather than an enemy, in the battle for survival.

It is unfortunate that in a mass democracy things seemingly must get much worse before they begin to get better. Democratic political institutions are generally responsive to the wishes of society, but politicians rarely take initiative to ferret out critical problems before they develop. In London, for example, smogs that caused thousands of deaths occurred before a decision was made to limit burning of soft coal in the city. In Los Angeles, school children are forbidden to exercise on many days each year because the polluted air is hazardous to health, but collective efforts to combat air pollution have remained insufficient. Weak smog control efforts are better than none at all, but smog problems cannot be effectively solved until collective decisions are made to overhaul the transportation system drastically. Until people see numerous corpses produced by environmental disasters, they will be unlikely to take initiative in upsetting established practices. Even after catastrophe has struck, they may refuse to assign responsibility to their own behavior and prefer to write off the event as an "act of God."

Glaring examples of such inertia serve to bring the point home. On the same day in 1971 that a destructive earthquake took many lives in Southern California, a bond election was held in San Jose (Northern California) on the question of earthquake-proofing the city's schools. A public relations firm could not have done a better job of manipulating the election in favor of the issue. The earthquake struck at six o'clock in the morning, and the news media brought the tragic story to the attention of voters, most of whom live within ten miles of one of the world's most active faults. Yet the measure failed to pass. Apparently the chief opponent of the measure carried the day with his argument that no serious earthquake in California history had occurred *during school hours.*

In September of the same year, the San Francisco Bay Area Pollution Control District called its first smog alert. The alert required only such voluntary actions as avoiding outdoor burning and leaving as many private automobiles at home as possible. On that day, however, traffic counts on the area's bridges revealed that the number of automobiles on the roads was as high or higher than usual.

Nationally, cost estimates of the bill for restoring what was once the natural environment have soared to approximately $100 billion, but no resolute action has been taken to restore environmental quality. Industry has been tagged as the worst polluter, contributing some 110 million tons of solid waste and one-third of all air pollution each year. It has been suggested that industry should foot much of the bill for cleaning up its own mess and that stockholders should be forced to relinquish some gains made at public expense. Far from being cooperative, however, industry has invested millions in fighting such "user charges" or "effluent taxes."

When the cost estimate for restoring the natural environment was released, no less a figure than the President of the United States announced that "it is simplistic to seek ecological perfection at the cost of bankrupting the very taxpaying enterprises which must pay for the social advances the nation takes." Institutionalized double-think thus defines environmental quality as "ecological perfection" and looks on social advances as distinct from maintenance of a quality environment.

Changing a social paradigm is a difficult task even when problems besetting society are as clear as those that now confront it. Only a small number of people look beyond today's predicaments to scan the future and to analyze the social roots of obvious surface problems. Too many are willing to risk continued deterioration of the total society to protect individual privileges, however minuscule they may be.

What Is to Be Done?

The transformation of a society like that of the United States implies the need for a massive educational effort toward a goal unique in history—the planned evolution of a new culture. But people must first be convinced of the necessity for change. It is extremely difficult to make meaningful the remote consequences of today's behavior. How, then, can the United States be hurried down the road to a new DSP?

Implicit in the approach discussed here is a belief that social change can take place both by working within the system and by continually pointing to the need for massive long-term structural transformations. Long-range solutions will require a revolution at least as significant as the dramatic shift that seems to have occurred in China in the past quarter-century. While working toward such drastic transformations, dedicated people should not lose sight of the many opportunities for changing things through progressive legislation. To attain long-term goals, however, means cultivating large numbers of well-informed, nonviolent revolutionaries. These people must use *all available peaceful strategies* to deflect industrial society from its suicidal course.

In succeeding chapters, the less-exposed areas of the socioenvironmental "iceberg" will be examined, and suggestions, both for policy shifts and major transformations, will be made to indicate the direction in which a new society must move. If mankind is fortunate over the next few years, those concerned with the future will be able to construct a revolutionary vision of a new world and to outline the ways in which society might make a transition to it. If those now entranced with simplistic and badly outdated visions of revolutionary confrontation can be persuaded to shift their sights, perhaps a substantial cadre of active and rational nonviolent revolutionaries can be assembled.

But even if a dedicated group can be assembled, a successful paradigm shift will ultimately depend on the actions of the majority in a democratic society. If each person fails to see and feel the long-term consequences of what he or she is doing, all will be lost. In the end, each person must be made to feel responsible for the present and future welfare of all mankind.

3

Growing Appetites: Limited Provisions

One of the vestiges of eighteenth-century Enlightenment optimism that has persisted as a fundamental economic principle in the dominant social paradigm (DSP) is the theory-turned-dogma of the free market and the laissez-faire economy. Adam Smith, the best-remembered spokesman for this free-wheeling approach to economic affairs, wrote against a background of royal regulation and privilege that strangled individual initiative and generously rewarded connections at court. The dominant economic theory of Smith's day, mercantilism, was aimed at enriching the government (in the person of a monarch) by increasing the amount of precious metal available to it. Smith recognized that the wealth of a nation would be better reckoned by the tools and skills of the citizenry than by the size of the pile of gold in the king's basement and that myopic restrictions aimed at enriching the already-established should be discontinued. The best-known example of the prevailing system of restriction and privilege was the Crown's decision to give the floundering British East India Company (a sort of eighteenth-century Lockheed or Penn Central) a monopoly on the sale of tea in the American colonies—a policy that did not work out too well. It is more than a coincidence that Smith's *Wealth of Nations* was published in the year 1776.

Smith's system of laissez-faire is in some respects a nonsystem. Its underlying principle is that society is best served if each individual's economic decisions are made by that individual on the basis of pecuniary self-interest. Hope for profit leads individuals to invest their wealth, talents, and energies where the demand, and therefore presumably the need, is greatest. In a free market, competition should guarantee that prices are kept down and that return on investment is maintained at reasonable levels. The collective good should be served by everyone taking care of himself. An "invisible hand" guides economic affairs in a supposedly harmonious society.

Smith's ideas make some sense in "cowboy" economies* where available resources and opportunities can be considered infinite, where there are no organized oligopolies or monopolies, and where purchasing power is fairly widely distributed. When there are wide-open opportunities for growth and many people are eager to invest, the role of government can be restricted to enacting a very few macroconstraints to govern entrepreneurs. Such freedom encourages individual initiative and the exploitation of open frontiers. Men work best when they can personally profit from their own ideas and hard labor. But today there are five times as many people as lived in Smith's world, and consequently there are very few resource-abundant societies left.

In Western industrial societies, laissez-faire development now means preserving inequities and special privileges similar to those that Smith originally attacked. Large blocs of wealth and thus significant entrepreneurial activity have remained concentrated in the hands of very few people. It should be obvious why variations on Smith's themes are still readily accepted as truisms by these individuals. They offer justification for self-seeking behavior and divert attention from ethical questions of distribution of wealth and equality of opportunity. They also focus dialogue about economic policy on growth and individual freedoms, while diverting attention away from ultimate constraints on economic growth.

Free competition and economic growth now serve to perpetuate many obviously unhealthy situations. In the United States today, lands that could belong to the people collectively as part of an inherited commons are snapped up for individual profit by land developers. Mineral rights to public lands —lands that should serve as a source of wealth for all—were given away in

---

*A cowboy economy is one in which the abundance of resources and opportunities is so great that little coordination or collective regulation are necessary for optimal allocation of resources. Hence, there is a resemblance to the open frontier where there were few laws governing individual behavior.

the past but now are auctioned off by government and exploited by entrepreneurs, who then escape heavy taxation through depletion allowances. Vast forests, once thought to be limitless and thus sold at very low prices, are now "owned" by lumber interests who are willing to sell parts of them back to the public at exorbitant prices for use as parks.

Because of increasing awareness of long-overlooked problems, Smith's theories are slowly losing influence. It is now recognized, for example, that laissez-faire economics is insensitive to the plight of the starving and poor. The poor have no resources with which to buy into the marketplace. A population explosion combined with rising aspirations presents serious problems for the free market. For many essential items, elasticity of supply* is already a thing of the past. In the near future, perhaps only the wealthiest will be able to afford what are now considered essential goods. In 1973, for instance, rising prices did not quickly lead to a significant increase in the supply of gasoline (inelasticity of supply) or to reductions in demand (inelasticity of demand). Similarly, prices for staple food commodities are expected to rise out of sight without significantly reducing demand. People must pay the price or starve. It is ironic that many countries, including the Soviet Union, have recently bought American wheat to provide cheap bread for the rich as well as the poor. In return, the poor in the United States might be forced to do without bread as its price rises to $1.00 per loaf because of a wheat shortage in the United States brought on by foreign purchases.

Today's economic world is very different from that envisioned by Adam Smith. In Smith's "ideal world," there would be many buyers and sellers, competition would be keen, and prices and profits would be held at reasonable levels by an "invisible hand." Today, however, huge conglomerate giants dominate many markets. In the automobile industry, as well as in metal, food processing, aircraft, and many other industries, there is little real competition. For instance, over the past forty years, General Motors, Ford, and Chrysler have sold approximately 90 percent of the domestically produced cars bought by Americans. If the buyer in the marketplace does not like what is offered, he or she can buy an increasingly expensive foreign car or do without. In view of the lack of adequate public transportation in most of the United States, doing without an automobile is not a very viable alternative. There is no way to ensure responsiveness to consumer demands in such situations.

---

*Elasticities of supply and demand refer to conditions in which an increase in price for a commodity leads to an increase in the quantity produced (elasticity of supply) and a decrease in the quantity consumed (elasticity of demand).

An unimpeded flow of information, essential for free competition, was another important aspect of Smith's ideal market. Today, of course, product information is power and is jealously guarded by manufacturers. Try to find out just how much profit there is in any particular product. Better yet, try to compare the quality of competing brands. Often manufacturers have not even been able to agree on meaningful categories of comparison, let alone measures of quality. "Let the buyer beware" has more than symbolic meaning in today's seller-controlled marketplace.

In an ideal free market, the number of potential sellers would not be restricted by heavy costs of market entry. In the less complex early industrial society, it was easier for artisans and other entrepreneurs to respond to consumer demands by establishing small enterprises. But, as society has become more complex, costs for a new business to enter the marketplace on a large scale have, in many economic sectors, become prohibitively high. Economic history has been flowing in one direction, from a large number of competitors in major industries to a much smaller number. Today it is almost impossible to conceive of an entrepreneur establishing a new automobile factory to compete with the "big three." The kind of money that would be needed to start the operation is not readily available; nor is the motivation. Similarly, few people have access to the funds needed to start a major new newspaper. In fact, over the last two decades a startling proportion of existing newspapers have merged, with a resulting decline in the competition of ideas in many large American cities. It is true, on the other hand, that it is just as easy or perhaps even easier now for individual entrepreneurs to set up very small operations, although these small operations have little impact in competition with economic giants.

Smith could know nothing about the role that advertising would come to play in manipulating consumer attitudes or the tremendous investments that manufacturers would make in merchandising their wares. Radio, television, magazines, and newspapers now carry messages that not only stimulate consumption, but often are designed to misrepresent products and further confuse an already confused market situation. Competition based on product quality has been replaced by media competition, which to date has been of little social value. Consumers are sold products on the basis of clever Madison Avenue pitches, usually aimed at ego needs or libidinal gratification. In the end society suffers through increased consumption, needless investment in advertising, and diminished competition based on product quality.

In summary, Smith's ideas were developed 200 years ago during the formative phase of the industrial paradigm and have been essential in providing its underpinnings. But the nature of society and its impact on the environment have changed so drastically that neither the original ideas nor their subsequent modifications any longer provide a suitable model for an economic system. Although Smith's theories have been modified by neoclassical economists, currently needed changes in economics must be much more fundamental.

Growth as Progress

No belief in industrial society is so pervasive and so essential to it as "progress" defined in terms of economic growth. It sustains faith in the industrial system and reinforces hope among the poor that they also may "strike it rich." There appear to be few social ills that cannot be remedied by a healthy dose of "development." Most Americans expect continued economic improvement during their lifetimes. Politicians strive to outdo each other in proving that the economy has grown tremendously during their terms in office and that their constituents have thereby improved their standards of living.

During most of the industrial revolution, there was little reason to question that growth was synonymous with progress. Growth permitted the wealthy to consent to improving the lot of the poor because it was much easier to yield a small portion of an expanding economic pie than it would have been to redistribute a fixed amount of wealth. Economic growth was the best kind of social cement. It permitted various antagonistic classes to bury differences while sharing in the fruits of increasing productivity.

Not only does mankind's present environmental predicament force a reassessment of growth policies, it also occasions a skeptical backward glance at what has been called economic progress. Progress is frequently measured, especially by politicians, in terms of increase in gross national product (GNP). Politicians point with pride to a growing GNP as an indication that society is prospering. People are told that GNP equals more than $1.3 trillion, up from only $300 million in the early fifties—a certain indication that capitalism and the free market still work and that Americans are enjoying a higher standard of living.

This is one of the reasons that suggestions for limiting growth in resource consumption raises such vehement political opposition. If traditional types of economic growth are curtailed, current economic inequities will become more apparent, and economic differences could become political issues. Two articles appearing in *Newsweek* in early 1972 stated the issue very clearly. Economist Henry Wallich laid the cards right on the table when he said that ". . . growth is a substitute for equality of income. . . . So long as there is growth, there is hope, and that makes large income differentials tolerable." Wallich went on to point out that continued growth is needed if the government is to be able to meet obligations without adding "painful" new taxes. Growth, he said, is "positively enjoyable." He failed to add, of course, that growth is positively enjoyable only for a limited period and then is not so enjoyable for the poor who will be the first to feel the effects of environmental deterioration. Political scientist and former presidential adviser Zbigniew Brzezinski took a somewhat more realistic view of the situation in March of the same year when he stated: ". . . that inequality exists in the United States is indisputable. . . . However, what has made inequality bearable is that in the American tradition (as well as myth) it is balanced by opportunity." However, Brzezinski gave no answer to the question of what will happen when this wide-open opportunity becomes constricted by the realities of resource availability.

An expanding GNP is not necessarily related to an increasing quality of life. Gross national product measures the value of all goods and services produced in any one year. Increases in total GNP, therefore, may not represent any increase in goods and services available to each individual, as increased production can easily be offset by increased population growth with no resultant improvement in each individual's standard of living. Even a substantial increase in *per capita* GNP can be misleading. For instance, most of the recent highly advertised yearly increases in United States GNP have not been *real* in the sense that they have been spurred by inflation (simple price increase) rather than by any increase in available goods and services. It is true that economists have developed other measures of economic health that take some of these factors into account, but in political discussions progress has been described most often simply in terms of increasing GNP.

Moreover, GNP does not adequately account for two very important factors, depreciation and obsolescence. It measures the flow of products through society but says little about the quality or quantity of existing stocks. In figuring net national product, economists do take account of depreciation on capital goods (facilities and equipment used to produce other goods), but even this more sophisticated measure ignores the rate at which manufactured goods deteriorate. It makes little sense to total the growth in goods and services produced, thereby implying that the sum is an index of an increasing level of living, without taking into consideration the average life expectancy of products and the need to replace worn-out goods. Every item that leaves the factory has a life expectancy known to the manufacturer but generally unknown to the public. If all goods produced fell apart in only one year, the entire production of goods could be devoted exclusively to maintaining a constant stock, and GNP would still be very high. Production of goods that endure is obviously both ecologically sound and in the public interest. In the present atmosphere of reduced competition, however, it is often in the manufacturer's interest to create a product that either will soon be out of style or will fall apart fairly rapidly. This guarantees a constant market for essential items and represents a modern-day crippling of Smith's invisible hand.

The American automobile industry offers striking examples of planned obsolescence and poor durability. There is no reason for restyling automobiles every model year except to accelerate the rate at which they are considered obsolete. Volkswagen, for instance, has been quite successful without making annual style changes. There certainly has been no voluntary movement by manufacturers toward designs that maximize durability and thus minimize the ecological damage attendant to the manufacture of automobiles. In fact, if warranty coverage is any indication, the movement has been in the opposite direction. Only a few years ago, automobile dealers were offering five-year/50,000-mile warranties. Today they offer one year or 12,000 miles. Each year millions of dollars are spent in making annual model changes designed to lure status-conscious consumers to buy the latest model. Everyone is happy when Detroit's sales reach new highs and the economy is said to be prospering, even though this type of prosperity threatens to bankrupt the ecosphere.

Obsolescence is also built into products through shoddy workmanship. When there is little room for annual style changes, the consumer can be stuck with products that need to be repaired often enough to be a nuisance. Components for most black-and-white television sets, for example, still come with one-year warranties; components for sets that provide color reception often have warranties of as little as three months. An electronics industry that can televise pictures from satellites orbiting Mars should be able to develop more durable and dependable television sets. Instead, the major research effort in this industry seems to be channeled into the development of new types of color sets, wall television, and other gimmicks for which new markets can be created. Furthermore, many types of major appliances are now being so designed that cheap repairs are impossible. When one small part burns out, a major part or even the entire unit must be replaced.

Changes in the composition of the nonservice portion of the growing GNP give further cause for reflection on the relation of GNP to the quality of life. Remember when most people lived close enough to their places of work that they could walk to them? And the fun that people used to have going into the woods to gather Yule logs or to cut a Christmas tree? Remember when children played with homemade toys or those carefully handed down from generation to generation? Those days are gone. Although many people lament their passing for sentimental reasons, a most intriguing economic quirk is that each move away from these traditions has resulted in an increase in measured GNP as well as an increased burden on the environment.

Today most Americans drive to work. Although daily journeys over miles of overcrowded freeway represent no great advance in the quality of life, constructing freeways has accounted for a considerable portion of recent growth in GNP. Many families now purchase two or three cars to make certain that each member of the family has one. Indeed, in many parts of the United States public transportation no longer exists, and automobiles have become a necessity. Using an automobile is attractive and convenient for each individual, but increasing traffic congestion and pollution lower the quality of life for everyone. The extra motor vehicles sold and the gasoline and oil necessary to fuel them, however, are all included in the growing GNP.

There are countless other examples of artificial growth in GNP that have accompanied greater societal complexity. Our "less-privileged" ancestors could stay thin by gathering their fireplace logs themselves. Today, firewood is gathered, boxed, wholesaled, retailed, and, of course, added to the GNP. So is the business of the reducing salon where overweight people pay for the privilege of exercising. Children no longer shoot marbles, play ball, or climb trees. Today's child "needs" a life-like Barbie Doll that will perform a number of tricks, or any of the hundreds of new $6.98 games that are constantly advertised on children's cartoon shows on television. Climbing trees entailed no special contribution to GNP, but sales of all the latest "kiddie items" are registered as significant additions to GNP and, by inference, to the quality of life.

As strange as it may seem, a real *decline* in the quality of life can be taken as a sign of health as defined in terms of present GNP. Crime, for example, can indirectly spur various types of consumption. A stolen automobile has to be replaced, usually by a newer model. Buildings damaged during violent demonstrations must be rebuilt. Weapons purchases become part of the GNP, as do burglar alarms, new locks, and private security services. When people cower behind locked doors, buy new protection devices, and are forced to hire private policemen for their safety, it is difficult to believe that the quality of life, as measured by these purchases, is improving.

In other words, past growth in GNP has not necessarily indicated progress toward a better life, nor does it always indicate such progress today. "Growth-maniacs" frequently focus on the need for simple increases in GNP, not on the mix of material goods and services produced. They also ignore the environmental costs of this growth and seem not to realize that a nation that produced nothing but hula hoops or hand guns would not be a very comfortable place to live. At a minimum, many new and more sophisticated indicators of *quality* of industrial production, as well as related environmental impact, are needed to replace simple GNP statistics.

Growth and Employment

In January, 1972, the very popular Children's Zoo in San Francisco's Golden Gate Park was closed as a result of a hiring freeze imposed by the mayor of that city. Ironically, a budget-cutting move came at a time when 7 percent of the work force in California was unemployed. During the previous year, the governor of the same state had imposed an austerity program to reduce the number of employees on the state payroll. The rationale for this move was that, in difficult economic times, we all need to "tighten our belts." The governor thought that the best place to start was with state employees. As a result of the employment freeze, no new instructors were added to the state college or university systems. Picking up the cue, many local school boards dismissed teachers as being nonessential, although they had been essential the year before, and the number of students per teacher increased. All this occurred as "official" unemployment in California hovered around 7 percent, and welfare rolls, which also represent people on the public payroll, reached their highest point since the Depression.

Nationally, the pattern was much the same. With nationwide unemployment averaging 6 percent, the Nixon administration was engaged in a belt-tightening program that meant firing thousands of federal employees and cutting back dozens of federal programs and social services. Many types of employment supported by public funds, including vital scientific research, fell before the presidential axe. At the same time, the President announced massive federal deficit spending, aimed at heating up the private sector, to get the country back on the road to prosperity.

In the early seventies, millions of Americans were still ill-housed and ill-fed, but the economy of the United States was only operating at approximately three-quarters of capacity. Factories were operating well below capacity, farmers were being paid not to grow crops, and the number of new housing starts was decreasing. Economists apparently could devise no method of matching unmet demands for the necessities of life with the unemployed pool of labor. Although idle factories are certainly no cause for alarm from an environmental point of view, a country with social goals such as those professed in the United States cannot afford to ignore basic human needs while labor and facilities sit idle.

By late 1973, Nixon administration economists, with their outmoded approaches to managing the economy, had created even more serious dislocations. New demand for industrial products fueled by government-backed campaigns, led to "gray" markets in several important sectors of the economy. The economic policies of the Nixon administration succeeded very well in stimulating the production and purchase of automobiles, but at the cost of creating impossible demands in other industries. The same Nixon administration arbitrarily relaxed environmental protection standards in 1973 because of excess demands for fuel. In late 1973, the steel industry could not meet orders from many customers and was carefully allocating available supplies. Petroleum refineries could not keep up with the increased demands for gasoline, caused in part by greater automobile travel and in part by pollution control devices that decreased gasoline mileage. Petroleum producers ordered great quantities of steel for refinery expansion, further exacerbating the steel supply problem. In addition, the rising expectations of Americans created demands that, when combined with environmental protection policies, could not be met by existing producers. Demand for paper, for example, rose at an annual rate of 17 percent, while the industry's facilities expanded at a rate of only 2 percent. But the critical point is that all this activity, much of it intended to increase employment, did very little to change unemployment figures.

While these economic maneuvers may seem illogical, they are an inevitable result of trying to apply old-paradigm economic thinking to new problems. A desire for profits and production "efficiency," a fetish for "private" enterprise and a "free market," and a preference for the production of goods rather than the provision of services are values that have led to considerable human suffering.

In Adam Smith's tradition, businesses try to maximize profits by employing as few people as possible. Employees must be paid regularly. Machines, after the initial cost of purchase, require only energy and maintenance, which, until now, have been extremely cheap. During the industrial revolution, as capital became more concentrated, machines replaced men and reduced the need for physical labor. The productivity of each worker was thus vastly increased through a fossil fuel subsidy. For a long period the exponential rate of economic expansion in industrializing countries overshadowed the declining role of labor in production as new businesses quickly took up the slack in employment. Rising output per man-hour was praised as a sure sign of progress, which it was, in a limited sense. During the years of resource plenty, particularly between 1800 and 1950, the abundance created by the fossil fuel subsidy certainly raised the quality of life for most Americans and made harsh and tedious toil largely obsolete. What is now deplorable, however, is America's failure to recognize that this narrow definition of efficiency, based on economies of scale and replacement of labor by fossil-fuel-driven machinery, no longer is appropriate.

Other factors contribute to the present unemployment problem. Traditional political values discourage economic activities in the public sector. It is considered inherently more proper for private enterprise to provide goods and services in the name of private profits than for government to provide them in the public sector. Consequently, the expansion of many needed services that could provide additional employment, such as education or public transportation, is retarded because of dependence on tax dollars. Thus, within the present dominant social paradigm, education is regarded as a frill, while the production of more automobiles in Detroit is considered essential. Excise taxes on large, polluting automobiles have been reduced to stimulate sales, while virtually no funds have been earmarked from tax revenues for public transit. Instead, tax monies are used to build new highways to serve the automobiles. The government provides large subsidies to failing, privately owned industries that produce nonessential products, while cutting back on much-needed educational programs, child-care services, research expenditures, and other public programs. Americans paradoxically live in the world's most affluent society, but the economy is unable to provide enough jobs to keep the population fully employed.

Labor itself also contributes to the unemployment picture. Rather than give up financial compensation in favor of more leisure, perhaps with a four-day work week, many employees work overtime while their fellow workers are unemployed. Instead of allowing available work to be spread among greater numbers, each person seems bent on accumulating as much money as possible.

Unless some fundamental changes can be made in this complex economic syndrome, Americans can look forward to continuing unemployment problems for at least the next decade. During this period, the labor force will continue to expand (reflecting the high birth rates of the preceding twenty years), while growing resource constraints and environmental protection legislation can be expected to slow traditional forms of economic growth.

The New Inflation

When this chapter was first drafted, the Nixonian economic "phase" vocabulary had not yet been invented. Although serious economic problems were already apparent, the American public was being assured that the economy was healthy and that only temporary measures were required to bring back economic health. Between 1971 and 1974, the economy moved from the verge of a recession, through an economic boom, and then bolted out of control with an inflationary thrust leading to measures to head the economy back toward recession. Most Americans watched with keen interest as the foremost economists of the old school wrote their prescriptions for economic health. Unfortunately, none of them has worked successfully; nor is there any indication that better results can be expected in the near future. The United States, as well as other industrial countries, is caught up in an inflationary spiral resulting from too much consumer demand, too little appropriate factory capacity, too many producers and intermediaries, and spiraling costs for natural resources and basic agricultural commodities. In this overheated condition, which undoubtedly will persist for some time to come, price increases do little to decrease consumption, and everyone involved in supplying essential commodities is able to take just a little more profit.

In the past, if an industrial economy became overheated and plagued by inflation (too much buying power chasing too few goods), one solution was to tighten credit (monetary policy) and raise taxes (fiscal policy). In combination, these actions would reduce the buying power of consumers and therefore would reduce demand. Similar results could be obtained in reverse; that is, if an economy were sluggish, credit could be eased and taxes lowered, thus freeing more buying power.

Employment levels are closely tied to such policies. When an economy contracts, a certain portion of the work force suffers directly through loss of jobs. As an economy heats up in times of prosperity, there are more jobs available. In the past, quite ruthless decisions have been made to deal with rising prices by cooling the economy and putting people out of work. The theory held that it was better for a few to suffer unemployment than for everyone to lose through inflation. Changing moral standards have made such policies less socially acceptable. In addition, it has now become difficult to deal with inflation with such a limited kit of economic tools.

The relationship between levels of inflation and levels of employment is depicted by what economists call a "Phillips curve," shown in Figure 3.1. The relationship between inflation and employment before 1970 is traced by the lower curve. Unemployment rates of 6 percent were associated with price increases of only 2 percent annually in the decade 1960–1970. Four percent unemployment could be traded for price increases of approximately 3 percent. In the decade of the seventies, however, the curve has shifted dramatically upward. In 1973, for example, unemployment rates of 5 percent corresponded to price increases of 8 or 9 percent. This new relationship is shown by the upper curve.

A number of factors can be blamed for an upward shift of the curve. The United States has apparently entered a new economic era in which old beliefs about supply and demand elasticities are much less applicable than they once were. The problems of maintaining supplies of gasoline and heating oil and

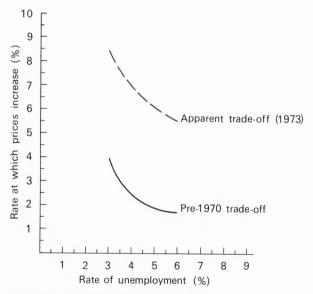

Figure 3.1   *The shifting Phillips curve*

the rises in food prices during 1972 and 1973 are obvious examples. In both situations many factors other than simple supply and demand were involved, and early economic planning might have averted the shortages and rising prices. Such dislocations are symptoms of more serious inflationary tendencies built into a situation where rising expectations collide with scarcity of vital resources of all types. Mineral resources and food undoubtedly will continue to become much more expensive over the next few decades, and an adequate supply will become increasingly more costly to maintain. Someone must determine that prices of essential commodities remain "fair"; otherwise, those few who now control them, the "haves," will be able to extract excess profits from the "have-nots."

We are entering a period in which price increases no longer have the same causes and do not serve the same function that they served in the past. When resources were in abundance, rising prices were useful to curb demand and induce capital to move into profitable areas. Under conditions of resource shortage, however, rising prices may not lead to increasing supplies, and in many situations they will not reduce demand. Demand for many items is inelastic; that is, people must have them at any price. Food, clothing, adequate shelter, and fuels for heating and cooking are needed by everyone. At the same time, substantial price increases may not elicit much greater supply. Greater profits sometimes can be gained from raising prices without increasing production, and this is something that the federal government must carefully monitor.

This is not mere conjecture. Major oil companies were able to use this situation to good advantage in 1973. Prices were increased on gasoline, but the increases led only to greater profits for many big oil companies, as well as the reduction of competition. The volume of gasoline produced did not markedly increase nor did consumption decrease, despite publicity campaigns and government requests for voluntary compliance. Manufacturing costs did not drastically increase, but prices at the pump certainly did. Clearly, new approaches are needed to deal with resource-related abuses, which will undoubtedly become more commonplace over the next decade.

The golden days of rapid economic expansion are coming to an end in all advanced industrial nations. Growth seems to be systematically slowing in these societies after the initial bursts of productivity that accompanied early economies of scale. In such highly developed economies as Great Britain, West Germany, and the United States, the average rate of economic growth has been less than 5 percent annually for the last decade. In countries that are in the "take-off" period of industrial growth, rates of increase in production close to 10 percent annually are not uncommon. Although Japan's economy grew at a rate of close to 10 percent per year in the sixties, now that Japan's level of industrialization is approaching those existing in Western Europe and the United States, a much lower figure may well prevail in the future.

Not only can advanced industrial economies expect to grow slowly in the future because of the difficulty of adding to an already large and complex industrial base, they can no longer expect to grow in traditional ways because of increasing costs of obtaining raw materials. In general, industrial societies have already depleted the richest deposits of resources within their borders. Western Europe and Japan are now almost entirely dependent on other areas of the world for supplies of critical raw materials, natural gas, and petroleum, resulting in increasingly unfavorable balances of payments for those nations. In addition, increasing economic and environmental costs of obtaining materials domestically, as well as costs of environmental clean-up, will restrict economic potential.

Some economists think that, from an environmental point of view, there is nothing wrong with inflation. They point out that, as raw materials become more difficult to obtain, they will rise in price, and problems of profligate consumption will thereby be solved. Unfortunately, there is no clear indication that inflation will cause declining levels of consumption for society as a whole, and particularly among the more privileged classes that consume most. The runaway inflation of 1973 did not reduce consumption at all; conversely, it seemed to spur it on.

Inflation hurts the young as well as the retired. Those who obtained property and other assets in the past can weather inflationary pressures, but the young must struggle with increasing prices and often cannot afford to buy adequate housing and other necessities. Price increases will be inevitable over the next few decades. But any rationing function performed by higher prices must be tempered with public policies designed to distribute inflation's impact fairly and to ensure the provision of basic necessities to all persons. Those who offer necessary and (sometimes artificially) scarce services, whether physicians or plumbers, will be relative immune to higher prices. Strong labor unions and large corporations can use their muscle to keep their earnings in step with inflation, while those who cannot deal with the economy from a position of strength will be unable to keep up with the pace. This group includes people on relatively fixed incomes. Teachers and some other public employees are forbidden by law to strike. Therefore, even though they provide essential services that consume very few scarce resources, they are at the mercy of the public when it comes to salary increases. During inflationary periods, the public is particularly hesitant to grant tax increases to increase services in the public sector. In the early seventies, for example, several school districts closed their doors for extended periods because voters would not pass bond issues to cover educational expenditures.

The picture of inflation that emerges is one of many mice nibbling away at an economic pie that is being blown up with air. The labor mice nibble faster, but the amount of nourishment they get does not drastically change. The corporate mice are also nibbling faster at the economic pie with similar lack of success. On the periphery, however, the aged mice, teaching mice, mice on the public payroll, and other mice on fixed incomes, eating at a relatively constant rate, are being slowly "moused" out of the banquet. Each mouse eats frantically out of self-interest, but no one really gets ahead. The inflationary world of the future may well be one characterized by brutal competition among people struggling just to keep up with rising prices. Those who are already at an economic disadvantage will continue to be the losers unless steps are taken to distribute the impact of inflation rationally and fairly.

When the underlying limits to growth are juxtaposed with rising expectations and the constraints imposed by a value preference for full employment, it is clear that prices must continue to rise. Arthur Okun, former chief adviser to President Johnson, has devised an economic "discomfort index," composed of the rate of unemployment added to the rate of inflation. The discomfort index has risen steadily over the last twenty years. It stood at 3.9 in 1952, moved to 7.1 in 1966, and jumped to 13.4 in 1971; it

Table 3.1   *Inflation and Unemployment in the United States, 1965–1973*

Year	Unemployment (Percent of Work Force)	Consumer Price Index (1967 = 100)
1965	4.5	94.5
1966	3.8	97.2
1967	3.8	100.0
1968	3.6	104.2
1969	3.5	109.8
1970	4.9	116.3
1971	5.9	121.3
1972	5.1 (December)	127.3 (December)
1973	5.0 (May)	131.5 (May)

appears to be approximately 14.0 for 1973. Politicians and establishment economists continue to argue that the old system is basically sound, but a twenty-year trend toward economic crisis suggests that their beliefs are based more on hope than on fact.

Most so-called solutions to persistent unemployment and inflation represent attempts to patch up an old economic paradigm rather than efforts to move toward a new one. The schizophrenic reversals of "Alice-in-Wonderland" economic policy during the Nixon years indicate a desperate attempt to find some combination of policies that will work short of replacing generally accepted economic policies. However, it is obvious that such patchwork solutions only postpone problems; they do not solve them. Politically acceptable solutions are timed to have short-term impact, and little thought is given to long-term solutions.

It is clear that a new economic program is needed that does more than attempt to boost employment through subsidies to big business and curb inflation through finger shaking and voluntary compliance. Many possible policy shifts and structural transformations could alleviate both problems and still maintain the principle of retaining as many microfreedoms as possible while increasing macroconstraints on the economy. At the very top, the division between "planned" and "free" segments of the economy must be reconsidered. The degree of market freedom that now prevails in the United States is higher than that in most other industrial societies, and too many people are presently left out of the marketplace. Too many essential public services are neglected while economic efforts are concentrated in bolstering the private sector of the economy.

Unregulated Giants

Many of the early successes of the industrial revolution resulted from mergers and the concentration of capital in fewer hands. Such consolidation was then beneficial and was responsible for large productivity increases. Today, however, the amount of competition in the industrial marketplace has drastically shrunk, and this has had serious implications for product quality and consumer relations in a free market economy. Giant corporations and wealthy financiers operate on the basis of self-interest, as they always did. But in the absence of competition, self-interest leads to callous attitudes toward consumers, needless abuses of the environment, and a general disregard for the public interest.

A quick glance at some figures indicates the scope of the problem. In 1948, the 100 largest manufacturers in the United States controlled 40 percent of all manufacturing assets held. By 1970 they controlled 49 percent of assets. In 1947 these 100 largest manufacturers were responsible for 23 percent of all value added in manufacturing. In 1967 the figure had increased to 33 percent. Between 1955 and 1959, there were 3,365 mergers and acquisitions in American industry. Between 1965 and 1969 there were 8,213. The rate of merging dropped slightly between 1969 and 1971 because of poor economic conditions, but it picked up again in 1973 in response to greater industrial profits.

It is difficult to justify the existence of large conglomerates that have their fingers in many different industrial pies. These organizations are certainly not more socially responsible, more efficient, or even more productive than conventional firms. The International Telephone and Telegraph Company used to be clearly in the communications business. After a decade of agglomeration, ITT has acquired Avis Rent-A-Car, Continental Baking, Aetna Finance, and Levitt and Sons Homebuilders, among dozens of other companies. Clearly, there are few social or even economic benefits to be obtained from such a conglomerate, except for its management. On the contrary, there are many good reasons that it should not be allowed to persist. In terms of natural resource efficiency, there is little reason for ITT to make telephone and electronics equipment, bake bread, and rent cars. These activities have little in common. Similarly, there is no logical reason for Textron to raise chickens, manufacture electrical equipment, or operate an ocean liner. Such conglomerates represent a serious threat to free competition. They are blocs of economic power that are difficult to regulate, that strangle smaller enterprises, and that frequently are unresponsive to any public interest or to consumer demands. The products and services these conglomerates offer are certainly no better than those offered previously by smaller independent firms.

Mergers once made economic sense. Large corporations could take advantage of economies of scale and avoid duplication of staff and facilities. These new efficiencies led to greater profits for both owners and society. Today, however, many conglomerate mergers take place for quite different reasons. The most obvious reason is to take advantage of tax laws by using capital that would otherwise be confiscated by taxation to acquire property. If the Smith Widget Corporation makes windfall profits in any tax year, it had better merge with another less successful company or it will be forced to pay considerable taxes. Conglomerates are also formed for diversification, to spread the risk of failure across several unrelated spheres of activity. Management is thereby protected from the economic consequences of mistakes if many different types of products are manufactured by different branches of a conglomerate. Another reason for merger often has been to manipulate favorable stock prices for executives who own a good deal of stock in companies to be merged. These advantages of mergers to corporations and management are real ones, but whatever advantages ever accrued to consumers or to society have mostly disappeared.

Many socially and ecologically desirable innovations are opposed by large corporations, for good reason from their private perspective. Inventions and discoveries often mean expensive changes in machine tools and other facilities. The steel industry has a tremendous investment in the open-hearth method of producing steel. Although this method is hard on workers and is responsible for considerable air pollution, a switch to new and more efficient electric furnaces would require millions of dollars of new equipment and would cut deeply into short-run profits. Since only three large steel producers in the United States (United States, Bethlehem, and Republic) control more than two-thirds of the market, new equipment can be kept out of the mills by gentlemen's agreements. Even though the new techniques are safer, cleaner, and almost four times as efficient in terms of energy used, as long as no big producer breaks ranks and modernizes its facilities there is no competition to force any of them to innovate.

The automobile industry also offers a clear-cut example of oligopoly and its attendant lack of concern for the environment and consumer safety. The mileage efficiency of the American automobile has not basically changed since World War II. Engines have been "souped up," but auto safety, fuel consumption, and repair records have not significantly improved. Those improvements that have taken place have largely been made under threat of government intervention or foreign competition. Seat belts, for example, have been used for decades in airplanes, but it was not until 1963 that Volvo pioneered them in automobiles. Not only was the seat belt pioneered by an import, the first American firm to install them was now-defunct Studebaker, the smallest of the auto producers at that time.

The Wankel rotary engine is another innovation that was for a long time rejected by Detroit. It is lighter, quieter, and likely to be more repair-free than conventional engines since it has fewer moving parts. By 1973 a Japanese version had been perfected to meet the Environmental Protection Agency's 1975 pollution standards. But it took the West Coast success of the Japanese

Mazda to interest Detroit in a Wankel engine as the costs of retooling presented a threat to short-run profits. The American consumer thus has been deprived of the savings of operating a trouble-free car.

Other large corporations persist in ignoring their own devastating impact on the environment. The steel and chemical oligopolies have traditionally despoiled the public domain by using the nation's streams to dump solid and liquid wastes and by using the atmosphere to disperse gases. The mining industry shows little regard for the environment or for working conditions. Both the efficiency and safety records of coal mines in the United States are well below those of Europe. In addition, strip-mining destroys a greater portion of the American countryside each year. In 1964, 31 percent of all soft coal produced in the United States was strip-mined. By 1972 the figure had grown to 47 percent.

The airline industry offers an example of the hazards of "quasi-public" control of large industries and the dangers resulting from half-measures. The United States stands almost alone among industrial countries in its reluctance to nationalize air transportation. Like other industries, airlines want to expand, merge, and increase their private profits. Since airlines are considered vital to the national well-being, however, their fares are regulated by the Civil Aeronautics Board (CAB) and computed to guarantee the airlines' stockholders a fair margin of profit. The CAB has a stated policy of permitting airlines to make a 10.5 percent profit on *total investment,* so there has been an understandable tendency for airlines to increase investment by using larger fleets and more extensive ground facilities. Although planes were flying at only 49 percent of capacity in 1971, the airlines continued to invest heavily in 747 jumbo jets and giant airbusses, even though existing equipment was far from obsolete. No concern was expressed for the tremendous amount of fuel being wasted by flying half-empty planes. Environmental scientist K. E. F. Watt has pointed out that aircraft manufacturers are planning to sell enough giant airplanes during the seventies to more than double the passenger capacity of all the airlines of the non-Communist world.

The reaction of the surface transportation industry to declining numbers of passengers has been to petition regulatory agencies for higher fares, which, when granted, lead to a further diminution of passenger business. Thus, while the need for surface transportation is growing, the available alternatives continue to shrink and fares increase. One commuter train can carry 500 passengers with one-fifth the consumption of fuel that would be required by 250 private automobiles. If the economy were run according to ecological principles, commuter fares would be reduced through public subsidies and public control of mass transportation industries. Instead, present policies permit private enterprise to skim the cream off the top with lucrative freight business, and the public is left with a badly mismanaged and highly inefficient passenger transportation system. Clearly, "quasi-public" regulation does not work much better than the free market when irresponsible, politically powerful interests are concerned.

Although there has been much talk about the "responsible corporation," large corporations are still run by executives who operate their businesses under old-paradigm rules. Corporate "success" is defined by profits, not by responsiveness to the public. Nor are stockholders paragons of social responsibility. Most stockholders are institutions: mutual funds, pension plans, banks, and so on. They also operate in self-interest and cannot be expected to pay much attention to anything other than their own balance sheets. Table 3.2 shows the results of civic-minded stockholder attempts to adopt environmental and other socially responsible initiatives in 1972. The table makes it clear that appeals to stockholders are not likely to alter the path being followed by corporate giants. The business world runs on self-interest, but this self-interest now rarely leads to social progress.

More evidence of irresponsible corporate behavior is offered by the activities of corporate executives during the wage and price freeze of 1972. While most Americans had to be content with maximum pay increases of 5.5 percent plus 0.7 percent for fringe benefits, business executives were handsomely rewarding themselves with huge salary increases. For leading the United States down the road to increased automobile-caused atmospheric pollution, Chrysler board chairman Lynn Townsend received a 209 percent increase in salary and fringe benefits. Ford executives Henry Ford II and Lee Iacocco contented themselves with "only" 27 percent increases in salary and fringe benefits but this meant total compensation of nearly $900,000 for each. On the average, top executives in all industries increased their total compensation by 13.5 percent in 1972, more than twice the percentage that was allowed under existing wage and price controls. As might be expected, those industries that, from an environmental point of view, should be least rewarded gave executives the greatest salary increases. Executives in the automobile industry received average compensation increases of 48 percent, transportation executives (including those in the airline industry, which claimed to be losing money) received 37 percent, and oil industry executives received 14 percent.

To sum up, industry in the United States is dominated by oligopolies. Today, free enterprise means freedom to stifle innovation and to manipulate markets out of self-interest; there are not enough competitors to make the invisible hand work. No institutions are present within the old economic

Table 3.2 *Voting Results on Social Issues in 1972*

Company	Proposal	Sponsoring Shareholder	Total Shares Voted in Favor	Percent of Total
American Metal Climax, Inc.	1. To require minimization of ecological damage from mining	Domestic and Foreign Missionary Society of the Protestant Episcopal Church	634,199	3.27
	2. To require disclosure of ecological program details	Same	712,983	3.68
American Telephone and Telegraph (AT & T)	To broaden representation on the Board of Directors	Project on Corporate Responsibility	14,259,710	3.80
Bristol Myers Co.	To conduct a study on drug abuse	Project on Corporate Responsibility	564,106	1.73
Chrysler Corp.	1. To broaden representation on the Board of Directors	Project on Corporate Responsibility	1,823,452	4.91
	2. To require disclosure of information on pollution control, product safety, and programs for hiring minorities and women	Same	1,647,695	4.45
Consumers Power Co.[a]	To broaden safety and insurance requirements for nuclear power plants	West Michigan Environmental Action Council	460	—
Control Data Corp.	To establish a committee to study economic conversion	Council for Corporate Review	274,595	2.68

Company	Proposal	Proposer	
Eli Lilly & Co.	1. To conduct a study of drug abuse	Project on Corporate Responsibility	330,817	.005
	2. To establish foreign labeling restrictions	Same	337,864	.006
FMC Corp.	To establish a committee to study economic conversion	Council for Corporate Review	1,539,436	5.40
Ford Motor Co.	1. To broaden representation on Board of Directors	Project on Corporate Responsibility	1,109,864	1.00
	2. To require disclosure on pollution control, product safety, and programs for hiring minorities and women	Same	1,781,762	1.63
General Motors Corp.	1. To establish a committee to study dividing the company	Project on Corporate Responsibility	2,426,243	1.04
	2. To require disclosure of Public Policy Committee activity	Same	2,598,655	1.12
Honeywell, Inc.	1. To require a report on military contract activity	Clergymen and Laymen Concerned	168,420	1.08
	2. To establish a committee to study economic conversion	Council for Corporate Review and Clergymen and Laymen Concerned	245,906	1.75
International Telephone and Telegraph Corp. (ITT)	1. To require a report on military contract activity	Clergymen and Laymen Concerned	2,053,856	2.35
	2. To establish a committee to study economic conversion	Same	2,210,834	2.53

(continued)

Table 3.2 *Voting Results on Social Issues in 1972* (*continued*)

Levi Strauss and Co.	To establish a committee to study social impact of the corporation	Rodney Shields	4.27
Merck and Co., Inc.	1. To establish foreign labeling restrictions	Project on Corporate Responsibility	1.2
	2. To conduct a study on drug abuse	Same	2.0
Smith Kline and French Laboratories	1. To require a study of drug abuse	Project on Corporate Responsibility	.80
	2. To establish foreign labeling restrictions	Same	.80
Warner-Lambert Co.	1. To require a study of drug abuse	Project on Corporate Responsibility	3.2
	2. To establish foreign labeling restrictions	Same	2.2

SOURCE: Council on Economic Priorities, *Economic Priorities Report*, Vol. 3, No. 3 (July–August, 1972).

ª Consumers Power Company refused to place the proposal by the West Michigan Environmental Action Council on the proxy statement. This action was affirmed by the Securities and Exchange Commission. The company did allow the group to introduce the measure on the floor of the annual meeting, which resulted in 460 favorable votes.

system to guarantee responsiveness to the public interest or to collective welfare. There are no macroconstraints to ensure corporate responsibility on environmental issues. The environment and public interest are ignored in the race for high profits. Today's oligopolistic corporations generally have little reason other than altruism to defer to the demands of consumers, and altruism has always been in short supply.

Big industries are still mainly interested in making big private profits. Justifying profit-seeking as the only function of the corporation, economist Milton Friedman argues that if the corporation obeys the existing laws of the land, it is being as "responsible" as it should be, and his views are echoed by many economic leaders. Any other socially valuable activities that used up profits would, in effect, be an "unfair tax" on the stockholders. It matters little that these same stockholders have been reaping profits at public expense through environmental deterioration for decades. And, of course, the argument becomes ludicrous when we consider the enormous role played by big business in drafting legislation to increase its own private profit at the expense of public welfare (see Chapter 4).

Many argue that, if society wants socially responsible corporations, it should pass laws forcing them to internalize some of the costs their products exact from the environment, either directly in the process of production, or indirectly through the products they manufacture. Much such legislation has been passed, especially since the late sixties, in response to increasing public pressure. Unfortunately, far from cooperating, industrial giants have often used their financial resources to control the passage and administration of antipollution legislation and to manipulate public opinion through advertising campaigns. Instead of investing funds in research and development designed to ease environmental and resource problems, big business would rather spend the money creating an image that something is being done. "Good will" advertising sells products more effectively than does action.

It would certainly boggle the mind of Adam Smith to hear his arguments and principles enunciated by the leaders of the American industrial and commercial establishment, who call to mind nothing so much as the coddled and privileged royal favorites of 200 years ago.

Who Directs Investment?

Widespread ownership of capital and thus citizen control of America's investment future is an important part of the American dream. Although one

American adult in six owns some stock, the total value of stock held by individuals in the United States declined in value by $10 billion between 1962 and 1970. An individual who owns 100 shares of IBM stock may get a pro forma invitation to the stockholders' meeting, but he has little to say about the direction of that corporation's affairs. Most large corporations have thousands of stockholders, but each is as powerless as the next. The owners of most stock are institutions, which are mainly concerned with traditional profits and payment of regular dividends. They have no interest in spearheading an economic revolution.

Self-interest and profits are the major motivating forces in investment decisions, and, in the absence of government initiative, there are no mechanisms to direct capital to areas of greatest social need. If higher dollar profits are obtained from producing more powerful automobiles, developing shopping centers, or building supersonic transports than from alternative activities, investment funds will be attracted to the high-profit areas. On the other hand, public needs, such as mass transport, education, and other social services that do not offer a good return on investment, are often ignored. Indeed, Americans are now caught in a situation in which corporations spend a substantial portion of their revenues on advertising to convince people that they really need the products that American industry now profitably produces. No funds exist for "counteradvertising" to make Americans aware of, and value, alternative types of production. Investment decisions are in the hands of a few individuals who control billions of dollars in institutional investment portfolios; and these individuals have no more appreciation of the environmental crisis that is facing the United States or of the nation's long-term needs for new investment priorities than do other people. Even if they did, they are bound to act in the interest of their clients; only the most farsighted among them might voluntarily channel funds into new and initially less profitable activities.

Many large American corporations are relatively independent of outside capital and can finance expansion without recourse to investors. Sears Roebuck offers one example. Through company-operated pension funds and employee profit-sharing arrangements, Sears' management controls nearly one-quarter of all Sears' stock. This is obviously a situation where there can be no outside control of investment. When corporations cannot generate expansion capital internally, the nation's large banks are ready to take up any slack. It is not at all unusual for banks to demand, and get, the right to appoint one or two members of corporate boards of directors in exchange for a sizable investment of expansion capital. In this way, big banks like Morgan Guaranty Trust maintain nominal control over the affairs of many corporations at one time. This particular bank controls $27 billion of capital and owns at least 5 percent of the stock in 72 corporations—a sizable empire by any standards. The 49 largest banks in the United States have officers on the boards of 300 of the 500 largest corporations. This is a particularly happy arrangement when it comes to financing mergers. This corporate-banking elite can readily manipulate more than $600 billion in investment funds in its own interest.

Nor is Morgan Guaranty Trust unusual. The ten largest financial institutions in the United States, all banks and insurance companies, control more than $160 billion in investment capital, enough dollar votes to control the economic destiny of the United States for a long time to come. This situation is extremely unhealthy for the economy and for the future of the ecosphere. Even if political leaders see the light and attempt to shift investment priorities in ecologically sound directions, this private paper government could well stand in the way. It is frightening to consider that nine of the fifteen largest American corporations, intimately tied to this investment directorate, are dedicated to the production or fueling of the automobile. No wonder the American economy shakes when Detroit sneezes! Americans like to believe that important decisions affecting the welfare of future generations are made in Washington when, in fact, many of the most essential decisions are made by a very small group of bank directors and corporate presidents.

This financial elite controls huge investment funds that are "expected" to earn a return of 10 or 12 percent each year. In 1973, institutions were responsible for 70 percent of the dollar volume on the New York Stock Exchange. This maintains strong pressures for traditional forms of industrial growth and explains why many stock prices have reached levels that are clearly not justified by corporate earning potential.

Perhaps the most disturbing aspect of institutional dominance is that the influx of institutional funds continues to keep prices of stocks well above the point of reasonable return on investment. In recent years the average dividend yield on common stocks has fluctuated between 2.8 and 3.8 percent of stock prices, a figure considerably lower than the interest paid to the typical savings account or by municipal bonds. Obviously, returns in the form of dividends are only part of the motivation for investment. Today's investors expect corporate growth to increase stock values and thus ensure a better total return on investment. But for many key speculative issues, current dividends, combined with more of their phenomenal price appreciation, will not yield economically acceptable returns for a period of at least ten years.

In addition to some $600 billion in directly controlled funds, the nation's banks indirectly control another $200 billion in private accounts and loan capital—more funds in search of hefty profits. Pension funds and mutual funds also contribute significantly to the institutional investment derby. Pension funds have soared to nearly $180 billion and are expected to hold $2.4 trillion by the year 2000. No pension fund is going to sit idly on its assets, so this capital must also find profits. Investment in mutual funds now totals nearly $53 billion, and there is every reason to expect investment of this type to increase. Including all sources, nearly $1 trillion in institutionally controlled investment capital is circulating in the United States economy today.

There are many complicated and important issues that must be faced in dealing with the question of $1 trillion of institutional investment. Only an agenda for future discussion can be established at this point, since there are no quick solutions or easy answers. Society sorely needs this capital to finance the development of new technologies and social innovations essential to its future. According to one estimate, exactly $1 trillion will be needed by world energy producers for exploration and development alone by 1985. But it is questionable whether so much capital should be invested in this type of energy strategy. It is clear that past profit levels cannot easily be sustained in a more frugal future and that the collective need is for investment in many areas that are not now especially profitable.

There is no reason to expect that investors in a future society will behave in other than a profit-maximizing manner. This could be especially unfortunate as shortages of essential commodities, minerals and consumer goods become apparent. In a society afflicted with "gray" and "black" markets, there is no reason to expect that the necessities of life will receive investment priority over luxury goods for the very wealthy. Mass starvation might well coexist with ever more fantastic electronic gadgets, new forms of personal transportation, and palatial, climatized homes for the rich and powerful.

Current approaches to credit rationing are only too illustrative of the lack of concern for humanity and even the irrational thinking characteristic of the makers of the nation's investment policies. When credit was contracted to stem inflationary tendencies in 1973, all potential borrowers were similarly affected. Interest rates rose for industries seeking capital for expansion as well as for young couples attempting to purchase housing. In general, industry had access to more money than did individuals. Thus, the already rich and powerful carried out expansion plans for their factories while hundreds of thousands of families were frozen out of the money market by high interest rates and large down payments.

As with other aspects of the old social paradigm, investment problems are rooted in the fact that behavior that has been rewarded and encouraged in the past is no longer beneficial to society. In the early stages of industrialization, there was a need for people to save, invest, and turn the world's seemingly boundless resources into useful products. Thrift and saving were rewarded; "a penny saved was a penny earned." Now, however, it is in the best interest of mankind to slow rates of growth in investment and consumption, particularly in the world's most overdeveloped countries. This implies completely new approaches.

In the present society, however, owning and investing capital are socially rewarded, and each investment dollar is expected to expand exponentially at a rate of at least 10 percent each year. Thus, investment funds are expected to double in size every seven years. Investment pressures behind economic—especially industrial—expansion are the impetus behind an attack on nature and her resources. Each stockholder and each corporation, in striving to maintain and expand profits, invests heavily in conditioning society to want more of what is being produced. Advertising creates rising expectations and perpetuates a culture based on consumption of material goods. The sum of individual demands funnels capital investment into traditional enterprises rather than in new directions. Future generations, unfortunately, have no advertising agency.

There are now very few ways in which American society collectively can direct investment so that it serves both a present and a future public interest. Budgetary allocations at federal, state, and local levels have some influence, but few of these expenditures are investments designed to produce future return. Funds in private hands are directed toward short-term payoff, and little is done to encourage investors to look two or three decades into the future. Therefore, dozens of institutions, thousands of large investors, and even millions of small investors, all seeking their own fortunes, contribute to the destruction of the ecosphere. Instead of directing investment into currently less lucrative, but more socially and ecologically desirable areas, these mechanisms exacerbate environmental problems and the depletion of natural resources.

Taming the Cowboy Economy

The discussion thus far has touched on only a sample of the critical economic problems that have been developing within what remains of the laissez-faire economic paradigm. These problems will be exacerbated by the multidimensional environmental crisis. As with many other aspects of the presently accepted dominant social paradigm, the practices responsible for early economic successes have become dysfunctional because of changes in the nature of industrial society. But old habits are very difficult to unlearn. This helps explain why the American people have been forced to ride an economic roller coaster in the early seventies while experts have been groping for simple solutions that do not exist. These experts live in an economic world of the past, and their myopia prevents them from seeing beyond the bounds of common wisdoms that they absorbed decades ago. Unfortunately, it apparently will be some time before political and economic leaders will be ready to come to grips with new realities, and economic turmoil can be expected to continue until they do.

There would be much less reason for concern about these various economic problems if the growth that hid them in the past could be sustained. In theory, in an ever-expanding economy, satisfying jobs could be available for everyone. But undirected, traditional forms of growth mean increased stress on ecosystems and vital natural resources. The problem is one of turning individual willingness to do something into binding collective action. Until a collective decision is made to formulate and enforce sound economic policies designed to preserve environmental integrity, even well-meaning individuals cannot be expected suddenly to change patterns of economic behavior that have been rewarded during most of the industrial revolution. Since the adverse consequences of this behavior will only appear in the relatively distant future, they are not effective in motivating present behavior. Furthermore, a natural reaction to predictions of disaster is to "get as much as possible while the getting is good." This strategy, if followed by everyone, will only hasten the arrival of the ultimate disaster.

The task for the future clearly is one of restructuring economic norms, values, and habits to move away from an economic model that encourages increased consumption of resources toward a model that limits growth in such consumption. We must also ensure that economic growth is carefully monitored and channeled in desired directions.

There are many different ways to modify economic behavior. The most obvious and most efficient method, at least in the long run, is to resocialize people–to encourage them to acquire new economic norms and values. However, several decades might be required to persuade significant numbers of people to alter their economic behavior, because the most efficient way of changing norms and values is to develop new attitudes among the young. If a crash program of education were begun in the schools now, however, there is no reason why a new economic consciousness could not be a significant factor by the year 2000. By then young people could have learned to govern their economic behavior according to a new set of expectations: to conserve rather than consume, to expect less rather than more, and to demand and support growth in services rather than in industries that consume natural resources. Unfortunately, substantial changes in the attitudes of many adults will be required well before such a crash educational program can be instituted.

Nevertheless, in the short run there are alternate methods of changing economic behavior and, eventually, economic attitudes and values. Economic situations can be structured so that the behavior of each person and each industry acting in self-interest will lead to environmental preservation and the collective good. This would require legislation aimed at rewarding ecologically sound behavior and penalizing various types of consumption that are not in the public interest. For example, new laws could be passed taxing automobiles according to weight or gasoline mileage. Thus, owners of gas-gulping Cadillacs and Lincolns would be heavily taxed, whereas owners of economy cars might not be taxed at all. If rates were made to escalate sharply enough, large, fuel-wasting vehicles might well become a thing of the past long before their present owners acquired any new economic morality. Similarly, the system of electric rates could be reversed so that those consumers using large quantities of electricity would pay much more per unit than those using the least amount. At present, of course, big consumers benefit from reduced rates, a vestige of old economies-of-scale thinking.

Some new legislation could deal with subsidies rather than penalties. For example, tax credits could be given to owners of four-cylinder automobiles or to industries that install ecologically desirable production processes or antipollution equipment. The essence of this approach to behavior modification is to structure economic rewards rationally so that people will change their behavior out of self-interest. Such an approach to economic engineering has not frequently been attempted because of America's infatuation with laissez-faire economics.

When other methods of behavior modification fail, sanctions can be prescribed and enforced. The automobile industry might be forbidden by law to manufacture automobiles that average less than eighteen miles per gallon over a standard test run. Unnecessary lighting and night advertising displays might be forbidden, to no aesthetic disadvantage. Certain industries might be forbidden to dump their wastes into streams, and heavy penalties could be applied if they should do so. When compliance with rules is exacted only as a result of fear of sanctions, however, beliefs and attitudes tend not to change.

Directing economic growth and modifying human behavior will require an increase in central economic planning and coordination, but economic planners must be very careful about the degree of centralization attained. Completely centralized control seems to function no more effectively than the present variant of a free economy. Experience has shown that highly centralized economies have serious weaknesses of their own. Neither one person, one board, nor a single computer can process and integrate all the information necessary to run an industrial economy. In principle it is fine to talk about an economy being run by government and therefore responsive to the people, but in practice the complexity of an industrial society makes complete centralization impossible. Therefore, whenever feasible, attempts should be made to design incentives that make self-interest among individuals in the free market coincide with the collective interest and the interest of future generations. Only when voluntarism clearly fails should direct centralized control of economic activity be considered.

Concern about overcontrol rests on more than speculation. It stems from numerous experiments in economic centralization that have been carried out in the Soviet Union and Eastern Europe during recent years. Total planning has led to warehouses overstuffed with goods for which there is no market, shortages of needed goods, shoddy production, and lack of innovation. Planned economies, moreover, have treated their environment just as harshly as their free market counterparts. In a completely controlled economy, demand for some commodities never seems to balance supply, whereas the oversupply of other commodities consumes needed resources and occupies storage space. Even the introduction of questionnaires and survey research to aid in future planning has not adequately replaced the workings of a relatively free market.

The most recent example of economic chaos caused by overcentralization occurred in Czechoslovakia. Party chief Antonin Novotny struggled for years to maintain control of one of the world's most highly centralized economies. He succeeded only in destroying the productive potential of what once had been a prosperous nation. Workers would not work, managers refused to manage, and planners bungled their jobs. Responsibility for deteriorating conditions was passed up and down the line. While warehouses were bulging with nonessential items, women were allowed only one new set of underwear each year and kitchen utensils were tightly rationed. Supply failed to meet demand in some areas and exceeded it in others. One important result of all this was that scarce resources were wasted in production that met no demand. Another was that Novotny finally was swept from office by the Dubcek reformers in the late sixties, who, in turn, were replaced by more orthodox comrades.

Although this type of bungling is a certain way to slow economic growth, it can hardly be recommended as a long-term solution to present problems. The United States must learn from its own and others' experiences and strike a judicious balance between completely centralized control (overcentralization and existing laissez-faire economic policies (undercentralization). A need also exists to partition the American economy more appropriately into public and private sectors in a manner consistent with new collective needs.

The time is ripe for the United States to establish an Economic Planning Board that would bear only faint resemblance to the one set up in the early seventies to oversee wages and prices. It should be located within the proposed Planning Branch of the federal government (Chapter 5) and be responsible for framing long-term, rational, and ecologically sound economic policies. Members of the Board should be selected for their independence, economic skills, environmental expertise, and ability to grapple with future problems. As with all other advisory and regulatory agencies, ways must be found to prevent it from becoming a political football, captured by the interests that it is supposed to regulate.

Membership on the Board should *not* be in accordance with any formulas based on existing conceptions of pluralism. The only interest to be represented should be the interest of the people as a whole. There should be no need to allot specified numbers of seats to labor, management, and consumers; if this type of pettiness remains unavoidable, there is little hope for the future of industrial society. As the environmental crisis deepens, public approval of such a Board will undoubtedly increase, as will the possibilities for appointing top-flight people. Appointments should be for a lengthy period to ensure political neutrality, and Board members' salaries should be adequate to keep them above the temptations of bribery.

Such a reconstituted Economic Planning Board would be primarily responsible for formulating economic sections of long-term plans produced by the new Planning Branch of the federal government. The Board should also be charged with issuing public reports on the economic situation, framing and introducing appropriate legislation directly to Congress, and helping to develop new measures of the quality of life. It could frame the major structural reforms that must take place in the near future to avoid economic disaster. Many possible areas of concern and appropriate policies are discussed in the following section.

Directing Growth and Investment

The issues that surround monopoly, oligopoly, conglomerate growth, and the direction of future investment might well be the first priority of the Economic Planning Board. Obviously, many things can be done within the present system of regulation and taxation to move in the direction of more citizen and government control over corporate affairs. Valuable steps toward an economy responsive to the public interest could be taken by passage of additional antitrust laws, particularly against powerful conglomerates, and strict enforcement of those that now exist. This proposed legislation and enforcement might well be backed by the business community at large, especially small businesses that are being forced out of the market by larger operations. Although these measures would not necessarily reduce resource consumption, they could make giant corporations more responsive to social demands and thus indirectly more likely to respond to social and environmental imperatives.

It is desirable to divide giant concerns into manageable entities and there are ways in which this can be done. The principle of progressive taxation is well accepted by the public in connection with the personal income tax. Modifications of this principle might well be applied to giant corporations. For example, large concerns could be identified by their gross sales or by the proportion of markets that they control. Since competition usually is socially desirable, taxation policies should be instituted that most heavily tax the largest corporations and those corporations that control a disproportionate share of any specific market. Progressive taxation schedules might help smaller industries overcome their present handicaps in competing with industrial giants.

The automobile industry offers a relevant example. An ideal outcome of such progressive taxation would be to give the underdog a competitive edge and restrict expansion capacity of the giants. On either basis (gross sales or percent of market), Ford and General Motors would have to pay taxes at a considerably higher rate than would Chrysler Corporation. American Motors would pay taxes at an even lower rate, thus gaining a competitive edge in a market now dominated by the other three. Similarly, in the steel industry, United States Steel and Bethlehem would pay higher taxes than would Republic and other smaller competitors.

There would certainly be critical problems, including some of definition, to solve in implementing any such system of taxation. The work of the Economic Board could include devising and overseeing such a scheme. Any difficulties encountered, however, should not serve as an excuse for failure to consider other variations on this theme.

Such tax policies could have several beneficial effects on the American economy. Most obviously, smart investors would be less inclined to invest in firms having limited potential for increased profits because of their already very large sales or their control of markets. There would be greater interest in backing smaller companies having higher potential profitability. Small, flexible companies would be able to compete with giants on more equal terms, spurring competition and innovation in stagnant markets. Differential taxation would also encourage the entry of new corporations into the competition. Most important of all, the historical trend toward larger and larger concentrations of economic power could be reversed.

The Economic Planning Board could also investigate taxation differentials designed on different principles. While size-dependent progressive taxation would direct investment into smaller corporations within an industry, taxation differentials *across* industries could also be considered as a vehicle to direct capital into socially desirable areas. For example, some industries in need of subsidy could simply be exempted from accelerated rates of taxation. Other, less desirable industries could be taxed at higher rates. Suppose, for example, that the Economic Board decided that it would be very sound environmental policy to reduce aluminum consumption. This could be accomplished by raising tax rates for the aluminum industry, a procedure that would drive up prices, discourage new investment, and lead consumers to look for less expensive substitutes. In the field of public transportation, by contrast, tax rates could be drastically reduced for railroads and buses, or outright government subsidies could be considered. This would make investments in such businesses much more attractive than they are now.

Under this system, small corporations in desirable industries would receive the biggest tax breaks. Large corporations in less desirable industries would pay the highest taxes. Less desirable industries might be defined by their large contributions to environmental deterioration (automobile and petrochemical industries), their heavy use of energy (aluminum and air-conditioning industries), their impact on limited resources (land developers), or their social disutility (weapons and strip-mining industries). Socially desirable industries would be those consuming few resources (repair, recycling, education, arts), those devoted to research and development (think tanks), those performing socially important functions (communications, food production, mass transit), and those working toward needed technological developments (solar power). Taxation would then fall most heavily on polluting, energy-consuming industries operating in areas where resources are becoming more difficult to find.

Although the operation of such systems of taxation seems complicated, most regulatory activity would be concerned with the top 500 corporations and could be accomplished relatively easily with the aid of computers. Only two major tasks would need to be performed by the Economic Planning Board. The first would be classifying corporations within industries, which should not prove too difficult, and the second would be tuning the mechanism to assure desired results. If exorbitant rates of taxation appeared to threaten many corporations, it would be necessary to juggle the rate structure. It might also be necessary to exempt certain corporations from accelerated taxation in the event of overwhelming national need. In general, however, it would be extremely important to maintain consistency over time and to refrain from modifying rates too frequently.

The Economic Planning Board should also have authority to form public corporations in intransigent industries. In deference to the ideal of minimal individual restraints, this procedure should be used only as a last resort. But there doubtless will be situations where any legislation aimed at modifying behavior through enlightened self-interest will do little to influence unsound corporate policies. When all else fails, it may be necessary to overcome traditional American taboos against public ownership and nationalize certain corporations. Among the major industrial powers, the United States has the fewest essential services owned and operated by government.

There are four reasons that certain industries might be owned and operated or more closely regulated by government:

1. Many industries, such as the aluminum and copper industries, the automobile industry, the aircraft industry, and the detergent industry, are now dominated by a small number of corporations. These corporations

might be relatively unaffected by differential taxation policies and might simply pass increased costs on to consumers in inelastic markets. Whenever a very small number of corporations approaches *de facto* monopoly control, a good case can be made for running them as public corporations and putting profits into the public treasury.

2. Certain types of industries must remain healthy in the national interest; at least that is what government officials say. These industries include the transportation and defense industries and certain utilities. In many such industries, the majority of corporate business is with the federal government. If corporations like Lockheed (88 percent government contracts) are so essential to the national interest that they are worthy of taxpayer loans, it would seem that taxpayers should have a direct voice in running the corporation and should also receive dividends in the form of reliable production and responsiveness to the public. No one has yet convincingly explained why taxpayers should guarantee private profits to a select few stockholders whose corporations often perform poorly in meeting government specifications. Corporations supplying the military have repeatedly asked for additional payments for cost overruns resulting from deliberate deception in bidding on contracts. They are obvious candidates for close public scrutiny.

3. Some firms have extraordinarily poor records of public service, responsiveness to consumer and public demands, and/or treatment of employees. Many corporations, including some in the strip-mining and lumbering industries, have simply ignored orders to reduce their environmental impact. Citizen groups might be encouraged by the Economic Planning Board to investigate these corporations and make their reports available to the public.

4. Many corporations have an unusual impact on the economy for a number of reasons, and these corporations should also be kept under scrutiny. Industries dealing with such essential resources as petroleum or foods immediately come to mind. As minerals and land become scarcer, abuses are likely to increase. At this writing the petroleum industry has already come under investigation for restraint of trade during the shortages of 1972–1973. When demand for a product can be expected to rise faster than supply, there are likely to be serious abuses.

In most situations, corporations that are possible targets for nationalization or closer regulation will clearly fall into more than one of these categories. Corporations that dominate an industry are also likely to have records of poor public service and to have an unusual impact on the economy. However, decisions to nationalize should not be taken lightly. Offenders should receive ample warning, and the threat of nationalization should be used as an ultimate deterrent to socially undesirable corporate behavior. For example, the stalling, deception, and engineering incompetence being displayed by the automobile industry in failing to meet federal emission control standards might, in the future, be grounds for nationalization.

Nationalization, even as a last resort, can only take place when some old taboos have been laid to rest. Industries that have been operated by the government in the past have usually been those found unattractive by private enterprise. In this way, government control has become linked in the public mind with unprofitable operations, even though frequently a valuable public service has been offered. There is absolutely no reason that government-controlled enterprises cannot be just as cost-efficient as existing private enterprise and even more responsive to social and environmental needs. Most public corporations in other industrial countries operate very efficiently.

Undoubtedly, if the government nationalized only bankrupt operations, such as Lockheed or Penn Central, there would be no immediate profits. But profit should not be defined only in dollars and cents but also in terms of public service. If transportation at low cost is desired, the public should not expect Amtrak or its successor to show profits. If Lockheed is to be preserved as an essential defense industry, profit considerations should be secondary to considerations of excellence. The only stockholders in government corporations would be taxpayers, and needed services would be a perfectly respectable public dividend.

In the end, of course, nothing will change unless the public demands more responsible behavior from American corporations. Progressive taxation of corporations based on size or social desirability, strict enforcement of existing and new antitrust and antimerger laws, and nationalization of certain key industries are policies that will be opposed by many powerful interests. But the economic crisis is destined to sharpen in the face of increasing citizen demands and environmental limits to growth. As the public begins to feel the effects of these constraints, there is likely to be increasing political activity in favor of economic reform.

Protecting Consumers

Another method of curbing the power of giant corporations is to give more leverage to consumers. The buyer in today's marketplace has few resources to devote to struggling with corporate giants. If a product does not work, an individual is largely at the mercy of the retail outlet that sold it. Retailers, in turn, are frequently at the mercy of industrial giants against which they have little leverage. There are no institutions with muscle devoted to protecting consumers from shoddy, defective, and overpriced merchandise. If a "lemon" is purchased, there is usually no redress without troublesome and sometimes expensive court action. The laws are biased in favor of big business, and the average consumer has few legal weapons.

The approach of a period of relative scarcity may signal even more callous treatment of consumers. A small number of producers who control a growing market can pass on increased costs with impunity. Future housing needs in urban areas offer a good example. People must have housing, and as prices rise there will be little consumer resistance. Home builders can keep profits high by raising prices or by substituting lower-quality workmanship and materials, and no individual consumer has the power to complain.

A lack of relevant information on product quality results partly from consumer inattention, partly from a lack of consumer testing laboratories, and partly from deliberate advertising efforts and very real industry taboos. How often, for example, do airlines publicly compare their safety records with those of other airlines or present comparative data on percentage of flights arriving late? Similarly, what is known about automobile repair statistics? More important, what is known about frequency-of-repair data for a host of items from ovens to television sets? Unfortunately, Americans know very little about the quality or performance characteristics of merchandise that they buy.

It should be possible for an organized activist citizenry to deal with these problems through political processes. Already the consumer movement has started to gain some ground, but sound laws designed to protect the consumer must have teeth, and laws with teeth will be vigorously contested by the regulated industries. A great deal can be done through less controversial legislation designed simply to provide consumers with more information about products than is now readily available.

Precedents have already been set by requiring an accurate listing of the contents of some food products. Certainly all consumers would profit from expanded labels or instruction booklets carrying relevant information. In the automobile industry, for example, new laws could require standardized performance and parts-cost data for all new models. These data might include estimated maintenance requirements, gasoline mileage statistics, exhaust emissions, frequency of repair of older models, and so forth. For large appliances, information could be required on average kilowatt hours of electricity used per month (or cubic feet of natural gas) during normal operation, parts costs, and frequency of repair.

From an environmental point of view, other data should be required to inform the potential purchaser adequately about all new products. To reverse the trend toward planned obsolescence, consumers could be provided with accurate data on product life expectancy. Such data requirements should be combined with stiff new warranty regulations. The automobile industry might be required to provide free repair service for new cars for at least five years or 50,000 miles. This might increase purchase cost, but it certainly would reduce maintenance costs. Eventually fewer cars would be produced per year if existing models performed well, and this would help lessen demand for nonrenewable resources needed to manufacture them. Other types of warranty protection could be required for large, resource-intensive items. Housing should also be regulated and buyers protected. National and regional standards for housing construction could help to raise the quality and durability of housing and preserve energy by requiring sound construction and insulation. New regional standards could reduce costs by superseding local laws that now require expensive but antiquated construction techniques. Noise pollution could be reduced in apartment complexes by making noise tests among units mandatory, as is now done in Switzerland.

In retail sales, additional price information could be added to price tags to help consumers fight inflation. At all stages of production, manufacturing, wholesaling, and retailing, careful records are usually kept, detailing such items as cost of production, wholesale mark-up, and retail mark-up. There is no reason that consumers cannot be apprised of these data. Huge mark-ups would then become obvious to all, and heavily marked-up products undoubtedly would be shunned. The mechanics would be simple; all that would be required would be to publicize accounting data that until now have been zealously guarded. Merchants undoubtedly would scream that such *private* information should not be made public, and it is very possible that consumers' lobbies would be in for a tough fight. Making this information public, however, would do much to inform consumers and to discourage unscrupulous business practices.

Although Congress has already recognized a need to create at least a modest consumer protection agency with public funds, a new agency should be created that does not at all resemble the sham that presently exists. Such a new Consumer Protection Agency would be in charge of establishing labeling standards, gathering and providing performance data, implementing congressional mandates, framing new consumer legislation, and coordinating an inspection system to check on violations. The management of this proposed agency could be drawn from consumer groups already active in the field. But the American public must be careful not to let historical precedent be a guide. The old pattern has been to appoint representatives of retailers, wholesalers, and producers, and even a few consumers, to important positions. Following this precedent would guarantee the ineffectiveness of the agency, because industry wolves would quickly devour the sheep.

The Consumer Protection Agency should also oversee the establishment of a Federal Products Testing Laboratory, part of which could make use of existing Food and Drug Administration facilities and experience. The laboratory would be in charge of testing and rating consumer items and spot-checking the validity of manufacturers' claims filed under new laws. It would also coordinate collection and publication of product data, which would be made available in a form easily understood by the American public. The laboratory could issue a regular report that could be given coverage on television news and consumer information programs and made available to the public through subscription and single copy sale at major retail outlets. Demand for such a service would undoubtedly grow as the amount of available information increased. Eventually, report revenues might pay much of the operating cost of the Federal Products Testing Laboratory.

Taken together, this collection of policy initiatives would do much to protect consumers and permit them to act in their own enlightened self-interest. These changes would inject a measure of rationality and competition into the largely irrational marketplace that we know today. These proposals are, moreover, in keeping with the desire for enforceable macroconstraints far upstream from consumers and the preservation of basic market freedoms. The primary objective would be to provide consumers with information, so there would be no need to establish a massive regulatory bureaucracy, and initially, the Consumer Protection Agency would require a fairly small staff. If public support for the agency grew and its activities were expanded, the staff could be enlarged; but an eventual operation five times the size of the present Consumers Union (which publishes *Consumer Reports*) should be adequate. The Consumers Union now operates on a budget of only $15 million annually. The federal agency could thus operate with an annual budget of less than $100 million.

The new legislation would be fairly simple to enforce. Retailers and wholesalers who cheated or broke laws would be revealed through the testing program or through consumer complaints, and appropriate charges could be filed. If penalties for deliberate falsification of data were tough enough and if the laws were enforced, consumers would no longer be at a complete disadvantage in dealing with retailers and manufacturers.

It would be desirable to have consumer protection legislation also promoted at state and local levels. If consumer protection organizations existed at these levels, offenders could be dealt with by local courts. This would take much of the enforcement burden off the federal government and leave it close to the consumer. Some might argue that such a procedure would never work, but a precedent has already been set in Yugoslavia, where local enforcement agencies do a remarkable job of checking reported violations. In Belgrade, for example, an eighty-man market inspection force equipped with police cars regularly checks out reports and issues court summons when necessary. It should not be necessary to have a socialist revolution before the American consumer can get similar action on complaints.

New Jobs in a New Society

Maintaining jobs for all who want them in a slowly growing economy will be difficult and will require considerable changes in social attitudes. Obviously, it will be necessary to halt population growth and thereby limit the number of people entering the labor force, but this is only a long-term answer to the problem. Until the late seventies, the number of young men and women entering the labor force each year will continue to grow. The birthrate decline of the sixties will ease this situation somewhat during the eighties, but pressure for additional jobs will not be entirely eliminated for perhaps forty-five years—until the number of new job seekers equals the number of people retiring each year.

One thing that the resource crisis makes clear is that the historical trend toward fewer blue-collar jobs will be accelerated, at least in the short run. Traditional forms of industrial expansion based on increasing consumption of natural resources will become more and more difficult as the costs of these resources rise. As industrial expansion slows, jobs will have to be found in other areas. Undoubtedly, the dissolution of large conglomerates and the encouragement of small, labor-intensive enterprises will create jobs for the same reasons that mergers tend to eliminate them. As the trend toward conglomeration is reversed, possibilities for employment in cottage industries, shops, restaurants, and other "old-fashioned" small businesses may be opened up. This could lead to a new kind of consumer culture. Opportunities in educational, cultural, and other services in both the public and private sectors can and should be greatly expanded as economic dependence on "throughput" (consumption) of critical materials is reduced.

Finally, there is much room for redistributing society's present workload and available compensation. Today, most people are still caught up in a derby to make more money each week, and leisure is not a highly valued commodity. Vacations are shorter in the United States than in any other industrialized nation except Japan because members of labor unions value overtime more highly. Labor unions could help ameliorate unemployment, in the short run, by negotiating for a four-day work week and longer vacations—changes that would mean foregoing wage increases in favor of leisure. Unfortunately, one reason that the shorter work week has not been adopted is that Americans have not learned to use leisure creatively, and many captives of the old economic paradigm are unable to deal with extra time on their hands.

Sabbatical years for further education could also be a great asset in decreasing unemployment. Today, once a person gets a high school diploma or college degree and enters the job market, educational development is usually frozen. There is little significant adult education in the United States, especially when compared with other industrial countries. Adult education could open a large new area of economic expansion and meaningful human endeavor while creating many temporary replacement jobs. Personnel in creative positions need to recycle themselves periodically to keep up with new developments. Others simply need an extended period of rest to recuperate from years of hard labor. A sabbatical year (Chapter 6) could become an accepted institution in "postindustrial" society just as it has been accepted in academic life. A sabbatical year would change old values and readjust the relative values of income and leisure. Executives and employees would have to accept somewhat lower salaries to implement a meaningful sabbatical program.

All these unemployment remedies are predicated on the development of what economist Herman Daly calls a new morality. Once it is accepted that cowboy growth cannot continue, fierce battles over the distribution of existing income appear inevitable unless a new cooperative morality can be developed. Both the rich and the poor must come to realize that a congruence of interests exists between them, that the environmental crisis is the great leveler, and that there are other values to be optimized in society besides dollar income. Such a change should be well within the grasp of a society bent on directing its own evolution.

Conserving Resources

The slowly developing crisis in energy resources is now very much on the public mind, and not all attention is being focused on increasing supply. In California, a legislative committee in 1972 commissioned a study of ways to reduce demand for energy. The legislature had suddenly realized that, by the year 2000, there might not be enough energy available to meet projected demand, even if available resources were used with maximum efficiency. The study, undertaken by the RAND Corporation, concluded that homeowners should pay higher prices for electricity and suggested many ways of reducing demand. It found demand for electricity in California to be increasing so rapidly that, by the year 2000, 130 huge 1,200 megawatt nuclear reactors will be needed to keep up with demand unless this projected growth is reduced. The cost of a crash program to build these installations would probably be more than Californians will be willing or able to pay. The concomitant environmental and health risks would be additional serious disadvantages.

On the national level, too, specialists have begun to assess the impact of growing needs for natural resources. Realization is growing that there are very real problems to be faced, and efforts are being made to anticipate the onset of crises to mitigate some of their harshest effects. For example, the Office of Fuels and Energy in the United States Department of State has suggested that the federal government may ask auto makers to produce automobiles that provide better gasoline mileage. The Environmental Protection Agency has published automobile mileage figures to guide consumers. There have been proposals to establish progressive rates for electricity and also to require better insulation for new homes to save on heating. An extensive report issued by the federal government in 1972 dealt with various aspects of curbing energy demand. Unfortunately, when President Nixon issued policy statements on the energy crisis in 1973, emphasis was put on increasing supplies (even at the explicit sacrifice of environmental quality). The possibility of reducing demand was limited to such weak, voluntary measures as encouraging citizens to turn out unused lights. Such appeals apparently fell on deaf ears as consumption has continued to escalate.

In addition to governmental initiatives, the semifree market has some mechanisms for dealing with approaching scarcities. The relatively mild fuel crisis of 1972–1974 has been a great learning experience, for it prepared the public for more serious unpleasant surprises that lie ahead. As supplies of nonrenewable resources become scarcer, prices will rise. This will provide some economic motivation for digging deeper, going further, and developing new technologies to meet rising demand. In many situations, however, price increases will be precipitous, causing minor crises. Although the free market will generally move in the right direction, this should not be cause for great rejoicing because tremendous price increases are not now a socially acceptable solution to resource shortages.

If no special planning is undertaken to handle the problem of rising costs, traditional free market morality will predominate. Scarcities will therefore have their first impact on the poor, those traditionally frozen out of Adam Smith's marketplace. The well-to-do will remain in the market while the poor, and eventually the middle class, bear the brunt of increased scarcity.

It may therefore be disastrous to wait for the free market and Smith's somewhat arthritic hand to allocate resources. The free market *responds* to a crisis of scarcity. It does very poorly at *anticipating* it. Furthermore, the free market takes neither immediate human costs nor the welfare of future generations into its calculations. It prices commodities for today, even though tomorrow many people may have to live at greatly reduced standards of living.

The United States, through its access to foreign resources, now enjoys relative abundance, although that may, before long, be transformed into relative scarcity by international political events. And, even in the international arena, problems of general depletion must be faced very soon. Now is the time to restrict consumption of key resources while there are still abundant supplies left. Since the prices of resources will inevitably be higher in the future, it makes sense to plan consumption carefully. Then, when ways of recycling resources and utilizing them more efficiently have been developed, there will still be something left for future generations besides remnants and low-grade deposits.

For these and other reasons that have previously been outlined in detail, designing and moving toward a "steady-state" (or "stationary-state") economy should be given top priority. Aside from maintaining the integrity of the Earth's ecosystems, the most pressing problem for the human race is to treat Earth's finite supply of resources with greater respect. Although a free market can make these resources more expensive, it cannot conserve them for use later on. Economic mechanisms are needed to provide for careful resource management and for translating future resource costs into current economic considerations. This means curbing certain types of consumption rather than encouraging them and giving generous subsidies to recycling industries and services, areas where the economy can grow without using up scarce resources. It also means curbing individual appetites in the interest of the general welfare, something that has rarely been done.

Economist Herman Daly's proposal for a steady-state economy is one plan for dealing with this complex of problems in the long run. He describes a steady state as follows:

> By "steady state" is meant a constant stock of *physical* wealth (capital), and a constant stock of people (population). Naturally these stocks do not remain constant by themselves. People die, and wealth is physically consumed—that is, worn out, and depreciated. Therefore the stocks must be maintained by a rate of inflow (birth, production) equal to the rate of outflow (death, consumption). But this equality may obtain, and stocks remain constant, with a high rate of throughput (equal to both the rate of inflow and the rate of outflow), or with a low rate. Our definition of steady state is not complete until we specify the rates of throughput by which the constant stocks are maintained. For a number of reasons we specify that the rate of throughput should be "as low as possible." For an equilibrium stock the average age at "death" of its members is the reciprocal of the rate of throughput. The faster the water flows through the tank, the less time an average drop spends in the tank. For the population a low rate of throughput (a low birth rate and an equally low death rate) means a high life expectancy, and is desirable for that reason alone—at least within limits. For the stock of wealth a low rate of throughput (low production and equally low consumption) means greater life expectancy or durability of goods and less time sacrificed to production.

A steady-state economy is therefore one in which throughput is held to a minimum. This is done by making resources into products that endure and by recycling no longer usable products. A steady state should not be confused with no growth. In reality, there can be plenty of growth in the sense of increased well-being within a steady state. But growth must be directed to areas that are not dependent on consumption of great quantities of energy and materials.

In essence, a steady-state economy would work as follows. Population size would be held constant (or gradually reduced), and material expectations would have to be curbed. The amount of material throughput available to society would remain constant over time. Such an economic system would be "closed" in the sense that few resources, other than energy, would be injected into the system. A steady state could be eventually powered by fusion, solar energy, or both, and might resemble the "hydrogen economy" suggested by many physicists. Society would make do with the mineral resources already mined, plus small additions to replace quantities that inevitably escape from the closed system. In such a situation, growth and progress could take place, not by increasing the throughput of mineral resources but by carefully managing the constant amount available. This would lead to a comprehensive recycling system, which would also eliminate many "waste disposal" problems. In such an environmentally utopian society, very little would be "wasted" because it could not be replaced by new raw materials. A steady-state economy would also encourage the development of new technologies, especially those that would ensure more efficient resource utilization. Finally, there would be diversion of talent, resources, and capital into areas of growth requiring no additional natural resources; progress would come from the more efficient use of existing materials and especially from the expansion of services and education.

Although such a utopian society would be very desirable, it is not a possibility for the United States in the near future. Complete conversion to such a system would probably take several generations—approximately the time needed to end population growth. However, some preliminary steps can be taken toward a steady state. One is to begin limiting consumption of twenty-five to thirty resources that are critical to the preservation of industrial society. This would mean, as Daly has proposed, setting national resource depletion quotas. An initial assault on the problem might be made by freezing American consumption of these critical materials at 1976 levels for at least a decade.

It is, of course, politically more realistic to use a self-sufficiency argument and first to establish an agency to set annual quotas for *domestic* resource depletion. This would drive industry into the world market to obtain scarce materials. In terms of realpolitik this would be a very desirable policy. It conserves remaining domestic resources until they can be used more profitably, and it guarantees the United States a resource stockpile in the event that foreign supplies become unavailable. Such policies could stretch available reserves in the United States for additional years. The negative aspect, of course, is that a simple freeze on domestic resource production does nothing to halt the resource imperialism characteristic of present United States and Western European foreign policy. But American political leaders do not yet recognize the serious and truly global nature of the resource problem; much enlightenment will be necessary before most of them are ready even to think seriously about domestic quotas. In fact, in late 1973, President Nixon announced an absurd policy intended to make the United States self-sufficient in fuels within five years, ignoring the great environmental costs that will be paid by future generations.

Eventually, of course, quotas should be applied to imports as well. The root of the problem is rising *world* consumption of limited *world* resources. Although domestic quotas would be a good beginning, the next step cannot take place until the United States is willing to institute quotas on all resource consumption regardless of point of origin. American adoption of resource quotas could set a tremendous moral example for the rest of the industrial nations. Since the United States is the world's largest per capita consumer of resources, this nation ought to be able to exact pledges from other countries to follow suit and develop steady-state economies of their own, at least once they approach current levels of consumption in the United States. Perhaps an international treaty specifying the establishment of such economies could be signed within and supervised by a revitalized United Nations or some new international agency. Because of the global nature of the resource depletion problem, it will have to be resolved internationally if it is to be resolved at all.

Such policies need not unduly restrict individual freedom, nor would they require large bureaucracies to administer them. A federal resource agency could ensure that the total United States consumption of resources designated "critical" remained at 1976 levels, for example. As demand rose in the face of constant supply, prices would artificially rise well before global resource shortages had an impact on the world market.

According to the Daly plan, rights to an annual resource quota could be auctioned to manufacturers and refiners by a federal resource agency under the jurisdiction of the Economic Planning Board. Some resources would have to be purchased abroad, and this would be a responsibility of the resource agency. Undoubtedly, the "auction" price would soon considerably exceed the free market price, but these dividends would accrue to the government and taxpayers rather than to private interests. Economists would have to establish rules for the auction if its results were to conform to public policy requirements. For example, restriction of the quantities of raw materials that any one firm could purchase might be useful. Otherwise, large corporations could hoard raw materials and drive competitors out of business. It might be possible to set these quantities low enough to exert additional pressures on extremely large corporations. Similarly, rules specifying the length of time that materials could be stockpiled should also be considered, as well as prohibitions against transfer of materials at higher-than-auction prices. It might be wise to require that purchased materials either be consumed within fifteen months or resold to the auctioning agency at the original price.

It is also possible that no formal auctioning activity would be needed. For example, if a decision were made to freeze consumption of certain resources at 1976 levels, resource agency economists could undoubtedly fix prices and corporate quotas so that consumption would be fairly close to desired levels. Again, in such a controlled market situation, careful regulation would be needed to prevent abuses.

There are other questions to be answered and problems to be faced. Legislation would be needed to deal with the import of resource-intensive semifinished and finished products. New tariffs and duties would be required to keep import prices as high as domestic prices, although this is the price that other trading nations would have to pay if the United States were to move toward a steady-state economy. American corporations could also be forbidden to import certain resource-intensive commodities from their foreign operations or to buy semifinished products from foreign suppliers. Such decisions would have to be made resource by resource, depending on the state of world and domestic supplies. These and other problems can be solved, and a careful research program should be organized to study them.

The suggested depletion quotas and related resource auction need not be extremely difficult to administer. Communist countries now routinely allocate resources to various enterprises. It would be much easier for the United States to do this in a semifree market. Furthermore, the number of corporations working directly with raw materials would undoubtedly be relatively small. Only the steel industry, for example, would be affected by quotas on iron ore. Prices for finished steel, of course, would rise, but these would then be passed on to other producers and then consumers. The same situation would exist for other resources because only primary producers would participate in the resource auction. Finally, since quotas would be fixed at 1976 consumption levels, there would be no severe dislocations among world producers of basic resources. Purchases of foreign resources by the United States would not decline but would increase more slowly in the future. Other countries would have adequate time to make required adjustments.

Although it may be impossible to approximate the ideal situation (one where additional inputs of nonrenewable resources would be exactly equal to the amounts of resources that are irretrievably lost within the economic system), movement toward a more perfect steady state, through a yearly decrease in input of new mineral resources, should be a long-term goal. Of course, attainment of this ideal is possible only with a stationary or declining population. Until population growth stops, additional resource inputs will have to be permitted to maintain constant per capita resource stocks.

There are many advantages to the adoption of depletion quotas at present. Since prices of raw materials will inevitably continue to rise, depletion quotas would encourage early development of new technologies to make recycling feasible and economical. Rising prices would also lead to pressures for substitution of less expensive materials, for conserving and recycling materials, and for manufacturing goods that use smaller quantities of scarce materials. Recycling could become a flourishing steady-state industry as mineral costs increased in advance of impending shortages. In addition, the high costs of resources would encourage a great deal of "pollution control" to recover expensive materials now discharged as effluents. It would be far better to develop these industries before the crunch arrived than to wait for severe dislocations within a free market.

Closely related developments would encourage substitutions and utilization of alternative fuels. Homes would undoubtedly be more sturdily constructed because use of stucco and bricks would become more widespread as the price of energy, wood, and other materials continued to rise. As prices of natural gas and electricity skyrocketed, consumers would demand better insulation to keep heating costs low. There would be much less tendency to illuminate cities with unneeded lights and garish advertisements all night. Enterprising producers of fuels might develop ecologically acceptable, economical ways of extracting oil from oil shales and tar sands to circumvent quotas on more readily available fuels. Of course, solar energy, on which there need be no quota, is always available as a practical and clean energy source that would become economically attractive because of the rising costs of alternatives.

In the words of Herman Daly,

> The depletion quota plan should appeal both to technological optimists and pessimists. The pessimist should be pleased by the conservation effect of the quotas, while the optimist should be pleased by the price inducement to resource-saving technology. The optimist tells us not to worry about running out of resources because technology embodied in reproducible capital is a nearly perfect substitute for resources. . . . This plan simply requires the optimist to live up to his faith in technology.

Other plans have been suggested for dealing with the resource crisis in different ways, but none feature the level of individual freedom found in the Daly approach. Two Australian ecologists, Walter Westman and Roger Gifford, have suggested a resource allocation plan that allots each citizen a certain number of national resource units each year, a parallel to the depletion quota concept. Others have suggested the use of baby licenses to restrict population growth and similar schemes to limit the aggregate environmental impact of a society by limiting individual impact. Many of these schemes are worth consideration, but all of them considerably restrict individual freedoms. Whenever possible, constraints should not be applied at the individual level where restrictions on freedom would be most heavily felt. The Daly plan meets this requirement.

Despite the contentions of conservative critics, in a steady-state economy, such as that proposed by Daly, only growth dependent on increased throughput of raw materials would be halted. This is the type of growth familiar to the clique of "steel-eaters" who now direct industrial societies. New growth could still be permitted in many other sectors of the economy. Industries would find themselves becoming far more efficient in their handling of resources, and fewer energy-intensive production processes would be developed. In some processes, the energy of human beings would once again replace that of energy-consuming machines, thus increasing employment. Most important of all, the quality of life would be enhanced through growth of "nonpolluting" cultural activities. A steady-state society could thus be designed that would provide a culturally rich life for all rather than a materially rich life for only a few.

A major structural transformation would certainly be required for a society to adjust to a steady state. Pressures for redistribution of wealth, previously checked by a rapidly growing economy, would have to be dealt with. This would not necessarily be unfortunate, unless perpetuating a highly stratified society and maintaining equality of opportunity as a myth only were felt to be required for several more generations. To grow means to mature. Just as physical growth in people levels off at approximately age twenty, so economic growth in society, based on increasing throughput, must give way to maturity, stability, and intellectual and moral growth.

Such economic changes in conformance with environmental imperatives would inevitably be accompanied by many changes in social life. Transformations in political and social thinking would have to occur if serious social strife were to be avoided. Educational and mass communications bureaucracies would have to begin to support and reinforce the new philosophy inherent in the steady state. Children and adults would, of necessity, learn to cooperate rather than compete and to conserve rather than consume. The development of an American steady state would have a tremendous impact on the international political and economic system. Most important of all, a shift to a new economic paradigm would have to be accompanied by parallel shifts in the political process. Politics, of, by, and for the wealthy would have to be replaced with a politics dedicated to the survival of society and *all* the people living in it.

4

Politics: Approaching the Narrows

Politics is frequently described by political scientists as "the authoritative allocation of values." It is the process by which individuals, each with separate sets of perceived needs and priorities, reach agreement on policies or laws by which an entire society is to be bound. The values allocated in the political process range from a very concrete distribution of economic rewards (such as increased social security benefits) and economic deprivations (such as increased taxes) to very symbolic values (such as military decorations or "hero of socialist labor" awards). This allocation of values is authoritative because it is backed by a monopoly of violence controlled by political leaders. In a mass democracy authority is said to come from the people, who choose many of their policy makers during periodic elections. In less democratic countries, the authority by which values are allocated is often found in the barrel of a dictator's gun.

The number of collective policies forged by political leaders, and thus the scope of government regulation, varies from one society to another. In some countries individual freedoms are held sacred, and very few constraints on personal behavior are enacted in the name of the collective. In other nations, however, the collective welfare is considered more important, and the scope of government regulation is very large. When a society is under stress, or when the authority of political leaders is widely questioned, there are usually many more constraints on individual behavior than when social harmony exists. The Soviet Union under Stalin offers an example of a closely regulated society. Societies under relatively little stress, such as the United States throughout much of its history, need fewer collective constraints, largely because in times of social peace the authority of political leaders is infrequently challenged and the number of difficult problems facing such societies is fairly small. Thus, the potential for individual freedoms is closely related to the number and seriousness of problems that need to be solved through collective regulation.

The environmental crisis presents American society with a need to frame many new collective policies and, in some respects, to restrict some individual freedoms. As insulating space among citizens continues to dwindle, it will be necessary for authorities to "reallocate" many of the values that have traditionally been taken for granted. In many urba.1 areas, for example, increased air pollution already means that, in the interest of the public welfare, individuals are forbidden to burn their rubbish. Laws have been passed restricting emissions from factory smokestacks to reduce industrial smog. Automobiles must meet ever higher antipollution standards. These are decisions that have been and are currently being made via the political process at national, state, and local levels. It is clear, however, that much more regulation will be needed to meet the environmental challenges of the future.

This chapter and the next are concerned with a new legislative agenda and questions of leadership response to environmental needs of the future. Two closely related issues are discussed: first, the possibility of designing needed collective policies within the present political framework and, second, the need for and possibilities of a major transformation in the process of political decision making itself. If it is not possible to change the methods by which leaders are now selected and by which decisions have traditionally been made, it may well prove impossible to change other self-destructive aspects of industrial society.

Industrial societies are composed of large numbers of individuals and groups with many competing desires and priorities. There is almost no issue on which all individuals and groups can agree completely. Because the problems are so complex and because so many individual interests would be affected by possible solutions, it is extremely difficult to reach a consensus on policies needed to cope with an increasing flood of environmental issues. Not only is there a diversity of attitudes toward environmental values; the manifestations and long-run consequences of environmental degradation are obscure to most citizens.

It is even difficult for people who realize that these problems exist to do something about them. As political economist Thomas Schelling has demonstrated, the need is to encourage appropriate "micromotives" among individuals and then to translate these motives into collective action. But collective action requires political leadership, and thus far political leaders have not distinguished themselves by framing policies within which concerned citizens can work together for change. The political response to environmental problems has been either to ignore them in favor of continued growth or to come up with stop-gap solutions that will not upset the status quo before the next election.

Partially as a result of lack of leadership, millions of families continue to buy second and third cars each year. Each family either chooses not to recognize the additional contribution to resource depletion and atmospheric pollution represented by another car or justifies the purchase by pointing to the lack of alternative transportation. The best of individual motives seemingly cannot be translated into collective decisions to establish cheap, efficient, and comfortable public transportation. Billions of dollars of public monies are spent each year on new freeways to carry automobiles, but diverting money from the public treasury to support mass transit—an environmentally sound but politically difficult move—seems to be nearly impossible.

Even as industrial society begins to feel the pinch and numerous minor crises alert people to growing environmental problems, barriers to effective political action remain formidable. There is nothing in the American political heritage to indicate that simple recognition of these problems will elicit wisdom and prompt action from decision makers. American politics has always been more competitive than cooperative, and scarcity can be expected to intensify competition. Political power is presently wielded by many people who, because of vested interests in the industrial system, are opposed to significant environmental legislation. They are convinced that technological fixes will solve impending problems. Furthermore, everyone, rich or poor, has at least some interest in continuing the old, familiar, predictable, and therefore comforting ways of doing things. More "environmental backlash" therefore can be expected in the future as people try to explain away problems rather than to cooperate and work actively to solve them through the political process.

Individual Interest and Collective Action

In the United States, as in most Western industrial societies, there are now relatively few collective constraints on personal behavior. This has been an important political result of the industrial revolution. Individualism can be tolerated by a society when the wolf is not perpetually at the door. Unfortunately, in the United States, individual freedom has often been synonymous with rugged individualism and little regard for the rights of others. A highly developed social conscience has not been a distinctively American trait. But an increasing interdependence of people and an obvious need for significant collective restraints to solve environmental problems conflict with this tradition of individual freedom.

In a nation of more than 210 million individuals, it is inevitable that there should be less than unanimous opinion even on the most crucial issues. Even in times of war, there always has been a sizable minority opposing common efforts against enemies. Unanimity might be expected in favor of something as clear-cut as the future survival of industrial society, but individual feelings vary tremendously even on this important issue. A few even view the prospect of a total societal collapse with equanimity. Among these could be numbered a wealthy student from Connecticut who, in a recent university seminar, claimed he would prefer a nuclear holocaust to collectivism because "his family had the best bomb shelter in the area," as well as many radicals who feel that a better society will rise from the ashes. Some academics have responded emotionally, claiming that mankind represents a "cancerous threat to the universe" and deserves to be wiped out.

Although most Americans put individual interests first and abhor governmental restrictions on their "freedoms" as they understand them, some general feeling of responsibility for the welfare of the nation exists. Most people support "law and order" because they believe that laws promote a general welfare and, in the process, individual welfare. Similarly, most Americans are willing to take action and some are even willing to die, if necessary, to protect society's interests, once it becomes clear that there are no other viable alternatives. At present, however, too few are convinced that there is a compelling need for radical change, and too little has been offered in the way of clear alternatives.

Thus, appeals for action in connection with the present crisis often seem to fall on deaf ears. It is no accident that smog alerts have no discernible effect on private automobile travel—it is a tragedy of the commons. No individual wants to be the first to surrender a privilege or freedom, particularly when there is even faint hope that some alternative will offer itself. Most individuals will agree to some limitations on their consumption and life-styles if everyone else is also limited and if no great sacrifice of convenience or cost is required. Great sacrifices can be demanded only when a need for them is obvious to a very great majority. The political problem, then, is one of demonstrating such need, providing reasonable alternatives, and *turning individual initiative and good will into binding collective action.*

Political philosophers use the term "social contract" to describe the idea of collective action. According to contract theory, men left a "state of Nature," which amounted to a "war of all against all," because agreeing to work together to promote some common interest seemed much more sensible than each person looking after his own welfare. The basis for the social contract is that organization and cooperation pay dividends and that survival of the group is enhanced if everyone can agree on a minimum number of basic principles. Now, however, new pages must be added to the old social contract, for, as population has grown and as society has become more complex, a greater number of agreed-on principles have become necessary.

In an industrial age, people are only now discovering that the world is one great commons and that any social contract must take into account the environment of that commons and the resources available within it. Environmentally speaking, human society has remained in a state of nature—a "war of all against all." Individuals feel free to pollute the atmospheric commons—or at least feel helpless to avoid doing so—with little regard for the welfare of others. Corporations continue to exploit forest and mineral resources with little regard for future generations, and every nation struggles to extract as much wealth from the Earth's "commons" as possible before time runs out.

This has resulted, in part, from the failure of political institutions and political leadership to meet the challenges of a complex, interdependent industrial society that is growing in a finite world. Even the word "politics" brings visions of competition. No one speaks of a political "council of understanding." Rather, phrases like "political arena," "political contest," and even "political corruption" pervade the language of politics and accurately reflect the role that political institutions play in modern society. Politics is now dedicated to satisfying individual appetites but is little concerned with future possibilities for meeting such desires. The type of politics that was nurtured in a cowboy society did not threaten the survival of that society, but under today's conditions, lack of planning and inadequate attention to the welfare of future generations are extremely dangerous. The American people need to develop a new set of political values and expectations to replace those that became accepted when political leaders did not have pressing environmental problems to solve.

The speed with which the physical environment is deteriorating and the social environment is changing in industrial societies is much greater than the apparent ability of present political systems to respond. Collective decision making is permeated with mechanisms that delay effective action and ensure that today's new policies will, at best, be answers to yesterday's problems. Political leaders respond to problems slowly; they rarely anticipate them. Those who, in one way or another, gain power over others generally use it to mold the law to serve their own interests, and they use the law and their financial power to impede change. All political systems are dominated to some degree by vested interests dedicated to preventing consideration of radical policy alternatives. In the United States, vested interest means money; in politics, money means power.

The old social contract, by which it was basically agreed that each person could seek his or her own interest, caring little for the welfare of others, is no longer an adequate guide. In politics, competition must be turned into cooperation; vested interests must be made to realize that their self-interest cannot be separated from the survival of the whole society. Long-range social planning must be substituted for the present system of muddling through—meeting problems on a piecemeal basis only after they have become apparent and painful. Most important, political institutions must operate to translate individual willingness to change, when it exists, into collective decisions to change, and political leaders must set good examples. These decisions must be preceded by a consensus recognizing the *need* for change, formation of intelligent alternatives, agreement as to the *direction* of change, and agreement as to the formulation and acceptance of appropriate policies. If political leaders fail to participate in developing this consensus, there is little hope that existing individual good will can result in social transformation of any consequence.

Although in a mass democracy the people theoretically possess power to change the political system, such a change surely requires skillful political leadership or a better understanding by the people of the responsibility of citizenship in a democracy. It is virtually certain, nevertheless, that significant reforms will not be initiated by many (if any) political leaders of this generation, for most politicians have too great a stake in the old system, their purpose in entering politics was too self-seeking, and their allegiance to vested interests is too well cemented.

Industrial Politics

In nineteenth-century America, a superabundance of human and natural resources provided wide latitude for error in decision making. Making collective decisions required no special expertise, for even fools could adequately carve up unlimited abundance. Exploitation of seemingly boundless resources on the frontier proceeded with little debate over public interest and private greed. Land and mineral wealth given away by government or taken from Indians came under the "ownership" of individual claimants, and today taxpayers and concerned citizens must buy back this governmental largesse for millions of dollars to create "open" spaces.

Before the twentieth century, few individuals or organizations spoke up for the environment. Buffalo hunters were permitted to slaughter and nearly to wipe out that animal for hides and tongues, often leaving the carcasses to rot. It seemed that the greatest good for society could be obtained by openly encouraging people to exploit natural resources. Little governmental planning and supervision was required and none was desired by powerful individuals who quickly rose to the top in a wide-open scramble for riches. At best, the style of politics that grew out of this situation has been called muddling through. At worst, it could accurately be described as the politics of interest-group warfare.

From the very beginning, men of great wealth, whether it was inherited, earned, or stolen, have dominated the American political process. They quite naturally have worked to create a system of government of the wealthy, by the wealthy, and for the wealthy. At the Constitutional Convention in 1787, for example, three-quarters of the delegates had sizable holdings in public securities. One-fifth were land speculators, one-half were money lenders and investors, and one-half were engaged in sizable commerce or owned plantations. This gathering was hardly likely to be concerned either with social justice or the establishment of a powerful central government, but it was not atypical of congressional gatherings that have occurred since then. The participants were mainly concerned with protecting their own interests and establishing a minimal, laissez-faire system in which government would regulate interstate and foreign commerce, unify the monetary system, operate a postal system, provide for some common defense, and do very little else.

Much has changed since the pattern of American politics was first established. The open frontier no longer exists, the abundance of domestic resources has diminished, and a complex, resource-hungry, rapidly changing industrial society has replaced the simple, slowly changing agrarian society that existed when the Constitution was framed. The process of political decision making, however, has changed very little over the past two centuries. The politics of self-interest and muddling through that evolved in a period of abundance has remained solidly entrenched in American society. The need to develop more efficient methods of decision making, to exert political leadership toward commonly held national goals, to overcome government by self-interest, and to inject an important element of expertise into the policy-making process has gradually come to be recognized, but no striking innovations have yet taken place.

The old system of interest-group, wealth-oriented politics now acts as a major roadblock to the framing of new policies that would increase chances for collective survival. Most politicians are still captives of the old political paradigm, more interested in defending individual interests than in promoting any long-term common interest of Americans or of mankind. People who own land and have amassed wealth are quite naturally found in the thick of the political struggle, protecting their own interests, as they understand them, and preventing the passage of legislation that might in any way alter the present system of prerogatives. For example, recent attempts have been made to eliminate the oil depletion allowance. Resistance to removing the depletion allowance, which exempts oilmen from paying taxes on a substantial percentage of their otherwise taxable profits, has been so vociferous that it has only been possible to reduce it from 27.5 to 22.0 percent, not to eliminate it.

Recent sessions of Congress have illustrated its inability to tackle important issues. While an unpopular and cruel war dragged on for years in Indochina, senators and representatives used various parliamentary tricks to forestall a clear-cut vote on ending the war. Important actions on civil rights and other critical areas have been frustrated again and again by stubborn minorities that were unwilling to yield to majority decisions. Much needed legislation on population and environmental protection has been watered down, killed in committee, or vetoed by the President.

Occasionally issues become pressing enough to warrant the appointment of presidential commissions to investigate and suggest action. These commissions could be a way of injecting more than superficial information into the political dialogue, but in reality they are often a polite way to bury controversial issues and postpone action, while giving the public the idea that serious soul-searching is taking place. Such commissions now have little long-term authority or impact. The most recent examples have been presidential commissions on marijuana, pornography, and population growth.

In 1972 a *conservative* panel returned a recommendation that penalties for the use of marijuana be considerably eased. On the federal level, the report was quietly shelved, but there have been a few related changes in public opinion. The report of the Commission on Pornography in 1971 received even ruder treatment: The findings were denounced by the President because they did not fit his conception of morality. The 1972 report of the Population Commission was also glossed over, even though it was very meekly phrased. The nation's Roman Catholic Bishops denounced its scientific findings as "beset with inconsistencies" and referred to those sections recommending liberalized abortion policies as "fundamentally immoral." The President also condemned two sections of the report, including the section on abortion, and remained silent on the others. Earlier, President Nixon had summarily reversed liberal abortion policies in military hospitals and interfered in state politics in an attempt to reverse New York's liberal abortion law, apparently in an attempt to impose his personal morality on others.

The resource-environment "commons" shared by all Americans will come under great pressure from the many interests that profit from and depend on its exploitation during the coming decade. Political institutions supposedly preserve order within this commons, but unfortunately this is analogous to appointing the proverbial fox to protect the chickens. Self-interest dominates political proceedings and the interest of the whole generally gets lost in a struggle among the parts. Scholars have observed that the congressional committee system often hinders rather than assists in a careful evaluation of proposed legislation, including that dealing with environmental problems. They also have pointed out that frequently the committees that should be legislating action against those who attack the environment are actually dominated by the attackers. Others have made the same point about federal regulatory agencies.

Political checks and balances were designed to discourage hasty, unreasoned actions, not to facilitate the transformation of a society headed for severe difficulties. Checks and balances now frequently operate to frustrate decisive action. The Chief Executive has the power to veto acts of Congress and to checkmate social and environmental initiatives from that branch. A two-thirds majority in the House and Senate, almost impossible to muster, is required to override a veto. Similarly, the executive branch depends on Congress for appropriations. Although the executive branch cannot by itself institute sweeping new programs, the President does have some power to act unilaterally in certain specific circumstances, such as meeting an economic crisis, responding to attack from another nation, responding to natural disasters, and in other similar emergencies. The crisis now facing mankind does not fit into this category as traditionally defined, and thus the President, even if he were inclined to take effective action, could only propose new legislation and administer those programs that already exist. To change the direction of this nation will require moving both the executive and legislative branches of government, and there is little indication that either branch is ready to budge.

Lack of attention to long-term goals and the interests of future generations is nothing new, but the consequences of such behavior are new and should not be overlooked. The industrial heritage of muddling through must be quickly replaced before the laws of physics and biology, over which politicians have no control, force changes that will benefit no none.

The Pluralist Trap

All societies have methods for collectively reaching decisions. The more complex a society and its problems, the greater the need for sophistication among decision makers and participation by informed citizens. Unfortunately, government by compassionate and intelligent leadership has been rare throughout history. Mass democracy as a form of government is a recent phenomenon. Historically, the majority has never been active in politics and has demanded no significant political role. Even the classical democracies in ancient Greece were democracies of the wealthy classes, not of the entire population. The extension of the vote to all citizens, whether or not they are interested in politics, has been a most important political result of the industrial revolution. Regardless of the reasons for expansion of the electorate, mass democracy is the system within which any change in politics must take place.

The term "democracy" must be used advisedly; the gap between theory and practice is large. Political theorist Roberto Michels has succinctly pointed out that "to say organization is to say oligarchy." Even so-called mass democracies have always been run by small oligarchies, groups of decision makers operating quite apart from direct consultation with the masses. The system cannot really work in any other way. Political scientist Robert Dahl calls it the efficiency principle, meaning that there must be some delegation of authority or nothing gets done.

In a democracy voters are given an opportunity to oust politicians from office in elections. In practice, however, permanent ouster of politicians rarely occurs in the United States, and the same faces reappear on either side of a porous curtain between official and "unofficial" government. Even a politician who suffers a severe electoral defeat often winds up in an appointed office or in a responsible position in business that permits him to remain close to centers of political power. There is room for only a few in the governing oligarchy, but, once admitted, an individual is a member for the duration of his good behavior. Thus, such well-known political names as Roosevelt, Acheson, Kennedy, Lodge, Harriman, Stevenson, Rockefeller, McNamara, and Bundy have either kept politics "in the family" for generations or have jumped from one important position to another throughout their individual careers. Various facets of "power elite" arguments will not be discussed here. Suffice it to say that relatively few people make decisions for everyone and that the selection of members of the oligarchy has never been particularly broad. The rules for entry have been based mainly on money and social position, and it has been unclear whether members of the oligarchy have acted as public masters or as public servants. It is certain, however, that they have rarely, if ever, made decisions that ran contrary to their own interests or the interests of their peers.

The most dangerous political belief nurtured by this ruling oligarchy has been that wise and fair policy decisions are best reached by maintaining a pluralist representation of interests in the political arena. In a young nation of apparent abundance, in which limits on potential growth were not an issue, there seemed to be every advantage in a system that allowed powerful groups to settle differences without involving the masses in violence. It was believed that the competition of powerful interests and the shifting of coalitions among them would prevent any one person or group from becoming all-powerful and that just decisions would somehow emerge from their struggles. In practice, the political power of these interests often allowed each of them to influence elements of the government and to carry on what was essentially an economic battle through legislation.

This system of minimal elite government established in the eighteenth century still exists in spirit today, even though the scope of its activities has since been vastly extended. It serves mainly to promote and protect a few strong interests. It is not surprising, then, that most politicians neglect one of the *stated* reasons for maintaining the union—to promote the *general welfare.* Although, in moments of fantasy, situations might be envisioned in which the actions of a few self-seeking power groups benefit the whole society, this result seems highly unlikely.

No purpose is served by attempting to affix blame for the present politics of corruption or by engaging in political name-calling. It is true that wealth almost guarantees access to the ruling oligarchy in the United States today. It is also understandable for "economic men" to try to protect and keep what they have or even to add to their fortunes. In fact, all of us tend to behave in this way. In a sense, "we have met the enemy and they is us." There is little indication that any powerful or potentially powerful group in our society would resist self-seeking temptations if given political power. Although it is possible to point to a small wealthy group that currently formulates and carries out most national policies, no group of unselfish philosopher kings is waiting in the wings to assume a leadership role.

It is important to stress that this represents one of the most serious dilemmas facing democratic government. Unless vested interests can be separated from political decision making (which seems unlikely) or a system designed that links their own welfare to the collective welfare, there is little hope that the needed social transformation can take place. It is clear that a new politics, a new allocation of responsibilities and privileges, as well as a new social contract will be necessary to meet coming challenges if the United States is to avoid falling into the traps of mob rule or dictatorship; but there are as yet few signs of a sudden "greening" of the political process.

Political scientist Theodore Lowi, in his classic indictment of interest group liberalism (democracy dependent on the clash of interest groups for persistence), points out that there are at least six reasons that pluralism and liberalism do not work as they should in theory. Roughly translated, they are as follows:

1. Liberalism-pluralism promotes principled decision making, but then detracts from decisions thus made. A pluralistic reconciliation of interests is fine for making important decisions, but liberal leaders lack the backbone to implement those decisions that are opposed to entrenched interests. Recent examples include the Philadelphia Plan for integration of labor unions or school busing to equalize educational opportunity. In both situations resolute decisions were made based on moral principle, but resolution was watered down during implementation as individual interests overcame the principled arguments.

2. Liberal-pluralist governments cannot adequately carry out plans. They can quickly formulate numerous programs but are frequently at a loss when required to choose one. Although people generally do not think of the Nixon

administration as being liberal, it is an example of liberal-pluralism weighted more heavily toward the economically powerful. The Nixon approach to the energy crisis offers a perfect example of how hesitant liberal governments are to carry out plans. Task forces have been organized, departments have been set up, studies have been commissioned, and exhortations have been made, but thus far no intelligent decisions have been made. The best that the White House has been able to do is to send a directive to federal departments ordering the relaxation of dress standards to reduce levels of air conditioning and to talk about fuel allotment plans for distribution of heating oil. No measures that would provoke any significant opposition have been proposed, and apparently the Nixon approach will be to continue trying to meet skyrocketing demand rather than to attempt to cut consumption.

3. Liberalism and pluralism corrupt democratic government by opposing formal legislative practices with informal bargaining. Issues are rarely resolved in a visible political struggle; more frequently the powerful wheel and deal behind the scenes. For example, on a series of important issues, legislation passed by Congress has been challenged in the courts or watered down by regulatory agencies, and enforcement has lagged as appeal proceedings have dragged on.

4. Liberalism and pluralism perpetuate faith that a system built on interest-group bargaining corrects abuses of power; but there is little indication that things really work this way. When millions of dollars of campaign funds are involved, monied interests are in a much better position to dictate legislation than are those without access to funds. The abuses of the system are well illustrated by the excesses of the Watergate affair, which, it must be remembered, nearly went undetected. We may never know of the number of similar activities, backed by millions of dollars, that have also gone undetected.

5. Pluralism cannot handle the issue of oligarchy. The political world is shaped by imperfect competition, and the necessary countervailing power to dominant groups is nonexistent. The role of the military-industrial-labor complex in dominating the political process illustrates this point. As in other social diseconomies of scale, the larger the aggregation of power, the greater the threat to open political competition.

6. Pluralism depends on the willingness of groups to compromise. However, there is much recent evidence to indicate that many groups do not wish to compromise. Battle lines between left and right and black and white have been hardening as a politics of confrontation has replaced a politics of compromise. The attitudes toward the opposition party evidenced by some of

the Watergate defendants, who equated Democratic candidates with Communists and other subversives, indicates that uncompromising attitudes can be traced right to the top in the political system. In a less affluent future, uncompromising attitudes may harden rather than soften, and the politics of pluralism might well become the politics of warfare.

Lowi's evaluation concludes that interest group liberalism has come to a dead end because it is an ineffective means of governing. However, Lowi was poorly acquainted with pressing environmental issues when he wrote. If interest group liberalism fails on so many counts to meet today's needs, it will fail even more miserably to meet the needs of the future.

Those in the oligarchy continue to write articles and books extolling the virtues of pluralism and political conflict. As a result, cooperation and long-term planning for collective welfare are ignored. When former Vice President Agnew argued that "Division may be the price of progress," he completely ignored the need for social consciousness in an industrial society. Frontier politics failed to foster any such social consciousness. In a less affluent world, pluralism and division might well lead to the extinction of whatever civility still remains in politics.

Common Wisdoms

Most stable societies are governed by leaders who make good use of folklore and conventional rhetoric to sustain dominant social paradigms. For example, almost all leaders claim to rule democratically, regardless of the actual amount of political power shared with those over whom they rule. It is important to understand some of the myths or folklore of democracy that provide the underpinnings for citizen support of our outmoded political system.

Ruling oligarchies in all countries use a variety of methods to maintain some limits on political thought and advocacy, and often these limits fluctuate. The United States Supreme Court has frequently vacillated in protecting free speech, being much more anxious to defend First Amendment freedoms when there is no clear and present danger to political stability. In times of conflict, orthodoxy is stressed, and radical ideas are not given much public hearing.

In the United States, the abundance of the past and the open frontier have helped to prevent much social strife of a kind that would have led to serious restrictions on freedom of expression. The degree to which the ideals of "free speech" and "freedom of thought" have been realized is very much a result of the lack of revolutionary threats to the oligarchy. Ideas planted by radicals make little difference as long as there is no fertile soil within which they can germinate. In rare times of danger, however, civil liberties have been easily curtailed: witness Lincoln's closing of "seditious" newspapers during the Civil War, the suppression of early attempts to organize labor, the post-World War I "Red scare" that closely followed the Bolshevik Revolution, the herding of Japanese-Americans into detention camps during World War II, and the havoc wreaked by Joseph McCarthy and other Communist-hunters in the early fifties after the Communist victory in China.

The matter of freedom of speech and political advocacy is very complicated. One of the functions a dominant social paradigm (DSP) serves is to set boundaries, mostly covert, on advocacy of change and freedom of speech. There are many issues that people refrain from discussing because of social inhibitions. Throughout most of American history, for example, people have seldom thought to question the meaning or wisdom of private property. Now that pressures on land and resources are becoming severe, more people are beginning to regard traditional concepts of ownership as inappropriate. Covert bounds on freedom of speech are quietly enforced by others in society. If there is no one with whom the issues can be debated, the man on the soapbox in the park may be in for a long and lonely Sunday.

Times of turmoil and change are times when society regards more overt restrictions on freedom of speech and advocacy as necessities. Political leaders are then much more likely to protect themselves by jailing those whose speech falls outside permissible bounds. Not all speech, of course, is censored. It is the rare political leader who demands that speech be censored within the family, although there have been reports of such censorship during periods of revolutionary ferment in the Soviet Union and Communist China. A ruling oligarchy is much more interested in censoring public speeches, newspaper articles, and television and radio broadcasts (communications that reach large audiences).

Throughout most of American history, covert social mechanisms limiting free speech and advocacy have served the oligarchy very well, and there has seldom been a need to resort to more overt restrictions. But if organized attacks on the mass media and education by both Nixon administrations are indicative of future trends, freedom of speech, and even thought, in the United States is bound to receive more overt political attention.

The DSP imparts some notions of the kinds of subjects that are acceptable in political debate. It is understood to be "safe" to argue for policies reforming the congressional seniority system. Although the idea might meet with intense opposition, its proponent is not likely to be beaten by mobs, socially ostracized, or detained by security police. On the other hand, no one who wants to make friends and influence people is likely to suggest abolishing existing political parties or nationalizing all major American industries.

Unfortunately, some of the most important questions regarding the declining quality of life and the survival of society are still defined as being outside the boundary of acceptable discussion. Bio-degradable detergents and lead-free gasoline represent the current limits of concern with the environment because they are remedies that pose no long-run threat to the distribution of wealth. To make political issues of resource depletion, a steady-state economy, or a new system for transferring wealth from the very rich nations to less-developed areas is now almost impossible because these ideas threaten the established system of privilege. Thus, when the Environmental Protection Agency in 1973 drew up plans that would permit major cities in the United States to meet clean air standards, the plans were shouted down by "political realists." When the 1972 report of the Council on Environmental Quality was made public, three chapters were missing. The chapters that dealt with the energy crisis, pollution in the Delaware Valley, and recycling, were for a time withheld from the public by the President on the grounds that they were too controversial for an election year.

Aside from implicit and explicit restrictions on political discussion, there are many potentially dangerous, commonly accepted wisdoms that directly sustain an increasingly outmoded political system. These constitute a part of the folklore of democracy that keeps people happy in an imaginary political world. A brief excursion through this jungle of maxims may be quite revealing.

1. *In the United States the People govern.* In democracies there is no question that power *ultimately* rests with the people, but there are many barriers to its effective use. As long as it is impossible to guarantee everyone a direct vote on all issues, efficiency in political processes dictates the selection of a few to represent the many. Wealth, experience, and support for accepted social wisdoms greatly enhance an individual's chances of becoming one of these select few. Once he or she is within the oligarchy, the deck is stacked in favor of incumbents. Financial resources, political organization, and access to the media give incumbents a considerable edge.

Given social realities, this arrangement has undoubtedly been functional in maintaining order throughout history. An entire school of political philosophy, going back to the time of Plato, has cautioned against putting power in the hands of people who possess no training, wisdom, or interest in affairs of state. Until this century, relatively few individuals have been knowledgeable enough to govern well, since education was available only to the wealthy. In the few instances when the uneducated masses have taken control, tyranny has ensued. Most people are not interested enough to be politically active. Moreover, forty-hour work weeks leave little time to keep fully informed on important issues.

Accepted rhetoric assures us that democracy is good and that the people should rule because most citizens are rational and intelligent. This is not supported by empirical evidence. An informed voter should at least be able to read newspaper articles, but data indicate that as many as ten million Americans are functionally illiterate, and another twenty million cannot handle material of news story difficulty. This is one reason why electoral campaigns are now in the hands of public relations firms. There is little reason to debate issues in depth when most voters cannot or do not follow the dialogue.

Radicals who genuinely desire to ensure "power for the people" in the long run should consider what the immediate effects of suddenly involving millions of "silent majority" voters directly in the political process would be. It is certain that policies designed to achieve social justice and ecological stability would require considerable economic redistribution and some form of social dislocation. There is little indication that the majority of Americans would support these new policies.

Whether a well-informed majority could be developed and whether it could govern a large nation effectively remain matters for conjecture. Presently, even though the United States possesses one of the world's largest educational establishments, politically sophisticated citizens remain in the minority. The people now rule only in a very indirect way, something for which those interested in rapid social change should be thankful. But because the number of activists in favor of any cause is small, minor changes can be initiated by a dedicated cadre of a few thousand people. If as many as ten million persons should become dedicated to transforming society, the job might be done.

On the other hand, the oligarchy that makes many crucial political decisions often seems just as unsophisticated and socially unconcerned as the average voter. The most propitious, and possibly the most feasible, goal would be to expand the present oligarchy into a broader one that includes more individuals who are socially concerned and who understand future environment constraints. Great efforts must be made to organize political action at all levels to involve more people in the political process and thus to broaden the oligarchy. Some progress has already been made in this direction, especially in the area of civil rights, but this must also be done on environmental and population issues.

2. *Voters are concerned and humane.* The folklore would have Americans believe that voters possess some kind of political wisdom. A corollary of this "truth" holds that the voter is the only person who can really tell the government what is wrong since only he or she feels the impact of government policies. Although it is true that restive voters have often turned incompetents out of office, it is less clear that they have replaced them with anything but other incompetents. Hunger, poverty, and oppression may be felt by everyone, but not all are sophisticated enough to uncover the sources. Furthermore, the subtle and complex issues on which society's survival depends often have "counterintuitive" solutions. What appears to be in society's or an individual's best interest may be counterproductive when all facts are critically analyzed.

Some observers contend that voters possess a sixth sense that permits them to choose wisely among political candidates, but there is little evidence to support this notion. By avoiding confrontations with other candidates and sticking to pallid prepared speeches, today's political candidates offer the public very little insight into their human qualities. Public opinion surveys repeatedly have shown that the public believes politicians to be generally dishonest, and the record of political corruption reveals good reason for such suspicion. Of twenty occupations listed in a recent study, the public ranked politicians nineteenth in honesty. Voters, however, continue to elect to political office persons whom they suspect will be crooked.

Although it is comforting to believe that all citizens are basically concerned and humane, this is not particularly a characteristic of the members of our present society. If people are basically humane, what is the explanation for the apparent public willingness to support an inhumane struggle in Vietnam for ten years, as well as the unjustified bombing of Cambodia for six months after the cease-fire was signed? Widespread popular support for the death penalty further calls into question the basic humanity of the electorate.

Social psychologists have investigated the depths of humane feelings in the laboratory, and the political and social implications of these experiments are chilling. Perhaps the most provocative study was reported by social psychologist Stanley Milgram in the early sixties. In his classic experiment, subjects were ushered into a control room where they could observe another person (actually the experimenter's assistant) strapped in a chair and strung with electric wires. The subjects were told that they were participating in a behavior modification "experiment" and that they were to shock the person in the chair upon orders from the scientist conducting the project. Each subject was then given a fairly painful 45-volt "sample" shock and was instructed to turn up the dial to shock the assistant. As the apparent amount of voltage was increased, the "shocked" person in the chair sobbed and moaned with pain. At an apparent 180 volts, the person in the chair screamed that he could take no more. At 300 volts the assistant apparently went into deep shock and refused to communicate. Actually, of course, he was not being shocked, but as far as the experiment's subjects knew, the pain was real.

Much to the dismay of those who would testify as to mankind's basically humane instincts, Milgram's subjects delivered the full dose of electricity two-thirds of the time. Only one-third of the subjects demurred from the scientist's requests and refused to torture fellow human beings. The more distant the control booth was from the person being shocked, the greater was the willingness of subjects to administer maximum shock. To emphasize a most important point, the subjects were not following orders in the military service, nor were they, for example, under the same pressures as people in Hitler's Germany. The sanctions for noncompliance were minimal.

Analogous situations frequently occur in the real world. During the conflict in Vietnam, many people remarked about the cool and efficient way that American pilots bombed both military and civilian targets. They did not have to face their victims. Other people in urban industrial societies are becoming increasingly faceless and distant—objects to be coped with, not human beings. Even supposedly close relatives often suffer the consequences of senseless violence, both overt and covert, wreaked by inhumane people. Many citizens beat each other and their children behind closed doors. In New York City alone there are more than 7,000 reported cases of child abuse annually, and many thousands more are believed to go unreported. Murders certainly are not uncommon occurrences in the United States. Even though one person's concern for another may have increased in some ways since the early days of the industrial revolution, the world is still a very inhumane place. A political system that depended on human compassion would quickly go bankrupt. This should not be taken to mean that it is impossible to build a higher level of social consciousness; evidence indicates that it is quite possible. Development of much higher levels of concern for the welfare of others might well be essential to the survival of industrial society.

3. *Politicians make wise decisions.* This common wisdom can, of course, be declared true by definition. On one hand, since the United States has not yet ceased to exist (although some would argue that it has recently been on the verge of collapse), it is difficult to demonstrate that political leaders have

made poor decisions. On the other hand, we have no idea what kind of society might exist if a different type of politics had been practiced. What would today's world be like if the United States and the Soviet Union had jointly decided to end the arms race twenty years ago? What might have been done at home with the many billions of dollars that could have been saved by learning from the mistakes made by the French and avoiding military involvement in Vietnam? What could be done with the $70–$80 billion now being spent annually for defense? What could have been done with the billions of dollars squandered in putting men on the moon? What could resolute political leadership have done for the country by following through on sensitive policies to equalize opportunity rather than backing down when political pressures mounted?

In the field of foreign policy, the United States has been bogged down in more expensive "holding actions" around the globe than taxpayers would like to contemplate. Korea, Cuba, the Dominican Republic, Guatemala, and Vietnam head a seemingly endless list of places where the United States has chosen to intervene actively on behalf of someone friendly to American interests. The list of passive interventions, clandestine operations, sabotage, undercover payments to friendly forces, and so forth is very much longer. While countless billions of dollars and tens of thousands of American lives have been expended, the prestige of the United States in world affairs has continued to decline. This is hardly a favorable comment on the wisdom of American foreign policy.

Much more to the point, the record of governmental success at all levels on environmental and social matters is open to serious criticism. Rarely have politicians resisted the lures of the quick dollar and undirected economic growth to consider what is happening to the quality of life. Riots in the ghettos, economic recessions coupled with inflation, growing ecological problems, and increased violence in everyday life attest to failures in social and environmental policy.

4. *Political leaders possess special expertise.* The average politician has no special training or preparation that renders him or her more astute than the majority of his (or her) constituents. Most are lawyers, bankers, and businessmen. They do not necessarily have educational backgrounds that broaden perspectives or provide preparation for wrestling with the world's critical problems. The skills that most legislators and presidents bring to their office are political skills: winning victories over opponents, giving speeches to spellbound audiences on the Fourth of July, lying to friend and foe alike with a straight face, and wheeling and dealing with campaign contributors in back

rooms. These are skills that might lead to successful horse-trading, political espionage, and compromise in decision making, but they seldom lead to visionary and enlightened policies.

The skills and perspectives that a politician fails to bring to office certainly will not be acquired during his or her tenure. There are simply too many routine political matters that require time and intellectual effort, such as meetings to attend, speeches to prepare, constituents to mollify, and a continuous stream of visitors to Washington. At best, a legislator can keep up with immediate business and learn the legislative ropes, but he or she certainly cannot take the time to amass the information crucial for understanding the social, economic, and environmental issues that must be faced in the near future.

5. *Public servants "serve" the public.* Political leaders and those who influence or control them are wealthy and powerful people. In general, they rise to the top by triumphing in Machiavellian struggles. There is no reason to believe that such recruitment leads to altruism in high places. On the contrary, the most self-seeking and cunning politicians are more likely to succeed, while relatively unselfish and compassionate people are more likely to be weeded out in a selection of the "least fit." Distinguished political scientist Harold Lasswell has even claimed that many politicians seek office because of a pathological desire for power—hardly a recommendation for public service. A tremendous shift in methods of political recruitment will be necessary to install true public servants in positions of power. At present, a public service rhetoric obscures self-seeking activities of politicians, most of whom leave office in much better financial position than when they were first elected.

6. *Democracy is a marketplace of ideas.* This myth assumes such importance in rhetoric, yet misses the mark so widely, that parts of Chapter 6 are devoted to it. Common wisdom holds that in a democracy there is a free competition of ideas resembling the competition of goods and services in Adam Smith's economic marketplace. The implication is that in this competition, good ideas win out over those of little merit. It is much more accurate to say that this is an age of unrestricted advertising in which the battle of ideas is heavily dependent on financial backing. Ideas rarely compete solely on their own merits; they have champions whose financial power helps determine the winner. The good idea that fails to be backed by wealth and power may never get a fair public hearing regardless of its importance to society's future.

7. *Planning restricts freedom.* An antiplanning bias has been etched very deeply in the American political conscience. It has resulted from the near

hysteria that has repeatedly been stirred up by domestic patriots and opponents of the "Communist conspiracy." "Patriotic" citizens know that
Communist and Socialist societies are planned. Since Communism and Socialism are supposedly evil, planning has been portrayed as a Communist
plot and a restriction of present liberties and those of future generations.
According to the dogma, planning today means closing off options that
might otherwise be held open for posterity. In reality the reverse is true.

Bias against planning is an excellent example of social lag. Planning must
be an integral part of any strategy for survival. A completely unplanned
society would be anarchic and certainly would not represent any kind of
freedom in an interdependent industrial society. Limited resources must
carefully be saved for the future; immediate desires should not be allowed to
overshadow rational considerations. Even squirrels know enough to gather
nuts for the winter. Lack of planning would leave us and our descendants
"free" to suffer the full consequences of irrational use of the physical and
social resources available to us.

Ignoring long-range planning and sticking with the politics of muddling
through will inexorably lead to the decline of industrial society. Judicious
planning for the future of the planet, on the other hand, can *open up an entirely
new series of options* that will not be available if population growth, resource
depletion, and environmental deterioration continue to be ignored. For every
freedom that might be restricted today, many freedoms will be made available
to succeeding generations who must live with the consequences of our
present behavior.

Selecting Political Leaders

The system of political representation that today is called mass democracy, as
originally established in the United States, was based on the assumption
that wealth, property, and experience were characteristics that distinguished
wise men from fools. Wealthy individuals were expected to participate more
actively in politics, both because they were considered superior to the common folk and because they had much more to lose if things went wrong. In
the midst of today's egalitarianism, it is easy to forget that the nation's
founders designed a system of representation that included restrictions on
voting, poll taxes, and other measures designed to keep voting power in the
hands of a few. In immediate post-Revolutionary America, this kind of
thinking made sense. The masses were largely illiterate, ill-informed, and

unable to grapple with the complexities of governance. The aristocracy was educated and had the time to engage in politics and the means to travel. There was neither a sizable intelligentsia nor an educated middle class to protest being left out of the political process. Thus, for a long period in United States history, women, slaves, and the poor had no vote at all, and at the time of the Constitutional Convention only approximately 5 percent of the population voted.

The ensuing years have been full of changes in American society, but there have been relatively few changes in our approach to representative government. The nation has grown to embrace a continent, the population has increased more than fiftyfold, education has become widespread, the social structure has changed considerably, and technology has created incredibly complex problems of social, environmental, and economic management. Political leaders, however, still come largely from the ranks of the wealthy. The cost of getting elected has risen sharply, partly as a consequence of the media and advertising explosion. A candidate must either be well-to-do or indebted to wealthy men to obtain the funds necessary for election. In 1968, $60 million was spent on political television and radio broadcasts alone. A sincere candidate faces real problems in finding money to finance his campaign without selling his soul. This is the reason that all politicians appear to be alike and to defend the interests of a small segment of society.

Politicians and their supporters spent more than $300 million in their quest for public office in 1968. When all returns are in for the 1972 elections, the total figure for campaign spending is likely to approach one-half billion dollars. The total for Richard Nixon's reelection drive was in the neighborhood of $60 million; the Democratic candidate spent a little over half that much. Even running in the primaries has become largely a game for rich men only. It is estimated that in 1972 each of the major Democratic candidates spent between $10 million and $12 million in the primary contests. Elections have become a major American industry; even the races for lesser offices have become extremely costly. In the 1970 California state elections, candidates spent a record total of $26 million.

In light of this runaway spending, it would seem sensible to pass legislation that would severely restrict campaign donations and spending, but many present incumbents have little desire to penalize themselves by making it easier for others to run for office. For 47 years (1925–1972), nothing at all was done to stop spiraling campaign costs. By 1970 the financial situation had so deteriorated that, in the seven largest states of the Union, eleven of the fifteen major candidates for the Senate were millionaires. The four nonmillionaires lost their elections. Congress finally recognized the issue in 1972 and passed a watered-down bill that did very little to change the situation. Today's presidential or vice-presidential candidate can invest "only" $50,000 of his personal or family wealth in his own campaign; senators and representatives are "restricted" to only $35,000 apiece. Each candidate is also denied the right to spend more than 10 cents for each potential voter on mass-media advertising. This means that presidential candidates, thus "deprived," will be able to spend *only* $13 million to $15 million on media advertising in future campaigns. Significantly, however, there is no overall ceiling on the amount that each candidate can spend in other ways. At this writing, a much tougher campaign spending bill has been passed by the Senate in the wake of the Watergate scandal, but it faces an uncertain future in the House.

This close link between money and politics represents a serious barrier to effective decision making in meeting future environmental problems and calls into question the willingness of political leaders to act resolutely when it might not be in their interest to do so. It is only reasonable that those who have made and are making profits within the old system that has led to environmental deterioration are going to be among the least willing to modify it to meet new survival imperatives. Furthermore, the need for an aspiring politician to be wealthy or have wealthy backers does not give society access to a very large pool of leadership talent at a time when innovative leadership is badly needed. Links between intelligence, compassion, and wealth disappeared long ago. These virtues are no longer a monopoly of the rich, if they ever were. Many of the wealthy have acquired their fortunes, not through skill or merit, but through inheritance or less-than-legal entrepreneurial schemes. Although there are many notable exceptions, neither the old wealthy nor the *nouveaux riches* are interested in transforming a society in which they "have it made." Indeed, it is their factories that are polluting the air and water, their mines and wells that are exploiting the resource commons, and their capital that is being reinvested in a continuing spiral of growth. It will be difficult to educate the wealthy and their political appointees to understand that their interests cannot be separated from the interests of society as a whole.

The unhealthy effects of money in politics may be even more severe on those who depend on the wealthy for their political careers. The security of wealth has permitted some men to turn their attention to curing the ills of society and promoting the common good. For instance, even their most determined detractors would admit that the Kennedys and Rockefellers have been concerned with questions of social justice. But the financially dependent politician may find little opportunity for exercising similar humanitarian instincts. Thus, it is difficult to see how Richard Nixon could make decisions that might attack the privileges of such financial backers as insurance executive W. Clement Stone, who gave Nixon $4.8 million over a four-year period, or Arthur Kroc, head of the McDonald's hamburger chain, who contributed $225,000 to Nixon's reelection effort, or Gulf Oil Company, which contributed $100,000 in 1972. Nor is it easy to see how the President could make decisions against the interests of other corporate executives, many of whom were asked to donate 1 percent of their *net worth* to the Nixon campaign. Quite the contrary, there is much evidence to indicate that many favors were directly purchased by these executives with their campaign contributions and that others purchased guarantees of access to the President if any economic or political problems should bother them. Survival in politics for the poor politician, like President Nixon, depends on keeping financial backers happy. For the enterprising politician there are ample opportunities to make money on the side through business deals engineered by wealthy friends, so that the pain of eventual retirement will be eased by possession of a sizable bankroll.

In addition to these abuses of money politics, winning candidates often staff the higher levels of government with their financial backers. In medieval France, an aspiring officeholder simply bought the office from the king for a sum of gold. Today the process is a little more complex, but the results are the same. Anyone desiring a prestigious appointment need only contribute enough money to the campaign of a winning candidate. When doubt exists as to who will win, contributions can be made to all likely candidates. Campaign contributions are repaid with ambassadorships, domestic political appointments, or official favor. When Richard Nixon took office in 1968, he handsomely rewarded ten of his strongest backers with prestigious ambassadorships. Arthur K. Watson, an IBM executive, earned the big plum, the post of Ambassador to France, by making a contribution of $55,000. Lesser ambassadorships were purchased by Guilford Dudley, Jr., an insurance company president, for $51,000 (Denmark), Vincent de Roulet for $45,000 (Jamaica), and John P. Humes, a New York lawyer, for $43,000 (Austria). In all these and many similar instances, it would be difficult to argue that the appointee possessed any expertise in diplomacy, world politics, or the affairs of the country to which he was assigned.

This practice is not restricted to diplomatic posts; the same spoils system extends throughout federal, state, and local politics. The Environmental Protection Agency, for example, was ostensibly set up to protect the environment, but President Nixon staffed it heavily with political appointees and very lightly with ecologists and environmentalists. In state and local politics, tales of the bequest of financially lucrative political appointments and plush contracts to supporters and relatives are commonplace—particularly, it seems, in the state of Maryland. The public interest and the interest of future generations suffer heavily when the incompetent are put on the public payroll as a reward for bankrolling a winner, especially when well-trained persons could easily take their place.

Today's huge campaign expenditures do little to elevate the level of political discussion, although campaign spending is sometimes justified on the grounds that it helps define issues and gives people a chance to make their own decisions. Campaign commercials do not consist of straightforward, well-reasoned speeches on important issues, backed with documented evidence. Instead, even televised debates have more to offer the theater buff than someone looking for an exposition of political philosophies and policy alternatives. The celebrated Republican commercial that was broadcast in the final week of the 1968 campaign, juxtaposing a laughing Hubert Humphrey with bloody war scenes from Vietnam, is a prime example. The naked appeal to authority inherent in the *Reelect the President* campaign of 1972 and the refusal of candidate Nixon to debate issues in public is another. But these abuses pale to insignificance when compared with those revealed by the Watergate Affair. In 1972 huge amounts of Nixon's campaign funds were used, not to present the case for reelection of President Nixon, but to finance an unprecedented series of illegal acts of political espionage and sabotage in a tragic subversion of the political process. To add insult to injury, additional campaign funds were then used to pay the legal fees of those indicted for illegal activities.

The inevitable result of a politics based on wealth is the overrepresentation of the interests of well-situated individuals who have "made it" according to existing rules. Visionaries elected to office are likely to be those with a good vision of the past. They then appoint like-minded supporters to high office, thereby reducing the effectiveness and vision of the bureaucracy. Most often, people having access to the kind of wealth required to get elected are older, relatively conservative, and have little interest in opening up a new dialogue or listening to those who point to a need for a radical transformation of society. Fortunes and connections are built up over a lifetime, and few people acquire them before they lose their enthusiasm for social change.

Homogeneous Legislators

Partly as a result of financial requirements, partly because of public acceptance of common political wisdoms, and partly because of publicity advantages accruing to incumbents, politics in the United States is dominated by a very narrow sample of the population, which has few imaginative ideas and limited substantive expertise outside the affairs of government and business. The upper echelons of the executive, legislative, and judicial branches of government, moreover, are dominated by men two to three times as old as the average citizen. Despite the recent burst of optimism surrounding the election of a few young people, there have been no substantial changes in congressional age distributions during the last decade. There were 59 members under 40 years old in the House of Representatives in 1961; in 1971 there were only 40. At the other end of the age distribution, however, there were 107 representatives over 60 years old in 1961. These retirement-age congressmen composed one-quarter of the House of Representatives then, as they did in 1971 when there were 108. In addition, 22 representatives in 1971 were over 70, an age at which most corporations have long since retired their key executives to make way for younger and more innovative talent.

The record in the Senate has been no better. In 1961 there was only one senator under the age of 40; in 1971 there were 4. At the other extreme, the number of senators over 70 rose from 9 in 1961 to 17 one decade later. In 1971, 2 out of every 5 senators were at least 60 years old.

Minority groups have not recently been favored with legislation beneficial to their causes, and the reasons are not difficult to find. In both the House and the Senate there has been only token representation of blacks and Mexican-Americans. Women have been even more underrepresented. There were 2 women in the Senate in 1961. There was only one left in 1971, and by 1973 none remained. In the House of Representatives, representation by women declined from 15 to 12 between 1961 and 1971.

The range of new ideas in politics is further narrowed by similarity of socioeconomic background. Political scientist Donald Matthews' extensive study of United States senators, completed in the early sixties, indicated that more than one-half of those interviewed had begun their careers as lawyers. An even greater percentage of senators had spent time practicing law by the time they were elected to office. An amazing one-quarter of all senators had begun their political careers by serving in law enforcement agencies. Of the remaining senators in the Matthews study, by far the greatest proportion had former careers in business. Among Republican senators, 40 percent came from business backgrounds. Although these specific figures would be slightly revised if the study were repeated today, a glance through the biographical section of the Congressional Directory for the 92nd Congress (1971–1972) reveals that occupational backgrounds for senators and representatives have remained much the same.

The combination of congressional age, occupational similarity, and slow-moving legislative practices greatly restricts the scope of political discussion and legislative innovation. Congressional machinery slows any initiative to a grinding halt. Most politicians will admit that ten years or more are usually required for an idea to be translated into legislation. In the picturesque words of the late Senator Everett Dirksen, "Congress is like an old waterlogged scow. It doesn't go far, it doesn't go fast. But it doesn't sink." Rather than providing leadership and initiative in developing needed social and environmental legislation, most politicians subscribe to old values, precisely those that are now leading toward destruction. These individuals often are out of touch with reality and resist new ideas, particularly those offered by younger constituents. Having grown up in different times, they are loath to recognize future constraints on growth and the fundamental weaknesses of the old social paradigm.

The tendency toward "gerontocracy" (government predominantly by the old) is further accentuated by the seniority system, which still dominates both houses of Congress. Assignments to key committees are made with an eye toward length of service and political orthodoxy. No young senator or representative who fails to honor the elders can expect to be assigned to a choice committee, and committees are where the day-to-day legislative work is done. When Representative Shirley Chisholm from urban New York City made her first appearance in the House, she had three strikes against her. She was female, she was black, and she made a lot of commotion. The "system" responded by initially giving her an assignment on the House Agriculture Committee, an area in which she had little competence or interest. This was normal treatment for a nonconformist first-term representative, but Representative Chisholm was able to use her double minority status to make a successful protest through the mass media and get a more appropriate committee assignment.

The all-important committee chairmanships have also been handed out on the basis of seniority. Particularly in the House, many years of service are required to reach a position of influence. There are simply too many incumbent representatives from "safe" districts—those in which the two-party system is in effect nonexistent. This explains the predominance of Southerners as committee chairmen. In many parts of the South there is no significant Republican party, so incumbent Democrats are automatically renominated and face no contest from the opposition. Thus, in the House, 11 representatives in the 92nd Congress (9 from the South) had served more than 16 consecutive terms (32 years), including: Wright Patman (Texas), 22 terms; William Colmer (Mississippi), 20 terms; George Mahon (Texas), 19 terms; W. R. Poage (Texas), 18 terms; John McMillan (South Carolina), 17 terms; Wilbur Mills (Arkansas), 17 terms; Edward Hébert (Louisiana), 16 terms; Robert Sikes (Florida), 16 terms; Jamie Whitten (Mississippi), 16 terms.

Table 4.1 lists the key committees and committee chairmen in the Senate and House of Representatives for the 92nd Congress. These data illustrate that powerful politicians come mostly from the conservative South, especially Louisiana, Mississippi, Texas, and Arkansas. Many would be judged well past their prime by any conventional standards. The average age of key committee chairmen in the Senate is 70. The average age of committee chairmen in the House is 71. The typical committee chairman has served as

Table 4.1   *Key Committees of the 92nd Congress (1971–1972)*

Committee	Chairman	State	Age	Length of Service in Years
Senate				
Appropriations	Allen Ellender [a]	Louisiana	82	35
Armed Services	John Stennis	Mississippi	71	25
Banking, Housing, and Urban Affairs	John Sparkman	Alabama	73	26
Commerce	Warren Magnuson	Washington	67	28
Finance	Russell Long	Louisiana	54	24
Foreign Relations	J. W. Fulbright	Arkansas	67	27
Judiciary	James Eastland	Mississippi	68	29
Rules	Everett Jordan	North Carolina	76	14
House				
Appropriations	George Mahon	Texas	72	38
Armed Services	Edward Hébert	Louisiana	71	32
Banking and Currency	Wright Patman	Texas	79	44
Education and Labor	Carl Perkins	Kentucky	60	24
Foreign Affairs	Thomas Morgan	Pennsylvania	66	28
Judiciary	Emanuel Celler	New York	84	50
Rules	William Colmer	Mississippi	70 [b]	40
Ways and Means	Wilbur Mills	Arkansas	63	34

[a] Deceased.

[b] No age listed in Congressional Directory. Figure represents an estimate.

a senator or representative for at least 25 years and was first elected in the late thirties or early forties, a time when the significant issues were quite different from those of today.

In 1971 efforts were initiated to reform the seniority system. Under new rules, committee chairmen were elected by secret ballot by their fellow committee members in both the House and the Senate in 1973. The results were exactly the same as if the formal rules had not been changed: The senior Democrats were elected chairmen, and senior Republicans were given top ranks within minority leadership. Politicians who have attained or who aspire to attain power under the old rules may formally change these rules, but they are not likely to change informal agreements and thus undermine their own power bases.

Although the problem of gerontocracy in the judicial and executive branches does not catch the public eye as easily as it does in the legislature, partly because aggregate data on age and advancement in these other branches are not readily available, age and seniority exact a similar toll there. Moving toward a position of power requires years of faithful service, patience, and a knack for not stepping on the wrong toes. An important appointment in the judicial branch normally requires a long record of distinguished service, although recent appointments to the Supreme Court indicate that social and political orthodoxy are just as important. Years are required to work slowly up through the bureaucratic system, and, in the meantime, an individual loses the innovative ideas and idealism characteristic of youth. Intelligent young people often join the civil service only as a last resort because they know that many years of slow advancement must take place before they can move into any position of influence.

Nor is the executive branch immune from creeping conservatism. Although the Nixon administration has appointed some younger people to key positions, they have been very carefully selected for orthodox and outmoded views, which mirror those of the President. It should also be noted that neither President Nixon nor former President Johnson would qualify as young when elected, either chronologically or in spirit. In fact, Richard Nixon won the White House after having spent his best years in a fruitless struggle to win other elections, and many of his speeches carry the indelible mark of a man who learned his social, economic, and political wisdom in days long gone. For example, he repeatedly attacked his Democratic opponent in the 1972 presidential elections as a man who "represents a challenge to our values." He also espoused the view that his opponent's policies would threaten the "work ethic" and thereby "weaken the American character."

Obviously, the President has not yet recognized that new values are needed if the United States is to be deflected from its very dangerous political and economic course.

This generation gap, which pervades contemporary politics, frustrates the purpose of representative government as well as its capacity for meeting future challenges. The typical congressman belongs to a different generation from that of most of his constituency. Although there have been many instances in which older people have championed new ideas, in general advanced age is associated with reactionary attitudes. Furthermore, the gap between the ideas of elderly congressmen and those of their much younger constituents is dangerous for democracy. When representatives do not adequately "represent," alienation and frustration with politics build up among the young. When the nation was first formed, built-in conservatism was an asset because it contributed to stability when few drastic changes were needed. Now, however, the very survival of these cherished political institutions may well depend on our ability to transcend rigid and reactionary attitudes.

New and unorthodox thinking must be introduced into a political dialogue that now trails behind social realities by many years. Today's problems are different in kind from those of yesterday, and tomorrow's problems will resemble those of today even less. The advantages of accumulated wisdom and expertise diminish when much social and scientific knowledge becomes obsolete every decade. People in many professions now claim to need sabbatical years merely to keep up with new developments. Can it be so different for government officials? If politics is to remain primarily concerned with relatively simply management problems and the reconciliation of group interests, then aged Solomons who specialize in knowing the political ropes can do the job; but in bringing about a political transformation, only those with youthful minds, regardless of their chronological age, will be able to make positive contributions.

Centralization of Power

The inability of the legislative branch to act decisively on major policy issues represents a time bomb of potentially greater consequence than the corruption induced by money politics. Legislative inaction leads to the centralization of initiative and power in fewer and fewer hands, and policy initiatives are transferred from Congress to the White House. In times of crisis, people tend to support demagogues and dictators. Germany in the late twenties and early thirties is an obvious example. Hitler could not have taken power so easily if the Germans had been well fed and economically prosperous. Given the developing crisis, it is not at all impossible that the dynamics leading to dictatorship could again be set in motion in this country.

The strength of the executive branch has varied throughout history according to the characteristics of the man in the White House. Thus, Franklin Roosevelt was able to see the nation through the turmoil of the Depression and World War II with a fairly free hand. In the late thirties, because he was dissatisfied with Supreme Court decisions, Roosevelt set about trying to remake the Court in his own image. His plan was voted down by the Senate. More recently, however, another strong President might have succeeded where Roosevelt failed.

Richard Nixon's position as a strong President during his first term resulted from the convergence of several trends in American society that have not been readily apparent. The most obvious is the degeneration of political campaigns into vicious athletic contests where the winner gets the spoils. The Nixon "mandate" in 1972 did not entirely originate with the people. In fact, it was engineered by the most skilled team of political saboteurs ever assembled in the United States. The Watergate caper justifiably received the most publicity, but the same group of Nixon supporters was responsible for using technology to ensure a political victory over a clearly more principled competitor. Public opinion polls, news releases, and letters that were faked, electronic listening devices, and organized heckling of opponents were among the more criminal aspects of that election. The Nixon campaign was orchestrated by a team of professionals whose goal was to win at all costs; and in that election, one of the hidden costs was the shift from issue politics to the use of political technology.

Aside from outright incidents of political sabotage, the centralization of power under the Nixon administration has been aided by what political scientist Thomas Cronin has described as an "image-tending theatrical presidency." The President now uses the expertise of media specialists and behavioral scientists to develop an acceptable public image independent of the merit of his policies. Public opinion polls show that presidential popularity rises every time a President does something of significance, irrespective of whether the consequences are good or bad. Thus, President Nixon froze wages and prices, and his popularity rose. He visited China, and the public opinion polls showed his stock to be rising. In the theatrical presidency, opinion managers use presidential access to media and critical timing on decisive initiatives to influence public opinion. In an age of instantaneous mass communication, a President must make very serious blunders to lose popularity. Thus, Eisenhower was a two-term President, Kennedy was assassinated, Johnson served more than the allotted four years, and Nixon has also been elected for a second term. This is not an accident. The President is in an extremely strong position to present a neatly tailored image to the public and, through his command of government services, has a great advantage over the opposition. The proof is found in President Nixon's ability to remain in office despite the early Watergate revelations, which would have swept away a parliamentary government.

Political scientist Cronin has drafted a list of "Presidential imperatives for the cosmetic presidency." Some of them are very thought-provoking:

1. Don't just stand there; do something!

2. Claim to be a consensus leader when polls are favorable and a "profile in courage" leader when your popularity drops in the polls.

3. Travel widely, be a statesman, and run for the Nobel Peace Prize.

4. Accentuate the role of symbolic leader: Do not delegate this source of strength and popularity to anyone outside the first family.

5. Proclaim an "open presidency" and an "open administration," but practice White House Government, decision-making centralization, and presidency by secrecy.

6. Hold numerous news conferences during your presidential honeymoon, but thereafter appeal directly to the people over the heads of the press (especially when too many unkept promises may make news conferences embarrassing).

7. History and historians will reward the man who protects and strengthens the powers of the presidency. Expand the Executive Office, defeat congressional measures to lessen presidential discretion, and minimize attention to the limits or weaknesses of the presidency.

8. If all else fails, wage war on the press, disparage its objectivity, undermine confidence in its fairness and integrity, impose prior restraint on the publication of news leaks (such as the Pentagon Papers), use subpoena power to coerce reporters to turn over their notes and to testify before grand juries on matters of which they learned in a confidential professional capacity.

Strong leaders are not, of course, necessarily evil. In fact, strong leadership will be necessary to solve the problems of the future. When all power is concentrated in the hands of one man, however, the abuse of that power becomes more likely, and the fate of the nation rides with him and his small group of confidants.

In these respects the Nixon administration might be a dire portent of events that may occur unless drastic action is taken to reorganize the government and elevate the level of political discourse. In the first four years of the Nixon presidency, the number of employees working directly under the President increased by 20 percent. The blank check given to President Nixon by Congress to freeze wages and prices is an indication of where power lies in times of crisis. Congress has indeed degenerated into what has been described as the "sapless branch" of government, internally divided into factions based on regional and party lines. Congress seems unable to act in concert even when directly defied. Thus, former Attorney General Richard Kleindienst could tell Congress with a straight face that because of "executive privilege," the President of the United States had the authority to block congressional demands for any document within the executive branch as well as for the testimony of any of 2.5 million federal employees. Kleindienst went on to tell Congress that the only checks that he could see on presidential power were public opinion (which the President can manipulate) and impeachment.

According to Cronin, the presidential establishment has become a "powerful inner sanctum of government isolated from traditional constitutional checks and balances." Credibility gaps have been created by what appears to be a callous disregard for truth in the White House. Information continues to come to light that the public has been deliberately misled on many serious issues including aspects of the conduct of the Vietnam War, the secret bombing of Cambodia, the level of public support for the mining of Haiphong harbor, and the extent of White House involvement in the Watergate Affair. The most important point is not that President Nixon and his cronies have treated the presidency as their own personal corporation, but rather that economic, technological, and social conditions are creating opportunities for individuals with totalitarian inclinations to abuse the power of the presidency.

This apparently inevitable concentration of power in very few hands offers both opportunity and danger. On the one hand, an insensitive President and his advisers could now easily lead the country down the road to destruction. On the other hand, such power in the hands of concerned men with long-term perspectives could be used to press for the initiatives and drastic changes that will be necessary in the near future. Knowledge, concern, and compassion must replace self-interest and greed at the center of power if appropriate steps are to be taken to frame enlightened collective policies. It is clear that this new power will be there for a long time to come. The questions are, who will exercise it, and to what end will it be exercised?

Vested Interests

In one way or another, thousands of organized groups in the United States bring pressure on politicians; of these groups, perhaps only a few hundred are sufficiently powerful to maintain permanent lobbying offices in Washington. But this rather small minority is able to wield disproportionate amounts of power in obtaining favorable decisions from the individuals and organizations that make up government.

Perhaps the most effective lobbying efforts are carried out by components of what has been called the military-industrial complex (MIC). This massive and complex group of interests has done much to shape a "warfare" society and to direct the distribution of public spending into weapons production. Big business and high-ranking military leaders have many interests in common, and they aggressively pursue policies aimed at maintaining high levels of military spending. The huge portion of the federal budget that goes into military affairs each year attests to their effectiveness. In some respects, the complex acts as a fourth branch of government.

As with other aspects of pluralist politics, no purpose is served by accusing those at the heart of the complex of self-seeking behavior, because unfortunately this is the way most people usually behave. However, an understanding of how the MIC operates is useful because it provides an example of a powerful vested interest that helps to sustain the present social paradigm. The critical problem is that, by using financial muscle and contacts in government, the members of the complex are able to influence the authoritative allocation of resources in one direction—theirs. There are no groups that can effectively counterbalance this constellation of private interests and break decision makers out of the uncritical patterns of thought that have characterized defense policies for the past two decades.

The MIC is worthy of special attention because its actions have been so blatant, its power so obvious, and what it stands for so typical of prevailing attitudes toward politics. It must be kept in mind, however, that the complex is simply the strongest coalition of vested interests in the United States at the present time. All lobbying organizations, as well as every citizen, represent vested interests. Everyone expects to be able to influence the allocation of values in his or her own favor. But large groups carry more weight than individuals, and the more powerful, of course, are much more successful than the powerless. Only a very small minority of the population refrains from playing by these competitive rules, and an even smaller minority sees the great dangers inherent in catering to many special interests and losing sight of the need for long-range planning and collective restraint.

Some observers have pointed out that the MIC should now be referred to as the MILC (military-industrial-labor complex). As labor has become more powerful, union leaders have begun to display a pattern of behavior remarkably similar to that exhibited by generals and corporation presidents. They are every bit as committed to full employment in defense industries as are other members of the complex. It is considered to be better to have jobs now, regardless of what is being produced, than to face the unemployment that accompanies a reordering of priorities. These are attitudes that extend right down to the union rank and file. The issues raised by environmental deterioration and exponential growth are much too remote to be pressing factors in present decisions. In the words of John Henning, Executive Secretary of the California State Federation of Labor, speaking at a labor conference in early 1973, "Thousands of workers throughout California have been displaced by environmental proposals, well-intentioned, but not related to the economic and social needs of the working people of this state. . . . There is not going to be any environmental program instituted in this state if that program is indifferent to the economic and social interests of the workers." Other speakers at the conference decried lawsuits that conservationists had brought against various construction projects around the state. They were far more concerned about keeping men at work than about the environmental impact of the projects. In a similar manner, the collection of individual interests that composes the MILC puts its own power, dividends, and paychecks ahead of the general welfare of the nation.

Military spending and fear of an "enemy" provide the cornerstones for the MILC. The military provides millions of individuals with jobs, paychecks, prestige, and frequently a complete way of life. Military expenditures in the United States appear to have stabilized at approximately 8 percent of gross national product, a percentage exceeded only by the military expenditures of the state of Israel, perpetually at war with her Arab neighbors. In 1970 there were slightly less than 3.5 million men and women in uniform, and civilian employees of the military numbered nearly 1.3 million. Totaling all relevant figures shows that nearly 5 million Americans received their incomes directly from the military in 1970. Although the number of men and women in uniform has declined since then, approximately 4 million people still receive incomes directly from the military. Millions of Americans are thus dependent for their livelihood on a high level of international tension and resultant high military spending. Most conspicuous among these are the 400,000 career officers and 675,000 classified Defense Department employees. Military and Defense Department personnel quite naturally do not appreciate talk of military cutbacks, as such reductions clearly are not in their economic interest.

Military appropriations will remain high as long as the public can be convinced that serious threats to the security of the United States exist. Fear of a Communist enemy has been a supporting pillar of the dominant social paradigm since the Russian Revolution. When Congress considers the budget of the Defense Department, the interest of all mankind in world peace is never a serious part of the deliberations. (Neither, of course, is it in the Soviet Union.) The bargaining for budget dollars is done on the basis of threats from new enemy weapons, which later often prove to have been based more on imagination than on fact. The Defense Department is helped by its allies in Congress who seek fat military contracts and bases for their own districts. New weapons mean more jobs both in the military and in industry. The Pentagon and big business often organize joint selling campaigns. Each year $4 million is spent for military "legislative liaison," a thinly disguised euphemism for Pentagon lobbying activities. Needless to say, this is an example of taxpayers' money being used to promote very private interests.

Aside from direct lobbying activities, the apparently private government in the Pentagon admitted in 1969 that nearly 3,000 employees were engaged in "public relations" work. Some experts claim that this estimate is much lower than the actual number of people who are directly involved in shaping public attitudes toward military activities and defense spending. The Pentagon also operates directly through a variety of people-to-people and mass media efforts, in which it is assisted by veterans organizations. In the past, armed forces reserve units have been urged to set up "community study programs" to acquaint people with the "Communist menace." The Office of Armed Forces Information and Education and the Defense Department's Public Affairs Office produce propaganda films that are freely disseminated throughout the country. For many years the armed forces produced their own television series, *The Big Picture*. They also produce and selectively disseminate film clips of battles for television news.

A wide variety of quasi-political services rounds out this impressive list of "information" activities. Included under this heading are the expense-paid junkets for newsmen (friendly newsmen, of course) to combat areas and trouble spots so that they might be properly informed about what is taking place. During the 1964–1965 escalation of hostilities in Vietnam, eighty-three correspondents were given "informational" trips to Vietnam under the auspices of the Department of Defense. Good-will trips are also organized for many politicians. An example is the infamous offer by the California National Guard in 1970 to fly any and all California Assemblymen to the Caribbean, ostensibly to study "hurricane protection." The armed forces also provide assistance, using taxpayers' money, to those making promilitary films, while denying the same assistance to film makers who are more critical of the military. *The Green Berets,* a John Wayne special glorifying the military, was filmed with full military assistance at Fort Benning, Georgia. The producers of *Fail Safe,* which had an antimilitary thrust, requested the same kind of assistance but were turned down.

It should also be noted that the military has operated its own "school" to which a substantial number of young male Americans have been exposed. The generals believe that there is little harm in throwing a healthy dose of "patriotism" into basic training. These young Americans have often been informally taught that Asian people are "gooks" and inferiors, while they formally learned that the various peoples' liberation movements around the world are part of a globally threatening Communist conspiracy. Although such indoctrination of combat troops is to be expected, there is no program for de-indoctrination when service is terminated.

Within the MILC, large defense industries do their part in cooperation with the Pentagon to keep military spending high and to influence the political debate so that it moves in favorable directions. In 1967 nearly three million people worked in industries that were almost entirely dependent on defense contracts, and the figures have changed very little since then. Table 4.2 lists these major industries and the percentage of business that came from defense orders from 1961 to 1967. Needless to say, these industries carry a very heavy political clout, particularly through their campaign contributions. Even though many of them are almost entirely dependent on public spending to maintain private profits, suggestions that they be nationalized meet with vehement opposition.

The Lockheed Corporation offers the best example of the cozy arrangement between government and defense industries. Lockheed, with 210 former high-ranking officers as advisers, not only does most of its business on government contract, including the contract for the habitually malfunctioning C-5A transport, but also has managed to soak the taxpayer for tremendous cost overruns. Inept management drove Lockheed to near bankruptcy

Table 4.2 Top Twenty Defense Contractors 1961-1967

Contractor	Military Sales 1961-1967 (Millions of Dollars)	Percent of Total Sales to Military	Number of Retired Military of Rank of Colonel, Navy Captain, or Higher Employed [a]
Lockheed Aircraft	10,619	88	210
McDonnell Douglas	7,681	75	141
Avco	2,295	75	23
General Dynamics	8,824	67	113
Grumman Aircraft	2,492	67	31
Martin-Marietta	3,682	62	40
North American Rockwell	6,265	57	104
United Aircraft	5,311	57	48
Raytheon	2,324	55	37
Boeing	7,183	54	169
Bendix	1,915	42	25
General Tire	2,347	37	32
Sperry-Rand	2,923	35	36
General Electric	7,066	19	80
RCA	2,019	16	35
Westinghouse	2,177	13	59
American Tel. and Tel.	4,167	9	9
Ford (Philco)	2,064	3	43 [b]
General Motors	2,818	2	17
Hughes Aircraft	2,200	?	55

[a] 1969.

[b] Ford Motor Company total.

before the government decided to bail out such an important member of the complex with a $250 million loan in the early seventies. The loan was justified on the grounds that the loss of an important defense contractor and so many jobs would be harmful to the national interest. Again, there were no serious suggestions to nationalize the bankrupt corporation.

When all employment figures are totaled, nearly ten million people are at least indirectly dependent on continued international tension for their employment. This represents nearly one out of every ten American jobs. No wonder that wasteful weapons procurement and military adventures so easily find public support. The "enemy" is not only generals in the Pentagon and their allies in big defense firms, the enemy is every citizen who is unwilling to make sacrifices or speak out of conscience for the good of the nation and all mankind. Too often people approach politics by asking what the country can do for them rather than what can be done by the people for the country and for future generations.

Thus, the arms race and wide-open defense spending continue, even though they are extremely wasteful of resources and increase the risk of war. This is another form of the tragedy of the commons: Everyone hopes to preserve personal financial security while contributing to collective catastrophe. The executives of large industries are not concerned whether industry's interests coincide with the long-term interests of society. They are in business to make money and to please stockholders. Stockholders are largely indifferent to whether their companies turn out weapons or television sets as long as dividends are regularly paid. Weapons production means jobs for millions of workers, who are not about to sacrifice themselves for posterity. They know that to protest is useless. Someone else will perform their jobs if they do not. Thus, the MILC continues to consume scarce resources to no social advantage and ties up a large portion of the federal budget that could be devoted to social services because political leaders seem unable to transcend short-term interests in favor of long-term collective welfare.

Waste and Irresponsibility

The theory of democracy is based on the assumption that intelligent voters periodically pass critical judgment on the decisions made by elected officials. In practice, however, voters have notoriously poor memories. Few remember who suggested what or which promises have been kept and which promises have been broken. Richard Nixon won the 1968 election by promising to *terminate* the war in Vietnam. He won the 1972 election by pointing with pride to the accomplishments of four years of fighting—especially to his substitution of American air power for American ground troops.

Passing the buck for bad decisions has become a tradition in the American system of government. But only a small percentage of voters normally holds incumbents responsible for errors that are made. Even in the depths of the Watergate scandal, one-third of the public credited the President with doing a good job. In foreign policy, almost any knowledgeable person would concede that the war in Vietnam and the isolation of both China and Cuba because of their revolutionary governments were major mistakes. In the early seventies the State Department completely bungled the United States role in the Indo-Pakistani conflict and was implicated (along with American business) in meddling in Chile's internal affairs. Blunders like these are only part of a pattern of mistakes that has been reducing American prestige around the globe. Such blunders also exact a heavy financial and resource toll that will not be tolerable in a more frugal society of the future. Alone among the major powers, the United States has expended billions of dollars and hundreds of thousands of lives in making the world safe for *something* and has usually suffered diplomatic defeats in return. Yet few officials have been called to account by the public or dismissed by the State Department for leading the people astray in the area of foreign policy.

Domestically, the Defense Department has cultivated the art of making wasteful decisions, investing billions of dollars in bad gambles, and sweeping mistakes under the rug. Few people still remember the intensive campaign to develop a nuclear-powered plane to "keep up with the Russians," the absolute necessity for several new wings of B-70s, or the huge "missile gap" that required all-out efforts in the early sixties. In each instance, billions of dollars were wasted because of faulty information, but those who pushed these programs were not demoted or fired for their mistakes. Many of them still occupy high posts in the Defense Department. Fiscal irresponsibility, cost overruns, and outwitting the public have become part of a very expensive political game.

Since World War II, many congressmen have been more than willing to cooperate in wasteful military spending. Many Southern congressmen and some of their Western counterparts act as funnels for defense funds to their districts. Names like Rivers of South Carolina, Vinson, Russell, and Talmadge of Georgia, Stennis of Mississippi, Hébert of Louisiana, Jackson of Washington, and Dole of Kansas have been so closely tied to military spending that it is difficult to imagine that they approached defense decisions with any concern for collective welfare. Too many people and too many incomes are dependent on the aircraft industry in Washington, California, and Georgia (Boeing and Lockheed) and on military bases in the South. In 1972 Senator Jackson went so far as to embarrass the Defense Department with his unsubstantiated horror stories about new missiles that were being deployed by the Soviet Union.

Waste in warfare society has been further supported by at least seventy congressmen who, at one time in the sixties, held reserve commissions in the armed forces. This elite corps was formerly headed by Senator Barry Goldwater (General in the Air Force Reserves) and Senator Strom Thurmond (General in the Army Reserves). Citizens who challenge defense spending have been told that members of the defense establishment are privy to "top secret" information that just cannot be passed on to the public. By the time each phony missile gap or mythical enemy weapons development is exposed, the money has been spent. And the public, long conditioned to accept fantasies about enemy behavior, awaits the next big lie.

Closer examination of two questionable decisions, one in military affairs and one in foreign policy, helps bring the point home. Not many people still recall the controversy and panic that surrounded a crash program to develop a nuclear-powered plane. The whole idea was initially "merchandised" at the end of World War II, when it occurred to military planners that nuclear energy should be harnessed to run a military aircraft. The apparent advantages of nuclear power were many. Such a plane would need very little refueling and could be kept in the air almost continuously. It could patrol near enemy territory and when necessary dart in and make a strike. But more important, planners reasoned that the United States must develop a nuclear plane or the Russians surely would, thus putting the United States a step behind in the arms race.

The development of a nuclear plane was highly problematic from the start. There were many ticklish technical problems to be solved. The plane was constructed on the principle that air was to pass through jet engines, but the heat to expand the air would come from a nuclear reactor in the plane. There was considerable doubt that the air could be passed directly through the reactor because of the danger of radioactive contamination. Yet glowing reports were written, feasibility studies were made, and the conclusion was reached that a nuclear-powered aircraft could be developed in only a few years.

Initial test results did not prove favorable. The biggest problem was shielding the crew from reactor radiation without adding too much weight to the plane. At one point the suggestion was made that the planes be flown by older men who were past child-bearing age to minimize the need for shielding them from genetically damaging radiation. Reactor materials had to be developed to guarantee that no radiation would leak into the airstream while the plane was in flight. This presented a problem because no known materials could withstand the temperatures, pressures, and nuclear bombardment that a direct heating technique required.

These setbacks did not stop the plane's proponents, however. The project, which was costing tens of millions of dollars yearly, was given priority status, the goal being to have an aircraft flying by 1957. Test results failed to measure up to expectations, and by the late fifties the suggested flight date was pushed back to the mid-sixties. Despite continuing setbacks, the Air Force demanded that the project be continued on a high-priority basis, even though nothing of note had been accomplished during the first ten years. Fourteen years after the decision was made to begin work on the nuclear plane, the project was terminated. No nuclear plane was ever developed, but the attempt cost the public nearly $1 billion.

The most disturbing aspects of the decision to develop a nuclear plane were that there were no pressing reasons to do it, and few experts could see any chances for success. But the project was backed by the Air Force-industry team, and little expense was spared in spreading propaganda. Falsehoods provided the basis for much of the debate that surrounded the work during the last few years of the program. In December, 1958, the industry journal, *Aviation Week,* claimed that the Soviets were already flying a prototype nuclear-powered bomber and bemoaned the fact that the enemy had beaten the United States to the punch. Nothing has since been heard about this miraculous Soviet achievement. Such phony intelligence is not infrequently created by trade journals, the aircraft industry, the Defense Department, and more militaristic members of Congress.

In the end, $1 billion was wasted on a very questionable project, taxpayers were frightened into thinking that the enemy already had such a weapon, and endless hours of committee hearings were required to kill the nuclear plane project. This is a perfect example of how the present political system is run by interest-group pressures and is wasteful of resources that could be used to meet other social needs. This is also far from being an isolated incident.

More recently, a similar series of mistakes was made in attempting to develop the Cheyenne attack helicopter. The helicopter gunship was dogged by a series of failures during development, including one fatal crash. Seven years of effort and $400 million went into development and only ten proto-types were produced. Finally the project was killed because the gunship would cost much more than it was worth. On that same day, however, Army officials asked Congress for another $36 million to start from scratch on a replacement.

Similar struggles have been waged over the deployment of an expensive antiballistic missile system, nuclear-powered aircraft carriers, and several planes and helicopters that have either failed to work properly or failed to work at all. In every such situation, the military has used the same techniques to convince the public that national security demands new weapons systems. The results have usually been much the same—most of the funded programs have turned into horrendously expensive boondoggles. Afterward no one acts as though a mistake has been made, and the same play is enacted time and again with a very similar cast of characters.

Many corporations have made ridiculously low bids on military projects to win contracts and to seduce Congress into appropriating more funds. When projects near completion, these corporations come back and ask for additional funds, threatening to close their doors if funds are not forthcoming. Thus, Litton Industries went before the House Armed Services Committee in 1972 to seek an additional $400 million to complete an original $1 billion contract for five amphibious assault ships. At the same time, the Grumman Corporation was pleading bankruptcy if its contract for F-14 fighter planes could not be renegotiated. It seemed that the initial $5 billion was not enough to cover the contract. In both instances the friendly House Armed Services Committee had no desire to set a precedent by making business live up to its commitments. In other documented cases, defense industries have deliberately falsified technological data to make it appear that their products met original contract specifications.

Vietnam represents the equivalent of the nuclear plane boondoggle in international affairs—an unnecessary, incredibly expensive mistake for which responsibility would be difficult to assign. Countless books have been written chronicling United States involvement, and the aim here is not to add to this overwhelming literature but simply to point out factors that seem built into foreign policy decision making that repeatedly lead to such mistakes.

American involvement in Vietnam stemmed from a mixture of naïveté, fervent ideology, and a power urge untempered by a sense of proportion and realpolitik. The Vietnamese people were fighting for self-determination long before American troops were introduced, a fact that was conveniently ignored by politicians. The French tried vainly for years to impose their own settlement terms on Vietnam. Not only was the objective evidence of French failure clearly before the United States when its role was expanded, but the French issued direct warnings that went unheeded.

Possibly only historians still recall the goals announced at the beginning of American involvement. Basically the United States claimed to be defending a "legitimate" government in South Vietnam from the incursions of Communists from the North. Certain essential aspects of legitimacy were, of course, overlooked, including the skipping of the promised general election of 1956 (President Eisenhower was afraid that Ho Chi Minh might win) and the fact that President Diem enjoyed the support of little more than the army, the Catholic church, and a few business interests. After the assassination of President Diem it became even more difficult to justify support of the "legitimate" government of South Vietnam as control of the government changed hands every few months.

The most revealing aspect of the Vietnam tragedy was the frequency with which the same errors were repeated and the stubbornness with which top-ranking political leaders resisted domestic public opinion. For how many years in a row was victory just around the corner? First the war was going to be won with technical assistance and advisers only. President Johnson stated categorically in the 1964 campaign that he would not send Americans overseas to do the job that Asians should do. But then he "found it necessary" to send limited assistance and subsequently to increase troop ceilings. Finally, he wound up with one-half million men on the battlefield doing what the advisers were to have finished years earlier. The reason was not that appropriate information was unavailable. Observers across a spectrum, ranging from members of the American military to radical revolutionaries, repeatedly predicted that these efforts would be costly and would amount to nothing. In the election campaign of 1968, both presidential candidates said that they were in favor of restricted military involvement and that they would bring the war to a quick end. But Nixon's secret plan for ending the war was only a convenient political gambit, and the same issues again came to the surface in the campaign of 1972.

The tenacity and blundering in Vietnam have been only too characteristic of the rigidity of old-paradigm leaders in the face of changing circumstances. The United States seems unable to refrain from sending good money after bad, whether for weapons development or in foreign policy. The French were equally unable to see the handwriting on the wall in Vietnam. The Soviets have similarly persisted in supplying the Israeli Army by providing equipment to the Arabs. Only repeated burning of fingers seems to get the message home. A political system that cannot adequately handle complex political situations when information is freely available is likely to be heavily handicapped when confronted with such a multifaceted problem as the population-resource-environment crisis, the ramifications of which are intricate and often obscure.

In summary, the present political system in the United States appears inadequate to cope with the critical problems of the future. It evolved in an environment of relative plenty, and the main task facing political leaders until now has been to exploit Nature's abundance to meet citizen demands. But now political leaders are confronted with the necessity of bringing citizen expectations into line with environmental possibilities. This means turning the political system inside out. Many of the attributes that have made the pluralist democratic society economically so successful could, if they are not changed, lead the United States to its own destruction.

5

Politics:
To Navigate or Drift?

A crucial question facing large, densely populated, complex industrial socie-ties in the latter part of the twentieth century is whether they can be governed both effectively and democratically. A tremendous number of problems must be solved in the American trillion dollar growth-oriented industrial economy as it enters an era of relative scarcity. Much dislocation and turmoil are to be expected, and there will undoubtedly be much pressure for simple solutions to complex problems. Whether this pressure leads to dictatorship or to a more sophisticated form of democracy depends on how well Americans plan for this uncertain future.

It must be remembered that experience with mass democracy is very limited. Mass democracy took root during the early period of the industrial revolution and flowered during a period of great material abundance. Political stability and democracy have been preserved by an expanding economy that offered a rising standard of living to most people. Whether political stability and democracy can be maintained under more austere conditions remains to be seen. Perhaps the industrial revolution represented only a very pleasant political interlude that is about to come to a grinding halt. At a minimum, it can be said that tremendous changes in political attitudes and political institutions will be necessary to maintain at least a semistable society in an unstable future world.

It is unfortunate that American political thinkers have been caught up in extolling the virtues of the existing pluralist democracy and have neglected many impending problems. As in economics, the study of politics in the United States begins with a given world of individual preferences and seeks to outline the best system for meeting these preferences (which, not unexpectedly, turns out to be pluralist democracy). Little attention is paid to the constraints of the physical world, with its limited possibilities for meeting these individual preferences, or to the types of political institutions that would be required to see industrial society through a period of austerity.

Political scientist Robert Dahl has outlined three important principles that explain how political authority can be maintained in a heterogeneous industrial society. According to Dahl, people are willing to defer to authority because:

1. Many political decisions correspond to choices that people would make personally. This has been especially true during periods of industrial abundance when few collective decisions requiring personal deprivation were necessary.

2. Some decisions are perceived to require expertise or competence that is only available among a very few specialists. Many people acknowledge that not everyone has the information required to make decisions on very technical matters and thus are quite willing to delegate authority.

3. It is recognized by many that not all citizens can possibly participate in every decision that is made because of the great numbers who would have to be consulted. A few must be selected to represent the rest in the interest of economy.

It is important to understand these principles because they are closely tied to the problem of maintaining authority with a democratic base in a future society. The frequency with which collective decisions can correspond to individual desires is likely to decrease as new collective deprivations are imposed by environmental constraints. In Garrett Hardin's words, future politics must be more concerned with providing "mutual coercion mutually agreed upon." Maintaining stable political authority and compliance with the law will be much more difficult under those conditions than in previous times when most legislation could be devoted to managing a constantly increasing quantity of economic wealth.

Long-range planning in a very complex society will require a much higher level of competence in politics. Governing must be transformed into a profession that is reserved for wise and dedicated individuals rather than being allowed to remain an arena where representatives of vested interests fight to retain their disproportionate share of the rewards. There will be little room for mistakes in coordinating the affairs of a densely populated and highly interdependent society, if that society is to survive future challenges.

The competence principle, however, stands in opposition to a trend toward greater mass participation in politics. Fed by a revolution in media and the rhetoric of democracy, this movement is leading to growing demands by larger numbers for a more direct voice in shaping society's future. Some have gone so far as to propose a direct democracy in which people vote on crucial issues through computer terminals in their own homes. Although this trend should be encouraged, especially if it leads to more informed political participation, at present too few people take the time to become thoroughly informed about the issues before voicing their opinions. In the short run, the critical problem to be faced in transforming politics might very well be to defend existing political institutions against a populist onslaught. Government by a moderately well-informed oligarchy is certainly preferable to government by an ill-informed mob. In the long run, of course, there can be no better goal than to create a more sophisticated electorate so that broadly representative political institutions can cope adequately with the more intricate problems of the future. It may be that future political stability can only be maintained through greater citizen participation. As the complex of problems becomes obvious, a small oligarchy may not be able to withstand citizen discontent. Within a real mass democracy, people would feel that they shared in making difficult decisions, and there would be no clear target for revolutionary violence.

Political Change: Myth and Reality

It is clear that the present American political system, with its cowboy economic policies, lethargic legislative practices, lack of respect for planning and expertise, and political philosophy developed over decades of relative plenty, is poorly suited to cope with the myriad new problems or to direct a major social transformation; neither are the political systems of most other advanced industrial nations.

The political problem is not limited to the self-interest found among the combination of the wealthy and the technocratic minority that runs industrial societies. A political system controlled by the poor would not operate much differently. Low-income groups have not been noticeably aware of environmental problems, nor have they been at the forefront of movements directed toward a transformation of society. In the United States, as well as in other countries, the working class has failed miserably to live up to Karl Marx's expectations. Instead of rising up to seize the means of production, the working class now forms the bulwark of defense against economic, social, and political change. Millions of American workers have great difficulty sorting out which issues and programs are in their own self-interest, let alone recognizing policies that promote any collective welfare. Polls indicate that most working-class people still believe that the present system is the optimal one and that supporting this system is in their best interest. An impetus for major political transformation will certainly not come from the American working class.

People who are seriously worried about present social and environmental conditions are discouraged from working within established political institutions by this lack of concern among the silent majority and by the slow rate of change characteristic of mass democracy. Given the political stagnation that has prevailed for the last two decades, it is understandable that some have been working toward change through revolution. For many reasons the efforts of such revolutionaries have been misguided. Not only can the United States not afford the costs of a bloody revolution; such an effort could easily lead to suicide for what remains of the "movement." Although a small portion of the population could pose a powerful threat, the number of people dedicated to violent revolution is far short of a critical mass and now seems to be declining. At present, any threat to the established order would be snuffed out with Prussian efficiency by the police, fully supported by the silent majority.

There are other reasons that a full-scale, violent revolution would do nothing to advance the cause of environmental sanity and societal survival. Revolutions exhaust material resources as well as human ones. The magnitude of dislocation that would be required to overturn the present political system may easily be underestimated. History shows that all such major revolutions have been extremely costly and wasteful. Another American Revolution would undoubtedly set new records for destructiveness and would occur at precisely the period in history when it is imperative to conserve natural, intellectual, and moral resources for the turbulent decades ahead.

There is a fringe group of radicals—latter-day nihilists—who see nothing disturbing about a complete political collapse, but these people are often noteworthy in their inability to suggest realistic alternatives to the system they wish to see destroyed. Often they suggest a return to the land and an agrarian society—a pleasant thought but one that would mean the death of millions by starvation. Nor is there any guarantee that any postrevolutionary regime would be less onerous or more intelligent than the present establishment. Individuals who might lead and survive a violent revolution do not necessarily possess attributes useful for building a new and environmentally sound society. They would doubtless possess the skills required for revolutionary success, including ruthlessness, cunning, and capacity for violence and killing. It seems highly unlikely that a new government formed by such a revolutionary committee would be any more sensible, egalitarian, visionary, or informed than that formed by present officeholders.

On the other hand, blind faith that recent small signs of change augur well for rapid *evolutionary* change is also misplaced. The young, the hopeful, and perhaps the naïve, find comfort in slogans and in a fervent belief that the old society is transforming itself. "Power to the people" is one of the slogans that have dominated radical politics over the last decade. The common assumption has been that "the people" can be liberated and will transform society once they get the message. Maybe so, but to date the message has not been getting through. America certainly is not rapidly "greening," and some critics suggest that it is "bluing" instead, as the sons and daughters of blue-collar families take on the attitudes and consumption patterns that have recently been denounced by some children of the wealthy.

The "power to the people" movement fails to recognize that the people do have considerable power in the United States, although most of them still fail to use it. Whereas actively involving the silent majority in politics is one way of attacking those entrenched in the political system, people-power is just as likely to be directed against change as for it. The average person in today's society is basically unaware of the major political issues and is preoccupied with making ends meet on a week-to-week basis. He or she may be fed up with political leaders and alienated from the political process, but this does not mean that such a person will suddenly become part of a major political transformation.

The phenomenal success of the candidacy of George Wallace in 1968 and his early successes in 1972 offer testimony to the futility of trying to build a social transformation on a working-class foundation. The simple populist solutions offered by Wallace seemed to find ready acceptance among a frustrated silent majority. Wallace would have the "little man" believe that all problems are caused by "big government." Wallace is thus a symbol of reaction, of a return to the "good old days" when there were fewer serious problems. Wallace's popularity indicates that many people are discouraged and ripe for an alternative to politics-as-usual, but the simple solutions offered by him would not solve any of the major new problems facing society.

There are viable alternatives to the naïve or daring solutions offered by revolutionaries, as well as by those who believe in a spontaneous greening of America, but they require dedication and persistence. There is little question that all citizens can and must take part in transforming the politics of mass democracy and building a new society, although this will require environmental and political education on a massive scale. Enlisting the support of millions of people will not be easy, but it is a job that must be done. In one sense, everyone in the United States now acts as a vested interest, just as military generals and corporation presidents do. Change is perceived by the poor as a threat, even though such change might well be objectively in their interest. Thus, the common sense that supposedly guides each voter at the polls must be transformed into an "uncommon" sense, or informed common sense, that takes into consideration an entire range of complicated and seemingly remote issues. Voters must develop a social conscience and learn to look beyond today's paycheck. Those who have "made it" and moved to the suburbs must realize that suburban life will not be available for their children unless major changes take place very soon.

Even knowledge, in the absence of clarified goals and a plan for action, will not provide enough impetus for a social transformation. The American people have never really clarified their collective goals, at least not in the 200 years that have elapsed since the Constitution was framed. This helps to explain an apparent inability to come to grips with long-term planning. If ends are undefined, it is difficult to choose appropriate means. What works today is pragmatically accepted, even though no one knows or seems to care if it will work tomorrow. There are many humanitarian values that most Americans do hold in common that can be used to build a coherent program of political and social change. It is necessary, however, to recognize them clearly and to reformulate them in ways that have relevance to present conditions. The right to life, liberty, and the pursuit of happiness, for example, should be more than an empty phrase found in historical documents. These values will have little meaning in a future of increasing scarcity unless they are redefined and incorporated into social planning.

Most Americans would agree that extending an equal opportunity for a full life, a maximum amount of individual freedom, and the pursuit of happiness to each individual is a worthwhile goal for which any society should strive. The greatest difficulty has been in living up to these principles when they were applied to all mankind. The result has often been adherence to a double standard: generating a smokescreen of common wisdoms and rhetoric while ignoring the implementation of ideals.

Political change thus is really dependent on living up to professed ideals and doing away with double standards. Rhetoric and fraudulent ethical theories that have grown up within the political process must be exposed, and people must see more clearly the human consequences of continuing to live by double standards in a future of scarcity and imbalance. Turning the political process around will require concern, compassion, and selflessness—virtues that have not been much cultivated in industrial society. A new breed of dedicated, actively engaged, citizen must be able to step back from the day-to-day struggle and cultivate the classical virtues of good citizenship. Good citizenship exacts its penalties and bestows its rewards. Transforming an outmoded and amoral political system will require dedication and tremendous efforts of the kind that many people are not yet willing to make. But if such efforts were successful, the reward would be a new feeling of progress and dedication to a series of desirable goals that could lead to the collective welfare of all citizens.

Today a new political value system is taking shape, albeit slowly, and we should do everything possible to encourage its development, bearing in mind that changing fundamental values takes decades, not years. Many things can be done to change the nature of present politics short of creating new political men, however, and many of these changes should find ready public support on the basis of enlightened self-interest alone.

Separating Money from Politics

Restricting the role that wealth plays in recruitment to the existing oligarchy is primary among presently available leverage points. Most Americans do not think of themselves as wealthy, and they are therefore not opposed to limiting political campaign spending. In fact, shortly after the Watergate scandal was exposed, a Gallup poll found that 58 percent of the American people favored governmental financing of presidential and congressional campaigns. Incumbents have already been forced to respond to public attacks against wealth in politics. In 1973 Senators Edward Kennedy and Hugh Scott introduced a bill requiring public campaign financing. Congress has handled this issue like a hot potato, trying to strike a balance between public pressure and the financial edge that most wealthy legislators hope to maintain, although the costs of major political contests have become excessive even for affluent politicians. It is clear that the real debate over limiting campaign spending has just begun, and public pressure against election-year extravaganzas in the wake of the Watergate and related scandals is likely to build.

If federal financing of campaigns cannot be immediately obtained, a first step should be to extend limits on campaign expenditures to *all* sources of funds, not only family wealth. Initial campaign-spending ceilings of $1 million for each presidential candidate, $50,000 for each candidate for senator, and $25,000 for each candidate for representative would not seem to be unduly restrictive. These figures are not precise; they simply represent a ball park estimate of sane limitations on campaign spending many times smaller than the sums now expended. As under present law, candidates should be required to keep highly detailed records of campaign contributions. But they should also be required to keep similar records of all candidate and committee expenditures. Contributions should be limited by law to personal contributions of not more than $50. Any contributor violating the law should be liable to heavy penalties, as should any knowing recipient. Those who violate election laws should be forbidden to take office or serve on campaign committees for a specified period. Serious violations should be punished by the imposition of prison sentences.

In addition to the new limits on the size of contributions, it is important that the names of contributors be regularly disclosed during the course of a campaign. Too often candidates now disclose the identity of contributors months after they are elected to office, when the political effect of such disclosures is negligible. The $200,000 secretly contributed to Richard Nixon in 1972 by Robert L. Vesco, who was at that time under investigation by the Securities and Exchange Commission for his part in an alleged international swindle, is a case in point, as are the many secret corporate contributions, apparently made in return for future favors, that came to light *after* the election.

Public office is a public trust, and there is no reason why candidates should not also be willing to disclose fully their sources of income and financial assets. Publication of recent tax returns and statements of net worth should be required of all candidates making a bid for office. This procedure would eliminate unsavory revelations, such as those surrounding President Nixon's land deals and the so-called repairs at the Western White House, by opening the record before a man runs for office. Candidates who are unwilling to open their financial records to public scrutiny can hardly be expected to be honest and open with their constituents after election. Disclosure of income would also alert the public to possible conflicts of interest and would help to eliminate much of the criminal and near-criminal element from politics.

A significant experiment along these lines was carried out by *The Los Angeles Times* in 1973 when the newspaper requested the California congressional delegation to open its financial record books. It is a hopeful sign that 36 of the state's 45 senators and representatives complied. As could be expected, the data revealed that the delegation included at least three millionaires and thirteen members whose net worth was at least $100,000. More important, the data also revealed that only a small portion of outside income need be reported under present federal disclosure laws. It was also made clear that those members who refused to make their financial dealings public were extremely wealthy and were among the more powerful members of Congress. One of those failing to comply with the request was Representative Chet Holifield, caucus chairman of the Democrats from California and a member of the House Ethics Committee, which oversees operation of the House disclosure law.

It is also poor policy to permit senators and representatives to maintain associations with law firms and banks while holding public office. Common Cause has reported that at least fifty-three members of the House of Representatives were still actively associated with law firms and thirty-nine were bank directors in 1972. These figures did not include those politicians who *informally* "commute" between Capitol Hill and their old law firms. It is difficult to see how any representative can serve the public interest in government while simultaneously serving private interests in banks and law firms.

Although it would be impossible to abolish informal connections between lawyers, bankers, and their old firms (such as John Mitchell's legal ties when he was Attorney General and Richard Nixon's ties with his Wall Street law firm), a minimal step in the right direction would be to outlaw all *formal* ties between public officials and any private business enterprise. Heavy legal penalties should be attached to any violation of these laws. Politics should be treated as a profession, not as a second job. Salaries and allowances in federal offices are now generous enough that officeholders need no large outside sources of income. Every effort should be made to discourage politicians who are motivated by greed from using public office to build private fortunes.

The proposed disclosure law should specifically prohibit congressmen who have holdings in banks and other enterprises from sitting on committees handling legislation that directly affects those enterprises. Common Cause also reported in 1972 that twenty-seven representatives sat on committees that supposedly regulated industries in which they had substantial interests. In the House Banking and Currency Committee and the House Committee on Ways and Means, thirteen representatives, a substantial part of the membership, had extensive holdings in banks and financial institutions. Disclosure statements would make these conflicts of interest abundantly clear.

Since political organizations are notoriously poor at self-discipline, the Senate and the House cannot be expected to police their own ranks. Therefore, a separate agency should be established to monitor the finances of federal officials. Perhaps this should be an office of "Watchkeeper" as suggested in the new Constitution proposed by political philosopher Rexford Tugwell, of the Center for the Study of Democratic Institutions, or an expanded General Accounting Office, or a branch of the Internal Revenue Service overseen by a civilian board. Any evidence of the use of office for personal gain should be made public and should lead to prompt investigation and criminal prosecution by the watchdog agency.

Opponents of this proposal will argue that such disclosures represent an "invasion of personal freedom." There is no defense against this argument except the one made by Plato centuries ago. He suggested that the decision to run for public office imposes extra burdens on a candidate and that one of these burdens is complete disclosure and honesty with the public. Although in Plato's ideal republic political leaders renounced all wealth in return for the privilege of leadership, to expect that to happen today would not be realistic. It is reasonable, however, to expect *complete disclosure and honesty* from those who seek public office. The era dominated by politicians who are owned and financed by special interest groups must come to an end and must give way to an era in which politicians become public servants who deserve public trust.

These suggestions represent changes that are quite possible or even likely, but a concerted public campaign to force congressmen to vote for such bills will be necessary. The proposed legislation is reasonable, lies within the presently accepted system of values, and would appeal to both the poor and the middle class—people who cannot now afford to run for office. It would also appeal to some honest incumbents who are hard pressed by the expense of fighting electoral battles every two to six years.

In the long run there is no reason why wealth should in any way be a criterion for seeking office. The best solution would be public funding of campaigns for high political office. Funding of campaigns would mean that fairly small amounts of cash, say, $50,000 for a Senate seat, would be allotted to all qualified candidates (those receiving nominations of their party or enough signatures by petition, for example). This would represent the total permitted expenditure, and private contributions would be excluded altogether. Such funding restrictions would certainly alter the structure of campaigns, once again introducing dependence on volunteer workers and door-to-door campaigning. Over time, these restrictions would significantly change the composition of the ruling oligarchy. Businesses might make a regular practice of allowing time off for employees to participate in elections instead of simply collecting money for campaign contributions. People power would replace money power, and ordinary citizens could again become an important political force.

Public financing of campaigns would require a new type of primary election designed to keep the number of candidates in the regular election reasonably small while opening up participation in the political process to those unwilling to join either of the two major political parties. Wealth does this within the present system, but in a new system petitions or more complex, but closely regulated primaries might be required to do an adequate job of narrowing down the political choices. Ultimately, a much-expanded multiparty system might perform the same function while allowing many more Americans to play an active role in the political process.

Financial restrictions would ultimately eliminate many of the three-ring-circus aspects of present elections. Expenditures for newspaper advertising, obnoxious television commercials, and garish billboards would be cut to a minimum. Additional legislation might outlaw short television spot commercials and subliminal advertising altogether. By strictly limiting expenditures, a financial and political climate would be created that would force public relations and advertising firms out of politics. Politicians would be compelled to run on their own words and ideas rather than depending on advertising agency images. Taking millions of dollars out of the campaigns would raise the caliber of political debate, as well as stem the senseless waste of resources and invasion of privacy characteristic of contemporary political commercialism.

An important result of such reforms would be to free politicians from the burden of pleasing wealthy interest groups to attract campaign funding. The role of the mass media would be restricted to presenting public service, face-to-face confrontations among candidates. An expanded public television could play an important role in organizing meaningful political debates. Finally, a balance among major political parties could be established. Funding problems have severely handicapped the Democrats in the last several elections, and the Republicans have been able to mount much more expensive campaigns. Most important of all, public funding would offer an opportunity for additional parties to become potent political forces and break the present political stagnation. If a diverse and flexible society is to be maintained, voters must be presented with a broader array of political choices and genuine alternatives.

A Planning Branch

Although changing the nature of the oligarchy through campaign restrictions would undoubtedly result in a somewhat more competent selection of lawmakers, the oligarchy should also be expanded by creation of a Planning Branch of the federal government charged with responsibility for the future welfare of society. The new Constitution proposed by Rexford Tugwell provides for such a branch as a way of overcoming the politics of muddling through. The Planning Branch would be charged with tackling the critical issues mentioned in previous chapters from a nonpartisan perspective. It would carry out extensive research projects with the help of citizen advisory boards and frame appropriate legislation that could then be introduced directly to Congress. The Planning Branch would inject much-needed expertise into government by replacing some of the 200,000 lawyers now working for the government with people knowledgeable in other fields.

The Planning Branch would be charged with several closely related tasks. One such task would be the formulation and regular revision of five-, ten-, and fifty-year plans for America's future. These plans would provide the basis for a continuing policy dialogue about short-, middle-, and long-term political, environmental, economic, and social goals. The five-year plan would, of course, be the most detailed and specific, for it would contain immediate recommendations for legislation as well as policy guidelines for the executive branch. The ten-year plan would be less specific and would include more discussion of alternatives, as well as numerous commissioned position papers. Various groups would be asked on a continuing basis to provide the Planning Branch with ten-year forecasts of anticipated trends and needs. The Planning Branch would serve as a clearinghouse for information essential to the development of such forecasts.

The fifty-year plan would necessarily be less detailed than the others. It would be considerably more speculative and perhaps would offer a spectrum of alternate pathways branching out from critical decision points. It would also outline long-term collective goals to be pursued through short-run policies. The full report would be rather lengthy and well documented and would include position papers and research documents submitted by various citizen groups, commissioned advisory boards, and other organizations within and outside government. The full document and similar reports of the Planning Branch should be made available from the United States Government Printing Office and sold at newstands at very low prices. Short summary versions of the plans might also be made available to all citizens in an attractive and readable format, perhaps published in the press or in paperback book form. Such summaries could provide an impetus for a dialogue about goals and directions among citizens as well as policy makers and could be made required reading in the schools.

The second major task of the Planning Branch would be to recommend legislation directly to Congress to implement new macroconstraints and to report to the people annually on the state of the nation. Thus the Planning Branch might be charged with recommending resource depletion quotas and levels of guaranteed annual incomes, outlining parameters for the federal budget, and proposing new environmental and social policies. Although the Planning Branch would be powerless in the sense that it could only *recommend* social policies and constraints, it would have the power to produce an official critique of legislative and executive policies. This body also would have the means of disseminating its findings to large groups of people, and in this way it could influence the political dialogue.

This raises questions of how the Planning Branch could be kept independent and prevented from becoming a victim of Washington's four-year syndrome. A number of devices could be used to minimize this danger. First, a minimal budget for the Planning Branch should be constitutionally established and pegged to total government revenues. (Tugwell, for example, suggests 0.5 percent of the federal budget.) This would prevent budgetary attacks from a Congress that might not approve of the critical reports of the planners. Second, the affairs of the Planning Branch might be overseen by a distinguished board of directors chosen for ten-year terms. These executives would be required to make the same disclosures as politicians and to divest themselves of all outside interests. If the board consisted of nine members, three might be appointed by senatorial committee, three by the President, and three by the United States Supreme Court. Their terms could be staggered to insulate the Planning Branch further from partisan politics. Although reappointment should be forbidden, generous pensions could be given after a decade of service.

Much of the work of the Planning Branch could be done by temporary citizen-government teams. Permanent employees of the Planning Branch would work together on appropriate tasks with people from universities, from think tanks, from city and state planning offices, and from the community at large. Citizen members of these task forces would serve for one or two years, perhaps while on sabbatical from their regular jobs. The Planning Branch could thus be dept from becoming a "technocracy" cut off from real life if politically interested citizens were encouraged to apply for short-term appointments on citizen task forces as well as positions within the Planning Branch itself.

Initially, the Planning Branch might be composed of five different sections:

1. The Office of Environmental Protection would be charged with evaluating environmental impact studies, making its own long-term projections, and outlining legislation to deal with environmental problems. It would be staffed by well-trained environmentalists and would draw heavily on environmental action groups for supplementary staffing and reports.

2. The Office of Natural Resources would be in charge of evaluating resource reserves, as well as future resource needs, and developing coherent resource-utilization plans. It would also recommend yearly resource depletion quotas. This section would be staffed by geologists, energy experts, economists, and specialists in international trade and resource planning.

3. The Office of Social Ecology would be charged with monitoring changing social conditions and overseeing the social aspects of the transition to a steady-state economy. It would suggest needed social legislation, especially for ameliorating the effects of increasing scarcity on the poor. It would also be particularly concerned with developing the educational programs that will be essential for moving toward a people-oriented rather than a profit-oriented society. This office would also deal with demographic matters and would recommend population policies. It would be staffed largely with social scientists.

4. The Office of Economic Priorities would perform many of the services that the President's Council of Economic Advisers should be performing now. It would propose legislation to move the economy in new directions. It would also concern itself with the allocation of capital and with restructuring the economic system of incentives and rewards. The staff would be composed of environmentalists, economists, and other social scientists.

5. The Office of Technology Assessment would critically evaluate all major new technologies, outline research and development priorities, and investigate the potential social, economic, and environmental impact of new discoveries.

Emphasis would be placed on developing new methods of meeting the energy and resource crisis and providing incentives for the adoption of the best of these. The staff within this branch would be heterogeneous but would consist mainly of competent scientists and engineers.

The headquarters of the Planning Branch should not be in the nation's capital but in some relatively pleasant location that would induce talented young people to choose careers in public service. Because the need for complete, up-to-date information would be crucial, the Planning Branch offices should have ready access to major universities as well as to good libraries and computer services. Branch offices could be strategically located throughout the United States to provide for contacts between Branch personnel and the public, especially with people serving on citizen task forces. Personnel within the Planning Branch should spend much of their time listening to people and should participate in the kind of planning exercises that have been pioneered by ecologist C. S. Holling at the University of British Columbia. Holling and his colleagues have enlisted the aid of a wide spectrum of the Vancouver community, including politicians, developers, and conservationists, in designing and building realistic computer models of areas near Vancouver. The computer has been used to forecast the results of various development strategies as applied to those areas.

The Planning Branch could thus become an informational and educational operation unlike anything yet seen in American government. The legislative and executive branches would surely profit from the activities of the Planning Branch and presumably would soon become responsive to its suggestions, particularly as environmental and economic conditions worsened and the public demanded new solutions. The Planning Branch should be able to establish a record of accuracy in predicting shortages, dislocations, and so forth, and consequently public confidence in its activities would grow.

Since the Planning Branch would have no enforcement powers of its own, the dangers of a Planning Branch dictatorship would be minimal. Protection against this eventuality would be further ensured by citizen participation in planning activities and by long-term appointments of nonpartisan personnel. The only interest served by the Planning Branch should be the collective interest of society; no partisan interests should receive special consideration.

The most important problem would be to keep the Planning Branch insulated from the politics in other branches of government. This could be done through adequate permanent funding, long-term appointments, and the hiring of competent specialists and generalists rather than political favorites. In the end, of course, the purpose of the Planning Branch could be thwarted if educated citizens failed to recognize the critical need for its independence and its functions.

Political Sabbaticals

There are many other ways in which additional knowledge and relevant information could be injected into political decision making. One most important innovation could be the introduction of sabbatical years for legislators, for high-level officials in the executive branch, and eventually for political officials at the state levels as well. Education is now designed to be a socialization process for the young and preparation for a career, rather than a lifetime pursuit and an intrinsically valuable experience. Today a person is expected to receive a dose of education before reaching adulthood. Once an appropriate quantity of education has been consumed—usually the quantity specified to obtain a well-paying job—the common assumption is that there is little need to return to the books again. This is one element in the "generation gap." The world changes very rapidly and the information passed on in educational processes changes almost daily. Those who have terminated their education often feel that they "know it all," even though the world they have learned about may no longer exist. This can be especially true of politicians who often have been carefully insulated from new perspectives by decades of service in the halls of Congress or in state legislatures.

Once a person is elected to office or appointed to a high-level position, legislating, administering, or running for office become more than full-time jobs. But not all officials ignore the need for further education. Some recognize that the world is constantly changing around them while they sit in their Washington offices. Many would like the time to follow through on research projects and periodically to return to the university for intellectual stimulation, but unfortunately the present political system makes no provision for such opportunities.

A sabbatical program would mean that one year in every seven, key government employees would be free to enroll for advanced study or to undertake research projects. On presentation of a satisfactory program for the sabbatical year, an official would receive full pay plus an allowance for additional costs of tuition, relocation, and other expenses. Sabbaticals would be voluntary, but those refusing to take them might find themselves in trouble when seeking promotion.

Elected officials need periodic educational leaves just as much as, if not more than, their bureaucratic counterparts, but legislative sabbaticals would present problems in terms of scheduling and representation of constituents. One-year leaves should be mandatory for all politicians at specified intervals. Officials should be forbidden to engage in partisan politics during this period. Legislators on sabbatical might be required to appoint an alternate for the sabbatical year, with the explicit intention of introducing "nonpoliticians" to the political process. Perhaps the logical sabbatical year for legislators would be every seventh year. For a senator, it could come at the end of the first term or, if he were reelected, it could be taken at the beginning of a second term. For a representative, it could occur at the end of the third term or, if he were reelected, it could be taken at the beginning of the fourth term. Such a procedure would cause staggering of election contests in the House of Representatives, since reelected representatives should get a sabbatical year plus a two-year term, but this would not necessarily be undesirable. In fact, it might diminish some of the "coattail" effects of presidential elections.

There would be many other incidental benefits to a sabbatical system. Congressmen would have an opportunity to become more familiar with current problems as well as the needs of their constituents. This would be especially true of congressmen who were reelected for a term to follow the sabbatical year. They undoubtedly would be much better informed legislators after spending a year away from Washington. Those congressmen spending "lame duck" sabbaticals could look upon this time as a reward for previous services rendered and as an opportunity to make a successful reentry to civilian life, possibly changing occupations or lifetime goals in the process.

Political sabbaticals would also significantly affect the American system of higher education. Government officials on sabbatical would be visible within the university community. This would help to develop more respect for further education among many Americans and could stimulate new demands for adult education as well as for sabbatical leaves in other occupations. In addition, a dialogue might open up between "egg-head" idealists on college campuses and cynical realists from the bureaucracy. Universities would no longer be four-year preserves for the young; they could become a social resource for all age groups. Lines of communication would open up among segments of society that had not formerly been communicating, and more contact with government officials might help dispel cynicism among students. Such integration of the academic ivory tower with the rest of society would benefit all concerned.

Secrecy in Politics

All voters need accurate information to make intelligent decisions; so do all legislators and bureaucrats. Unfortunately, undoctored information, especially information about what is taking place within the government, is becoming a very scarce commodity. Recent figures show that 41 percent of all congressional committee meetings were held in secret session in 1970 and 36 percent were so held in 1971. This means that the "informed citizen" often cannot find out what is going on in the legislative branch of government, even if he or she makes the effort. Since approximately one-half of legislative business is routine, and therefore likely to be open to the public, these figures indicate that a very high proportion of crucial policy decisions are made behind closed doors. The House Committee on Ways and Means is one of the most powerful committees in Congress, but it has traditionally thwarted the purpose of democracy by closing all of its sessions. This may permit each congressman latitude to wheel and deal, but it certainly does a disservice to information-starved citizens.

There are only two valid excuses for holding closed committee meetings. The first is when critical issues of defense policy must be dealt with; discussion of technical details of new defense systems in public would clearly be inappropriate. The second is the rare occasion when an individual testifies before a committee at great personal risk. When identities must be masked for protection or when the information given might somehow compromise a witness, there is obviously a need for secrecy.

Aside from these two exceptions, voters have the right to demand that records of all political dealings in the legislature be made public. Many of the transcripts of meetings that take place in the executive branch should also be made public. In the wake of the Watergate Affair, the concepts of executive privilege and governmental secrecy must be reexamined. All important governmental decisions should be openly reached, and, with the exceptions noted, no excuse for secrecy should be permitted. Since a democracy is supposedly run by the people, withholding critical information from the public can lead to serious abuses. Closed meetings usually are held so that politicians can act without the public ever knowing the positions taken on issues. If politicians are unwilling to defend these positions in public, they hardly merit public trust. Whereas there are few excuses for closed legislative hearings, there are no valid excuses for secret or disguised votes. All votes taken in any committee or any legislative body should immediately be made public. The only way to develop public trust in government is to open it up for inspection and demand that officials keep their constituents fully informed.

Even on those few occasions when closed committee meetings might be permitted, the proceedings should not be kept secret for more than two years. Throughout the entire United States government, the "top secret" stamp has been put on the most trivial of documents. It has also been used to keep government blunders from becoming public knowledge. The Pentagon Papers, for example, represented nothing but a critical analysis of foreign policy mistakes and deceit, but they would have been kept forever secret were it not for the courageous acts of Daniel Ellsberg. Merely keeping secret documents in order costs the American taxpayer between $60 million and $80 million annually.

Currently, if a scholar, author, or any other individual wishes to see secret papers, he or she must demonstrate a *need to know* before receiving access. The public has a *right to demand* that nothing of importance be kept classified for any length of time. There can be no "open" politics without unhindered public access to current and accurate information. It is a sad commentary on the state of American politics that people have been imprisoned for making possible the publishing of documents like the Pentagon Papers. If democracy were working appropriately, the Government Printing Office should have sold copies to all citizens and abridged editions should have been made available on newsstands. If voters are not permitted to read such documents, even well-informed citizens will be unable to affix correct responsibility for policy mistakes, particularly as political affairs become more complex and as "media management" becomes an ever-greater temptation.

The dangers of secrecy were well illustrated by the secret and illegal bombing of Cambodia that took place in the spring of 1970. That action was concealed not only from the American public but from Congress and even from the Assistant Secretary of the Air Force. Knowledge of the Cambodian affair would have profoundly influenced the attitudes and votes of many congressmen and might well have influenced the outcome of the 1972 election. There is no justification for concealing the bombing of another nation from the American public while that nation obviously knows that it is being bombed.

On a more basic level, there are no grounds for secret meetings and caucuses within political parties (to say nothing of special campaign committees and burglary squads). The two major political parties enjoy a virtual monopoly in the United States, even though there is no provision for them in the Constitution. The Democratic and Republican parties now control much essential information, dominate the political debate, and control access to high office. Today it is questionable whether these parties should be permitted to retain their present monopoly in view of their long and dismal record of irresponsibility. If the system of two major political parties is retained, however, all their records and meetings should be made open to the public. It would be only a half measure to open up the official governmental process if unofficial political decisions, which often are every bit as important as official ones, are made in secret. A working democracy requires an "open" politics, and this means open decisions openly made at all levels.

Freedom of the press is closely related to the question of governmental secrecy. Stringent new laws are needed to protect newsmen from intimidation by political officials. Legislation should also be framed to guarantee newsmen the right to keep identities of informants confidential and to protect newsmen from being forced to divulge information gained in the line of duty to grand juries and other judicial bodies. In a sense, newsmen should be regarded as the "paid snoops" of democracy, and one of their functions should be to ferret out information that political leaders try to cover up.

It is ridiculous to claim to be practicing democracy when vital information is withheld from the public. The many abuses of the media and the deliberate distortion or suppression of facts by the Nixon administration are only a sample of what may happen unless *all* governmental secrecy is abolished.

Thoughts for the Future

It is also worthwhile to consider some ideas whose time may not yet have come, although they might soon become more acceptable among a better educated citizenry. The need for a critical reevaluation of the two-party system has become increasingly obvious. The present system might be replaced by a multiparty system that would give a broader spectrum of representation in politics. Although it is not clear whether such a development would necessarily lead to more socially and environmentally sound laws, the resulting legislation certainly would not be worse than that produced by the present system. If politics could be separated from money, a multitude of parties might spring up and new ideas could make their way into politics. The outmoded nominating process might well be replaced by petition or the holding of open primaries in all parties.

The nature of voting and the definitions of constituencies might well be reconsidered. Perhaps the trend toward complete political leveling might be halted by putting some emphasis on a system of weighted voting if appropriate criteria could be developed for offering additional votes to politically active and informed citizens. Representation by geographical areas might be replaced by a different definition of constituency. The principle of representation by area was a necessary compromise at the time the Constitution was written, but such representation discourages broad planning across administrative units. It also leads to decisions that benefit one geographical area at the expense of others. In defense matters, for example, many senators and representatives vote for legislation that will benefit local industries, regardless of the quality of the proposals. Environmental protection measures are often opposed by districts that include big mining interests or polluting industries within their boundaries. In a nation of increasingly interdependent and overlapping units, it may not be possible to preserve geography as the principal basis for representation.

There are various alternate ways of reorganizing constituencies that could be very effective in facilitating the development of a new politics. One of the most appealing alternatives is to combine broader geographic representation with age. For example, one-third of all senators and representatives could be nominated and elected by those who are between 18 and 35, an age group that in the past has been very much neglected in the political process. A second category of representatives could be elected by the 35- to 55-year-old group, and the last category could represent citizens over 55. A Constitutional amendment should be passed, lowering the age requirement for all elective offices to 18. It seems unlikely that, say, a 20-year-old would acquire the experience (and following) to be elected President; but, like sex, religion, and race, age *in itself* should not bar any legally eligible adult from elective office.

Variations on this theme might prove more acceptable. For example, the Senate might remain a body with representation based solely on geographic area; the House could be divided according to large geographical regions and age. Or a certain portion of legislators might be selected *from* as well as *by* these new age constituencies. Incidental benefits of such redivided constituencies could include dismantling the seniority system of congressional committee assignments, as well as waging an indirect attack on wealth in politics. If one-third of the members of the Senate and House were under the age of 35, the traditional seniority system would be disrupted. Similarly, such a reconstituted legislature would be more likely to vote for legislation that would strictly regulate campaign expenditures and for other innovations that would help to separate wealth from politics.

Much could be done immediately to reform the inner workings of both the Senate and the House. The seniority system is an obvious place to begin. This practice in no way serves the public, and voters should demand that it be discontinued. Committee chairmen should be selected in open elections by all senators or representatives. If Congress were reconstituted so that one-third of the membership was under 35 years of age, open election of committee chairmen might provide some real surprises.

In the same vein, committee assignments could be made by lot. At the beginning of a session, each congressman could draw a number giving him or her an opportunity to pick a committee slot in sequence. Committee assignments could then be chosen by this rotation until all available slots were filled. This system of assignment would help break up the collections of cronies who have supported private interests through their control of assignments to key committees. It would also give young representatives and senators an opportunity to compete equally with older members for service on committees of their choice. Composition of key committees would be determined by desire to serve combined with the luck of the draw in the congressional lottery.

This proposal is not quite as extreme as it seems. It is doubtful, for example, that any senator would be denied membership on a committee of his or her first preference under this system. Many important committee slots would be open, and even a senator holding number 100 would undoubtedly serve on at least one committee of his choice. On the second, third, and succeeding rounds, however, there would certainly be some disappointments as committees began to fill up. It might be useful to permit some committee members from the preceding Congress, chosen by committee vote, automatically to continue service to provide continuity from session to session. But this privilege should be extended only *once* for each legislator on each committee, thus preventing any politician from "automatically" serving more than four years on any committee.

As for the highest office in the land, it is worthwhile at least to consider the possibility of a new division of executive responsibility. Originally, the framers of the Constitution intended both the President and Vice President to be strong figures. The President was to be chosen by a majority of the voters, whereas the Vice President would be the runner-up. This system could have resulted in a division of executive labor between two strong and capable political leaders or might even have evolved into the sharing of executive responsibility by a larger group. As political parties and interest-group politics began to change the design of the Constitution, however, the executive branch was modified to guarantee that the top officeholders would have the same political philosophies. Today, of course, the President and Vice President are nominated from the same political party and run on a single ticket.

In practice, this arrangement has led to a series of frustrated Vice Presidents who frequently have been chosen mainly because of their appeal to a selected minority. Most Vice Presidents have had little opportunity to use their talents because they have been given little responsibility. One of the reasons that Richard Nixon was originally chosen as a vice presidential nominee was to balance an Eisenhower ticket that was tipped toward the East. Spiro Agnew received the vice presidential nomination to create a ticket that would appeal to conservatives and to the South. It is well documented that Dwight Eisenhower regarded Nixon as somewhat incompetent and entrusted few important tasks to him. Agnew was assigned to be the administration propaganda and antimedia machine during Nixon's first term. John Kennedy regarded Lyndon Johnson as a political liability, but Johnson was certainly instrumental in carrying Southern and border states.

The irony is that Eisenhower's selection of Nixon made it possible for Nixon eventually to become President. Kennedy's selection of Johnson gave the nation a Johnson administration for five years via an assassin's bullets. In both instances the Vice President was selected out of political expedience, not necessarily because he had outstanding leadership qualifications. It could be argued that Lyndon Johnson, for example, was certainly better qualified to be Vice President than most politicians, but he was not selected because of those qualifications, and no attempt was made by Kennedy to take advantage of them.

The President is often said to be overworked. It is ridiculous to maintain the vice presidency as a ceremonial office when the Chief Executive has so much to do. Capable Vice Presidents could take much of the load off the President's shoulders. The man who is only a heartbeat away from the presidency should enjoy public confidence, be an asset to the President, and be perfectly prepared to step into the President's shoes at any moment.

One solution to these problems might be to create a dual executive, with each part having a well-defined sphere of competence. The most logical division would be between foreign and domestic affairs. The President for Foreign Affairs would be in charge of the nation's foreign policy. He would be able to concentrate his energies on this area and would remain quite apart from the press of domestic issues. He would perform all executive foreign policy functions, including signing congressional bills and treaties. The President for Domestic Affairs would concentrate his energies on internal problems. He would serve all the current functions of the President with the exception of those defined as being within the jurisdiction of the President for Foreign Affairs. There is little doubt that he could be fully occupied with domestic problems during the next few decades.

A dual executive would offer the additional advantage of helping to guarantee that men competent in foreign affairs would be candidates for the office of President for Foreign Affairs and that those specializing in domestic matters would be likely to be President for Domestic Affairs. Too often in the past a President has been a specialist in one sphere or the other. Richard Nixon turned his attentions outward, much to the neglect of internal matters. Lyndon Johnson, on the other hand, was very astute at handling domestic affairs but failed tragically in the field of foreign policy. This dual arrangement would also ease the problem of succession in the event of presidential death. The President for Foreign Affairs, for example, could assume the dual role until a new President for Domestic Affairs could be elected. Finally, voters would be given a more refined choice; they would not be forced to accept poor foreign policy to get the domestic package of their choice, and vice versa.

Finally, one of the best ways to renew dedication to basic ideals and to begin a political transformation would be to call a second Constitutional Convention. There is no reason to limit the United States to one time-worn document. An excellent time to convene this convention would be July 4, 1976—200 years after the founding of this nation. There could be no better way to celebrate this occasion than by admitting that times and society have changed in the last two centuries. A new social contract, written in a new spirit and containing new rights and obligations, is clearly needed for a postindustrial society. The drafting of this new Constitution would force Americans to sit down together and redefine the goals and values that they hold in common. These could then be embodied in a more modern Constitution designed for a society of the future rather than a society of the past. Rexford Tugwell has developed a new Model Constitution for the United States. This model, which has now gone through more than thirty drafts, is designed to stimulate discussion of desirable structural changes to be made in the American system of government. It might well serve as a preparatory document to be read by all those attending the Second Constitutional Convention.

A Note to Skeptics

This chapter concludes with a note addressed to skeptics. Anything suggested in the preceding paragraphs can be attacked as "not new," "naïve," "politically infeasible," "not really leading to fundamental change," and so forth. "Realists" will point out that politics simply cannot be changed and that self-interest is the only principle on which politics can be organized. Within the context of the current political paradigm, there is some validity to such charges. After all, the present oligarchy is unlikely to allow to go unchallenged any changes that represent threats to its power. But the objective need for a new politics is growing, and concerned citizens are getting restive. The trends discussed in previous chapters and the numerous disclosures of political corruption surrounding the Watergate Affair are rapidly leading to a situation where the public might be very receptive to such suggestions. Today, more than ever before, educated citizens have the power and are developing the will to transform their politics and their society.

Other skeptics will point out that nothing new will work and will apply for more research grants to study politics as usual. They will argue that it is better not to experiment and risk disturbing the system that presently exists. Life still seems pleasant for most of the members of our society, so why worry about the future? Muddling through has always worked in the past; why should it fail now? Those individuals who predict increasingly troubled times must be wrong, so why not stick with the present system and accept the rewards that it has to offer?

Interconnected global problems like the ones anticipated in these chapters have never before been faced. Expectations for so many have never been raised so high, and the possibility of fulfilling these expectations has never been so remote. Within the present pluralist system predicated on self-interest, *each day is a new experiment in system elasticity.* No one knows how far the old system can be stretched before it snaps, but many individuals seem determined to find out. The preceding suggestions are offered in the hope that a dialogue for survival can be developed and with the trust that reasonable men can devise more workable political alternatives for directing their own social evolution.

In the end, however, new ideas must find public acceptance in a democracy before they can be implemented. In a mass democracy, people get the government they deserve. The changes that have been suggested would go far toward opening up opportunities to establish a new society, but if citizens continue to expect corruption in government, that government will remain corrupt. If they continue to support a pluralist spoils system, it will remain. The important thing about political change is that all the reforms in the world will have little effect unless people really believe that alteration of the old political paradigm is both necessary and feasible. The most intricate system of democratic political structures can easily be subverted if the people continue to tolerate apathy, stupidity, abuses of power, and corruption in government.

6

Scanning the Horizon: Education and Information

Large-scale social change can take place only when a significant number of people perceive some alternative to be preferable to the existing state of affairs. Discontent or satisfaction with the status quo is a function of the information received. Most Americans believe that the information they receive is accurate and related to "truth," that it is objectively gathered and transmitted, and that it helps to make them well informed. This, unfortunately, is not necessarily true. In a complex society in which most communications are "mediated" (transmitted by processes other than face-to-face conversation), there is not necessarily a perfect correlation between the information each person receives and events that occur. This is particularly true when subjective evaluations are made of conditions and events that are not easily observed and defined, such as levels of discontent in the ghettos, the extent of participation in public demonstrations, the number of casualties in distant military battles, or the state of the nation's economy. News about a five-alarm fire in the center of a large city is likely to be fairly accurate because there is not much room for individual interpretation of what takes place. Wherever people have discretion in analyzing and reporting social data, however, there is a danger that reports will be based on false premises. Therefore, truth about a society is often relative, because news can be carefully selected, manipulated, or even neglected by those working within that society's communications network.

For convenience, the types of information citizens receive can be divided into two categories. The first is information that is directly received through sensory mechanisms. Information about smog levels, for example, is perceived by the eyes, nose, and throat. Accurate news about the availability of gasoline or other commodities is best received by attempting to purchase them. Even this kind of information, received directly from the environment, is often perceived differently by different people. There is an extensive literature in social psychology documenting that social pressures can change individual perceptions of clearly observable situations.

The second category of information on which beliefs are based comes through what could be called the social information system. In a large society, each individual cannot experience all the important events that make up the news and cannot receive firsthand all the information needed to make decisions. Much of this information comes through the "nerves" of society, the printed and electronic media. The forms in which information is received vary from high school classes in ecology to stock market reports heard on the evening news.

The information that has flowed through society's nerves in the past has not dealt much with environmental deterioration or a host of other issues that could lead to large-scale social change. The dominant social paradigm shapes this information flow, and most of the people who influence media operations have little interest in raising potentially embarrassing questions about the present social, economic, and political system. Simple self-interest dictates that those who have, in one way or another, profited from the old system of cowboy growth would not be the first to call attention to its faults. Furthermore, the mass media and the school system, both of which are of critical importance in shaping views of the social and physical world, are largely controlled by a small and influential group that also controls local political and economic life. It takes money to operate a newspaper, and it takes both political influence and money to operate a television station. The annual operating costs of large television stations are in the vicinity of $1 million. The media and the schools have historically been the instruments through which the DSP is preserved and transmitted to future generations. Properly operated, however, each could serve as a vehicle for rapid changes in social attitudes.

Learning the Ropes

The role of education in American society has been the subject of a voluminous literature, both laudatory and critical. The laudatory literature usually emphasizes the quantity of education provided to young Americans and stresses the number of people receiving high school diplomas, bachelor's degrees, and doctorates. The record shows that Americans are, indeed, among the most literate peoples in the world. In 1968 less than 2 percent of Americans fifteen years old and over could not read or write—a figure comparable to the percentages in other industrial countries. Quality of education is less emphasized, although America's superiority in advanced training in many disciplines is frequently mentioned. The critical literature is perhaps more voluminous than the laudatory. It has dealt with a variety of ills ranging from the low quality of education in ghetto schools to the "failure of schools to teach the Biblical version of creation."

Whatever the pros and cons, the school system is now clearly a vast, complex apparatus for transmitting the DSP. As Ivan Illich has succinctly written, "School is the advertising agency which makes you believe you need society the way it is." It would be very desirable if the school system could be transformed to teach students how society "ought to be."

Formal education has two different aspects. The first is the straightforward transfer of information from teacher to student, part of the process by which a person is "trained" for life in the outside world. Most education trains people for the job market. This aspect of education includes learning to add and subtract, memorizing chemistry formulas, and learning to type and take shorthand. The second aspect of education deals with learning to question assumptions, analyze statements, draw conclusions, and develop new perspectives. This is the broadening aspect of education, which supposedly teaches people how to think. It is much praised but too little practiced in most school systems. Education that broadens perspectives seems to be a sideline, even in colleges, which remain devoted to education in the knowledge-transfer sense and to the production of specialists: engineers, scientists, physicians, teachers, attorneys, corporation executives, and other cogs for the industrial machine. As society has grown more complex, the "need" for compartmentalized specialists has supposedly become paramount, and the academic machinery has been used to turn out precisely such products. Little time or attention has been given to careful analysis of why such a limited array of career opportunities should exist or to the many alternative patterns that could be created. The educational system produces replacement parts and sometimes parts that expand the existing apparatus; it does little or nothing to engender its own redesign or redirection.

The American educational system neglects another extremely important aspect of education that is very directly related to environmental problems: the development of social consciousness or concern for others among students, a task from which school administrators shrink. This hesitation has largely resulted from the historical separation between church and state. Now a moral vacuum exists in which the public school system claims no mandate for dealing with such delicate subjects as the way people act toward one another. The churches have lost a great deal of influence among the young, and the family depends on other institutions to do the job since children spend little time at home. Perhaps this has been most manifest in moralistic skirmishes over sex education. Most educators now recognize that sex education for young people is imperative, particularly if an escalation of premarital pregnancy and venereal disease among teenagers is to be avoided; yet sex education is often considered *too controversial* for the classroom. Few parents have sufficient knowledge of sex to teach it to their children, even if they are willing. (After all, where could the parents learn?) The churches are often repositories of a grotesque sexual morality that, if inculcated in the young, frequently leads to unhappiness or tragedy. The schools are generally not allowed to develop the expertise to provide comprehensive sex education. Thus our laissez-faire society carries an unnecessary burden of ignorance and disease.

One of the most pressing needs in our competitive industrial society is the enhancement of individual feelings of responsibility for the entire society. When there was plenty of insulating space among people, the need for concern for others was less apparent, although it certainly existed. In recent decades, manifestations of such concern for others have become increasingly rare. In the near future, however, such concern will become a necessary part of a transition to a new social paradigm. Children must be socialized to cooperate rather than to compete, to be concerned for the welfare of others rather than simply for the welfare of self, and to learn that the world and its resources must be treated as a big commons to be shared by all rather than as a private preserve to be exploited for individual gain.

Cornell University psychologist Urie Bronfenbrenner has made an extensive comparison of the educational systems of the Soviet Union and the United States. He notes in his study that one of the striking differences between the two systems is the Soviet emphasis on character building, the development of concern for the group rather than the individual, and the promotion of a new communist morality rooted in a "new socialist man." By contrast, in the United States children are socialized to be little "rugged individualists," and personal success is much preferred to group success.

Bronfenbrenner's work is mentioned here not in defense of the Soviet system but because the Soviet emphasis on the collective in education offers an alternative model that has much relevance for the future of American society. If we are seriously interested in the creation of a new social model and in the development of young citizens who are environmentally aware and socially concerned, the Soviet experience bears careful consideration.

Children in Soviet schools are systematically taught group loyalty. Discipline is centered on withdrawal of approval from the peer group rather than on a paddle in the principal's office. Classrooms are divided into little "cooperatives"—groups of children assigned to work together. If one child in the group fails to pull his or her weight, the entire group suffers the consequences and privileges are lost. Although teachers provide guidance, much decision making rests with the peer group. Competition is encouraged, but only among groups. It is discouraged among individuals. Undoubtedly, this feature of the Soviet system is pushed too far for American tastes, but it stands out in stark contrast to the American classroom, where emphasis on concern for one's fellow human being is neglected from kindergarten through graduate training.

Bronfenbrenner has found that the resulting behavior of Russian children contrasts sharply with that of American or Western European children. Russian children tend to be less aggressive and violent, more cooperative, to have friendlier and more affectionate relationships with children of different ages, parents, and teachers, and in general to be better behaved. Test situations show them to be much less ready to engage in such antisocial behavior as cheating on exams or refusing to admit to inflicting property damage than are Western children.

Some Soviet-style changes in the American system of bringing up children might very well have salutary effects on the level of social consciousness among young Americans. Bronfenbrenner contends that "the most needed innovation in the American classroom is the involvement of pupils in responsible tasks on behalf of others within the classroom, the school, the neighborhood, and the community." Such changes would doubtless help to reduce the rampant competition in American society and induce greater social consciousness and responsibility in future citizens. However, in adopting Soviet child-rearing and education techniques, great care would have to be taken to avoid the excesses of the Russian system. Particularly to be avoided are overemphasis on conformity and obedience, since openness to change will be absolutely necessary if a new social system is to be developed.

During any such social transition, much human energy must be diverted toward intellectual growth, which does not seem to be encouraged in either the Soviet or American system. Today both school systems do far too little to produce analytical, independent thinkers. In fact, a good case could be made that most school boards in both nations would prefer to maintain a system in which no student ever raised any critical social questions. There is much room for criticism and questioning of assumptions at all educational levels, but teaching children to question orthodoxies is now almost entirely lacking in elementary and secondary schools in the United States. In traditional civics classes the United States government is depicted as working precisely as the Constitution prescribes. If students got all their political education in school, they would remain blissfully unaware of what really goes on by the Potomac. A sanitized, ethnocentric version of history is also pervasive. All too often the young student is taught that he or she lives in the best of all possible worlds and that those who question the established order are simply misfits to be disregarded. Of course, many teachers never raise questions about the value of the present educational system, nor are students encouraged to consider whether they might be better educated if school systems, as they now exist, disappeared.

The average student who leaves the educational system after high school has learned enough to permit him or her to function in a household, an office, on the assembly line, or in the bread line. High school graduates have acquired some limited knowledge of their world, knowledge shaped by a social information system the existence of which they are usually unaware. Those who continue on to college are sometimes permitted exposure to ideas that are less acceptable in the mainstream of society. Many read Marx, Marcuse, Fanon, and Mao; they hear lectures from radicals and "subversive" ecologists. They may learn that religion can be understood as a culturally evolved device for social control and that Communism represents an alternative type of economic system. They may even be told about many assumptions that scientists accept on faith. These revelations, however, cause society less worry because most university students have been exposed to orthodoxies for the preceding eighteen years. Thus, the university is permitted to act as a mild introduction to thinking for those who survive the dreary socialization of the grade school and high school years and still manage to retain a spark of intellectual curiosity. Clearly, curricula at all levels must be revamped, and teachers must become devoted to educating people so that they will be capable of coping with future problems.

A major step toward transforming the educational system and present society could be taken by encouraging people to participate in a broadening educational process throughout their lifetimes, rather than continuing to restrict education mainly to people under twenty-one. The United States rates very poorly among industrial countries in providing for adult education. Sabbatical leaves for the explicit purpose of intellectual improvement should become more common. Such a renewal process for politicians has already been recommended in Chapter 5. If a transition is to be made to a functioning mass democracy capable of dealing with future problems, continuing education for all members of society will be important. Sabbaticals could be spent in universities, in government or community service, or in some other form of educational enterprise. Whatever the precise form of learning experiences, the economic "costs" could easily be borne in a society in which material throughput was minimized and improving the quality of the stock of human capital had become an important goal.

It will be essential in a steady-state society, with its short work week and lower production of material goods, to find substitutes for today's frantic, high-consumption, "leisure" activities. Emphasis must shift to a variety of cultural activities to occupy the human mind and body. Such activities as reading, composing poetry, engaging in new forms of interpersonal encounters, becoming active in civic affairs, creating artistic or handmade articles, listening to (or performing in) musical groups or orchestras, sewing, sailing, gardening, and participating in nonmechanized sports must supplant the motor boat–camper–dune-buggy–motorcycle–trailbike–type of activity that now generally dominates periods of leisure and recreation. People must be encouraged to develop intellectual resources that will permit them to find fulfillment in themselves, through development of their own abilities, rather than vicariously through the purchase of energy-devouring mechanical devices.

A sabbatical could well become an important part of the educational system, even though a classical pedant might not recognize some of these sabbatical activities as "education." After all, learning to play a musical instrument, do a fine woodcarving, write a book, or maintain a garden are just as "educational" as memorizing the names of long-dead kings. Can anyone claim that serving on a city council, helping a legislator to do research, or taking a job in social work is any less educational than doing a year of graduate study in biology? By such extension, the educational system could be made broader, less structured, and very much more practical and useful in shaping a new society.

The American educational system is now so designed that each person goes through an "educational period" in his or her life that lasts approximately thirteen years, at which time formal education ends. Unfortunately for many people, this means that intellectual curiosity then enters a steady decline. Society, however, does not stand still, and neither does the production of new information or the development of new perspectives. Periodic exposure to various types of further education would shake many people out of their comfortable ruts and make them think about the problems of today and tomorrow rather than those of yesterday; it would also help eliminate the generation gap created by one-shot exposure to education. This would be an uncomfortable experience for many, but the process of transforming a society cannot take place without intellectual inquiry and much soul searching.

Changing the University

If any part of the educational system can serve as a vehicle for *immediate* social change, it is the universities. A major part of the nation's future leadership will, in the coming decade, be exposed to four or more years of higher education in prestige institutions. This may be unfortunate, since many able women and members of minorities will be excluded, but it will occur nonetheless. These future opinion leaders could well initiate a major social transformation if they became convinced that it was in their interest and the interest of society as a whole to move toward a more ecologically sound social model. Unfortunately, colleges and universities do not now do a very good job of educating in the broader sense, or of preparing students for a future very different from the present or the past. The lion's share of major university resources is devoted to mission-oriented research and teaching, and very little time is left for the debate and interchange that lead to critical thinking.

There are three sets of major problems that must be faced if colleges and universities are ever to become forums for open social inquiry and an asset in solving future, more difficult social and environmental problems. First, a means must be found to finance the university apart from the carefully negotiated handouts from state legislatures or donations from wealthy alumni. Funds from both sources tend to come with strings attached, and administrators are instructed that educational activities should not stray outside carefully prescribed bounds. Second, some method must be found to overcome the myopia of academic disciplines. In a world that is becoming increasingly difficult to understand and where major social problems cross conventional discipline lines, it is ridiculous to preserve disciplinary hierarchies that have vested interests in attempting to keep the world divided into "manageable" academic parcels. Finally, new reward systems and curricula must be arranged for students, who universally condemn the course and grade system that now circumscribes intellectual development. In most schools students are in effect penalized for taking challenging courses, as a B+ grade in a difficult subject may keep a student out of graduate school.

Let us first turn to the critical problem of funding. The American university has four basic sources of funds. Most state schools submit annual requests for financial appropriation to state legislatures. When economic times are good and when students have not been restive, the handouts have often been sizable. When economic times have been bad, however, or when students have challenged authority, the handouts have been meager. There is no question that this type of budgetary coercion has had an important impact on state university structures, particularly since the cutting of funds results directly in a freeze on hiring, one of the few sources of innovation in a university structure beset with academic *rigor mortis.*

The second source of funds is donations from wealthy alumni, foundations, and other charitable institutions. These gifts make up a small part of the educational budget of public institutions. For private institutions, however, they often represent the vital margin between survival and slow death. These funds do not come to the university without strings attached either. People make charitable donations to universities because universities seem to be "doing good things," as defined by the people making the donations. The threat of withholding money may thus be used as pressure to stem teaching and research activities that might be thought to be "subversive" by the alumni. It is unfortunate that there are at present so few charitable sources that reward universities for futuristic studies, for organizing programs that may be critical of the social drift of industrial society, or for developing probing programs in environmental studies. It is well known that the total amount of alumni contributions to many important American universities is highly correlated with the success of the school's football team!

Tuition, the third source of money, plays a relatively minor role in funding most institutions. Tuition pays a very small part of the total costs of public institutions. This is by design, because the belief that the major part of public higher education should be financed by taxpayers has received general acceptance. Private institutions depend more heavily on tuition, but tuition still meets no more than a quarter of the bills of these colleges or universities. The reasons are largely economic. Education is not so highly valued in American society that parents are willing to mortgage the family home to pay Junior's tuition. In many private institutions, annual tuition now exceeds $4,000. If tuition were to cover all student costs, the yearly figure would be in excess of $15,000, a sum that clearly would price education out of the reach of all but the wealthiest.

The last major source of university funds is the federal government. Most of this money is now given in the form of grants for mission-oriented research. Universities extract a considerable "overhead" figure from such grants and finance other operations with this money. Like state legislatures, the federal government waxes and wanes in its support to higher education, depending on the mood in Washington at any particular time. Under the Nixon administration graduate training and academic research, particularly social research and research of an interdisciplinary nature, have suffered considerably as funds have been tightened and allocated only to those projects where a very concrete product of immediate value is expected to be derived from the research.

The tenuous nature of federal support for higher education was clearly revealed in a White House memorandum of April, 1972, which was later published in the journal *Science.* The memo dealt with the subject of "disciplining" the Massachusetts Institute of Technology because of the "antidefense" bias on the part of MIT's president, Jerome Wiesner. The memo suggested that almost all federal support to MIT be discontinued, including the funding of a laser program ($40 million) and all other funding of nondefense programs, both present and future ($62 million). It should be noted that MIT at this time housed the controversial "Limits to Growth" study, which was also not favorably received by White House bureaucrats. Freedom of inquiry is indeed very difficult to preserve when federal funds are so closely tied to political concerns.

In summary, the American university is not the autonomous center of free thinking that it is portrayed to be. In reality, it is subject to many financial constraints that attempt to keep the university as an adjunct of the high school, a socializing institution overseen by the keepers of the old social paradigm. To keep the university solvent, obeisance must be paid to those who control the purse strings. And, as might be expected, those who control the purse strings are usually most deeply enmeshed in old ways of thinking. University boards of trustees, for example, have never been noted for their radical perspectives; nor have they been noted for steadfast support of university programs that could in some way result in social criticism.

There are solutions to this financial dilemma that should appeal to taxpayers and university presidents alike. One obvious part of a solution would be to increase university income through fellowships that would permit adults to attend universities during their sabbatical years. Both government and private corporations might be asked to pay the *full cost* of sabbatical years for employees. This would result in a considerable pool of tuition money with no strings attached, should the sabbatical program ever become a reality.

Another partial answer is to phase out the "begging" system altogether by guaranteeing every child born in the United States a *fully paid* higher education as his or her birthright. This could be an integral part of a plan to equalize educational opportunity in the United States. Under such a program, every child in the United States would be guaranteed tuition and living expenses for four years at the college or university of his or her choice, so long as the entrance requirements for the selected school were met. Tuition rates could then be raised so that the amount of the birthright more nearly reflected the cost of the education. This program would not only free schools from financial burdens, but it would also raise the quality of education and make each university compete for the best students, rather than just the wealthiest ones. If the federal government dragged its feet on such a proposal, forward-looking state legislatures could enact such legislation in their own states.

Money for the program could be generated from federal and state funds that now are funneled into higher education by different routes. In addition, steep new inheritance taxes might be imposed to help cover any deficits. It would seem fitting to tie efforts to equalize educational opportunity with a program aimed at equalizing economic opportunity for each new generation as well. Surprising changes in attitudes toward higher education and social stratification might result from a system in which the *starting place* for all young people was much more nearly the same than it is at present.

Under a new tuition system, the decision whether to obtain a higher education would be left entirely up to the student. Family finances would have little relationship to the choice of colleges or universities since each student would have four guaranteed years. Students not choosing to exercise their educational rights would lose them at age thirty, and the money would be returned to the general fund. Universities would become more cosmopolitan places because economic status would disappear as a selection criterion. Prestige institutions would no longer be populated by homogenous student bodies drawn largely from the upper classes.

Financing graduate education might be handled in a similar fashion. A national task force could establish minimum quotas for graduate training in various fields. Fellowships might then be created to match these numbers and an open national competition for them could be held. Fellows would then be free to select the graduate program of their choice, and it would be financed with fellowship money. Conventional means of financing graduate education, such as family funds, corporation grants, research contracts, and loans, would continue to be used. The sabbatical program in government and private industry should also eventually prove to be a lucrative source of revenue to finance graduate programs of education.

Abolishing disciplinary compartmentalization and changing the structure of student rewards could well prove more difficult. In a sense the two problems are linked since reorganizing the structure of academic disciplines could lead to different kinds of student rewards and a different role for the university. It is critical that the university become a much more valued and active part of society. This necessity is understandably perplexing to many academicians because it is an inevitable result of their having ignored the changing character of society for far too long. When university educations were luxuries reserved for children of a narrow segment of society, little attention was paid to whether the education received was at all relevant to society's problems. Students attended the university to "become cultured," make future business contacts, and perhaps find a mate. Today, universities have become much more egalitarian, and their function in society must be quite different.

The primary task for the university of the future will be to so reorganize its internal structure that economic rewards are no longer controlled by old disciplinary hierarchies. This task will require a mammoth effort. The old structure of disciplines artificially divides knowledge into little compartments that can be offered to students in bite-sized courses. But it is becoming increasingly obvious that these artificial boundaries make little sense; the real world is "interdisciplinary" in nature, and its problems often cross the lines of many established disciplines. Many interdisciplinary programs have recently been established, and many have failed for lack of faculty support. The academic community exacts penalties from scholars who stray from the straight and narrow, and the wise professor asks no interdisciplinary questions but remains securely attached to the concerns of each discipline.

There are no easy answers to the question of how the university structure should be transformed. Student demands often prod faculty members to change their teaching and research perspectives. In addition the budgetary crunch in research is leading many professors back to the classroom and into contact with inquiring young minds. Outside financial support of innovative university programs could also be crucial in inducing faculty members to break out of their old molds. Too often, however, new programs are really old programs with new covers. Given the financial boost that could accrue from adoption of the suggested sabbatical year program, as well as the additional revenues that could be generated from the previously mentioned educational birthright program, enough funding might be made available to lead today's starving universities to develop new programs that are more suited to the society of the future.

Society's Nerves—The Mass Media

Once the student in the United States is disgorged by the learning machine, meal ticket in hand, he or she anticipates little further contact with formal education. The knowledge picked up in high school or college becomes frozen. It is as if all intellectual development and change suddenly stopped on graduation day. From that point on, most people receive their information from the mass communications network. Everyone in American society is constantly barraged with processed information from a variety of communications sources—television, radio, magazines, and newspapers—known collectively as the mass media. Television is obviously the most used media; it is estimated that American households averaged *seven hours* of viewing time daily in 1972. Unfortunately, the existing media are controlled in large part by those people in society who have the greatest interest in maintaining the status quo. The tradition of poor but honest editors producing staunchly independent local newspapers is all but dead. Most newspapers have merged into chains, and the small independent sources of news have largely been squeezed out of existence. They have been replaced by large media complexes, in which local radio and television stations as well as newspapers are often controlled by one individual or a small group of wealthy individuals with an interest in not rocking the boat. Thus, the nature of information or "truth" as it moves through the nerves of society is often subtly altered in ways that are supportive of the existing dominant social paradigm.

As with most aspects of economic activity, the prime concern of television executives is making money, and the major goal of television programming is to keep advertising revenues continuously growing. Thus, soap operas or reruns of "B" movies often take precedence over important news events, because the potential audience for these programs is larger. One observer has written that "during the critical moments of the United Nations debate over Vietnam in 1966, CBS News provided a special half-hour summary on important developments in the Security Council, but the CBS television station in New York did not carry the program because this would have meant delaying the start of its afternoon movie." More recently, outraged viewers besieged local television stations when the Senate Watergate Hearings took air time away from soap operas.

Presidential telecommunications adviser Clay Whitehead hit the nail right on the head when, in an unusually frank speech to a media group in 1971, he remarked:

> Look at the current state of the broadcasting business. *You sell audiences to advertisers* [italics ours]. There's nothing immoral about that, but your audience thinks your business is providing them with programs. And the FCC regulates you much in the way the public sees you. It requires no blinding flash of originality on my part to see that this creates a very basic conflict.

Whitehead went on to criticize efforts to open the media to a wider diversity of opinions:

> However nice they sound in the abstract, the Fairness Doctrine and the new judicially contrived access rights are simply *more* government control masquerading as an expansion of the public's right of free expression. Only the literary imagination can reflect such developments adequately—Kafka sits on the Court of Appeals and Orwell works in the FCC's Office of Opinions and Reviews. Has anyone pointed out that the fiftieth anniversary of the Communications Act is 1984?

The White House thus sees the electronic media as a big business in which audiences are delivered to advertising agencies. Attempts to open the media to vital communication concerning pressing issues become equated with censorship in another example of establishment doublethink.

It is commonplace for media management to contend that television belongs to all the people and that programming of the kind that FCC Commissioner Newton Minnow has described as a "vast wasteland" is just what people want. The tragedy of television's slavish obedience to advertising is represented by A. C. Nielsen's 1,200 families. What these families like sets standards for the whole nation. Many billions of dollars worth of advertising decisions are made annually on the basis of these audience ratings, but such ratings tell only which sets were tuned to what and do not attempt to measure audience satisfaction, audience desires for better programming, or even degree of sponsor association. If three poor programs are aired at 8:00 P.M., one undoubtedly will receive an excellent rating. Even if the ratings truly represented the preference of viewers, such preference should not be assumed to reflect the total potential interest of the audience or even a healthy state of affairs. Fred Friendly, for several years president of CBS News, wrote in 1966 that "The stock answer of network apologists for the current television schedule is 'We give the people what they want' but what has actually happened is that those viewers who have been brainwashed select their own brand of popcorn, while those of more discerning tastes simply give up watching or listening."

The situation, if it has changed at all, has deteriorated since Friendly made his observation. Corny situation comedies, fantasy police-detective shows, variety hours, and sports are the choices presented by commercial channels in most prime-time slots. Programs dealing with serious social problems or with environmental issues are widely scattered through the schedule as specials and often are not presented during prime time. Given the apparent preferences of present audiences, it is true that networks find their ratings dropping when they present specials, but a substantial part of the audience is still deprived of the opportunity of seeing them. Recently the frequency of such programs has been decreasing, and many of them have been criticized by the federal government. Furthermore, programs scheduled outside prime time that attempt to deal with serious problems, such as NBC's *Today* show, are unable to give sufficient time to their topics. Commercials eat up large amounts of time and continually break up the discussion. Today the viewer in search of quality prime-time television must often do without unless the Public Broadcasting System happens to be showing a program of interest; and the Public Broadcasting System has recently been forced to cut back its programs because of reductions in its budget.

The quality of commercial television raises the questions of whether today's broadcasters can be considered suitable guardians of society's nerves and whether they can be trusted to report the news objectively. Robert Cirino, in his book *Don't Blame the People,* contends that the news media have a permanent conservative bias that is related to the composition of ownership. This bias leads to continuous covert manipulation of public opinion and protection of the DSP. Cirino points out that simply keeping certain problems from getting media exposure is as effective as outright propaganda. He validly asks, "Could America have ignored the hungry if the poor had their own ABC, NBC, or CBS? Could Americans have ignored racism if the blacks had had at their disposal communication technology and techniques equal to those of the Establishment? Did the white newspaper, news-magazine, radio or television audience receive the black man's viewpoint in an arena where all ideas had an equal chance to be presented?"

That Cirino and others document a persuasive case for media bias comes as no surprise to those who have had an opportunity to watch news made and then to watch it reported by the press. There is a series of filters between the story and its reception by the reader or listener. Reporters are basically honest and hard working and are less wed to old ideas than the average person in other professions, but their stories are reviewed by editors, executives, owners, and sponsors, all of whom have a direct or indirect role in determining output. They filter all the news that is seen, heard, or read. Many subjective judgments about "importance," "newsworthiness," and financial or legal complications that might result from the dissemination of a story are made in the process of reducing the voluminous input to a much more restricted output.

If the loss of information during these filtering processes were more or less random, it could be accepted with equanimity. After all, it is not necessary, or even possible, for every member of society to be accurately apprised of all important events. But as Cirino has documented, there is much more to media distortion than honest filtering. Organized religion, for example, has been consistently protected from any adverse publicity because attacks on religion are specifically forbidden by the Television Code. Religious groups also control many television stations and censor their program content. Certain comments on the economy, particularly those favorable to socialism, are rarely broadcast. Pro-abortion forces, minority groups, and advocates of disarmament have at times been rudely treated by the media.

Sander Vanocur, former correspondent for NBC News, referred to this situation when he wrote in *Esquire* in 1972:

> Corporately, the image projected—at least to me—was not that of Big Brother but rather Big Mother. . . . [NBC] feeds you (rather more than you need for your own good), she rewards you, and she punishes you in the sense that for years during the period of prolonged adolescence you tend to feel that you must not do anything or say anything which she will not approve. You find more and more that your journalistic behavior pattern tends more and more to be shaped towards an expression not of what you believe, but rather towards what Big Mother will find acceptable.

Is it possible, then, for the media to become a positive force for social transformation, given its existing orientation? Perhaps, if only because many of the changes that are needed are already being demanded by groups that have until now been systematically excluded from ownership of the electronic media. A conflict has been recognized between the public nature of the limited frequencies available for television broadcasting and the interests of the private businesses that now enjoy the use of those channels. Many suggestions have already been made for increasing the "public service" aspects of broadcasting and for allowing more public exposure of minority views. Both the opening of more television channels through the use of UHF and the trend toward cable television may broaden control of the electronic media. New FCC regulations, however, could immediately move the news and important informational shows into prime-time slots.

Future steps that should be taken include returning of the airwaves to the public via federal government subsidy. Programming on the BBC in England, for example, is far superior in quality to that of any commercial network in the United States. There seems to be little indication that the British government uses the BBC channels for partisan programming, one of the objections often expressed to governmental support of an American network. This objection may be a valid one, especially in view of recent attempts by the Nixon administration to control the media, but there is every bit as much danger of a subtle government takeover of supposedly "private" networks through political pressures. In addition, there are many diverse cultural, ethnic, and geographic groups in the United States that should be guaranteed access to the airwaves. Satisfactorily running a federal network that attempts to serve the needs of all people might prove to be an immensely difficult task. It is, however, one worth trying, given the necessity of getting important information to the American public. Public control of major segments of the electronic media, particularly television, might be the only way to open new channels of information.

There may, however, be less drastic ways of achieving these ends. One possibility is to separate profits from programming, perhaps by having the Federal Communications Commission (FCC) rule that all commercials be shown at random. Thus, a manufacturer could buy programming and prime advertising time from a network but would have no way of knowing, until notified, on what day or with what program his advertisement would be shown. This practice might lead to screams of anguish from networks and advertisers, both of whom seem to feel that the advertiser has a God-given right to dictate what program the public views adjacent to his commercial message. Nevertheless, advertisers do not try to control the news adjacent to their newspaper or television ads or the articles surrounding their space in magazines, although they would undoubtedly try if they thought they had any chance of success.

The amount of time devoted to commercials should also be more strictly limited. All commercials might be shown in groups at half-hour intervals to reduce the annoyance of constant interruptions. Strict standards of truth should be made mandatory for all television commercials, and subliminal gimmicks should be outlawed. Furthermore, advertising aimed at children should be completely eliminated; young consumers do not need to be encouraged to develop bad habits. Although the idea now sounds utopian, television commercials might someday be eliminated altogether. This would be a forward step in the movement toward a steady-state economy, as it would help reduce consumer demands. Funding could come from government grants and subscription fees. Television would be much cheaper if private profits were removed from it, and air time could be sold at lower prices. An active FCC could upgrade program content and see that the airwaves are used in the public interest by demanding that a large proportion of prime time be devoted to public information programs. Part of that time could be devoted to exposing the public to the environmental and social problems previously discussed. It is possible that some of the funds allocated to the proposed Planning Branch of government could be used to produce regularly appearing important and serious programs on critical issues, and networks might be required to show these programs during prime time.

There can be no doubt that media management problems are complex, and until the private profit motive is checked, little improvement in the accuracy of public information can be expected and the extent of media criticism of commonly accepted social wisdoms will probably remain unchanged.

Science, Information, and the Citizen

The close relationships that exist between the wisdom of the electorate, the quality of government, the excellence of education, and the objectivity of the information establishment are both a curse and a blessing. They are a curse because of the difficulty of changing one without causing repercussions in the others. The blessing is that improvement in any of these areas may have significant positive effects on the others. There can be little question, for instance, that the use of radio and television has raised the level of public political awareness in the United States far above that of earlier days. The media have also clearly increased public recognition of environmental problems. A generation of ecology-minded teachers has begun to alter the perspectives of young people. One result of these changes is a generation relatively dissatisfied with things as they have always been—a generation that may continue to sow the seeds of a major social transformation.

Thus far the discussion has touched on two important aspects of the social information system that are primarily concerned with the dissemination of facts and ideas; but little has been said about the origins of these facts and ideas. Their sources are diverse, ranging from cultural wisdoms to advertising agencies and news reporters. Perhaps the most important information-producing institution in society today is a collection of individuals, methods, activities, and attitudes that comprises what is called science. No institution has had a greater impact on society over the past century, and none seems destined to have greater influence in the future. All citizens must have some understanding of science and how scientists operate if they are to maintain a proper perspective on both the promise and the peril of science in the critical decades ahead. Science greatly influences social priorities—especially by encouraging a favorable view of "progress" and supporting the premise that there are technological solutions to all problems. Science could well be called the religion of industrial society, and it is as badly in need of reformation as the fifteenth-century Church.

Science and technology are woven into the political processes of society in subtle ways. In a sense science and technology are as political as the legislative process, for science legislates through the innovations produced by research. Some innovations are entirely the result of initiative by private research organizations. Others are the result of technologies developed through public funding or are the unforeseen offshoots of these new technologies. In the future, critical problems will require research and development funds in amounts that only the federal government can provide. Hence, society will have increasing opportunities for collective control of research and development.

Science also often legislates directly in the present political arena. Many decisions involving social values are made solely on the basis of scientific expertise, or at least under the guise of scientific expertise. Nuclear power plant siting is a value-laden issue, especially to residents of adjacent areas, but often issues that concern human values are ignored as attention is focused on simpler questions of technical feasibility and topography. The use of massive data banks for dealing with consumer credit and the computerization of tax information represent other forms of legislation by technical capability. Since the capacity exists, it becomes "needed." Political decisions are often made with little thought being given to the whole range of value trade-offs that occur. Thus, such questions as whether computerization of society is desirable have been raised mostly after the fact.

This situation is now slowly changing, however. The antiballistic missile (ABM) decision and the debate over the supersonic transport in the early seventies presented similar value choices in technological disguise. Scientific experts were lined up on both sides of each of these issues, but in the end political battles were fought over *both* technological feasibility and social desirability. Some attention was called to the sacrifices that would be made in social programs as well as the social impact of the innovations in question, although the discussion of future trade-offs was basically superficial.

Science also legislates by setting limits within which social choices can be made. Feasibility studies and expert testimony are frequently used to bolster or reject value choices before debate begins. This procedure works in two different ways. First, the testimony of "experts" restricts the universe of political discussion because such experts are drawn from the narrow stratum of society that is usually most dedicated to scientific progress. Quite naturally, their solutions and suggestions often reflect a technological-optimist bias and seldom raise questions of trade-offs or social values. Expert testimony also narrows choice by reducing benefits and values to technological terms. Values that cannot be realized immediately with available technology are rejected as being too costly. Little effort is devoted to finding technological means of meeting people's social and environmental demands if appropriate technologies do not already exist. It is also true that unmet demands frequently go unexpressed when a way to meet them is not immediately available.

The claim could be made with considerable justification that the overdevelopment of military technology and nuclear weaponry brought the question of the political and social role of scientists clearly into focus for the first time. Certainly these events caused a sizable group of scientists, primarily nuclear physicists, to begin questioning the relationship between progress in science and technology and the uses to which such progress was put.

Many attitudes have changed in the thirty years since the developers of the atomic bomb agonized over the morality of their activities. Perhaps this change is best symbolized by two actions of the Swedes. In 1948 the Nobel Prize was given by the Swedish Nobel Committee to Paul Muller, the inventor of DDT; in 1970 the use of DDT in Sweden was banned. In the West, where first a population explosion and then an affluence explosion have been detonated by science-based technological advances, negative aspects of scientific progress have been recognized even by those with a quasi-religious commitment to science. Scientists increasingly have been forced to examine critically two fundamental dogmas of their faith. The first is that "pure" scientists are simply seeking "truths," expanding man's knowledge, and going wherever the search leads them. The second is that the use society makes of scientific discoveries is of little or no concern to the scientist.

Although it is perfectly correct that some science remains a "pure" search for truth, it is equally clear that the vast majority of some 300,000 scientists in the United States—pure and applied—are engaged in nothing of the sort. The direction of their research is heavily influenced or even controlled by various private and government organizations. Sometimes the pressure is only partial and subtle, as when federal government funds are allocated to various divisions and panels of the National Science Foundation or National Institutes of Health. Sometimes it is very unsubtle, as when a physicist working for the Department of Defense (or a civilian corporation under contract to the Department of Defense) is told to design a warhead that will withstand a given dose of X-rays coming from an anti-ABM weapon, or when a psychologist working with a cosmetic firm is told to dream up a product name that will evoke images of orgasm (at least subliminally) in the mind of a television viewer. In addition, the government, through its control of vast amounts of funds, is able to influence the numbers of people who become scientists, as well as the fields they enter.

The point is not that such control is necessarily good or bad, but that it exists—indeed, it is nearly ubiquitous. There is no such thing as "science" standing aloof from society, autonomously producing facts or discoveries that may or may not be useful to mankind. Science is channeled in certain directions by what appear to be the needs of the moment. The problem is not one of "science and society," but of scientists *in* society. Science, like the school system and the media, is a social institution. "Science" cannot have social responsibility, but scientists can.

Most scientists feel that the uses to which society puts their discoveries are not a scientist's concern. Although statements like "anything that might be possible should be tried for its own sake" and "any experiment that expands human knowledge is legitimate" are occasionally still heard, most scientists now at least realize that they have *some* responsibility in choosing the direction of their research. No one would field test a doomsday machine, nor would anyone (at least openly) recommend that experiments be conducted on the limits of pain that can be suffered by babies. But some socially concerned scientists have begun to demand that the scientific establishment use the potential *social impact* of research as a criterion for evaluating research projects.

This aspect of scientific responsibility has received considerable attention on university campuses, where the question of war-related research has repeatedly been raised. It represents a difficult dilemma because the results of virtually *any* research can be put to evil ends. For example, seemingly innocent work on the interactions between butterflies and their larval food-plants *could* be put to use by generals interested in waging war on crops. Consequently, there has been a nihilistic outcry from some radical groups for a ban on *all* research. The results of such a move on an overpopulated planet, where new kinds and applications of technology may be able to save billions of lives, can well be imagined. But absurdity on the part of radicals should not be used as an excuse for another absurdity—the idea that society collectively has no right to direct scientific research.

If civilization is to survive, the necessity of imposing some restrictions on the activities of scientists and technologists seems inevitable. But how are these restrictions to be applied, and by whom? The suggestion is often made that science ought to police itself—that boards or committees of scientists should be set up to determine what kinds of research should be undertaken and what kinds deserve support. Why not let "distinguished" scientists make these judgments; after all, are they not the ones with the requisite background?

Experience indicates that this would be the worst possible way to achieve rational control of the scientific enterprise. First, there is overwhelming evidence that professionals never adequately "police" themselves. The dismal record of the American Medical Association in creating an inequitable, overpriced health-care delivery system in the United States is a testimonial to that fact. In a nation that badly needs a better distribution of health care, the A.M.A. has worked to limit the number of physicians that are trained, to limit the number of female physicians, and to prevent the employment of paramedical personnel so that sizable incomes will be ensured for those already in the guild. Another example is the record of trial lawyers in opposing a constructive change in automobile liability insurance systems—adoption of "no-fault" insurance. A third is the almost total refusal of teachers to permit hopelessly incompetent, lazy, *but tenured* colleagues to be fired (even though tenure does not legally extend to such dead wood). In short, "professionalism" consistently triumphs over public good when governing is left entirely to members of the group itself.

Science is no different. By the standards of their disciplines, the best scientists are members of the National Academy of Sciences. The members of the Academy can be roughly divided into two categories: those who are so interested in their research and so devoted to science that they pay little attention to politics within science, and those who are interested in political power and who use the Academy as a vehicle to acquire it. The latter group would, of course, busy itself with any proposed regulation of science. This group has been noted not for the breadth of its grasp of societal problems, but rather for its tough-minded defense of old-line thinking. The current president of the Academy and leader of the group that runs it appears to have great faith in the rightness of existing science and to be deeply offended at suggestions that not all scientific "miracles" have been unmixed blessings. His reactions to environmental problems have ranged from helping block the election to the Academy of a distinguished ecologist from Cornell University to making silly public statements defending the use of DDT.

The unblushing incompetence in ecological matters among many such scientists is easily explained by the training available in the narrow professional-graduate school mill. Perhaps the selection process leading to power in the National Academy of Sciences ensures that those with the most limited background will be chosen. This could also explain the attitude of those in charge of "rendering unto Caesar" in Academy policies.

The Academy has sponsored secret military research through its subsidiary, the National Research Council. Richard Lewontin, a brilliant geneticist, resigned from the Academy because it was sponsoring secret military research about which most of its members were not informed. In a statement issued at the time of his resignation, he dealt with several fundamental issues that are of concern here:

> The particular issue of secret research is so deeply embedded in the nature of the Academy that its resolution would require a resolution of the fundamental contradiction implicit in the organization. The coupling of the highest prestige with unquestioned service to the state is a scheme of legitimation of state service on the one hand, and, on the other, a mechanism of coopting into the establishment system a professional group, which because of its own elitist, internationalist and intellectually rebellious tendencies, contains germs of dissidence and obstructionism. For the Academy to refuse classified work, whether industrial or governmental, would destroy the legitimation scheme and alienate the government. It would affirm the political content of technological and scientific research, because it would raise criteria other than scientific competence for the acceptability of research. *More deeply, it would affirm that men and women will refuse to assent blindly to acts of which they have no knowledge or over which they have no power.* On this last issue there can be no compromise on either side. It is an issue that is beyond reform. It is the issue around which a social revolution must be fought.

Is the issue, as Lewontin states, beyond reform? Considering the possible results of attempts at revolution (abject failure and witch hunts would be highly probable), reform would seem to be worth trying. Indeed, Lewontin's own willingness to resign from the Academy (and the willingness of several of his colleagues, all "young" men in an organization where the average age is over sixty, to follow him) is just part of a trend developing among scientists to forsake standard disciplinary rewards. Although much dissent has been channeled along doctrinaire radical lines, the upsurge in unemployment among young scientists is now causing painful and overdue reevaluations of the relationship of scientists to society. In times of budgetary stress, only the more orthodox prosper.

The key to reforming science is to reform its relationship with society through the political process. The active participation of scientists—social scientists as well as their physical science colleagues—in politics should be increased, as should the familiarity of all citizens with the scientific enterprise. The educational process must be reformed to minimize the number of scientists who emerge from it with tunnel vision and to maximize citizen understanding of what science is all about. As more people become capable of understanding science, its activities will undoubtedly fall under close public scrutiny, and nonscientists will be able to play an active and intelligent role in directing science toward desired social ends. In short, such a development would force scientists to make their assumptions and guiding principles explicit; these assumptions could then be the subject of intelligent public debate and criticism. The priesthood aspects of science would, it is hoped, wither, and scientific activity would come under the control of society in an open arena, rather than being conducted behind closed doors.

Once the impotence of existing planning and control mechanisms is understood, new institutions can be created to bring the scientific enterprise under social control. These new institutions should be built around participatory technology, which means "citizen participation in the use and regulation of technology." Participatory technology can take many forms, but all of them depend on construction of a political system within which new science-citizen relationships can be forged.

The beginnings of a kind of participatory technology have already been seen on some college campuses, where protests forced a halt to war-related research. The application of similar public pressures to industrial firms may have lessened corporate enthusiasm for weapons research. Political action leading to further restriction is needed but is fraught with dangers and difficulties. Somehow, research that is "pure" and useful in the sense that it is designed to enhance knowledge of ourselves and the universe must be protected, even if it should occasionally lead to perverted potential applications. For that reason, the applications of such research must be carefully directed.

Those familiar with research know how difficult and complex the task of making science socially responsible will be. Society must not be deterred, however, by platitudes about the fragility of the scientific enterprise. Science has survived under a wide variety of conditions, including military and industrial secrecy. Virtually all scientists have by now adjusted to the masses of paperwork that are required to obtain funds. In the future, scientists will also need to learn how to explain and defend their research and its potential to their colleagues in the humanities, to politicians, and to the public.

The greatest challenges and opportunities will face scientists in the universities. Research is more open to public scrutiny in universities than in government and industry, and universities tend to attract those who do innovative research. It is there that the initiative could be taken to open research operations to the scrutiny of others by the establishment of research review boards from a diverse constituency—scientists, scholars in other disciplines, students, and members of the community at large. Such boards could serve to review potential projects and investment of public funds and issue advisory reports.

Before such boards can become effective, however, many scientists must learn how to present their findings to the public. They must be able to relate what they are doing to social needs, present or future, and they must be able to justify the expenditures of public funds that are being made. If scientists cannot convince the public that their findings will eventually benefit society, they will not be deserving of taxpayer support.

As the population-resource-environment crisis has deepened, more and more scientists have taken steps, not only to investigate problems of immediate importance to humanity, but also to communicate their results to their colleagues and directly to the public. This is a risky process, since at the moment the public is poorly trained to evaluate the statements of scientists. But because time is very short, both scientists and laymen must struggle to overcome this problem so that society can begin a rational evaluation of its present options.

This difficulty has been typified by the controversy surrounding the publication of Meadows *et al., Limits to Growth*. Written for laymen, *Limits to Growth* represented an ambitious attempt to increase understanding of global problems by incorporating ecological and demographic factors into a computer model of the world system. The computer model had the advantage that all its assumptions were explicit and open to criticism. In contrast, the mental models now used by politicians in debates over public policy are based on many covert assumptions, often so hidden that decision makers are unaware of them.

The *Limits to Growth* study had tremendous impact. Numerous critical articles were written, but its basic conclusions helped spark a new environmental awareness on college campuses and among the public. The authors used good judgment in presenting their findings and letting their results speak for themselves.

Limits to Growth showed that science can play a major role in creating shifts in public attitudes if scientists are willing to address the public directly and intelligently. By the same token, the public must be prepared to listen. Increasingly, concerned scientists are directly addressing the public at large, using plain English instead of the language of the priesthood. This is a healthy trend and should be encouraged.

Times are changing, and participatory technology is already making itself felt in two different arenas of the political process. Many public interest groups have taken to the courts in an attempt to force a public debate over value choices inherent in technological decisions, but the language of the law and the rules of the court are not always amenable to a thorough review of issues. Judicial decisions have given many citizens' groups an opening to fight technology's challenges to the environment, but more legislation is needed to bring science and technology under public control.

In another sector, government has begun to show interest in long-term planning and technology assessment. Technology assessment is a method for identifying and dealing with the implications of applied research. Through technology assessment processes, citizens can be informed of the impact and desirability of various technological developments taking place. Although methods of assessment are still in their infancy, new forms of technology assessment could place scientific decision making in the center of the political arena and make research priorities more explicit. Technology assessment must become a routine part of the political process, and concerned citizens and scientists should be given every opportunity to examine the merits of scientific research in an open forum.

Educating the public to participate in a politicized science means developing new channels of communication and emphasizing lifetime education. One such method of communication would be the practice of "adversary science." The format could be that of a courtroom-style forum in which the public serves as a jury. When an issue arises in the area of science and public policy, the entire matter should be aired in laymen's terms. For example, the merits of both fission and fusion reactors versus solar power should be thoroughly examined in public before further large investments are made. The Wisconsin DDT hearings in 1969 and the airing of scientific questions on the Public Broadcasting System's television program, "The Advocates," represent small beginnings in this direction. Greater efforts are needed and are possible if the media can be reformed along the lines suggested earlier.

In summary, there are three areas in which the social information system can be changed to facilitate a more general social transformation. Drastic changes in the nature of the educational system, including an alteration of the role of the university by opening it to community needs, would be a good beginning. Education must become a lifetime pursuit if citizens are to play an active role in managing the present complex industrial democracy. Adequate funding must be made available so that innovative and broadening programs of interdisciplinary education can be established.

At the same time, the mass media must be made responsive to the public, and the content of the media must be changed. Although pure entertainment is a legitimate function of radio and television, the intellectual and educational quality of the media could be upgraded while preserving entertainment value. The public can learn to appreciate educational programs, especially if good ones are offered during prime time. The role of educational television must be reassessed and funding must be made available so that important informational programs can remain on the air. The role of advertising on television must also be reevaluated and programming standards must be revised.

Finally, the scientific establishment must become more closely regulated by collective decision-making processes. Upgrading the educational system and revising the role of the mass media would prepare the public to play a much more active role in directing scientific activities.

In combination, such changes could help to halt a laissez-faire proliferation of technology and establish a more equal balance between science and society. Restoring the balance, however, means asserting the priority of social values over those of the scientific establishment. There is a pressing need for the establishment of social assessment panels to identify critical *social problems*. For example, decades were required for American society to recognize that discrimination was a serious social problem. New social indicators and methods of monitoring social conditions are clearly needed to develop a social technology that is comparable to the physical technology that now exists.

Most important of all, social priorities must be drastically altered to turn science inward to the study of man, his values, and his institutions. This area of inquiry will be vital to future survival, given the need to redirect human aspirations and consumption patterns. If social expectations and behavior are not altered, even the most earnest technological efforts will be unable to keep pace with growing human demands.

7

Sailing Troubled Waters: The International System

Historically, international considerations have played only a minor role in shaping American policies. The United States remained well isolated from the mainstream of world affairs until World War I. Geographically isolated from European intrigues, the United States possessed an open frontier with seemingly abundant land and natural resources and could look to growing markets for its products both at home and in the western hemisphere. There was little need to engage in trade in the world's resources, and there were few economic incentives to participate in international commerce to obtain finished goods. Throughout most of its history the United States was content to be left alone and to play policeman of the Caribbean. The struggle for colonies, markets, and resources could be left to the European powers in need of them.

Since World War II, the international posture of the United States has dramatically changed. World War II made the United States heir apparent to a position as a world power. The European nations were in ruin, and it would be more than a decade before they could get back on their feet. American corporations, having massively increased production during the war, stepped into the breach, supplying Europe with needed commodities and also picking up the slack in trade with less-developed countries (LDCs). Much of this postwar development was financed by the Marshall Plan and other forms of United States economic aid. As a result of the economic expansion thus afforded American industry, the United States emerged as a major international trading power, and the dollar became the accepted currency in international commerce. In the late sixties and early seventies, however, the United States has found itself in an increasingly uncomfortable position. European nations have recovered from the war and are offering the United States some real competition in the international marketplace. More important, the Soviet Union has also recovered from the war and has developed a military threat that has been taken very seriously by American military planners—perhaps a bit too seriously. Old alliance systems and balance-of-power arrangements have been upset as one nation after another has developed nuclear and thermonuclear capabilities. Isolationism is no longer a possibility for the United States or any other nation. But American policies do not yet fully reflect the new realities of the international system.

The seventies have brought the dawning realization that Fortress America does not have unlimited supplies of the resources that represent the building blocks of industrial civilization. Although the population of the United States represents only 6 percent of the world's population, it consumes nearly one-third of the total global production of natural resources. The United States is fast becoming dependent on other countries to maintain its present high levels of resource consumption. The domestic supply of natural gas is rapidly being depleted, and existing petroleum stocks will not be able to meet domestic needs for more than two or three decades. Today the United States is dependent on other nations for its supplies of manganese, nickel, platinum, tin, zinc, bauxite, beryllium, chromium, cobalt, and fluorspar. Between 1966 and 1970, the United States met more than half its domestic requirements with imports of these materials and imported more than 30 percent of its mercury, titanium, iron ore, and copper.

Relative to its chief international competitor, the United States is in a less-than-enviable position. A recent study has pointed out that, of the thirty-six minerals considered essential to industrial societies, the Soviet Union is self-sufficient in twenty-six and the United States is self-sufficient in only seven. The United States now supplies only 90 percent of its energy requirements with domestically produced fuels, whereas the Soviet Union exports considerable quantities of fuels and other resources. It is no wonder that the United States has been reaching outward to find new sources of raw materials and that the Nixon administration has put ideological considerations aside for some "businesslike" negotiations with the Soviet Union over natural gas reserves in Siberia.

The United States is not alone in facing these new resource problems; Western Europe and Japan are currently in a much more serious predicament. Almost all industrial nations are competing for the natural resources of the LDCs. At the same time, the economic gap between industrial nations and their resource suppliers continues to grow. The rich get richer while the poor struggle along, accumulating what capital they can from the sale of resources and meager handouts of "foreign aid." Thus, tensions between the rich and the poor continue to mount as third-world leaders come to realize that the development gap is widening rather than narrowing. Because of the time-lag in the perception of these new realities, however, the United States and other overdeveloped countries (ODCs) continue to behave as if they were living in a world that no longer exists.

The Increasing Costs of War

Conflict among nations did not spring from the industrial revolution. In fact, people have been quarreling and killing since the beginning of recorded history. There has been no substantial period during which there has been an absence of significant bloodletting on the face of the Earth. Economically speaking, few other activities have absorbed so much of mankind's time and energy.

The amount of destruction brought about by local quarrels throughout history is rather small by present standards. Before the advent of modern communications and transportation, most wars were restricted to limited geographical areas and were fought among a small number of adversaries. A century ago, conflicts like the Arab-Israeli wars, the Korean war, and the Vietnamese war would have been of concern only to the belligerent participants. Although the fighting might have been just as bloody as present-day hostilities, or even more so, the impact of such destruction on the rest of the world was relatively small.

The industrial revolution significantly changed the meaning, the extent, the costs, and even the causes of organized warfare. The present nation-state system has become economically interdependent and interconnected as new forms of transportation and communication have made the world a much smaller place. Local wars now send shock waves throughout the international system, and even minor conflicts can easily erupt into large-scale conflagrations. Weapons developments have made long-distance warfare and push-button destruction of entire civilizations a reality. The twentieth century has already produced two wars of sufficient magnitude to upset the entire international system; a third world war could preclude the possibility of a fourth. Today, five nations (France, Great Britain, the United States, the People's Republic of China, and the Soviet Union) have the power to wage war with nuclear and thermonuclear weapons. Many others (Japan, Israel, and India among them) are developing or could easily develop this capability. Other LDCs do not yet possess the technical sophistication to produce these weapons on a large scale, but they can compensate by developing bacteriological weapons–"poor man's H-bombs."

While the nature of warfare has been rapidly changing, possibilities for serious confrontations have increased. Today the interests of major powers more and more often intersect at remote spots around the globe. Industrial nations need food, natural resources, and foreign markets for their products. Only the Soviet Union, among industrial powers, approaches self-sufficiency in energy and resource production. Western Europe, the United States, and Japan must maintain access to supplies of vital materials in the less-developed areas of the world. The potential for dangerous confrontations among major powers in these areas will grow apace with their increasing need for energy and other resources.

In the old international system, each major power attempted to build security and maintain access to resources through the formation of complex alliances. With alliance systems of nearly equal strength, a rough "balance" of power could be maintained, and major powers were thus theoretically discouraged from initiating violence that could not be successfully concluded. The United States and other major powers found it in their self-interest to seek protection in numbers. No nation would be foolish enough to attack a strong alliance. In the present international system, however, such thinking has less validity.

In 1970 the United States was committed to mutual security pacts with no fewer than seventy-two nations. American policy makers did not realize that, after World War II, balance-of-power arrangements were becoming increasingly useless even as new allies were signing them. Asian allies such as South Korea, South Vietnam, and Taiwan have not proved to be a boon to the United States. Instead of adding to American power, alliances with small, unstable countries have committed American troops and American tax dollars to several brushfire wars, each of which could have led to an escalation and international conflagration. The probability that the United States will be drawn into more and more such conflicts will increase as the world economic situation deteriorates and as social revolutions in "allied" countries become more common.

Preoccupation with stability and the conclusion of military arrangements to ensure dependable access to resources has frequently led the United States to support politicians and political movements that seem opposed to announced American value preferences. Often these politicians have little domestic public support. Franklin Roosevelt expressed the American philosophy concisely when he remarked about one such leader, "Sure he's an S.O.B., but he's *our* S.O.B." The United States has supported some of the modern world's most corrupt and nonresponsive dictatorships, including Batista in Cuba, Chiang Kai-shek in Formosa, the Somoza family in Nicaragua, Salazar in Portugal, and Diem in South Vietnam. Popular actions against such dictators often become identified with "leftist" subversion, and these allies ask the United States to live up to treaty commitments and send in troops to oppose social revolutions.

For the present and the foreseeable future, international affairs must be so conducted that such confrontations and interventions in civil wars are avoided. In the post-Vietnam world, the notions of "winning" or "losing" a war no longer have any validity, and the number of military allies a nation possesses is meaningless. Everyone, perhaps most of all the United States and the Soviet Union, now realizes that any future conflict holds the seeds for a third world war and possible total destruction.

As with other aspects of the old world view, United States foreign policy is out of touch with the realities of the seventies. Strategists still insist on "thinking the unthinkable." Billions of dollars are spent on new weapons systems so that the United States will not "fall behind" the enemy. No one, of course, can explain how a nation can fall behind an enemy while possessing enough power to destroy him many times over. One sizable thermonuclear warhead, for example, could wipe out ten million Americans or Russians if it were dropped on the right target. Each nation possesses thousands of such warheads. No antimissile system now on the drawing board could begin to keep out all enemy warheads. Leaders both in the Soviet Union and in the United States nevertheless cling to obsolete definitions of security and pour billions of dollars into efforts to build the ultimate system. Yet, in this era of thermonuclear terror, life seems more insecure than at any other time in history.

Not only is thermonuclear war an impossible arbiter of disputes because of the tremendous destruction that would be wrought, conventional warfare is becoming practically outmoded because of the large quantities of resources and heavy cash outlays necessitated by military preparations and operations. When resources were abundant, there was little concern with the amount of fuel or metal that was needed to kill enemies. Today, however, no nation can afford both guns and butter for any length of time. The high cost of "security" can bankrupt even the world's strongest economy, and, indeed, seems to be doing so.

In the fiscal year 1970 the United States spent $76.5 billion on the military. This represented 6.5 percent of total gross national product–$373 for each American. Defense expenditures make up one-third of all federal spending and a much greater proportion of federal spending if social security payments are excluded from the computations. The United Nations has calculated that during the period 1967–1969, the United States spent 8.8 percent of its gross domestic product for the military, while only 6.1 percent was spent for education at all levels, both public and private. The Soviet Union spent an estimated $270 per person on the military in 1973 and devoted 6.7 percent of its gross domestic product to education. Expenditures for both military and education were somewhat lower than those of the United States.

Continued reliance on military preparedness as a major element of foreign policy will be even more costly in the future. Each F-4 fighter bomber now costs the American taxpayer $4 million, enough to pay the annual salaries of 300 teachers. Diverting this money from military expenditures could keep open one of the American school systems that have been forced to close for "lack of funds." Operation of each fighter plane costs more than $800 an hour. The even more expensive B-52 bombers cost taxpayers $1,300 for each hour spent in the air. Huge quantities of petroleum are burned each time one of these giants takes off on a mission. The demand for military jet fuel used in Asian adventures in late 1972 contributed to serious shortages of fuel for domestic airlines and eventually for automobiles. With each round of the arms race, equipment becomes more costly and security becomes more elusive. Each new tank now costs taxpayers $1 million; an aircraft carrier can cost as much as $1 billion. There is no longer any way that security can be technologically purchased by either conventional means of defense or nuclear weapons.

Analysis of such expenditures on a global scale reveals that the world spent nearly $150 billion directly on armaments in 1960. By 1970 direct defense spending had climbed to $203 billion. The United States was responsible for more than one-third of the total, and the Soviet Union followed close behind. The six biggest military spenders (the United States, the Soviet Union, France, the People's Republic of China, the United Kingdom, and Germany) accounted for four-fifths of all military spending. In 1970 the world spent nearly 6.5 percent of total world product on arms, which was 2.5 times the amount spent on education and 1.5 times the amount spent on health. From a statistical perspective the world would have to be classified as a "garrison planet." The irony of all this spending is that the vast quantities of military equipment produced will never be put to any useful purpose. Use of a significant proportion of it would mean suicide for mankind. Political and military leaders nevertheless remain trapped in their old-paradigm modes of thinking and continue their frustrating attempt to buy security with additional superweapons. Rather than moving toward new forms of cooperation—a social solution to an arms race that cannot be solved technologically—the major powers remain locked in a competition of military power. They seem bent on spending each other into oblivion and refuse to recognize the role that military spending and weapons proliferation play in perpetuating world poverty.

The Widening Gap

There are, of course, reasons other than fear and paranoia that maintain military spending at high levels. Many of them are economic and have been well documented in the literature on neoimperialism. Suffice it to say that many jobs in the ODCs depend on continued military spending and that the economies of these nations are ill-prepared to make a transition to a more peaceful world. In addition, as the costs of obtaining resources skyrocket during the next decade, military force may well become the winning hand in an imperialistic game in which the rich nations use their military strength to obtain resources from the LDCs. In 1973 Senator William Fulbright warned the United States Senate that the energy crisis might lead the United States, or its military surrogates such as Iran or Israel, to use force in obtaining what could not otherwise be obtained in the Middle East. Fulbright went on to state that there was little question that the United States could overwhelm the Arab countries by force and that it might be possible to have surrogates do it for us. Fulbright was alarmed by discussion in very high places that emphasized a role for United States troops in maintaining access to petroleum.

There is a growing belief in the ODCs that military force will be necessary to maintain the present stratified international system. This cold and "realistic" view of the world is predicated on the slight progress that the LDCs have made in their efforts to industrialize and the needs of ODCs for LDC resources to sustain their high standards of living. Conventional wisdoms tend to conceal the widening gap between the rich and the poor countries at a time when major problems of resource distribution are becoming critical. The press frequently uses the term "developing nations" to refer to those areas of the world that now supply the United States, Japan, and Western Europe with raw materials, but within the present system of international priorities there is no way that these nations can begin to close the gap between themselves and their overdeveloped trade partners.

United Nations statistics highlight the extent of the gap between the rich nations and the poor nations. Per capita gross national product represents a readily available crude measure of a nation's standard of living. Between 1958 and 1966, per capita GNP in the United States increased by $1,272, from $2,602 to $3,874. During this same period, per capita GNP increased from $110 to $160 in Africa, an increase of $50 per person. In Asia the corresponding increase was from $120 to $200, an increase of $80, deceptively large because Japan (hardly an LDC) is included in these figures. Similar statistics for Latin American nations show an average increase of $140 for the same period. These figures include no correction for inflation, which has been much more rampant in LDCs (especially those in Latin America) than in industrialized nations.

The LDCs are therefore moving very slowly, at best, toward attaining higher standards of living. Development over this eight-year period is measured in tens of dollars per capita. Although the figures are not precisely comparable because dollar increases tend to have more meaning at lower levels of development, it is clear that the huge absolute increase in GNP per capita in the United States dwarfs the $50 to $140 increases in the LDCs. No miracle is going to narrow this gap substantially without concerted action on the part of the ODCs. After all, if per capita GNP in the United States had *ceased growing in 1966* (it had increased by $880 to $4,754 by 1970) while that of the African nations continued to grow exponentially at the 1958–1966 rate, this gap could not be closed until after the year 2025. Optimistic estimates of LDC growth project a per capita GNP of only $363 for Africa, $328 for Asia, and $1,083 for Latin America by the year 2000. By that time per capita GNP in the United States is projected to be in the neighborhood of $10,000. Less-developed countries produced only 15.3 percent of global GNP in 1965.

Given current growth rates, these countries can at best be expected to produce 18.3 percent of global GNP by the year 2000; and by that time three-quarters of the world's population will be living in these countries.

With all the talk about a green revolution, the LDCs would surely be expected at least to have begun to narrow the gap in production of food, but they have not. Between 1963 and 1969, per capita food production grew by 4 percent for the world as a whole and by 9 percent in Western Europe. Food production in Africa actually *declined* by 5 percent on a per capita basis during this period. Latin America and the Near East exhibited no per capita increase in food production, and production increased by only 3 percent in the Far East, even though during the latter part of this period weather was excellent for global agricultural production. In the early seventies, bad weather once again caused serious drops in production in many countries.

These and countless other statistics indicate that, unless effective action is taken, the gulf between the rich and poor nations will continue to widen. To date there have been few political crises related to this growing chasm, because people in the LDCs as well as the ODCs have believed that "development" would somehow narrow it. This fiction will not persist much longer in a world where resources are in short supply. Although coalitions of the wealthy may be able to maintain power in the LDCs for a short time, revolutionary movements could well sweep them (and with them, United States interests) from power within the next decade.

In addition, as each ODC begins to feel the economic pressures brought on by resource scarcity, "new priorities" are likely to dry up what little aid is now channeled to the LDCs. Indeed, this process already seems to have begun in the United States. In 1965, according to United Nations sources, the United States transferred $5.2 billion in aid and long-term credits to less-developed areas. Of this amount, $3.2 billion represented governmental transactions of a bilateral nature. By 1969 total United States transfers had dropped to $4.4 billion, and governmental transactions had dropped to $2.9 billion. On a global scale, however, the transfer of funds from the ODCs to the LDCs showed a very small increase during this four-year period.

The gap between the rich and poor nations is certain to be a factor in increasing tensions in a two-tiered world of the future. The less-developed world will not be content to remain an economic colony of the United States, Western Europe, and Japan. As ODC puppets are replaced by more revolutionary leaders in these countries, there will be dramatic shifts in international alignments as well as major economic crises in the ODCs. The Arab world has begun to forge a common policy with regard to oil exports to the overdeveloped world. Saudi Arabia announced in 1973 that it would not expand production capacity to meet the petroleum needs of the United States until the United States changed its pro-Israeli foreign policy. The countries belonging to the Organization of Petroleum Exporting Countries (OPEC), which produces 80 percent of the world's oil, have become a potent force and have begun collective negotiations to obtain higher prices for their oil. These nations have already engaged in withholding actions for political-economic purposes. Several of these countries did not wait for collective action when they began cutting oil exports in October, 1973. Venezuela used the occasion to double taxes on exported oil.

As the strategies of the LDCs become more organized, these resource-rich nations will be able to fight the ODCs through boycotts, nationalization, and rising prices, although they cannot possibly prevail against the troops of NATO or the United States, should such troops be employed. Even while the Arabs have been overtly threatening future American interests, however, the United States has been trapped into supplying some Arab nations (Saudi Arabia and Kuwait) with billions of dollars' worth of advanced weapons. To refuse to supply these weapons now would have immediate resource repercussions, whereas to supply them means that there will be greater repercussions in the long run. But even if all or many groups of LDCs organize and attempt to withhold vital resources from the ODCs, there is little prospect for success. Furthermore, substantial numbers of the LDCs have no vital resources to withhold. At worst, resource manipulation could drag all nations down to the level of the poorest by leading to a nuclear or biological war. At best, such actions might throw the international system into a new era of colonial wars if ODC troops were sent in to pacify "revolutionary" forces in the LDCs.

Table 7.1 illustrates some important aspects of the international development gap and the related energy crisis. In this table, countries are arranged vertically according to levels of industrialization as indexed by per capita energy consumption. Horizontally, the table is divided into the "haves" and the "have nots," according to each nation's self-sufficiency in energy production. Those nations on the left side are relatively self-sufficient, whereas those on the right are very dependent on imports. The figures in the first two columns represent the ratio between energy resources produced and consumed in each country in 1965 and 1970. The third column shows the percentage increase or decrease in energy production between 1965 and 1970, an indication of recent discoveries or development of energy reserves. The fourth column lists per capita energy consumption in 1970. The last column

Table 7.1   *The World Energy Situation*

Resource "Haves"	Energy Production-Consumption Ratios		Percentage Increase or Decrease in Energy Production	Per capita Energy Consumption (kg of Coal Equivalent)	Percentage Increase in Per Capita Consumption
	1965	1970	1965–1970	1970	1965–1970
ODCs					
United States	.91	.90	26	11,128	21
Canada	.89	1.07	63	8,997	25
Czechoslovakia	.92	.87	8	6,274	12
East Germany	.84	.79	5	5,944	9
Australia	.74	1.00	77	5,374	18
Netherlands	.40	.74	190	5,080	48
U.S.S.R.	1.12	1.12	31	4,436	24
Poland	1.15	1.14	23	4,246	21
Developing Countries					
Rumania	1.18	1.04	34	2,808	42
South Africa	.89	.87	13	2,769	3
Venezuela	10.74	9.81	7	2,573	−3
North Korea	.97	.94	61	2,212	45
Argentina	.80	.89	45	1,686	21
Mexico	1.02	1.00	40	1,203	25
LDCs					
Iran	12.92	10.39	113	887	128
Saudi Arabia	53.85	36.41	75	827	126
Libya	165.22	166.67	176	647	130
Iraq	20.49	17.24	19	617	20
Colombia	1.86	1.63	15	602	12
China	.99	.98	23	522	14
Algeria	9.79	10.11	80	460	33
Syria	.00	1.90	916	457	−15
Egypt	.96	2.52	153	262	21
Tunisia	.02	4.06	269	259	21
India	.89	.86	17	189	8

Table 7.1   *(continued)*

Resource "Have Nots"	Energy Production-Consumption Ratios		Percentage Increase or Decrease in Energy Production	Per Capita Energy Consumption (kg of Coal Equivalent)	Percentage Increase in Per Capita Consumption
	1965	1970	1965–1970	1970	1965–1970
ODCs					
Sweden	.17	.10	−12	6,304	41
Belgium-Luxembourg	.43	.19	−42	5,955	26
Denmark	.04	.00	−93	5,862	43
United Kingdom	.69	.55	−15	5,358	5
West Germany	.74	.55	−5	5,151	21
Norway	.49	.41	17	4,813	35
Finland	.10	.06	1	4,177	82
Developing Countries					
France	.48	.31	−15	3,799	28
Bulgaria	.64	.48	21	4,021	56
Austria	.57	.42	−1	3,430	30
Switzerland	.19	.17	32	3,390	27
Japan	.35	.17	−12	3,215	80
Hungary	.76	.70	5	3,174	12
Ireland	.32	.28	20	2,994	33
Italy	.22	.18	29	2,685	49
Spain	.51	.32	−5	1,478	44
Yugoslavia	.85	.73	8	1,440	21
Greece	.26	.26	61	1,259	60
Chile	.72	.61	16	1,228	22
Cuba	.01	.03	263	1,090	9
LDCs					
South Korea	.81	.50	21	785	75
Portugal	.21	.15	4	687	38
Peru	.81	.70	15	630	15
Zambia	.03	.67	2133	515	5
Brazil	.41	.44	62	468	28
Turkey	.71	.64	41	429	22
Ecuador	.49	.18	−41	293	37
Philippines	.04	.03	00	291	39
Thailand	.04	.04	113	245	91
Guatemala	.01	.02	300	239	19
Dominican Republic	.01	.01	133	237	51
Ivory Coast	.04	.03	50	227	59

shows the percentage increase in per capita consumption between 1965 and 1970. The table indicates that few overdeveloped or developing countries remain even close to energy self-sufficiency; only a very few countries produce and export the greatest share of the world's energy resources. Significant among these, of course, are members of OPEC, recognized by their very high production-consumption ratios. Saudi Arabia, for example, produced approximately thirty-six times as much energy as was consumed domestically in 1970. In the same year, Iraq produced seventeen times and Iran produced ten times their domestic consumption.

Those countries with adequate energy resources generally exhibit substantial increases in energy production over time. In other words, the rich seem to be getting richer. The combination of high production-consumption ratios and increasing energy production indicates a favorable situation, at least in the short term. In general, energy production figures are highly correlated with production of other essential minerals, and those countries with inadequate reserves of petroleum and natural gas usually are also lacking in copper, iron, aluminum, and so on.

Scanning Table 7.1 reveals that, among the 15 ODCs, only the Soviet Union, Canada, and Poland are self-sufficient in production of energy and able to export it. Energy-exporting countries are found almost exclusively among the LDCs, the ODCs having expanded their industrial production well beyond levels that could be sustained by domestic resources. Western Europe, for example, is resource deficient and has been for some time. Western Europe imported 791 million metric tons (mmt) coal equivalent of energy in 1970. The amount of this imported energy is increasing every year. In 1950 Western Europe used 1.2 million barrels of petroleum daily. By 1970 consumption had reached 12 million barrels daily, and import costs were $9.5 billion yearly. By 1980 Western Europe will be consuming approximately 23 million barrels of petroleum daily and, of course, will be paying much more for each barrel. Of the 23 LDCs only 9 are net exporters of energy. With demand for energy increasing exponentially in the ODCs, prices will rise, and the resource-deficient LDCs could well be left out of the economic bargaining. Figure 7.1 summarizes world trade in petroleum and clearly reveals the LDC–ODC direction of flow.

A most critical situation is faced by resource-deficient countries. Most of the ODCs in this category have been experiencing a yearly *decrease* in energy production. These nations are going to find themselves in increasingly poor competitive positions as the price for fuels rises.

Less-developed countries lacking energy resources face another set of problems. Nations like the Philippines, the Dominican Republic, and Por-

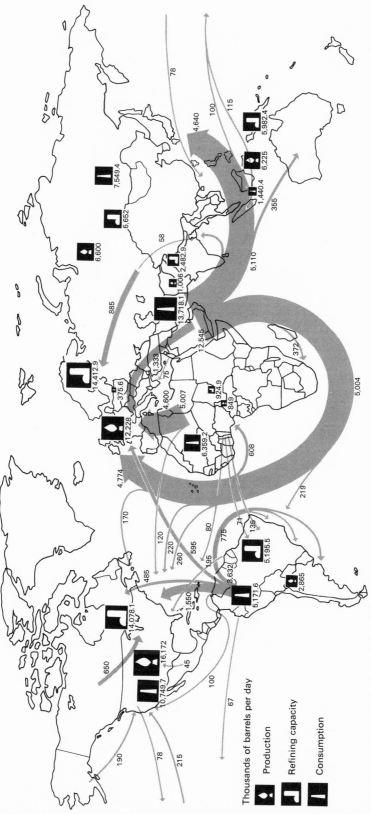

Figure 7.1 Worldwide patterns of oil production, refining, shipping, and consumption summarized from maps in the International Petroleum Encyclopedia. The data are for 1970. All quantities are in thousands of barrels per day. Export figures for eastern Europe, the USSR, and China refer only to exports from those areas to other parts of the world. The arrows indicate the origins and destinations of the principal international oil movements, not the specific routes. The U.S. is a heavy net importer. (From Luten, "The Economic Geography of Energy." Copyright © 1971 by Scientific American, Inc. All rights reserved.)

tugal have little hope for improving their economies without massive aid from the developed world. Unlike petroleum producers, they have little to exchange for technological assistance, and most of them have few minerals that are of interest to the industrial nations. These nations seem destined to remain in the ranks of the never-to-be-developed nations unless there is a large shift in international attitudes.

Most of the less-developed nations, although they are, politically speaking, no longer colonies, are still at the mercy of the ODCs. With the exception of the few that are rich in resources, there is not much that most of these countries can do to improve their lot substantially. Their economies were geared to serve the interests of the former colonial powers, especially to supply basic commodities like tin, sugar, copper, petroleum, and rubber. Rail and road networks were built to move commodities to seaports rather than to meet domestic needs. Furthermore, many of these countries have "one-crop" or "one-resource" economies and are badly in need of economic diversification. All these problems are exacerbated in areas where new national boundaries do not enclose logical economic (or ethnic) units. Such problems often reflect the result of past conflict and negotiation among European colonial powers, especially in Africa.

The situation is made more serious by competition among the LDCs themselves and by the relative inelasticity of demand for certain commodities, at least in the short run. Brazil, for example, can do little about the price of coffee. If Brazil withheld its coffee from the market, some other country would make up the difference and the Brazilian economy could collapse. Historically Brazilians have been plagued by one-crop surpluses, produced at enormous ecological and human cost. Cuba, with a surplus of sugar, offers another example. If the Soviet Union had not stepped in when the United States cut off sugar imports from the Castro government, the Cuban economy could well have collapsed. Chile is highly dependent on the export of copper, a large proportion of which goes to the United States. If the United States should choose to shop elsewhere, the Chilean economy could be devastated.

Aggregate data for the LDCs reveal that, for the average poor country, the principal export accounted for 44 percent of total exports in 1965. This was down only slightly from 47 percent in 1953. In North Africa the principal export accounted for more than one-half of all foreign trade. In the rest of Africa, the principal export accounted for exactly one-half of all trade. In the ODCs, the corresponding figure was only 14 percent of exports, indicating much greater trade diversification. In addition, the LDC portion of international trade is presently dropping, making it even more difficult for those countries to obtain needed capital goods. In 1950 the LDC portion of international trade was 31 percent. By 1969 it had dropped to 18 percent.

In many countries, particularly those where minerals are a chief export, this situation could change drastically by the year 2000 as the principal exports in these countries become more highly valued. For the time being, since there are still competing sources of supply, the world remains a buyer's market, and the LDCs are in poor financial position to resist the prices dictated by the "Rich Man's Club" in the ODCs.

Georg Borgstrom has pointed out that the net flow of protein in the world currently follows a path from the poor, protein-starved nations of the world to the rich, overfed nations. Seven units of protein move from the LDCs to the ODCs for every five that move in the opposite direction. Few citizens in countries like Japan, the Netherlands, Denmark, Great Britain, or even the United States realize the growing degree of dependency on food and mineral imports. The Netherlands, for example, has eighteen times the population density of the United States and is often used as "proof" that the United States could support a much larger population. Suffice it to say that the Netherlands is now the second largest per capita importer of protein in the world. It also imports all of its cotton, 77 percent of all wool consumed, all of its iron ore, antimony, bauxite, copper, gold, nickel, tin, zinc, phosphate and potash fertilizers, and a host of other essential resources. In 1969 the Netherlands also consumed 60 mmt of coal equivalent in energy but produced only 37 million tons. These figures would be even more out of balance were it not for North Sea gas discoveries.

The United States, although it is not nearly as dependent on imports as the Netherlands, is still "resource poor" when its production and consumption figures are compared. In 1968 the United States, with 6 percent of the world's population, consumed 61 percent of world production of natural gas, 53 percent of the world's silver production, 54 percent of the world's uranium production, 35 percent of the world's petroleum production, 40 percent of the world's lead production, and an average of one-third of world production of other important minerals. United States domestic consumption of many minerals was dependent on imports from abroad. Between 1966 and 1970, the United States imported 85 percent of asbestos used, 91 percent of all bauxite used, 85 percent of chromium, 90 percent of manganese, 90 percent of tin, and slightly smaller percentages of many other minerals used domestically.

Such statistics have important implications for future development gaps. Given current international patterns of resource consumption, there is *no way* that the LDCs can begin to approach the levels of living in today's ODCs.

Consider, for example, what would happen to world resource demands if consumption levels in the world's most populous country were brought up to the levels found in the United States. If the level of industrialization in the People's Republic of China could miraculously be increased to the point where each Chinese family possessed amenities similar to those available to families in the United States, the effect on the ecosphere would be catastrophic. There are now more than 750 million people in mainland China. This means that there are 3.5 Chinese for every American and that therefore China would consume resources at a rate 3.5 times the rate of the United States if the Chinese became "just like us."

In 1969 the entire world consumed 6.5 billion metric tons of coal equivalent in energy. The United States consumed 2.2 billion metric tons (11 tons per capita). This was approximately one-third of world consumption. The Chinese, on the other hand, consumed in the neighborhood of 400 mmt, approximately 6 percent of world consumption, or one-half ton per capita. Thus it "cost" the environment approximately 22 times as much to sustain one American as to sustain one Chinese in 1969.

This imaginary industrialization of mainland China would mean Chinese energy consumption of nearly 8 billion metric tons of coal equivalent each year, which is more than the *total* 1969 energy consumption of the world. Energy consumption is a reasonable indicator of overall environmental impact, and these figures therefore indicate that raising consumption levels in only this one country to those of the United States would double the human impact on an already strained ecosphere. Industrialized China would require 460 million tons of steel annually, which is two-thirds of present world production. And these annual "stay even" consumption figures do not take into account the tremendous investment in capital stocks that would be necessary to raise China to United States levels. For example, huge amounts of petroleum, steel, aluminum, and other materials invested in railroads, buildings, machinery, and other permanent artifacts would be required to make China capable of sustaining United States levels of production.

Bringing *all the nations* of the world to the American level of affluence would require a much bigger resource investment than that outlined for mainland China. To accomplish this, if world population growth had halted around 1970, the world's annual production of steel would have to be increased six times. Copper production would have to be increased sixfold, and lead production would have to increase by eight times. But these annual consumption figures are dwarfed by the requirements for "catching up"—the amount of minerals that would be needed to provide all the people on the globe with the stock of equipment necessary to sustain American production and consumption levels. To produce the per capita United States stock for the entire world would require mining 250 times the present United States annual production of tin, 200 times as much lead, 100 times as much copper, and 75 times as much zinc and iron. In theory the needed iron is still available, but its usefulness could well be limited by lack of molybdenum, which is required for the process that converts iron to steel. The needed quantities of other metals are much greater than *all* known or inferred reserves.

In summary, it is clear that cherished beliefs that the LDCs can some day catch up with the industrial countries are nothing more than myths propagated by the "haves" to keep the "have nots" in line. The data show that the gap between the rich nations and the poor nations is widening, not narrowing. Furthermore, leaders in the ODCs believe that they must deal with the LDCs from a position of strength, since the industrial countries are becoming increasingly dependent on them for oil and minerals to keep the wheels of industry humming. Indeed, if the LDCs unilaterally decided to cut off supplies of raw materials to the ODCs, economic collapse would ensue. During the Arab-Israeli crisis of 1970, Western Europe had only a sixty-day supply of petroleum in reserve.

The United States has traditionally enunciated major policy decisions in the form of such policies as the Monroe Doctrine and the Truman Doctrine, both of which served notice on other countries that there were certain territories and rights for which the United States was willing to fight. It is not at all unlikely that sometime in the 1980s the United States will announce a "Doctrine of Implied Supply." It may state that "a favor thrice conferred becomes an obligation" and that those countries that have been supplying the United States with vital fuels and raw materials must continue to do so or face military consequences. The reasoning behind such a doctrine, although it may now sound like tortured logic, would be that the United States has come to depend on certain suppliers to maintain present living standards. To deny the resources necessary to sustain these standards would be considered an act of war. Although this pronouncement may sound implausible now, within a few years it could become a reality, especially given the acceleration of pressures on conventional sources of fuels.

The United States and some parts of the overdeveloped world are dependent on the less-developed world not only for the energy and minerals necessary to sustain high living standards but also to sustain the dying expansionist economic paradigm. Economies of scale led to factories, to corporations, then to conglomerates, and eventually to huge multinational corporations. It was inevitable that billions of dollars of ODC investment capital would seek opportunities and new markets in the less-developed world. This would not have been an international and development problem except that the investments made in the LDCs do not result in any great increase in the industrial wealth of those countries. Rather, most of the profits make their way back to the countries in which stockholders in the multinational corporations live. And, in 1969, debt service payments, public and private, amounted to 70 percent of the money being lent to LDCs; within a few years the LDCs will be paying out more money in interest than they will take in.

To the multinational corporations, the less-developed world offers virgin territory for exploitation. Labor costs in these countries are low, unemployment is high, natural resources are close by, and, most important, the LDCs themselves offer a tremendous market for the products of these corporations. (At present the LDCs produce only 60 percent of the consumer goods they require, 45 percent of semifinished goods, and one-quarter of the required capital goods.) In a sense this represents a more gentlemanly economic extension of nineteenth-century colonialism. The multinationals set up operations in the LDCs, pay workers minimal wages, use indigenous natural resources, and repatriate large profits to the overdeveloped world. Admittedly, they may supply material goods to the local people, but many times they are precisely the products that these people could do without. Soft drinks, for example, are hardly a necessity for people living under conditions of extreme poverty.

One of the essential aspects of capitalism is that investors seek opportunities that offer the highest return on investment. In the present international system, this means that industries in the overdeveloped nations, facing market saturation at home, look greedily to the LDCs as future markets. Sometimes this means dumping less desirable merchandise abroad under the guise of "foreign aid agreements" or surplus military hardware "assistance programs," and sometimes it means market penetration by ODC firms and the generation of rising expectations through advertising.

The scale of multinational economic activity is already mammoth and is destined to increase in the absence of any effective controls on the international flow of investment capital. For example, if corporate sales were treated as "national income," 51 of the world's 100 biggest financial powers would be multinational corporations, and only 49 would be nation-states. Multinational corporations currently do approximately $500 billion worth of business on foreign territories. This represents about one-sixth of the gross world product. Thus, ITT, Ford Motor Company, IBM, Nestle, Leverhulme, and dozens of other corporations move unhampered about the globe in a never-ending search for new markets and new profits. In an international economic environment that resembles Garret Hardin's "commons," no authority exists to keep the multinationals in line. In fact, there are very few ways in which less-developed nations can protect themselves against exploitation by the multinationals without risking reprisals by the ODCs.

Large corporations, particularly those in Western Europe, have long realized that their future depends on obtaining raw materials from Africa and the Middle East. To do so, they must sell finished products to those countries to maintain a favorable balance of trade. United States industry has also come to see this more clearly as domestic resources no longer seem to be in unlimited supply. Merchandising campaigns are thus aimed at the LDCs to interest them in the fruits of industrial society. Coca-Cola bottles are found in almost all corners of the globe, and General Motors, Shell, Volkswagen, and ITT have become common symbols in virtually every capital, as corporations based in the industrial nations stretch out their tentacles and open up new markets. Little does it matter that the LDCs cannot afford the luxury of automobiles and other consumer goods and that the influx of such luxuries actually may hinder local development. The need among the ODCs to grow and invest eclipses concern for fostering rational patterns of consumption. This need contributes to a revolution of rising expectations in nations with plummeting prospects, a situation with which democratically elected leaders have difficulty coping. Thus, political instability is characteristic of many of the LDCs as the masses expect political leaders to be able to emulate ODC affluence and provide them with quantities of consumer goods.

Richard Barnet of the Institute for Policy Studies in Washington, D.C., claims that much post-World War II foreign policy can be explained by this desire to open up new markets abroad and protect American investments in those countries. According to Barnet, even the apparently "unselfish" Marshall Plan was consciously designed to benefit American industry. The plan was conceived to deny Western Europe to the Communists and to open up the area to United States business. At the time the Marshall Plan was being discussed, the Council of Economic Advisers quite openly warned that:

> Without new foreign aid Europe is threatened with starvation and disease.... Moreover, Europe would be forced into an entirely different character of production and a reorientation of trade. European resources would have to be organized in such a manner that all but the most essential imports from the Western Hemisphere would be dispensed with. This would have a detrimental effect on a number of our export industries which have been accustomed to considerable exports to Europe.

Barnet could be accused of some selective perception, although his basic thesis, that much apparently altruistic United States foreign policy has very clear roots in the needs of big business, seems to be valid.

American foreign aid also has frequently been used to compel receiving countries to buy American products. In 1966, 44 percent of all United States aid to developing areas was used simply to service previous debts, and more than 80 percent of the remainder was spent on American products. A substantial portion of American exports during the sixties can be directly tied to United States aid agreements, including 30 percent of total exports of fertilizer and railroad equipment and 24 percent of iron and steel products, all of which were not very competitively priced on the world market.

Exporting offers American industries a way of making profits now that the market for certain products has been saturated at home. "Between 1950 and 1964 United States commodity exports, including sales of overseas facilities of U.S. corporations, rose nearly 270 percent, while commodity sales at home increased only 125 percent. As could be expected, earnings on foreign investments make up a rising portion of after-tax profits—ten percent in 1950, and twenty-two percent in 1964."

Corporations based in the United States apparently reap good profits from their overseas activities. After-tax earnings for corporations with extensive multinational sales were 7.2 percent of sales in 1964. The comparable figure for top United States corporations without large overseas sales was only 5.9 percent. For those corporations not on *Fortune* magazine's list of the top 500, the profit level was only 3.1 percent. In 1946 direct foreign investment originating in the United States totaled only $7.2 billion, roughly the same as in 1929. Today the total foreign investment is ten times as large. American inflow of profits from investments abroad has exceeded capital outflow every year since World War II.

The flow of American and other ODC investment capital abroad, as well as the bombardment of LDCs with commercial propaganda, continues. Markets are opened in these countries to release the expansion pressures of ODC industry, and ODC advertising skill is the vehicle by which such markets can be created. The ODCs thus export their problems of overdevelopment to the rest of the world. The United States, in particular, exports an "American way of life," including the outrageous habits of consumption that have led directly to serious environmental deterioration and exponentially increasing consumption of a large share of the world's nonrenewable resources. All overdeveloped countries have, of course, pursued such policies, but major responsibility for these activities since World War II rests with the United States.

The International Tragedy of the Commons

We thus find a "tragedy of the commons" in the international system. Most of the countries of the world need more resources today and will demand even greater quantities tomorrow. These resources must be drawn from what may be considered a global resource commons. Resource deposits are uneven, and their distribution tends to be unrelated to political boundaries or to the distribution of human population. Many of the most densely populated countries have relatively small resource endowments. The rich nations, because of their long histories of industrial development, have depleted their domestic resource bases and are now exploiting the resources still available in poor nations. If the less-developed world could successfully industrialize, the result would be loss of markets as well as a possible loss of resources for the overdeveloped countries. Therefore, the ODCs compete for LDC markets, each competitor being determined to milk as much profit as possible from the situation before the present arrangement collapses.

An international tragedy of the commons also is taking place through exploitation of oceanic fish stocks and exploitation of petroleum reserves under the continental shelf. Many nations, including Japan, the Soviet Union, and the Scandinavian countries, are heavily dependent on protein from the sea and have developed increasingly efficient methods of harvesting the world's fish populations. In keeping with the tragedy of the commons, it is apparently in each fisherman's own interest to get as much of the fish catch as possible, using finer and finer mesh nets in the process. There is no social conscience or even "mutual coercion mutually agreed upon" in this international commons. Similarly, at the national level each nation pushes its territorial boundaries further out to sea in hopes of claiming more fisheries and seabed resources for itself.

The results of lack of control over the international commons are apparent in the whaling industry. Since World War II, in spite of repeated warnings and accurate predictions of the biologists hired by the International Whaling Commission, the nations engaged in whaling have systematically hunted many of the largest species of whales until they are on the verge of extinction. The recent history of the whaling industry might lead to the conclusion that the owners of the fleets have been incredibly stupid, since they seem willing to jeopardize the entire future of their industry for quick profits. The decisions that have led to wide-open hunting of whales are nevertheless rational to those who made them. More money can be made by hunting whales to extermination now and then investing the profits in other enterprises. This is merely another example of how unfortunate long-run consequences of present behavior are ignored by profiteers who exploit the commons.

The inability of mankind to establish controls over use of the ocean has already resulted in overfishing of approximately one-half of the exploitable fish stocks. It has also led to a massive assault on the capacity of the oceans to absorb wastes without undergoing irreversible and, from man's point of view, catastrophic changes. Because of the heavy dependence of humanity on the oceans for high-quality protein, a sharp decline in productivity of salt-water fisheries could lead to a calamity of unprecedented magnitude. The integrity of oceanic ecosystems must be recognized as a matter of vital concern to all nations.

The oceanic commons does not exist in isolation but has a large interface with another commons, that of the atmosphere. The ocean, for instance, contributes 100 million billion gallons of water to the atmospheric commons annually in the form of evaporation and receives 91.5 million billion gallons back in the form of rain. The difference, 9.5 million billion gallons, falls as rain on terrestrial areas and is the basic source of the world's freshwater supplies. Needless to say, it is absolutely essential to prevent any of the pollutants now being added to the oceans from significantly altering this moisture cycle, for the world is also facing a widespread shortage of fresh water.

Pollution of the atmosphere also affects the oceans. For instance, clouds formed from the contrails of jet aircraft flying over the North Atlantic have been suspected of reducing photosynthesis in the oceans beneath air corridors.

Many pollutants reach the oceans through runoff from the land, especially via rivers. Any effective control of the oceanic commons also requires control of activities on the land. In short, mankind can no longer afford to treat any part of the ecosphere as a common garbage dump. The rate at which resources are mobilized, whether they be copper, fish, petroleum, or timber, must be of international concern; so must the rate at which pollutants are released into soil, fresh water, the atmosphere, or the oceans.

Dust raised by poorly designed and often overly intensive agricultural systems in both underdeveloped and developed countries affects the weather of the entire planet; so do the smoke of both industry and agriculture and the building of cities and highways. Pesticides sprayed in Japan can affect the complexity of California's ecosystems. The dumping of industrial chemicals into the Rhine by Germans can reduce the yields harvested by English fishermen. Smoke from England can increase a Swede's chance of dying of emphysema. Nuclear weapons tests in China or Polynesia blanket the globe with radioactive fallout. The escalating energy demands of the overdeveloped nations lead to oil exploration that destroys the way of life of Alaskan Eskimos and desert tribesmen and to oil spills that threaten the ecology of the seas.

Thanks to the nature of the planet's ecological systems, the nations of the world have intertwined fates, a fact that they consistently fail to recognize. The global ecosystem is now suffering under the impact of many past decisions made by overdeveloped nations. A partial solution to contemporary problems would be to convince the leaders of wealthy nations that traditional types of development are now becoming impossible for the LDCs because of actions taken in the past by the ODCs and that, therefore, new types of aid and development will be necessary. The accessible (and inexpensive) resources the ODCs have consumed will not be available for future industrial development in poor nations.

The fate of the world's life-support systems, however, rests in the hands of many individual actors, and there are no institutions within the present international system capable of dealing with this most serious of all international problems. Obviously, these problems could best be handled by a strong and rejuvenated United Nations or similar successor organization, but it still appears unlikely that the major powers would support an international agency with significant enforcement power.

Turning Liabilities into Assets

The attitudes and accepted values that presently shape international politics certainly will not be transformed overnight. Unlike many other aspects of the accepted world view, they are not necessarily the products of the industrial revolution. The overdeveloped as well as the less-developed countries are guilty of dealing with other countries mainly in terms of self-interest. These attitudes existed long before factory chimneys began to dominate the landscape. Nations have been dealing with each other from positions of power and in a spirit of distrust since they came into being.

Two world wars, a costly "police action" in Korea, and a seemingly interminable struggle in Indochina have led many Americans to question some of the fundamental principles that now guide American foreign policy. Revulsion at the destruction and carnage that follow major wars leaves people ripe for change. After the destruction wrought by World War I, concerned nations formed the League of Nations to avoid a repetition of the slaughter. The League failed in that task, largely because of lack of United States support and the desire of the other nations to punish Germany. After the horror of World War II, the United Nations was formed to ensure that bloodshed would not be repeated. For the first two decades following its establishment, the United Nations was dominated by the United States and a few other developed nations, but the admission of many new members, including the People's Republic of China, has altered the balance. The United Nations no longer acts as an auxiliary agent of the United States government. The United States is deserving of some credit because it has continued to supply a major portion of United Nations financial support, even though it has not recently been willing to strengthen the United Nations by submitting all disputes to that organization's judgment since a favorable outcome is no longer assured.

The human and economic costs of the Vietnam tragedy have recently led Americans to question the link between lofty expressed principles of foreign policy and its recent implementation. The American people supposedly believe in self-determination for all peoples, but apparently only when such self-determination leads to outcomes favorable to American policy. The United States covertly refused to recognize the right of the Vietnamese nation to govern itself and stood steadfastly against nationwide elections that were originally scheduled as part of the Geneva Accords. In South Vietnam the United States backed one dictator after another and stood by and watched General Thieu (our S.O.B.) destroy all political parties but his own. Policy makers in the United States claim to believe in disarmament but continue to demand numerical superiority over the Soviet Union in nuclear weapons. The "peace-loving" government of the United States turns out to be the only superpower directly involved in a protracted war since the Korean conflict. The doublethink inherent in United States policies was clearly revealed by Secretary of Defense Melvin Laird in 1972 when he explained that the indiscriminate Christmas bombing of Hanoi was undertaken because "we believe that to attain a generation of peace certain risks must be taken." It would be difficult to argue that American international behavior since World War II has been more peace-loving than that of other nations. Nor can it be argued that this behavior can be traced to the corruption of a particular administration. The United States, through both Democratic and Republican administrations, has acted in its own perceived self-interest, and even this perception has been terribly misguided.

The losses incurred by acting in accordance with the old view of the world are not unrecognized by a nation that is sick of pouring billions of dollars and thousands of lives into dubious military ventures in foreign lands. Even the United States Congress reacted very strongly in 1973 in cutting off funds for bombing in Southeast Asia. The American people seem ripe for a change in foreign policy, but constructive alternatives have not been offered by either of the major political parties. The time has come for a new foreign policy, one that does not confuse national security with world domination.

A beginning might be made by emphasizing the errors in the assumption that the good of each nation can be separated from the good of all mankind. Before the advent of nuclear weapons, resource pressures, and rapid international communication, this belief had some validity, but today the fates of all nations, large or small, are inextricably intertwined. When the Arabs and Israelis confront one another, the major powers watch with nervous anticipation. A Marxist electoral victory in Latin America spoils cocktail parties in Washington. Liberalization in Czechoslovakia leads to a potential East-West confrontation in Eastern Europe. Declarations of unity by the OPEC send economic shivers through Western Europe. Growing numbers of discontented individuals struggling to extract the most from a finite international commons, bathing in each others' wastes, breathing each other's factory exhausts, and threatening each other's lives and health are proof of the necessity of moving to a new and more enduring international model based on the principle of the unity of all mankind.

Needed changes must take place very rapidly by international standards. There is little time to wait for a new system to "evolve" to replace the one that exists. Tiny steps in the right direction—treaties to keep nuclear weapons from outer space and off the seabed, the SALT talks, public relations visits to Moscow and Peking by American presidents—are useful, but they also tend to lull mankind into a false sense of security. Such incrementalism does not address the basic problems facing mankind, such as the inequitable distribution of wealth, the growing gap between the rich and poor nations, growing populations and rising expectations, shrinking resource reserves, and environmental deterioration.

The United States can and must act unilaterally on a number of issues because it is important to international stability that the world's most overdeveloped and most powerful nation seize the initiative in international affairs. But this time seizing the initiative must mean serving as a model for other nations by acting to benefit all mankind, rather than simply throwing military and economic weight around for its own benefit. The American people like to believe that the United States acts in a moral and rational manner, and there is no question that the United States has frequently acted at least partly out of such considerations, as it did after

World War II in helping to rebuild shattered economies. But much-needed third-world development programs will not coincide as closely with the pure economic self-interest of the United States as they did after World War II.

It is in the self-interest of the United States to set such a moral example for other ODCs, for Americans will have the most to lose in a tumultuous future. The United States will feel the pinch of shrinking resource reserves long before the Soviet Union or the People's Republic of China. American corporations will be among the first to be confiscated as nationalistic leaders seize properties belonging to "neoimperialist" powers. And, if there is no change in its perspectives, the United States can expect to see its position of world leadership continue to deteriorate as one former ally after another becomes disillusioned with American policies.

Self-interest alone would dictate a new approach to international relations, but such an approach would be viewed in a better light if the United States were able to make such adjustments because of the visionary and generous qualities of the American people. Whatever the justification, however, some very fundamental principles should be understood. *First,* the United States cannot go on consuming one-third of the world's yearly resource output indefinitely. Drastic readjustments will have to be made in patterns of consumption as reserves shrink and demands from the third world for more resources rise. *Second,* some portion of the future potential wealth of industrial countries will have to be transferred to the less-developed areas if international stability is to be maintained. *Third,* maintenance of peace and stability will be increasingly difficult, and this can be better accomplished by winning over the minds of people with new ideas and good examples, rather than by dominating their bodies with the pressure of military force. Future political alliances cannot be held together by economic blackmail; consensus will become much more important. The idea that thermonuclear threats are a guarantee of future stability must be discarded and replaced with a politics of compromise and idealism. It is obvious that even so-called second- and third-rate powers will soon possess the requisite technology (nuclear or bacteriological) to threaten the major powers. The only sensible defense against Armageddon is the establishment of an atmosphere of compromise, trust, empathy, and progress for *all* in the international system.

The ideas outlined in the following paragraphs represent the beginnings of a program to achieve these new ends in foreign policy. Within the old model of international thinking, they might well be considered outrageous or unworkable. They are, however, in keeping with America's professed tradition of altruistic behavior and generous treatment. They might find favor among a war-weary populace, but whether this populace has the interest, the power, or the will to encourage its leaders to act in behalf of all mankind, or whether these leaders are willing to take initiatives themselves, remains to be seen.

A Development Quarter

Although it may seem to contradict the arguments against resource consumption advanced in the rest of this book, a most crucial task for the next decade is to *develop* the economies that are presently on the "wrong side" of the development gap. Leaders of LDCs cannot realistically be expected to refrain from seeking a better life for their ill-housed and ill-fed people. Greater strains will, of course, inevitably be placed on the world's heavily taxed supply of nonrenewable resources as well as its agricultural production. The United States nonetheless should take the initiative and declare the last quarter of the twentieth century a development quarter for the LDCs. The United States could pledge not to increase its consumption of any of the basic and scarce resources during that twenty-five year period and to reduce consumption wherever possible.

The development quarter should concentrate not only on developing the economies of the poor countries but also on reorienting economic priorities in the rich countries. An alteration in the prevailing patterns of resource utilization will be essential for any narrowing of the development gap. To be realistic, the idea of drastically reorganizing advanced industrial economies will not appeal to those still unconvinced of the severity of the alternatives. At the present time, few can be expected to support a program that encourages them to consume less. Ecological realities dictate that, at the very least, however, the industrialized countries refrain from escalating their impact on the ecosphere and reorient their resource priorities while the LDCs increase their standards of living. It is also essential that the LDCs develop industries that are less resource intensive and that they not slavishly follow the heavy industry path that has been chosen by today's ODCs.

To meet the challenge of world poverty, the present developmental gap must be narrowed by a three-pronged effort. First, the industrial countries must cease increasing their consumption of the world's scarce and non-renewable resources. Second, in addition to an alteration of the world's lop-sided pattern of resource consumption, there must be a massive transfer of development capital from the ODCs to the LDCs. Finally, rising expectations in both ODCs and LDCs must be dampened. This, of course, includes enlisting support for programs of population limitation to hasten a demographic transition in the LDCs. Citizens of industrial countries must learn to live within slowly growing economies and to base their consumption patterns in part on concerns for international equity. There is little point in drumming up demand in the LDCs for energy-consuming products that 90 percent of the people could never hope to own. Therefore, market penetration and international advertising by ODC firms should be restricted. Instead, these firms should be encouraged to manufacture and promote products that are needed and useful in the LDCs, and, as far as possible, to manufacture those products in the LDCs also.

Closing the development gap will be impossible without a reconsideration of priorities on the part of the LDCs as well. They must give up their ideas of emulating the industrial giants, they must solve problems of corruption inherent in the "soft state" left over from colonial days, and they must forge a unified approach toward developmental goals and toward the industrial world.

Many leaders of the poor countries now have their minds set on repeating the mistakes that have been made by overdeveloped nations. They want polluting steel mills, automobile factories, and other types of heavy industry. They want to free themselves of dependence on the ODCs for manufactured goods and even to compete with the ODCs in some markets. It will be virtually impossible for a significant number of the LDCs ever to become industrialized along traditional lines for reasons that have been previously discussed. If, by some miracle, the job did get done, humanity would have to pay a terrible price in terms of environmental destruction.

It is possible for the nonindustrial areas of the world to enjoy the necessities produced by factories without building these factories themselves, but this requires a social and political solution, one designed to change the structure of international trade and traditional concepts of profit. The Marxist law of uneven development must be turned on its head. The overdeveloped world must begin supplying essentials to the LDCs at or near cost and forsake the profits to be gained by the exploitation of less-developed nations. Perhaps the governments in the ODCs could adopt policies that would facilitate sale of essential finished products at cost by subsidizing such sales through grants to ODC industries. This would help ease economic and unemployment burdens in ODCs and would also result in much more favorable terms of trade for the LDCs. The whole process could be aided by rising resource prices toward the end of the development quarter. At present, natural resources are priced extremely low in relation to the price of finished goods. In fact, in the late fifties and early sixties, the developed nations were able to depress prices of LDC commodities by as much as 13 percent, a situation that is now being altered by increasing resource scarcity.

The LDCs do not require many of the trinkets that seem to be essential in the overdeveloped areas of the world, and an immediate problem that can be tackled is setting new developmental priorities. Poor countries need effective mass transit and freight systems, bicycles, small motor scooters, farm-to-market roads, pest-proof storage facilities, and fertilizer plants. Most of them will have to depend on agriculture as a major source of income simply because they lack domestic deposits of minerals and fuels. Thus, leaders of LDCs might well consider moving in new directions and developing new types of societies that are not heavily dependent on consumption of material goods.

New satisfactions might be found in new forms of interpersonal relations, meditation, and appreciation of the natural environment, as well as turning inward to personal development rather than outward to the material world. In many countries this would simply mean reinstating traditional life-styles that have been displaced by the industrial onslaught. It might result in a reversal of the "flow of expertise and assistance" from the industrial world to the less-developed world as leaders in the LDCs shaped new types of societies in which personal satisfactions were more suited to the ecological realities of the future. The LDCs might then assist the ODCs in coming to terms with their own problems.

In an oversimplified analogy, the world today can be viewed as one in which a few wealthy people drive powerful automobiles and a lot of poor people walk but *want* powerful automobiles. Ways must be found to change this picture to that of a world in which everyone does some walking but may also have a motor scooter; where some people have small economical cars, many people ride on trains and buses, but nobody has or really desires a powerful automobile.

The second problem for the LDCs to solve revolves around what Gunnar Myrdal describes as the "soft state." Corruption and incompetent leadership plague many LDCs just as much as they plague the ODCs, but the LDCs can little afford this kind of political drain. In 1968 the Indian Minister for Foreign Affairs and Labor, S. Rajaratnorm, described the prevalent form of LDC government as "kleptocracy." He stated:

> It is amazing how otherwise excellent studies on development problems in Asia and Africa avoid any serious reference to the fact of corruption. It is not that the

writers do not know of its existence but its relevance to the question of political stability and rapid economic development appears not to have been fully appreciated. It may also be that a serious probing of the subject has been avoided lest it should offend the sensibilities of Asians.

The lot of the poor nations will not easily be improved as long as they are victimized by their own leadership. In poor countries the inequitable division of the available wealth hurts even more than in the wealthy countries because the amount is so much smaller.

The third problem is that of unity. Solidarity of the third world exists primarily in the minds of members of the New Left. Lack of unity has been a major cause of the failure of the Arab nations in their military struggles with Israel and the inability of the OPEC at first to bargain effectively with oil-consuming nations. Africa has been torn by rivalries and wars of tribal origin. "Peace-loving" India has repeatedly gone to war with Pakistan, and both of these hungry nations have wasted inordinate amounts of their limited resources on weapons. India has even been reported to be giving "nuclear weapons serious thought in the framework of the nation's security needs." Since the mid-sixties, military expenditures in LDCs have increased much more rapidly than in the ODCs, and such expenditures frequently have exceeded expenditures for health and education.

As long as the LDCs continue to squabble among themselves, it will prove extremely difficult for them to negotiate needed changes in the world trade system from a position of strength. The LDCs must begin to organize into regional and transregional entities to increase their political and economic bargaining power, as well as to facilitate regional approaches to development. Small steps in this direction have been attempted in the past and have failed. A great deal of the fate of the LDCs (and of the world) will rest on how successful these efforts are in the future.

Although a unilateral declaration of a development quarter is desirable, the United States also should attempt to negotiate with other overdeveloped nations a multilateral pact governing future consumption of resources. These international initiatives could be closely linked to development of a steady-state economy in the United States. Other countries would be encouraged to face up to their own resource constraints by a move to limit American consumption, and pressures would undoubtedly grow, particularly among the LDCs, for an international agreement establishing maximums for per capita consumption of key resources, perhaps based on 1976 United States standards. It is possible that other industrial nations would undertake to institute limited steady-state economies of their own at levels of resource consumption lower than those now prevailing in the United States. Undoubtedly such a-greements would be for a limited period, perhaps for the first decade of the development quarter, at the end of which the United Nations and each individual nation would reassess the situation. The important point is that these initiatives and "social solutions" would start the ball rolling and once again would give the United States moral leadership in international affairs.

The modified steady-state economy proposed for the United States should include an agency that controls resource purchases on the world market and superintends their domestic distribution. The agency would sell resources destined for the free market to the highest bidder. In a free-market situation, the prices of resources would rise in the face of high domestic demand and constant levels of supply. The resource distribution agency would thus fall heir to a considerable amount of money—eventually billions of dollars—representing the gap between prices paid on the world market and prices paid in the United States after free-market bidding.

In keeping with the spirit of the development quarter it would be only fitting to pledge a healthy portion of this revenue, perhaps 50 percent, to a fund for international development. This type of aid would certainly be less painful and more politically palatable than schemes that have been suggested for an outright transfer of a percentage of GNP to LDCs. It would not come from tax revenues; rather it would be a hidden tax reflected only in the pricing of resource-intensive items and would represent a relatively painless way of repaying the LDCs for years of resource exploitation.

Such a program would be of limited usefulness unless parallel institutions could be established to channel funds effectively to the LDCs. It is important that the organization responsible for allocating development funds be es-tablished not by the ODCs but by the LDCs themselves, perhaps under the auspices of the United Nations. The United States should offer to turn development funds over to such an organization as soon as one is established. Within this agency the LDCs could establish their own developmental priorities without being forced to take into consideration the wishes of the ODCs. The LDCs would thus be forced to confront their problems of cooperation.

Although the LDCs alone should determine the structure of this agency, it could eventually become a body dedicated to planning for global develop-ment rather than the development of only one set of nations. Membership in the organization might be made available to all nations, but the decision-making system should certainly give the most voting power to those countries in greatest economic need. Organization of such a system would be one challenge for the LDCs that their enlightened self-interest might permit them to meet successfully.

Other industrial powers might be enticed (or blackmailed) to follow the example set by the United States and channel development funds through the third-world agency. Perhaps these transfers would be in the form of outright grants, or perhaps they would result from the establishment of "partial" steady-state economies in the other ODCs. Regardless of the manner in which they were given, however, significant grants of capital could be made to the agency as pressures grew for more development funds to offset debt repayment. The most important point is that the agency would be under the control of the LDCs, and therefore only a minimal role would be played by donor countries.

As the agency became more established, members would find it useful to make developmental goals explicit. For example, the use of developmental funds for armaments should certainly be prohibited, and aid should be cut off from any country that in any way used development funds to accelerate arms procurement. Violations would be determined by other third-world countries. This sanction should prove highly effective in blocking wasteful arms races in the LDCs if the agency were prompt and fair in its application. The LDCs might also wish to dedicate themselves to funding greater numbers of projects in those countries that made the greatest strides in reducing domestic income differentials between the rich and the poor. Whatever the goals of the third-world agency, the members should make them explicit and should use the development fund to build a socially just world *according to their own definitions.*

Obviously, the United States and other industrial countries would maintain some control over development funds, but this control would rest entirely on a decision to give or not to give. Countries that controlled the purse strings ultimately would have a final veto over expenditures, but within the development agency the important day-to-day investment decisions would be made by agency members. With proper organization, considerable pressures could be applied by the development agency to any ODC desiring to withdraw funding. For example, if the United States unilaterally decided to cut off funds, the OPEC might retaliate by denying petroleum to the United States.

There is another source of development funds that might well become important over time. Mankind has just begun to exploit the resources of the ocean floor. The nations of the world could agree by treaty to impose international supervision over seabed and oceanic resources. An agency of the United Nations could administer the ecologically sound development of seabed projects and could be empowered to license corporations to undertake them. This agency would have the difficult task of calculating total costs and benefits of various kinds of exploitation of the oceanic commons and pricing the resources thus extracted. For instance, it might attempt to estimate the threat to oceanic fisheries represented by the recovery of a given amount of oil or manganese and then determine the price that should be charged for these resources. The revenues from mining of the seabed could be dedicated to the development of the third world.

The likelihood of the conclusion of such an agreement will doubtless increase as the need for seabed supervision becomes apparent. The oceans already are threatened by industrial wastes. Pollution problems will become much more serious as large-scale mining and drilling are undertaken by resource-hungry countries. Unless some agreement is reached, open resource warfare may occur, leading to rapid deterioration of oceanic ecosystems. An economic incentive for the LDCs would encourage their support for such a treaty, and the combination of self-interest and growing environmental concern might well make the signing of such an agreement inevitable.

The plan outlined in the preceding paragraphs can be expressed only in very general terms at this time. Much refinement would have to be done by diplomats and economists before any accords could take shape, and a fundamental change of the attitudes of industrial nations would be necessary. The important thing is not that the future international system unfold precisely as suggested here but that the United States seize the initiative in moving toward an international system in which such fundamental shifts in perspective become possible.

A New Type of Security

There are many immediately practical initiatives that can and should be taken by the United States to increase international security. As the most overdeveloped and overarmed country in the world, the United States is the only country that can take them. There is no reason that per capita military expenditures in the United States should remain at their current insane level. Such paranoia not only leads to needless exhaustion of resources and perverted priorities at home, it also creates pressures for military adventurism and arms races in all corners of the world. A country that relies on military strength to maintain a position of world dominance in the future will find its position slowly eaten away. Vietnam could be only the first in a series of tragedies that might take place, should the United States ignore these obvious lessons.

Since the Korean war, the United States has increasingly gambled its future on the efficacy of nuclear deterrence. It is important to understand the flaws in deterrence theory. Most people assume that deterrence really works, that the only reason the United States has not been reduced to nuclear ash is that the Russians and Chinese are afraid of nuclear retaliation. The underlying principle is simple: It would be suicidal for anyone to attack the United States because the United States can destroy the attacker. But the premise that underlies deterrence theory is that men and their governments can be depended on to act rationally—a shaky assumption at best.

There is a long list of examples of irrational behavior that have occurred over the years in international affairs. Before the sixties, who would have thought that "rational" American leaders would commit the United States to a ten-year land war in Asia, particularly after watching the French experience in Vietnam? Who would have predicted that President Nixon would try to raze Hanoi, completely ignoring the condemnation of almost the entire world community, or that he would bomb Cambodia to protect a dictator from his own people? Would anyone have considered it rational for the North Vietnamese to hold out for so long while their country was being slowly destroyed from the air? Who would have considered it a rational act for Nikita Khrushchev to send missiles to Cuba? There are presently no guarantees that the Chinese would be unwilling to absorb very substantial nuclear destruction if, for instance, the integrity of their border with the USSR were involved. All that is needed is one irrational or unstable leader for deterrence theory to fall apart. And recent political history has been spiced with many examples of highly unstable leaders. Some observers even claim that political leaders must be psychopathic just to weather the selection process and that only an obsessed man can go through the rigors of campaigning or conspiring for high office in any country.

Deterrence enthusiasts now have developed computerized detection and launch systems so that retaliatory strikes can be ordered when enemy warheads first appear on radar screens. Civilization's fate might rest with a computer, the ultimate in supposed rationality and lack of discrimination. Today, with human beings still in the system, the world's safety rests on "fool-proof" fail-safe procedures. It is useful to remember the maxim credited to the father of the H-bomb, Edward Teller: "The fool will always prove greater than the foolproof."

In the face of such risks an appropriate question to ask might be whether a different set of risks might be substituted for those inherent in the old international paradigm. This new set of risks would demand winding down the arms race rather than winding it up. Twenty years of nuclear and thermonuclear "progress" have failed to make anyone more secure. It makes a great deal of sense to take the initiative in breaking out of the arms race entirely, although the United States need not opt for unilateral disarmament. It should, however, take unilateral action to stop deployment of new weapons systems and challenge other countries to follow suit.

One possible disarmament proposal might call for the cutting of United States military spending by 10 percent each year and urge the Soviet Union to do the same. The United States could also announce a freeze in the deployment of new weapons and enter into expanded SALT talks with the avowed aim of reducing military strength rather than simply agreeing to curb arms excesses. International pressure could be put on the Soviet Union to respond, and Kremlin leaders might welcome such a proposal as a method of freeing funds for more consumer goods. Even if there were no immediate results, the risk factor would be so small as to be negligible. There would still be plenty of nuclear punch left in the United States arsenal to satisfy militaristic critics.

Most important, such actions must be linked with a resolve to untangle the United States from the affairs of other countries. *Pax Americana* has become outmoded, and the costs of imposing it have become prohibitive. The only interests now served by the vast military establishment are those of American industry and the various cliques that are being supported in Vietnam, Taiwan, and other United States outposts around the globe. It is ridiculous to ask each American taxpayer to cough up $380 in defense spending every year so that policymakers can continue to wield the big stick in world affairs.

A giant step forward would be taken if the United States were to announce support of peaceful resolution of all disputes through the United Nations and a policy of self-determination for all nations, regardless of their chosen political and economic systems. It is impossible to impose the "American way" on people who have no desire to be so blessed and who more often than not loathe the United States for its attempts. Real security can come from abstaining from military involvement with others just as readily as it can come from an open-ended arms race.

This would permit substantial reductions in Pentagon spending to well below the $60 billion level proposed in the Urban Coalition's *Counterbudget*. Such a cut would have a salutary effect on the military establishment with its renowned waste and inefficiency. In the words of I. F. Stone, "The United

States is like a man with a brood of hungry children who insists upon keeping an elephant as a housepet. The pet is the Pentagon. . . ." One of the immediate benefits of freezing deployment of strategic weapons would be to trim some of the fat off the elephant. The immediate effects on security would not be serious, given that the United States spends one-third of all the monies spent on armaments in the entire world and $10 billion a year more than the Soviets. In fact, the United States always has enjoyed and continues to maintain a superiority in most categories of destructive weapons; the "overkill threshold" was passed long ago.

In addition to trimming defense expenditures, the United States should rededicate itself to the United Nations because no successor to it appears on the horizon. The problems that accompany the gap between the rich and poor nations, the deterioration of the oceanic and atmospheric commons, world-wide hunger and resource depletion, and the conclusion of any viable disarmament agreements cannot be handled on a nation-to-nation basis. They require international agreements signed by all members of the international community.

Thus Congress, rather than discussing decreasing the contribution of the United States to the United Nations, should immediately consider *increasing* it. True, the United States has been the largest financial contributor to the United Nations and has probably supported that organization in all ways more faithfully than any other major power. Many other nations, including the Soviet Union, have been much more lax in meeting their obligations. If America is to act as a world leader, however, it must not permit the irresponsible behavior of others to be an excuse for similar behavior. The $63 million dollar assessment of the United States for general support of the United Nations in 1972 is approximately the cost of one Lockheed C-5A transport. Thus, although the United States contribution to the United Nations is large in proportion to other nations (32 percent of the United Nations budget as opposed to 14 percent for the Soviet Union, 6 percent for Great Britain, and .04 percent for many LDCs), it is nothing compared with the amount that has been and is being plowed into military boondoggles that do nothing to increase American security. For less than the cost of an additional seven C-5As annually, the United States could *double* the entire United Nations budget as well as that of the three major specialized agencies, the Food and Agriculture Organization (FAO), the Educational, Scientific, and Cultural Organization (UNESCO), and the World Health Organization (WHO). *That* would be a gesture worthy of a nation seeking to take the lead in the search for world peace.

Finally, there is a series of less glamorous actions that Congress could undertake in regulating United States activities abroad. Although the establishment of an international development agency would obviate the need for much private investment, to attempt to impose a complete prohibition on American investment abroad would be foolish. Rather, Congress should establish specific guidelines for United States corporations abroad. The first might be to require 51 percent ownership by the country in which any facility is to be located, the rationale being that everyone's interest is served when each country controls foreign investment on its own territory. Events such as the attempted ITT intervention in Chilean affairs might thus be halted and the amazing growth of multinational corporations curbed. American corporations that desire to invest abroad must be willing to transfer control of investment decisions to the people of the country invested in. This requirement would make certain that a good share of corporate profits remained in the country in which investments were made rather than being channeled back to the United States.

Congress might also consider legislation that would limit profits repatriated by American corporations from abroad. These profits could be held to a certain fixed level (perhaps 6 percent of investment), or they could be pegged to the level of domestic profits, thus preventing corporations from earning higher profits from foreign operations than those earned in the United States. Such legislation would, of course, limit the incentive to invest capital abroad in search of quick profits.

These changes in corporate investment policies would find support not only among those concerned with environmental deterioration and social justice; they might also be supported by the American labor movement. Many American industries have established branches in foreign countries to take advantage of cheap labor and lenient pollution-control laws: Lower costs for labor and facilities mean that a higher profit can be returned. Obviously, the United States pays for this in jobs at a time when domestic unemployment is a major problem. The foreign branches of United States corporations often "export" their cheaper products to the American market. If the profitability of foreign investments were limited, there would naturally be much less incentive to take advantage of cheap labor and lenient corporate restrictions and more jobs would remain in the hands of Americans. The end result of these new investment policies would be less corporate meddling in foreign policy, more capital retained in foreign hands, and more incentive for American industries to meet antipollution standards at home.

It is obvious that a tremendous educational effort will be necessary to get the American public to accept this new kind of international thinking. Most people still do not understand that there can be no real security in the world as long as an immense economic chasm separates the rich nations and the poor nations, particularly when that gap is increasing rather than diminishing. Security is to be found in asserting moral leadership, in curbing the appetites and imperialistic urges inherent in a capitalist economic system, in developing programs to narrow the gap between the ODCs and LDCs, and, most important, in setting an example by diminishing armament levels and opening a peaceful competition to equalize living standards throughout the world. These steps require resolute action aimed at changing a perspective of fear to one of fairness and confidence in dealing with other nations. There never has been much reason to believe that either the Soviet Union or the People's Republic of China wishes to burn the United States to a crisp in a nuclear holocaust. Like all nations they want the opportunity to develop their resources—natural and human—without interference.

A new foreign policy means a major shift in ways of thinking in the United States, from fear and suspicion to trust and understanding. That the time may be right for such a shift is indicated by President Nixon's moves toward détente with both the Soviet Union and the People's Republic of China and the public's approval of these moves. If Americans can eventually see that their interests are served by moving in this direction, chances are good that the rest of the world would follow suit. No wealthy country has ever made a serious effort to transfer wealth to the poor without economic self-interest in mind. No powerful nation has ever attempted to end an armaments race by unilaterally beginning to disarm and then challenging others to do likewise. Once the governments of the world were convinced that the United States was serious, there should be enormous pressures to follow its example.

The United States has very little to lose and everything to gain from taking these kinds of initiatives. Betting on the stability of a balance of terror as competition for resources becomes more severe is a bad investment. Thermonuclear disaster results if the bet is lost, and the balance of terror, with all its adverse consequences, continues if the bet is won. The money that is bet benefits primarily the military weapons salesmen. Gambling that the world would follow the United States lead toward disarmament and economic reorganization also has risks, but if the gamble were won, the result would be a peaceful and stable world caught up in a spiral of international cooperation rather than competition. What if, in the worst of all possible futures, the gamble were lost? The only penalty would be further erosion of the American power base, which is already collapsing under present international competition and balance-of-terror policies.

8

The Animals Come Two by Two

It is cold and bleak in San Francisco at 5:00 A.M. as damp fog begins to lift, revealing a strange assortment of individuals standing in front of a shabby building on Mission Street. To many it would appear that the skid row bars had just closed their doors. To those in the know, however, the daily lineup represents another side of the American dream. These shabby individuals, standing as if in procession to the capitalist altar, are part of a blood line. They sell blood as frequently as possible for $5 a pint.

The line forms early because those at the head are first to get in out of the cold. Inside they find free coffee, and perhaps a little food, a welcome change from the hunger and cold most of them suffer during the long foggy nights. Although $5 a pint is not a very substantial income, some of the leeched make as much as $40 a month bleeding for profit. The blood is processed and in turn is sold for $25 a pint, or more.

Such unpleasant scenes might easily be dismissed as social aberrations, but the numbers of individuals participating give pause for further consideration. In San Francisco, this particular establishment processes more than 1,000 persons each month. Some efforts are made to limit visits and to keep the quality of the blood high, but a man or woman is usually allowed to give as much blood as his or her body can produce. For them being leeched is a way of life. This scene is repeated in other clinics and major cities across the United States.

Sale of blood by the poor to maintain a marginal existence is symbolic of human relationships that exist today, both within and between nations. Elaborate ideologies and ethical theories promote a global system in which a few live in luxury while most live in utter poverty. There have always been large gaps between the world's rich and poor, and competitive, socially stratified societies are considered to be a natural phenomenon. Little attention has been paid to alternatives and very little thought has been given to the impact of increasing scarcity on the ability of industrial society to sustain large differences in living standards. The affluence provided for a few by the industrial revolution has led many to forget that cooperation among individuals and social groups is the basis for organized society.

It seems as though only 200 years of laissez-faire industrialization has succeeded in canceling the social contract that bound people together over the centuries. This is unfortunate because a much stronger type of social contract or social cement will be needed to bind people in industrial societies together if a transition is to be made to a less materialistic way of life. Even though we may now abhor the rigidity and inequality of feudal society, the nobility felt at least some concern for the welfare of all, and the serfs could expect at least minimal levels of decent treatment. Human relationships at that time were much closer and more personal. Serfs felt a personal attachment to their lord, and to a certain degree the relationship was reciprocal.

The development of the factory system of production has slowly destroyed the primary ties that held traditional society together. The essence of capitalism is to compete, to accumulate, and to expand. People have become less concerned about the welfare of others as they themselves have been freed from poverty by the fruits of the industrial revolution. The upwardly mobile seem to develop contempt for those left behind in the struggle.

Double standards have historically prevailed in all societies, and despite propaganda to the contrary, many aspects of old double standards still prevail in industrial society. The wealthy live by one set of rules, but the poor are forced to conform to quite different standards. The scales of justice are tipped toward the rich, who, even in democracies, write the laws for themselves and their representatives and then see that these same laws are enforced for their own benefit. Since the beginning of the industrial revolution, the poor have not actively sought to eliminate these double standards and have voiced little complaint.

In the twentieth century, the growth of modern communications and greater mobility, among other developments, have led to an increased awareness of double standards and a growing resentment on the part of those who have been discriminated against. However, it has proven difficult for those being discriminated against to mobilize and attack. Part of the problem has been that the same disadvantages that are suffered by minority groups often impede effective political action. Thus, lack of organization, lack of unity, and lack of financial resources have plagued minority efforts.

There is now much talk about "equality of opportunity," but few who perceive themselves among the "haves" are willing to make serious sacrifices to create equal opportunities for the "have nots." People profess a desire to work together to find acceptable solutions to social crises. But when it comes time to take action, these exhortations are conveniently forgotten. There is a lot of "take" in American society and very little "give." In their neighborhoods people either strive to outdo the Joneses or ignore them completely. The typical office, university department, or government bureau is filled with competition, conspiracy, gossip, and struggles for promotion. Getting ahead of others has become an accepted part of the American dream. When the evidence is weighed, contemporary industrial society seems a nasty, cruel, lonely, and competitive place. And, as more and more people discover that they are feeding on a fixed (or even shrinking) economic pie, nastiness and competition may escalate accordingly.

American society has become a place where governmental corruption is assumed to the point that President Nixon could easily be reelected in spite of the ITT and wheat scandals as well as the burglary of the Democratic party national headquarters. These events were dismissed by many with a shrug of the shoulders and the comment, "That's politics." Even when the blatant criminality in high places symbolized by the Watergate Affair was fully exposed, a considerable segment of the public remained unperturbed. Indeed, many objected to the amount of attention paid by the media to such a mundane matter, and Ronald Reagan, Governor of California, stated publicly that he did not think this kind of governmental corruption was really criminal. In contemporary society many people vote in favor of restoring the death penalty, since to do otherwise would be "going soft on crime." The wealthy build fences around their communities and hire armed guards as protection against the rabble who might seek to steal or damage their property. Honesty and concern have become objects of derision; an honest man is often regarded as a "sucker" who will never get ahead. The harsh realities of the "blood market" are more characteristic of present society than most people would like to believe. And it is this society that must face a tremendous challenge to its cohesion, without the benefit of much experience, a reserve of good will, or future-oriented, well-respected social institutions.

New Social Priorities

In the United States the result of laissez-faire economic development, largely untempered by humanitarianism, has been the continuation of an unequal distribution of wealth, which has led to perverse social priorities in using America's existing resources. New automobiles with huge eight-cylinder engines that average less than twelve miles to a gallon of gasoline clog the highways. Meanwhile, millions of poor people subsist without adequate food and shelter and are told to consume less energy. Large blocks of discretionary income remain, often untaxed, in the hands of the affluent while legislators complain that the funds available for education, welfare, and social programs are inadequate. Interest rates are raised to "stem inflation," thereby denying millions of families the opportunity to own their own homes, while entrepreneurs buy up these homes and rent them out.

At a time when many Americans cannot afford adequate medical care, much discretionary income is plowed into such frills as new pet hospitals. In San Jose, California, for example, one pet hospital currently in operation has a 24-hour emergency ward with enough space for 40 small animals. It houses a cardiac monitoring machine, an X-ray unit, and television monitors for the canine and feline patients. Pet cemeteries are now popping up across the United States. It is estimated that more than 400 of these establishments are now scattered across the nation, and their number is growing at the rate of approximately 35 each year. At the Imperial Pet Cemetery in St. Louis, the average cost of pet funerals ranges between $80 and $120. There are more than 7,000 gravesites in this cemetery and some individuals have paid as much as $275 for their pet's funeral, complete with satin-lined coffin.

Such perverted priorities are nothing new or peculiar to present society. The rich have always engaged in ostentatious displays while the poor have starved. In fact, largely because of more abundant production, industrial societies evidence a more equitable distribution of wealth than did their predecessors, or indeed, than do most contemporary agricultural societies.

The critical point here is not that more significant gaps have existed, but rather that people now know that these gaps exist, and many believe that they are fundamentally wrong. *Relative deprivation* is much more important than any absolute income differences.

That Western man has long permitted the rich to take from the poor (Robin Hood to the contrary) provides little justification for perpetuating such injustice. The environmental and economic situation that exists in contemporary industrial society makes persistence of such large inequities highly unlikely. Expectations run high among the lower and middle classes, and people base their expectations on continuing the upward mobility they have recently enjoyed. Given the limited potential for continued economic expansion, however, everyone may well have to settle for less in the decades ahead, at least for *less of the goods that are valued within the present dominant social paradigm*. This is precisely why significant social turmoil can be expected. Polls show that most Americans expect *their own* lives to improve over the next decade, although they simultaneously feel that conditions will get worse for society as a whole.

People in the Los Angeles Basin were indignant when they were told by the Environmental Protection Agency in 1973 that the only way to clean up the air to meet national standards would be to install a system of gasoline rationing and to eliminate private automobiles in favor of public transportation. They would be even more indignant if they realized that the price of gasoline is expected to rise by at least 33 percent by 1981, an estimate that may be on the optimistic side. At this writing, oil companies are predicting that there might not be enough gasoline on hand to meet future needs anyway. Gas prices have risen 10 percent or more, many independent dealers have been eliminated, utility rates in California have increased six times in the last nine months, and there has been at least one murder related to the widespread rationing of gasoline. On May 26, 1973, a resident of Oakland, California, was denied more than ten gallons of gasoline at a local station. Acting in the frontier tradition, he returned with a shotgun and blew the head off the attendant who had refused him.

Technological and environmental constraints mean that other essential goods are also becoming scarce, leading to higher prices that the *rich will be able to afford but that the poor soon will not*. And under the present capitalist system there is no provision guaranteeing that the price of necessities will be within reach of the poor. Food is needed by everyone and food prices have been skyrocketing, but as yet no system guaranteeing adequate protein to all people has been designed. A pound of beef cost the American shopper 80 shopper 80 cents in 1967 and $1.15 in 1972. By the end of 1973 it is estimated that the same pound will cost $2.00. A 65-item monthly basket of food that cost $1,071 per year in 1967 cost $1,273 in 1972 and is likely to cost $1,500 at the beginning of 1974. Even the price of lumber, which is necessary for home building, has become inordinately high, partly because of the profitability of exporting it to Japan, but also because of huge increases in the value of land. As a result, rising costs have put home ownership out of the reach of many middle-class Americans.

During the coming decades of increasing scarcity and social unrest, old priorities are certain to be called into question in light of serious economic problems. These problems can be anticipated and a careful, systematic discussion and analysis of new priorities can be begun now. The current social paradigm establishes priorities, assumptions, and behavior patterns that gravely threaten the future of society. Problems surrounding these misguided priorities can be roughly grouped into six areas.

1. The interests of the rich are carefully protected, whereas relatively few resources are devoted to improving opportunities for the poor. Current data indicate that, objectively, the lot of the very poor may be slightly improving, but the gap between the poorest and the richest is widening. Advertising has accentuated feelings of frustration, necessitating bold new approaches to income redistribution.

Housing offers a relevant example of how the system protects the interests of the wealthy. As adequate housing becomes more difficult to find, landlords will be able to raise rents and prices of homes at will. Most tenants will have no right to appeal rent increases to any economic board of control. Those purchasing homes may have no choice but to pay increasing costs as well as increasing rates of interest. The inelastic supply of homes has already led to a national vacancy rate of less than 1 percent. Rental housing seems to be the wave of the future because young people will not be able to afford to make large down payments on their own homes.

Even if a person is fortunate enough to be able to buy property now, the standard mortgage and conditions for obtaining loans are so restrictive as to burden the new property owner with heavy responsibilities, and the lending agency is bound by few regulations favoring the borrower. Furthermore, income tax laws favor property owners by permitting interest on mortgages to be deducted, whereas rent is not.

Price controls on rental properties were removed in 1973, after a short freeze that was part of the illusory Nixon anti-inflation policy. In California, as in the rest of the nation, removal of controls led to large rent increases that tenants were powerless to protest. In San Francisco many rents were doubled. The Internal Revenue Service reported that it received more than 2,000 complaints in a one-month period but said it could do nothing about the massive increases. Tenants were faced with the choice of paying outrageous rents—a further spark for real estate speculation—or moving out of their apartments. There is always someone else willing to pay the price in crowded urban areas.

The property situation in the United States, however, with the possible exception of New York City, has not yet deteriorated to the point that it has in some European capitals. In London, for example, prices for homes and rentals rose 4 to 8 percent each month in 1972. In addition to the rental cost, payment of special fees was often required to obtain the right to bid on property. The wife of an American executive was asked to pay $12,000 just for the right to get a lease on a five-room flat. What is happening in London could very well be the wave of the laissez-faire future in the United States unless something is done to reverse priorities and protect the interests of the poor and the middle class.

2. Private interests often assume priority over the public interest. Private enterprise is considered to be the only "reasonable" way to get things done. Government operation of anything but the most unprofitable of economic activities is usually condemned as "anti-American" or "creeping socialism." The federal government has always been instrumental in creating private fortunes for clever individuals and has reserved few revenue-producing activities for itself. Government largesse has assumed many forms, including direct benefits, jobs, occupational licenses, franchises, special contracts, subsidies, and gifts of public resources. People benefiting from these privileges act as though government has given them nothing and often complain about high rates of taxation. Because the government has kept virtually no economic activities for itself, high taxes are necessary.

Throughout American history, land has been given away in many different forms ranging from homesteads to oil leases and railroad rights-of-way. Now, after this land has appreciated many hundreds of times in value (sometimes after simply lying idle), the government rushes back in to "repurchase" its original gift to "preserve open spaces." The windfall profits that accrue from simply holding these gifts are taxable at reduced rates as capital gains, and taxpayers foot the bill to repurchase what was once public land.

As the energy crisis has worsened, government-owned land containing oil shale in Wyoming and Utah has appreciated in value, as have off-shore drilling sites. The government could retain these lands and develop ecologically sound techniques for refining shale as a publicly owned industry. Instead, the lands are auctioned off to the highest bidder for uncontrolled development by private enterprise. The government could produce oil from off-shore wells. Instead, drilling sites are auctioned off to private enterprise. The oil industry is one of the largest, most capital-intensive, and profitable industries, and it has a terrible record of social responsibility. But suggestions that it be run by the federal government are met with horror.

In 1972 the San Francisco Bay Area Pollution Control District decreed that no more construction of new gas stations would be allowed within its area of jurisdiction. Ostensibly, this seemed to be a fine move to help combat pollution; but local government actually was creating an ideal situation for those who already owned gas stations. This move, combined with gas shortages and the related elimination of independent dealers, caused the value of franchises to rise, and individual owners and large service-station chains have profited. To date the public has not been adequately protected against price increases by price controls or public ownership of such facilities.

3. Within the present system both bigness and consumption are glorified, leading to perverse utilization of resources and little concern for the individual small consumer. No institutions exist to protect the rights of small concerns or individual citizens against the power of business. The energy crisis again is a case in point. With fuels in such short supply, it seems reasonable that national planning should give priorities to homeowners, schools, and so forth, and that mammoth consumers such as industrial establishments should receive a low priority. It furthermore seems reasonable that those who consume more should pay higher rates. However, few priorities have been set, and industry and homeowners compete for the same fuels. Furthermore, price rate structures reward the big user with low rates and penalize the small consumer with high rates. In California, the Pacific Gas and Electric Company charges homeowners more for natural gas than it charges industry. In 1972 homeowners paid nearly 8.0 cents per therm for the first 23 therms of gas used monthly, whereas industries using more than 50,000 therms of gas monthly paid only 6.7 cents per therm. Thus, the price of gas, instead of rising or remaining constant per unit, becomes progressively cheaper with increased usage. The same relationship holds for electricity. Nationwide, the average price for the first 100 kilowatt hours consumed monthly was 4.3 cents in 1970. When more than 250 kilowatt hours were used, the average price dropped to 3.1 cents. If more than 1,000 kilowatt hours were used monthly, the price dropped to 1.9 cents per kilowatt hour.

Thus, even though fuels are in short supply, the large consumers receive a discount and the small consumers pay more. Although prices of industrial goods obviously would be raised slightly if progressive prices were based on total consumption, such a move certainly would make environmental sense. It would be a particularly wise move if utilities responded by implementing a highly progressive rate structure for individual homeowners, so that those who do not conserve pay more, but there are few signs that this will soon happen.

4. The social welfare system is designed to perpetuate poverty and unemployment, not to offer the poor a chance to improve their condition. Big bureaucracies are set up to funnel "subsistence" money into the hands of the poor. This money is not enough to guarantee any equality of opportunity to children of poor families, and the cost of supporting the bureaucracy often exceeds the total amount that actually reaches the poor.

American attitudes toward equality and equality of opportunity are ambiguous at best. Most Americans claim to believe that "all men are created equal" and that everyone should enjoy equality of opportunity. On the other hand, Americans fear complete equality of opportunity like the plague. For example, equality in education is a goal that most Americans support, but there is a notable lack of enthusiasm for changing the basis on which public education is financed so that such equality might be achieved. As long as local taxes are the primary method of financing, schools in wealthy communities will be better funded than those in ghettos. Upper-class Americans have an interest in retaining a system that guarantees their children more opportunity than it offers to the children of the poor. This explains why the wealthy often oppose programs that will help to make equality of opportunity a social reality. It also explains how Americans can tolerate a complicated and costly patchwork welfare program that barely permits the poor to subsist. In one sense, welfare money is almost totally wasted because it keeps families on the dole but too poor to do anything about their condition. These programs, complete with watchdog bureaus to catch ineligible offenders, serve no function other than to provide minimal help to the needy while keeping them out of sight and ensuring that they do not become a threat to the affluent.

5. Financial compensation tends to be adjusted as the result of economic struggles, and there are no collective mechanisms to apportion wages and salaries in relation to the value of a person's contribution to society. Indeed, in today's interdependent society there are no accepted criteria for making such judgments. Old labor and capital theories of value have lost their meaning, and economists have not developed new theories to replace them. Obvious inequities exist everywhere. Policemen, for example, are on the

public payroll and are paid relatively little; starting salaries in many areas are in the vicinity of $9,000 per year, and even maximum salaries are relatively low. This situation persists even though society demands of the police considerable patience, restraint, judgment, legal expertise, and, of course, acceptance of hazardous duty. Teachers have even lower starting and maximum salaries but are required to spend many years in preparation for teaching. Many workers who are members of powerful unions and who have less education and safer, less responsible jobs receive higher wages. They are permitted to strike and exact a ransom by inconveniencing the public, whereas teachers and policemen are forbidden by law to strike and remain at the mercy of public generosity.

No question of priorities has the potential to divide Americans in the future as much as the question of pay. Economists need to develop a new rationale for deciding what is to be considered adequate compensation for various jobs. For example, high salaries could be paid to those with special qualifications, to those who have spent long periods in preparation, to those who do extremely dangerous work, and to those whose jobs are important to the national welfare. Unfortunately, studies show that each occupational group thinks that its work is most important and that its members deserve the highest wages. Because there is no set of accepted standards and because opportunities for real increases are rapidly diminishing, strife and conflict over wages and salaries can be expected to increase drastically. Labor strife like that occurring in Great Britian during the last few years could well be repeated in the United States in the very near future. American labor unions have never been noted for their restraint. As economic conditions become much tougher in a highly interdependent society, labor strife can be expected to become much more frequent and much less tolerable.

There are no simple answers to the wage dilemma. It is clear, however, that if Americans are to live together peacefully and weather the economic storms of the next few decades, a national wages and incomes policy must be formulated. Society can no longer afford to rely on open combat in the labor marketplace to decide levels of compensation. If a steady-state economy is established, a fantastic wage spiral for factory labor will not be sustainable. Unless an expanded board of wages and prices obtains public confidence and acts resolutely, a series of crippling strikes will be unavoidable.

6. Social resources are wasted in useless attempts to enforce organized religion's concepts of morality and to prevent victimless crimes. In keeping with the American tradition of overregulating individual behavior while ignoring more serious problems, the state often attempts to regulate private

individual behavior rather than concentrating on curbing organized crime. Hundreds of millions of tax dollars are spent annually for arresting and jailing some four million drunks, marijuana smokers, drug addicts, prostitutes, gamblers, and people who engage in unconventional sexual behavior.

Similarly, American society expends far too much effort and far too many resources supporting bureaucracies that persecute people who commit these victimless crimes. But this is the result of bringing old-fashioned religion into politics; many clerics do not mind helping God out by giving "sinners" a preview of things to come. While the rates of violent crime have been increasing and the fraction of cases solved has been decreasing, expenditures for law enforcement in the United States have been rising precipitously. In 1960 United States taxpayers spent $3.3 billion on controlling crime. By 1970 the figure had grown to $8.6 billion, which represented a per capita expenditure of $42. This figure, when combined with the $373 per capita United States military expenditure in that year, means that a total of $415 per person was spent for "security" in a country that is becoming less secure all the time. *A typical family of four was thus "protected" by a public expenditure of $1,660, which was approximately one-sixth of the mean family income for that year,* and that figure does not include large amounts invested by individuals and corporations to pay for security guards, fencing, burglar alarms, bomb shelters, and the like.

Close examination of the relevant data reveals that police spend most of their time arresting people to protect them from their own vices. Approximately 56 percent of all arrests are for drunkenness, gambling, or prostitution. The result is an absurd situation in which jails are filled with people waiting for trials in overloaded courts for trivial offenses. Figures from the California Bureau of Criminal Statistics reveal that half the inmates in that state's city and county jails at any one time are legally innocent. Many of these people cannot raise bail and serve weeks and months in jail until they come up for trial. No one compensates the innocent for these delays.

The simplest kind of policy shift would serve to unclog the courts, release police to catch serious offenders, and stop the skyrocketing social investment in law and order. There is no reason for police to send harmless alcoholics through the courts simply because they are happily drunk, jail marijuana smokers who are disturbing no one, or arrest prostitutes who conduct their business discreetly off the street. Society can no longer afford this indulgence in overregulation of individual behavior when there are so many other matters directly related to survival that require attention. Nor does the public support the arresting of people who commit victimless crimes. A national survey conducted for the National Commission on Marijuana and Drug Abuse revealed that more than half of all Americans believe that marijuana is at most a medical problem, not a crime. In addition, the survey showed that at least 24 million Americans are "criminals" by virtue of having smoked marijuana. If the numbers of individuals who have broken any of the various archaic sex laws that are still on the books could be tallied, there is no doubt that the majority of American adults technically could be classified as lawbreakers.

Legalization of some of these presently illegal activities is receiving increased public support, but unfortunately, in this matter the actions of political leaders and the police trail behind public opinion. Police bureaucracies depend on large numbers of arrests to keep arrest statistics high because government appropriations are partly based on these figures. Until policy changes are made, society's resources will continue to be plowed needlessly into activities that drain the public treasury, deflect attention from important issues, nurture large bureaucracies, and conceal the extent of really serious crime that permeates society and claims large numbers of victims.

Equalizing Opportunity

Equality of opportunity is an important psychological underpinning of industrial society. It provides some justification for continued real inequities, just as economic growth provides some hope that these inequities will some day disappear or become unimportant. A belief that objective failures and successes are linked to a person's own efforts is deeply ingrained in industrial culture. Those who are wealthy and successful supposedly have achieved their success through their own hard work and by developing their own talents in some conveniently obscure type of "open" competition. The poor, the weak, and the failures are in sad straits because they have not worked hard or taken advantage of opportunities.

Sustaining this myth of equality of opportunity has been essential to the maintenance of the secular industrial order. As long as the dispossessed have believed that equality of opportunity exists for them and their children, they have been able to rationalize their poverty. The growing economy has created intergenerational social mobility, and poor parents have been able to "succeed" vicariously through their children. As economic growth slows, however, such mobility will decrease, and existing inequalities of opportunity will come under increasing scrutiny and criticism.

Social Darwinism and the equal opportunity myth have been closely linked in American society. Taking the cue from theories of evolution, Social Darwinists have contended that, just as the "fittest" survive in Nature, the "fittest" people in society also flourish and multiply. Horatio Alger stories, stressing that the intelligent and thrifty child is rewarded for his or her–but mostly *his*–perseverance in the most adverse of circumstances, offer examples of the American success myth in action. The poor newsboy on the corner parlays his nickles and dimes into a newsstand. Then fortune rewards him, he eventually comes to own a chain of newsstands, and through thrift, clever-ness, and connections he becomes chairman of the board of a publishing house. Typical Alger titles from the late nineteenth century are colorful, to say the least. An aspiring young capitalist in those days might be exposed to stories like *Mark the Match Boy* and *Strive and Succeed: The Story of Walter Conrad's Success.* He could then move on to such classics as *Risen from the Ranks.* If he had missed the message, the aspiring young man could finish up with *Strong and Steady, or Paddle Your Own Canoe.*

Social Darwinists are still very much with us today, although they are not quite as easy to recognize in their equal-opportunity disguises. Most people still teach their children that everyone has approximately the same chance for success, that the economic and social reward system is rational, and that talent and intelligence are more important than connections. Conservatives still preach the virtues of initiative, competition, and free enterprise and rail against the vices of socialism, even though for many "initiative" consisted of inheriting the family's millions. Although "the poor will always be with us," they are supposedly people who fail to take advantage of rather than victims of a system that fails to give an opportunity. That the well-to-do and successful cling to this view is hardly surprising. As B. F. Skinner and others have pointed out, if some individuals cannot be blamed for their failures, it becomes much more difficult for others to take credit for their successes.

There has never been true equality of opportunity in the United States or in any other country. Opportunities are far from equal in the United States at the present time, although conditions are somewhat better than they were in the past. Many of the great fortunes of the past were accumulated through luck, which included being in the right place at the right time, and above all by taking advantage of connections to bend the rules by which the rest of society abided. Hard work and initiative certainly played a role in fortune building, but many who worked like slaves and showed great initiative went broke. Lenient tax laws now permit these fortunes, which are no longer linked to hard work or misdeeds, to be passed almost intact from generation to generation and to perpetuate inequality of opportunity as well as rigid social stratification. In this manner only 13 families have gained control over 8 percent of the stock in America's 200 largest corporations. In addition, 80 of these top 200 corporations are each controlled by only one family, with sufficient voting power to direct corporate affairs.

It is not necessary to detail the tremendous inequities and related inequalities of opportunity that exist in the United States or point out the links between today's big fortunes and past misdeeds. Ferdinand Lundberg has already done an admirable job of this in his book, *The Rich and the Super-Rich.* He points out that much of today's inherited money was originally earned by engaging in less-than-legal activities, exploiting political connections, land grabbing, and so forth. Such activities were looked on with disfavor at the time they took place, and all of them would be roundly condemned by today's moral standards. Thus, much money was made running rum or selling liquor during Prohibition, and is now made selling hard drugs. Other fortunes were accrued through the operation of sweat shops, and still others were and are being made through stock manipulations and other types of fraud. Where there is a great fortune there is also likely to be a trail of corruption, broken laws, pay-offs, disregard for the rights of others, and in some instances, corpses of hapless victims. So much for the myths that today's big fortunes have been earned by hard work and the theory that working hard, following society's rules, and adhering to accepted moral values will ensure success.

Today many of the wealthy are unquestionably hard-working, honest, and even generous. Their behavior, however, is overshadowed by that of others who are wheeling and dealing in Washington, who live in heavily protected enclaves, and who do not seem to mind ignoring the law when to do so seems expedient. Society could tolerate the corruption and large income differences that are now leading to formation of armed camps if the wealthy were leading a campaign to equalize opportunity and to soften the class differences that exist. But unfortunately they are not. For most people the old maxim, "the more you get the more you want," seems to hold true.

Wealth is only one of a host of factors that ensure success. A growing literature reveals that family background, race, sex, geography, and parents' education are also extremely important in determining the probabilities of success. The black female born into a poor farm family in southern Mississippi has very little chance of reaching the top or even overcoming the racial barriers that have been designed to perpetuate bondage. There can be no doubt where opportunity lies, particularly when the poor black Southern female is compared with a white Anglo-Saxon Protestant child of wealthy parents. Children born into poor families receive very little early intellectual stimulation in the home, may suffer mental retardation from undernourishment, must attend poorly equipped and poorly staffed schools where they meet other similarly deprived children, and have little opportunity to develop skills necessary for college or even to hold more than a menial job.

The Nixon veto of the child-care program in 1972 and related administration actions represent major blows against equalization of opportunities and indicate where true priorities lie. Many studies have shown that intellectually impoverished family situations have a stultifying effect on early development of intelligence. Day-care centers offer an opportunity for poor children to enter a different environment and develop skills necessary to cope successfully with the modern world. Day-care centers also offer a subsidy to low-income families when both parents work and encourage the liberation of women from household duties. The President, however, unable or unwilling to look beyond his personal view of society, charged that day-care centers had "family-weakening implications" and objected to committing "the vast moral authority of the national government to the side of communal approaches to child rearing over [*sic*] against the family-centered approach." In other words, it is very dangerous to offer this type of educational opportunity even though participation in such programs is voluntary. Little does it matter that children have hardly any family life anyway when both parents work. It is all right to send children to public schools daily for twelve years, but subsidized day-care centers have more radical implications since they help equalize opportunity during the formative years.

The perpetuation of this system is constantly reflected in statistics. Unemployment statistics reveal that 10 percent of eligible blacks were unemployed in 1972, whereas unemployment for the labor force as a whole was half that figure. This reflects job discrimination as well as a lack of appropriate educational opportunities. All minorities start life with two strikes against them, and this is reflected in poorer jobs and much lower annual earnings. In 1972 the median income of black families was only 59 percent of that of white families ($6,864 as opposed to $11,549). This gap has been widening recently. In 1971, the income of black families was 61 percent that of white families.

Now that an initial assault on unequal educational facilities has been made, oppressed minorities are beginning to understand how the system has been stacked against them. However, there is no frontier to which minorities can now move and seek their fortune. The worsening economic situation and the desirability of moving toward a steady-state economy, juxtaposed with a new awareness and rising minority expectations, mean there is no way short of brute force to preserve existing inequality of opportunity. As the poor begin to realize that social mobility is coming to a standstill, pressures to destroy the institutions responsible for perpetuating unequal opportunity will become intense. It is clear that to provide any semblance of equal epportunity for American children, the opportunities both to be born either extremely rich or desperately poor must be eliminated. The present income gap must narrow, and some equalization of wealth will be necessary. This means turning to new policies that will not be popular among the wealthy: taxation aimed at redistribution of income (including substantial inheritance taxes), new educational programs for the poor, a general upgrading of all public facilities, and new methods of financing education that are not tied to property taxes alone. Such a transformation would be difficult in times of abundance, and will be even more difficult during a period of relative scarcity.

Income and Scarcity

Any attempt to equalize opportunity and come to terms with impending scarcities must deal with the very sticky issue of how to distribute income. The present distribution of wealth has developed in haphazard fashion, largely as a result of economic warfare. There is unfortunately no way that social scientists can determine an "optimal" distribution of income. Income distributions *per se* seem to have little relationship to social discontent, violence, and revolution. It is much more important to understand relative deprivation when examining questions of income and social stability, because people apparently anchor their expectations in what others receive–they seem to need differences in economic rewards as incentives. The income differences currently found in the United States, however, are well in excess of those required to maintain a viable economy.

Today the average family income of the wealthiest fifth of the population in the United States is a little more than seven times the average of the poorest fifth. The average family income of the very wealthy (the top 5 percent of income recipients) is more than twenty times that of the poorest 5 percent. Before-tax income in other Western industrial societies does not differ much from one country to another. The United States, Sweden, the United Kingdom, and West Germany all have income distributions in which the richest fifth receive about eight times the income of the poorest fifth.

These figures stand in contrast to those for socialist Eastern Europe and the Soviet Union. In the Soviet Union and Poland, for example, similar income ratios are only four or five to one. Immediately preceding the economic collapse in the mid-sixties in Czechoslovakia, a country in which the income range was clearly too narrow, four-fifths of all employees in the national economy were encompassed within an earning ratio of 2.5 to 1. These figures, however, give a somewhat misleading impression of egalitarianism in the socialist nations. Money income does not have exactly the same meaning in socialist countries as it does in capitalist nations because many other factors must be considered in the distribution of amenities. Housing, for example, is very cheap and some citizens, usually members of trade unions, find that they are more favored than others when waiting in line. It is fair to say that inequities persist in all societies, but they are smaller in socialist countries. Equality of opportunity is, moreover, much greater in countries where conscious efforts have been made to elevate sons and daughters of the working class to positions of power and prominence for ideological reasons.

After-tax distribution of income is more important and tells a different story. In the United States, contrary to popular myth, supposedly progressive taxation does virtually nothing to alter income ratios. The top 20 percent of all families receives nearly the same proportion of income after taxes relative to other income groups. The impact of taxation, then, is not redistributive, but maintains approximately the same level of inequality. In Sweden and the United Kingdom, by contrast, rates of taxation are extremely progressive and do substantially alter the distribution of income. In those countries, in Eastern Europe, and in the Soviet Union, in return for paying heavy taxes, citizens also receive a social dividend in the form of basic goods and services that are provided at subsidized rates by the state. These goods and services are considered essential for society and are provided cheaply, a practice that the United States government could well emulate. In virtually all these countries, for example, medical care is given free to the poor as well as the rich. In Eastern Europe and the Soviet Union, the cost of housing is kept extremely low since housing is considered to be a basic human need. Indeed, the problem is to find adequate housing, since there is little problem in affording it. Although before-tax income distributions may not *seem* out of line in the United States, when the lack of social dividends and lack of progressive taxation are considered, the after-tax distribution is much more highly stratified in the United States than in other industrial countries, a matter that will be a source of persistent friction as possibilities for "becoming rich" diminish in the future.

It is important to point out that consciousness of income differences in industrial societies marks a big improvement over historical lack of concern. Throughout most of history, the upper classes lived very well indeed while the poor toiled to sustain the good life led by the very rich. Organized religion has helped cement such income differences by justifying them as God's will. A gradual diffusion of wealth has taken place as part of the industrial revolution, but this has not been the result of any benevolence on the part of the economic elite. Rather it has resulted from the organized demands of the working class as well as from the increasingly secular nature of society.

This fact should give little cause for rejoicing, however. Gradual improvement of the lot of the poor is certainly progress in the right direction, but it bears little relationship to human happiness. The standard of living among the poor has risen, but expectations have risen faster. Poverty is never absolute, it is a relative condition. Today's poor do not compare their living standards with those of the poor of thirty years ago. Their definitions of adequate living conditions are shaped by what they perceive others to be getting. From the subjective point of view, it is virtually meaningless to point out that only 12 percent of all Americans lived below the "officially defined" poverty line in 1969 as opposed to 22 percent in 1959. In the minds of persons with low incomes the important point is that a $4,000 income for a family of four might be much less tolerable in today's society than the pittance received by the poor in sixteenth-century England.

It is more pertinent to talk about the direction in which income inequality is moving in the United States than to discuss absolute figures. A "Gini" index is often used in determining the degree of equality in a national income distribution. In a mythical society where everyone received about the same amount of income, this index would stand at zero. In a society in which almost all income was in the hands of a very few, the figure would be close to 1.00. Changes in the index over time indicate whether income distribution in a society is becoming more or less equal. In 1947 the Gini figure for all households in the United States was .42. In 1970 the Gini index was .41, hardly a startling shift in income distribution in twenty years. But these gross figures can be a bit misleading. Part of the reason that there has been any shift at all is that more middle- and lower-middle-class women now have jobs. This has raised family incomes in the middle of the distribution but has done little to alter the extremes. The percentage of the population with incomes less than half that of the median family income was 18.9 in 1947 and still was 18.9 in 1970.

There are other important facts that must be considered in discussing income distribution. Although the ratio between incomes received by the top and bottom 20 percent of the population has slightly narrowed in recent years, this has resulted not from a leveling at the top but rather from putting a subsistence floor under the very poor. The rich get even richer while the very poor become only slightly less poor. In addition, it is essential to point out that the actual size of the gap between the income of the richest fifth and the poorest fifth has steadily grown. It is not unlike the growing gap between the rich countries and the poor countries. In 1947 the mean income of the richest 20 percent was $10,600 higher, in 1969 dollars, than the mean income of the poorest 20 percent. By 1969 the gap between mean incomes of the richest 20 percent and the poorest 20 percent stood at $19,000. The gap between the richest 5 percent and poorest 5 percent increased even faster.

Determination of what is a "just" distribution of income is difficult, although people do have some concepts of fairness. It is clear that most people do not consider the present poverty level ($4,275) to be an adequate income for a family of four. In a recent public survey, respondents pegged the lowest income at which a family of four could "get along" at $7,586. In addition, the majority opinion was that top executives should receive compensation at rates only 3.5 times as high as unskilled blue-collar workers. Public support thus seems to exist for the leveling of incomes by putting more realistic floors under lower incomes and skimming the excess off the top.

Pressures for a new income policy will certainly increase as the public realizes that opportunities for economic mobility are decreasing. Presently few people raise an eyebrow over the fact that Harold Geneen, President of ITT, receives an annual salary of more than $800,000, including bonuses, or that Richard Gerstenberg of General Motors receives more than $750,000 annually, although it is far from obvious that such mammoth salaries are needed to motivate executives. Not only are such tremendous incomes received by only a small segment of society, often these incomes are subject to very little taxation. In 1970, for example, 1,203 Americans had adjusted gross incomes in excess of $1 million, and 53 of them paid no income tax at all. The only tax bracket with a similar proportion of nontaxpayers was that consisting of people whose income was less than $5,000. In 1970, 394 Americans with incomes in excess of $100,000 paid no federal income tax. Of the 18,646 other Americans with incomes of this size, the average rate of income tax paid was less than 7 percent of earnings. Some of these people, of course, paid "hidden taxes" by buying tax-free municipal bonds. However, most of them evaded taxation through the many loopholes that have been written into the law to keep actual rates of taxation from being progressive in higher-income brackets.

Thus, in principle the majority of Americans believes in a graduated income tax, but in practice the wealthy benefit from policies that negate the graduated principle. They have their tax returns prepared by specialists who know the loopholes. Ralph Nader's Tax Reform Research Group has found that the wealthy take advantage of available tax loopholes whereas the middle class does not. In 1970, for example, middle-income taxpayers deducted an average of $33 for medical expenses, while the deductions of the 78,000 taxpayers in the highest brackets averaged $449. Similarly, the group found that the very rich take full advantage of capital gains provisions, by which income from the sale of capital assets is taxed at only 50 percent of normal rates. Taxpayers in the $10,000 to $15,000 range average $1,631 in capital gains. The top 0.1 percent of all taxpayers average $38,000 in capital gains.

A new taxation and incomes policy should have several goals. It should minimize the bureaucracy required for its administration and maximize simplicity for the taxpayer. Enormous simplification of tax forms is needed; *all* loopholes should be eliminated, including those for the rich, elderly, oilmen, cattlemen, and philanthropists. This might put a lot of tax-advising companies out of business, but many of them have been found to abet cheating anyway. Another goal would be to eliminate special incentives for investment, which often leads directly to environmental deterioration. This means treating capital gains just like other forms of income. Such changes would operate to make the income tax more truly progressive. A simplified, progressive system of taxation might permit the establishment of realistic income floors (and perhaps even ceilings) and would go far to restore shattered public confidence in the fairness of the tax system.

Abolishing Welfare

Some coherent new policy is clearly needed to supplant the present jumbled welfare system. Most Americans favor some type of national family assistance plan, and nearly everyone thinks that those who want jobs should have them and be justly compensated. It is now clear that jobs are not being provided for all who want them. Pressure will undoubtedly continue to mount for a livable guaranteed annual income for all American families; but it is not clear what the political response will be to these demands.

A complex combination of welfare programs now exists to aid the poor, and each has its own separate bureaucracy and its own forces for checking on welfare violations. The federal government offers old-age pensions through social security, pays benefits to the unemployed, and aids destitute families through the Aid to Dependent Children program (ADC). Much of what the federal government does is supplemented by the individual states, but benefits vary tremendously from one state to another. Welfare incomes that prevail in Mississippi would be totally unacceptable in California or New York. In addition, much of the money budgeted for welfare winds up going into program overhead; that, is, to support the administrators, social workers, and clerical help. Most important of all, welfare programs are now designed to offer recipients only a subsistence income. Children born into welfare families have little chance to better their conditions because present welfare programs guarantee them no access to an adequate education. In this sense a vicious circle of poverty underlies the whole welfare tragedy.

A much better way to handle the welfare problem is to admit that poverty is as much the fault of the present economic and social system as it is a result of human failings. There are very few people who will refuse a decent job, if offered, or who will refuse an educational opportunity. The old idea that people, rather than the system, are at fault is a convenient moral crutch that offers a supporting ethical theory to those who oppose higher taxes and the redistribution of wealth. Instead of attempting to eradicate poverty with grudging charity, it would make much more sense to guarantee every American family an annual income adequate to sustain more than subsistence living. There are many social advantages to such a policy in addition to its moral justifications.

The credit tax, a relative of the negative income tax, represents a very promising social innovation and could be an enduring solution to the problem of poverty. The idea of the credit tax goes back more than thirty years, but most recently it surfaced briefly during the McGovern campaign for the Democratic presidential nomination. The credit tax would be administered through the Internal Revenue Service. Under a credit tax system, most people would pay while some would receive. Each individual in the United States would be guaranteed a sizable tax credit. For example, if it were decided that everyone should be guaranteed $1,000, a family of four would have a total credit of $4,000. To those families of four earning less than $4,000, the Internal Revenue Service would issue a check at the end of the tax year to make up the difference between money earned and $4,000. It would be better, of course, to set this minimum income somewhat higher, perhaps at $6,000 for the family of four.

For a majority of families, those earning more than the established minimum, the credit income tax would work differently. Each individual would have a credit of $1,000 to be used to pay income tax. A four-person family would thus be credited with $4,000. If a family of four had an income of $15,000, leading to a tax bill of $5,000, the income tax credit would take care of the first $4,000, leaving only a $1,000 tax burden.

Sociologist Lee Rainwater has proposed adopting this type of credit tax and has worked out some rough estimates of costs. If every American were given a tax credit of $1,000 (or, should they earn no income, a payment of $1,000), which would seem to be the lowest acceptable standard, the total cost of the program would be $220 billion for 220 million Americans. This would be roughly 25 percent of national income. Current federal expenditures, other than transfer payments, make up 9 percent of national income. Thus, the new total federal tax bill would be approximately one-third of national income. In very general terms, this means that approximately one-third of all personal and corporate income would have to be paid in taxes under the proposed system. Although there certainly would have to be a period of economic readjustment, there is no reason to think that such a system of taxation would be unworkable.

Under the credit tax system, *all* income would be taxed. Capital gains would be treated as ordinary income, and none of the deductions, including those for dependents, that have made the tax system so complicated and inequitable would be permitted. Every family of four earning $25,000 a year (whether from salaries, interest, capital gains, or any other source) would pay exactly the same amount in taxes. Changes in the existing tax code would expose a much greater portion of income, particularly income in the higher brackets, to taxation. The entire program would represent a major step toward the redistribution of income and would guarantee a minimum income to all citizens.

The burden of such a system would fall most heavily on the wealthy, and therefore it would be a boon to America's lower and middle-class families. A hypothetical family of four having total tax credits of $4,000 could earn up to $12,000 without paying any taxes. The suggested tax burden would be one-third of income, in this case $4,000, which would be precisely equal to the tax credit. Even a family of four with earnings of $25,000 would benefit from the credit tax, since the net tax burden for such a family would be only $4,000. Those with larger incomes, however, would pay more than they do at present, particularly because of closed loopholes. It would also seem desirable to make the new tax scale sharply progressive in the higher income brackets to finance other important social programs. Perhaps the 33 percent general rate should break at $30,000 and escalate gradually to 50 percent of income, where it is now, in the very highest brackets. Some consideration should be given to the idea of imposing an absolute ceiling on individual annual income, perhaps in the vicinity of $100,000 (1973 dollars).

One very important objection to such a tax is that its focus on the individual as recipient of credit might lead to more births. If a credit of $1,000 were attached to each additional child, families might be encouraged to have more children. This problem could be overcome in part by amending the tax credit system to limit credit given to children in all but the poorest families. (Care must be taken not to penalize children for the reproductive irresponsibility of the parents.) The number of children's tax credits per family, above a certain income minimum, could be restricted to two, thus discouraging large families. If social conditions justify even stronger antinatalist policies in the future, penalties instead of credits could be attached to each child born in excess of two. Affluent couples could still have as many children as they liked, but costs, rather than benefits, would be attached to these extra children. This system would represent a big improvement over the present pronatalist tax system, which permits equal deductions for all children, regardless of their numbers or the financial status of the parents.

The social impact of such a tax credit system would be tremendous, and it would solve two of our most nagging social problems at once. Both the welfare and social security bureaucracies would be abolished, and the income tax system would be simplified. The tax credit system would guarantee an income much higher than mere subsistence to all Americans. It would equalize welfare payments in all states, thereby stemming "welfare migration." Today, benefits paid to a typical welfare family with dependent children vary from a high of $350 per month in Alaska to a low of $75 a month in Alabama and Mississippi. Although costs of living vary from one locale to another, these variations are small compared with existing welfare differences.

Because the proposed scheme would also eliminate the patchwork of bureaucracies that now administers these programs, there would be a substantial saving to the taxpayer because operating expenses would be reduced. The credit system would also give a psychological boost to welfare recipients. Humiliating "means" tests would no longer have to be passed to qualify for charity. Thousands of federal, state, and local welfare bureaucrats would be free to seek more worthwhile types of employment. Individual freedom and dignity would be preserved because the only welfare elegibility test would be the annual income tax statement. The only snooping needed would be that on the part of the Internal Revenue Service, and that should be reduced by the simplified tax forms.

Moreover, this approach to welfare would free the states from their heavy welfare burdens and would be an effective way of transferring revenue from the federal government to the states. States would be free to use these extra revenues for other needed programs.

Finally, under the new plan, life would become tolerable for welfare recipients who are the real victims of the present system. They would be treated as human beings and would merely fill out their income tax forms every year to qualify for payments (although special provisions would have to be made for those suddenly out of work or otherwise impoverished). Enough purchasing power would be put in the hands of the poor to guarantee them a decent standard of living and increased ability to compete for educational and job opportunities. This would be especially important for poor children. Such a plan, if combined with the educational birthright described in Chapter 6, would help to equalize opportunities for each new generation. The aged would also qualify for the guaranteed income, thus making the whole social security program obsolete. Higher levels of income would enable individuals over sixty-five years of age to remain closer to society's mainstream.

Critics of the generous income floor and the tax credit scheme are certain to portray them as methods of encouraging loafing, particularly among the young. If, for example, the individual income floor were set at $1,500, what, they would ask, would keep hordes of young people from simply dropping out? Although the values of industrial society encourage people to seek traditional types of employment, the need for these jobs is declining, and forcing people to work does not now seem to be one of society's critical problems. There is nothing inherently immoral about enjoying increased leisure or exploring new careers. In fact, a $6,000 incentive for the head of a family of four to drop out for a year might well be useful to individuals who wish to try a new kind of life or to develop new creative skills that might not now be economically rewarded. More leisure time could spark the development of a new culture dedicated to personal enrichment through art, poetry, literature, music, participation in physical activities, and other forms of personal expression that would represent a sharp contrast to the present culture, which requires hitching personalities to the industrial system. Furthermore, there is little indication that large numbers of young people would suddenly rush to welfare. The industrial world is still very much with us, and there is every indication that most of today's young people still prefer material goods and the luxuries that usually accompany high incomes. In fact, the most pressing need may be to educate the young to want less.

A thorough reform of the tax system, including the imposition of a much larger inheritance tax, would provide additional revenues for other needed social programs. In a society ostensibly dedicated to equality of opportunity, there is no justification for passing great quantities of wealth from generation to generation. Large inheritances could be taxed at extremely high rates to provide revenue for the educational birthright discussed in Chapter 6. The combination of a respectable welfare program and a new tax system that is simple, fair, and progressive would go far toward the construction of a new society, one that might be capable of dealing with future social problems.

A New Society

According to legend, all the animals boarded the first ark in pairs. Launching Ark II will require a new society and new social relationships. The industrial revolution in the West has destroyed the extended family arrangements commonly found in agricultural societies. It has left industrial society with hundreds of millions of isolated and competitive family units, adults living in pairs with their young offspring. Children acquire the worst of traits in the nuclear family: competitiveness, selfishness, greed, and in-group–out-group distinctions. The small family comes to represent security, whereas other human beings are labeled as outsiders and enemies. Most people never out-grow the perspectives they acquired in childhood and spend the better part of a lifetime clinging to one other adult and competing with the millions of other family units.

A new society capable of overcoming industrial habits must be radically different from that in which we now live. Philosopher Ivan Illich has suggested that the main task before us is to move toward a "convivial" society, one in which human beings engage in autonomous and creative intercourse, rather than simply responding to the needs of the machine. A new society and a new culture must stress the potential, the value, and the dignity of the inner person, rather than mankind's outer shell. The potential of each human being, rather than each factory, must be developed. Industrial culture today is the culture of steel-eaters—"socialist realism" on a planetary scale. A new society could be based on development of human characteristics that are now lacking. Creation of a convivial society would require a transfor-mation of the social and cultural norms that have been bequeathed by the industrial revolution. The future survival of humanity depends on deflection of industrial society from its present materialistic course. People in the industrial world do not require more material artifacts; rather they require a pause to let bodies, minds, and culture catch up with and assert control over a technology that has gone wild.

This new society cannot be created without new people to live in it. Unless we learn to cooperate rather than compete, to do unto others as we would have done unto ourselves, to see other people to be like us, and to work for the good of all mankind rather than just for the good of a few, little of significance can be accomplished. Empathy must become a universal quality. People must identify their fate with the fate of all mankind, or there will be no way to overcome the global tragedy of the commons. For many this would mean small sacrifices; for others it might mean very large sacrifices. But some compensation for sacrifices made would be gained from seeing a chance for prosperity and happiness made available to all mankind.

The transformation of society could begin with the unit on which it is based–the nuclear family. Within a new society, variations of the extended family could replace present family structures to great social and personal advantage. Large, commune-type living units could help reduce competitiveness. Children reared in communal environments have been observed to share more, to develop more concern for others, and to develop more cooperative rather than competitive habits than children in nuclear families. Such children would have the advantage of interacting with large numbers of other children and adults of all ages. Adults living in extended families would also profit from a rich variety of interpersonal contacts not available in the present society. The economic benefits of communal living arrangements will become more significant as the economic situation deteriorates. The main barriers to the establishment of new family units have always been inertia and fear of the unknown. But such fear is slowly being overcome, and these alternative forms of family life should be given every opportunity to flourish.

In times of stress, people have historically turned to religion and promises of the next world for consolation. New forms of religion will be inevitable in the trying times that lie ahead. Indeed, humanistic faiths, stressing the unity of all mankind and of human beings with nature, could be an essential part of a major social transformation. However, there are some pitfalls that must be avoided. Irrational religious fervor could distract people from coping with the critical problems that lie ahead. Turning attention to the next world to the neglect of this one could mark the beginning of an antirationalism that would lead only to more poverty, hunger, and death rather than to any "second coming." It must be kept in mind that some of history's greatest crimes have been committed by religious zealots content to look to another world for their rewards. These include not only such classic events as the Inquisition and the Crusades with their attendant murders and massacres of "infidels," but also the "God is on our side" approach to all wars. Old-style religion offers industrial mankind a crutch, a set of precepts that, if closely followed, will presumably lead to other-world salvation. The true believer blindly follows dogmas, when to do so is suitable, and gives little critical thought to them or to improving the quality of life for others in this world. It may be no accident that some of the major figures in the Watergate scandal were church-going, prayer-reciting, Christian folks who believed they and their cause was "right."

There is every indication that a revival of old-time religion will soon be upon us. "Jesus freaks" are popping up among the young, and slightly older individuals are once again "laying on hands," speaking in tongues, and engaging in other bizarre practices. Billy Graham attracts millions with his war-loving and antisexual "morality," mixed with promises of salvation for those who accept his simplistic religion. Snake cults hold national conventions where people die from rattlesnake bites and strychnine poisoning while waiting for the Lord to work a miracle. In 1973, parents mesmerized by a "faith healer" killed their diabetic son by depriving him of his insulin. There obviously is little that is constructive in such primitive rites and stale doctrines.

A second type of religious revival could be labeled the new "Bambiism." It counsels mankind to drop everything and return to Mother Nature and the forest primeval for solace. Many well-meaning people are eager to lead humanity to the happiness of the forest, forgetting that Bambi eventually saw the forest burn to the ground. The thought that any substantial portion of today's urban population could find contentment and sustenance communing with Nature in a shack in the woods is a romantic notion. Clearly, no religious answer for industrial society can be found in a retreat to the idyllic forest.

On the other hand, a humanistic religion, one that dignifies the person and stresses the unity of all mankind and Nature, could give a great boost to a new culture. This person-centered religion must engage real-world problems, however, and not encourage avoidance of them. It must be concerned with alleviating the present suffering of all mankind rather than focusing its attention on some vague, mysterious after-life.

Twentieth-century society is witnessing a revolt against the machine. People are now searching for the lost tribalism of preindustrial society. They are seeking the joy of sharing and living with others. They are ready to forsake the glut of materialism that now threatens the existence of important human qualities. The expansion of this movement could result in a society based on love and trust, rather than materialism, and a religion embracing all mankind. The growth of the human potential movement, communes, free universities, cooperatives, and humanistic religion indicates that millions of people are looking for alternatives, for a way out of the present predicament. Perhaps they will find it in a second Ark, a society that nurtures improvement of human beings and a spirit of unity rather than one that embraces the cult of the machine.

Epilogue

When we began to work on this book it was still necessary to make a case that various types of environmental deterioration and resource scarcity were close at hand, that the world food problem was acute and would soon worsen, that the economic situation was deteriorating badly, and that political institutions were ill-equipped to solve these problems. The American public entered the seventies with very little appreciation of the magnitude of the crisis that would have to be faced. At that time agricultural experts were still praising the green revolution, politicians were dismissing predictions of energy short-ages as sensationalism, and economists were making their customary pre-dictions of better times ahead. But the onset of scarcity has occurred much more rapidly than most people expected.

It has been fascinating to see how rapidly ideas that were unthinkable in 1970 have become matters for open debate and discussion. A fuel shortage materialized quickly, and people who had been accustomed to pulling up to the pumps and saying, "Fill 'er up" were suddenly faced with ten-gallon limits or closed gas stations. At this writing, a shortage of fuel oil and natural gas threatens to close school districts and major industries and to leave homes unheated, especially in the event of a very cold winter. Further uncertainty is introduced by the possibility that Arab nations might, as a result of the Yom Kippur war, withhold petroleum from the United States. Because of incredi-bly incompetent planning, no additional refineries will be on line before 1975, and some fuel refined in the United States has been shipped to Europe, where prices are much higher. World wide hunger, never of much concern to Americans, has suddenly become a topic of conversation as the world's supply of wheat for 1973 turned out to be some 300 million bushels short. The Common Market banned the export of wheat by its members, and the Soviet Union drove up prices for wheat in the United States by making huge purchases to overcome Russian shortages. Serious crop failures have once again been reported in India, China, and considerable portions of North Africa.

These larger scarcities have been complemented by smaller ones as the demands of an industrial society have outstripped supply in the United States. Iron and steel have been in short supply, farmers have had great difficulty getting enough baling wire to bring in their crops, and needed amounts of fertilizer and seeds have been sporadically unavailable. Lumber and newsprint have also been scarce, and prices are soaring while supply has increased only very slowly. It is ironic to look back less than a decade and recall how Americans, on returning from visits to Eastern Europe and the Soviet Union, made snide comments about the shortages that seemed to beset those "planned" economies. The free enterprise system worked so much better! But those countries, which have been coping with various kinds of scarcities since World War II, may be in better shape to handle future problems than are the undisciplined and unplanned economies of the West.

The effort to help overextended populations in countries around the world will increasingly result in the decline of living standards in the United States. Present trade policies permit private interests in the United States to export scarce commodities to those countries willing to pay the highest prices, thus causing an upward spiral of prices in the United States. When the Soviet Union buys American grain to provide subsidized bread to Soviet citizens, the American public must pay higher prices for a wide variety of commodities ranging from bread to beef. When Japan buys American lumber at very high prices, the domestically available supply shrinks and prices rise.

For better or for worse, there is no effective way to isolate Fortress America from the rest of the world. Planetary problems have become our problems. Prices for key commodities have been rising precipitously around the globe. Between September 1972 and September 1973, the Reuter's Commodity Index, which monitors world agricultural prices, more than doubled, and these prices will inevitably be translated into higher prices in the United States. In the present increasingly interdependent world, there is no way that the United States can avoid becoming very dependent on foreign suppliers of critical resources, unless Americans are willing to reduce their consumption dramatically. This dependency means selling agricultural commodities to the highest bidders in exchange. As competition for scarce commodities becomes more intense around the world, prices can be expected to rise even higher and living standards will dip even lower in the absence of effective action to modify planetary demands and patterns of distribution.

The global agricultural crisis may be even worse than is now apparent. The relatively good weather of the last few decades, which played a large part in increasing food production, may well have been an aberration, and a return to more normal conditions in the late seventies may extinguish a significant part of the badly overextended world population. According to meteorologist Reid Bryson, the climatic conditions that existed between 1930 and 1960 were the most unusual of the last 1,000 years. He speculates that the planet may be returning to climatic conditions more typical of recent centuries—conditions quite different from those to which modern high-yield agricultural systems are attuned. Bryson also expects that climatic changes, partly caused by human activities, are likely to cause more frequent monsoon failures in sub-Saharan Africa and Southern Asia. If he is correct, regional collapses such as the one now beginning on the southern fringes of the Sahara Desert may occur in much more heavily populated areas such as the Indian subcontinent. If this occurs hundreds of millions of people will die.

Recent economic and political setbacks in the United States have been both discouraging and encouraging. They have been encouraging because the folly of ignoring critical problems has been made so obvious through a series of easily observable incidents. In many ways a review of recent history is like watching guerilla theater, almost as if events have been orchestrated to arouse public awareness in time to do something before still more serious problems arise. The Watergate scandal and the exposure of a "law and order" Vice President as a felon revealed the Emperors to be without clothes (or good judgment) and demonstrated a clear need for a complete restructuring of American politics. Many Americans have been understandably shaken by the corruption of high officeholders and their use of Constitutional niceties to keep relevant facts from becoming known. But this shock could easily turn into complacency if people resigned themselves to expect more of the same, rather than demanding an entirely new cast of characters and appropriate structural changes to prevent future corruption.

In other ways, however, political inaction has worsened our plight as irresolute politicians have repeatedly demonstrated unwillingness to act on principle in confronting major social and environmental issues. Rampant inflation, for example, has in no small part been spurred by a crisis of confidence in the ability of those in power to control inflation. The sorry fact is that most of the governments of the world, including that of the United States, are still run by people skilled in self-enrichment and maintaining power but hopelessly ignorant of the many forces that are moving industrial society toward the brink. They are abetted by economists who are caught up in growthmania and cannot understand the world that exists outside their formulas, by many scientists who are much more interested in technological circuses and weapons development than in meeting the basic human needs for food, clothing, and shelter, and by "community leaders" who work harder to maintain personal privilege and established hierarchies than to ensure social justice. At a time when resolute, forthright and honest leadership is badly needed, very few individuals seem equal to the task.

It has been most discouraging to see the continued refusal of political and economic leaders to take steps toward solving critical long-term problems. The apparent Nixon policy (if it can be called that) for dealing with resource shortages is hopelessly inadequate, a relic of an era when there was an open frontier to exploit. The energy crisis will not be solved by lowering pollution standards and drilling more offshore oil wells; it will only be delayed slightly while another set of serious problems is created. Clear-cutting American forest lands will not solve the lumber shortage; it will merely put it off for another day. This failure is not exclusively American. Recently, Prime Minister Heath of Great Britain berated the man whom he had appointed to supervise government planning for making a "pessimistic" speech about the future of the British economy. It seems that the government's top planner had failed to "clear" this future with the Prime Minister, who was busy assuring political supporters that the future had never looked more rosy.

This tendency to hide heads in the sand is extremely unfortunate because inaction now will make it far more difficult to cope with problems in the future. The Nixon administration's original plan for "solving" the energy crisis included both easing antipollution standards, which were at best barely adequate, and giving in to the powerful petroleum industry on such things as the Alaska pipeline. This plan represented a convenient way to duck the more serious issues until another administration is in office. By late 1973, however, the seriousness of the crisis was so evident that even the Nixon administration had to start talking about fuel rationing and the production of smaller cars. It is hoped that the next administration will adopt a long-range policy designed to limit energy consumption drastically. If it does not, the air will become more polluted by high-sulphur fuels, more drilling in offshore waters will take place as part of a frantic search for more domestic oil supplies, most federal regulation of strip mining will be eliminated, and the deployment of the extremely dangerous nuclear fission power technology will be rapidly accelerated, all in an effort to keep up with energy appetites that are continually stimulated by American industry and Madison Avenue. All these measures will certainly increase energy production in the short run, but they will leave a legacy of resource depletion and environmental destruction for future generations.

The energy crisis now clearly illustrates for the American people how various aspects of environmental problems are interconnected and how difficult it is to "solve" them easily. For example, in the interest of cleaning up the air, the new mandatory smog devices on automobiles reduce automobile mileage and exert additional pressure on gasoline supplies, indirectly leading to a decision to burn fuels high in sulphur content to heat American homes. This, of course, adds to the pollution that the smog devices were designed to prevent. Shortages of petroleum and natural gas may also soon affect the ability of farmers to harvest and dry their crops and thus may reduce food supplies. In addition, almost all new energy technologies, ranging from nuclear power to coal gasification, require enormous quantities of water, which, in some parts of the country, is also in limited supply. In short, there are no easy ways to solve these complex problems, and the politically acceptable solutions of today barely scratch the surface.

The agenda for a sane future is a long one, and mankind seems to be fumbling even the most elementary decisions. What is happening and what has been happening in the United States and around the world are symptomatic of an impending massive collapse of the industrial order. We are all now caught in a gigantic tragedy of the commons; each person, each family, and each nation is struggling to stay ahead while the whole system is on the verge of collapse. Many people are now coming to realize the predicament, but it remains to be seen if enough people are willing to break the individual patterns of behavior that are leading to social destruction.

The claim is often made that human beings are rational creatures, that people are capable of planning ahead and regulating their affairs accordingly, and that the world can be shaped to satisfy all human desires. But the evidence calls these beliefs into question. Population explosions and associated overshoots of the carrying capacity of the environment have been common throughout human history, and the cancerous growth of industrial society casts considerable doubt on the notion that the situation has fundamentally changed. What is now needed is a bold new step in social evolution that will put man's favorable view of himself to the test. To make this step, a preferred and ecologically sound human future must be outlined, and social efforts and expectations must be modified to conform to it. This is not an impossibility, but it will require marshaling the intellectual resources of all societies and the acceptance of some sacrifices on the part of many individuals, especially in the overdeveloped countries.

The alternatives for mankind are now very clear. People can continue to ignore the dangerous consequences of present behavior and painfully adjust to the inevitable through a series of crises. Or mankind can face up to the challenges and begin now to manage the future of the planet and the ecosphere. There can be no doubt that mankind must eventually come to terms with environmental imperatives; the only question that remains is which path will be taken.

Suggested Readings

The Notes that follow this section are keyed to the numbers preceding these references.

Chapter 1

1. Borgstrom, Georg. *Focal Points: A Global Food Strategy.* New York: Macmillan, 1973. The most recent book by an outstanding expert on the world food problem. His two previous books are also highly recommended.

2. Borgstrom, Georg. *The Hungry Planet: The Modern World at the Edge of Famine.* New York: Macmillan, 1972.

3. Borgstrom, Georg. *Too Many: A Study of Earth's Biological Limitations.* New York: Macmillan, 1969.

4. Cloud, Preston, ed. *Resources and Man.* San Francisco: W. H. Freeman and Company, 1969. Although this collection is somewhat out of date, it gives excellent coverage of the international and domestic resource situation.

5. Ehrlich, Paul, and Ehrlich, Anne. *Population, Resources, Environment: Issues in Human Ecology.* San Francisco: W. H. Freeman and Company, 1972. A comprehensive treatment of many of the subjects touched on in this chapter. Extensive references provide an entry point into the more detailed literature.

6. Ehrlich, Paul, Ehrlich, Anne, and Holdren, John. *Human Ecology: Problems and Solutions.* San Francisco: W. H. Freeman and Company, 1973. A somewhat

shorter treatment of these subjects that is more suited for supplemental reading and for the nonspecialist.

7. Hammond, Allen, Metz, William, and Maugh, Thomas. *Energy and the Future.* Washington D.C.: American Association for the Advancement of Science, 1973. A compendium dealing with various new energy-producing technologies. Includes a brief but useful section on energy conservation.

8. Holdren, John, and Herrera, Philip. *Energy.* New York: Sierra Club Books, 1972. A readable and well-documented treatment of the energy crisis, new technologies, and environmental impact. Includes case histories of utility-environmentalist confrontations. By far the best popular treatment of this important subject.

9. Hunt, Cynthia, and Garrels, Robert. *Water: The Web of Life.* New York: W. W. Norton, 1972. A detailed treatment of one of mankind's most formidable problems, the water supply.

10. Kormondy, E. J. *Concepts of Ecology.* Englewood Cliffs, N.J.: Prentice-Hall, 1969. A basic introduction to the science of ecology, in paperback.

11. Meadows, Donella, Meadows, Dennis, Randers, Jorgen, and Behrens, William. *The Limits to Growth.* New York: Universe Books, 1972. A well-written and unduly maligned report based on computer simulations of possible environmental futures. This book has probably been subjected to more unjustified criticism than any other recent work in this field because of its pessimistic findings. The results, however, are congruent with the findings of many scientists studying global ecology.

12. Ricklefs, R. *Ecology.* Newton, Mass.: Chiron Press, 1973. A highly recommended text for further reading in ecology. Ricklefs' modern treatment includes the critically important interface between ecology and population genetics.

13. Study of Critical Environmental Problems (SCEP), *Man's Impact on the Global Environment.* Cambridge, Mass.: MIT Press, 1972. An excellent assessment of some of the most pressing and pervasive environmental dangers.

Chapter 2

14. Berger, Peter, and Luckmann, Thomas. *The Social Construction of Reality.* New York: Doubleday, 1966. Closely related to Thomas Kuhn's work on paradigms and the structure of science but directly concerned with the social construction of individual perspectives on society. A sophisticated study in the sociology of knowledge.

15. Hardin, Garrett. *Exploring New Ethics for Survival.* New York: Viking, 1972. A very entertaining, but very serious extension of ideas originally exposed in Hardin's classic essay on the tragedy of the commons.

16. Kuhn, Thomas. *The Structure of Scientific Revolutions.* Chicago: University of

Chicago Press, 1962. A classic work outlining the role that dominant paradigms play in structuring scientific inquiry. Must reading for those interested in understanding more completely the role of social paradigms in shaping social thought.

17. Skinner, B. F. *Beyond Freedom and Dignity*. New York: Alfred A. Knopf, 1971. Skinner's well-known and often misunderstood argument for developing a technology of behavior to deal with contemporary social problems. He puts concepts of freedom and dignity in a realistic perspective. Much of his argument is relevant to issues of human values and behavior lying at the root of the environmental crisis.

18. Taylor, Gordon Rattray. *Rethink: A Paraprimitive Solution*. New York: E. P. Dutton, 1973. Puts many modern trends in historical perspective and argues for the development of a new type of society based on different standards of consumption and different ideas of community.

Chapter 3

19. Barber, Richard. *The American Corporation*. New York: E. P. Dutton, 1970. Offers extensive documentation of the concentration of control within American corporations. An excellent and somewhat frightening portrayal of the new domestic and international environments within which corporate empires are growing.

20. Daly, Herman. ed. *Toward a Steady-State Economy*. San Francisco: W. H. Freeman and Company, 1973. An excellent collection dealing with the need for and possibilities for limiting traditional forms of economic growth. Many of the steady-state concepts mentioned in this chapter are discussed by Daly in further detail.

21. Dolan, Edwin. *TANSTAAFL*. New York: Holt, Rinehart and Winston, 1971. This short and very readable book offers a nontechnical introduction to ecological economics and the agenda of problems created for economists by the environmental crisis. Especially recommended for those who have done little detailed reading in the area.

22. Georgescu-Roegen, Nicholas. *The Entropy Law and the Economic Process*. Cambridge, Mass.: Harvard University Press, 1971. A highly specialized book challenging the basis for standard models of economic thought. The author begins his economic analysis with the laws of thermodynamics and demonstrates that all economic processes lead to greater system entropy and are irreversible. This theory contradicts much contemporary economic thought, which assumes the reversibility of such processes.

23. Heilbroner, Robert, et al. *In the Name of Profit*. New York: Doubleday, 1972. A collection of case studies documenting corporate irresponsibility and criminal neglect in the name of private profits.

24. Lundberg, Ferdinand. *The Rich and the Super Rich.* New York: Bantam Books, 1969. Analyzes the extent to which a small group of wealthy individuals dominates control of America's corporate affairs. Unique in its documentation of the origins of America's great fortunes.

25. Mintz, Morton, and Cohen, Jerry. *America, Inc.* New York: Dial Press, 1971. A detailed assault on the American corporate structure, outlining the use and abuse of corporate power in shaping economic and political institutions. A strong case is made that private "governments," including corporations, banks, and holding companies, now have more power in shaping our lives than do political institutions.

26. Mishan, E. J. *Technology and Growth.* New York: Praeger, 1970. A lucid and well-written argument against growth for growth's sake. Mishan's contention is that much growth in industrial society is not related to any increase in the quality of life and that it exacts a tremendous toll in terms of overcrowding, congestion, and other social ills.

27. Galbraith, John Kenneth. *Economics and the Public Purpose.* Boston: Houghton Mifflin, 1973. The most recent book by one of the foremost critics of the present economic system. Galbraith suggests that present economic beliefs are predicated on consumer sovereignty, which exists mainly in people's minds. He recommends more detailed planning and a complete reorientation of the concerns of economists to enable them to come to terms with new economic realities.

28. Weisskopf, Walter. *Alienation and Economics.* New York: E. P. Dutton, 1971. Argues for a new approach to economics that stresses new scarce resources including time, life, and energy, rather than material wealth.

Chapter 4

29. Chamberlain, Neil. *Beyond Malthus.* New York: Basic Books, 1970. A scholarly treatment of the impact of population growth on social structures. Chamberlain concentrates on population and its effects on the distribution of power within societies as well as among nations.

30. Domhoff, G. William. *Who Rules America?* Englewood Cliffs, N.J.: Prentice-Hall, 1967. Dedicated to identifying a monied elite that controls American politics and written in the tradition of C. Wright Mills. Although it is now somewhat dated, this book is must reading for those who still believe that the common man has a lot to say in American politics.

31. Dunn, Delmer. *Financing Presidential Campaigns.* Washington, D.C.: The Brookings Institution, 1972. A thorough review of campaign spending practices. Concentrates most heavily on expenditures for mass media.

32. Fellmeth, Robert C. *Politics of Land.* New York: Grossman, 1973. The report issued by Ralph Nader's study group on land use in California. It is a detailed and

unprecedented investigation of who owns the land and how they use politics to enhance its value while frequently ignoring environmental consequences.

33. Gilson, Lawrence. *Money and Secrecy*. New York: Praeger, 1972. A survey of existing federal and state laws that deal with campaign finance, conflict of interest, and secrecy in government. Includes citizen action plans for enforcement of existing laws as well as suggestions for new ones.

34. Green, Mark, Fellows, James, and Zwick, David. *Who Runs Congress?* New York: Grossman, 1972. An investigation of the private interests and activities of supposedly "public" servants in Washington. Paints a very unflattering picture of American legislators and the legislative process.

35. Lowi, Theodore. *The End of Liberalism*. New York: W. W. Norton, 1969. A well reasoned indictment of contemporary interest group liberalism. Lowi calls for reforms that would permit adequate planning by the federal government and that would permit the government to carry out plans once they have been formulated.

36. McConnel, Grant. *Private Power and American Democracy*. New York: Alfred A. Knopf, 1966. A detailed and carefully reasoned analysis of the erosion of governmental power by private interests in American democracy.

37. McGinness, Joe. *The Selling of the President 1968*. New York: Trident Press, 1969. Although this book is now somewhat dated, it remains a classic documentation of Richard Nixon's political tactics as well as of the Madison Avenue techniques that he has employed in presidential campaigns. The book details many of the campaign practices that were later refined for use in 1972.

38. Wise, David. *The Politics of Lying*. New York: Random House, 1973. An enlightening portrayal of many of the methods now used by the federal government to hide information from the American people.

39. Yarmolinsky, Adam. *The Military Establishment*. New York: Harper and Row, 1971. This detailed study of the impact of the military on American society covers a number of important topics, including government-military relations.

Chapter 5

40. Bell, Daniel, and Perloff, Harvey, eds. *The Future of the United States Government: Toward the Year 2000*. New York: George Braziller, 1971. This collection of essays was produced by a working group of the Commission on the Year 2000 of the American Academy of Arts and Sciences. It deals with the problems of governmental organization and public policy to the year 2000. Like most collections of this sort, the essays are uneven in quality, but this does represent one of very few attempts to speculate in this area.

41. Burns, James MacGregor. *Uncommon Sense*. New York: Harper and Row, 1972. This book argues that the biggest tragedy in the present political system is the inability to make long-term plans. Uncommon sense is needed to break out of a

system in which everyone is tending to private interests and no one is looking out for the collective welfare. Americans need to spell out their values clearly and plan accordingly.

42. Dahl, Robert. *After the Revolution?* New Haven, Conn.: Yale University Press, 1970. This is a scholarly treatment of classical questions of democratic theory as they pertain to postindustrial society. The author seeks to explain what types of authority will be possible in a complex society and how this authority can be maintained.

43. Lakey, George. *Strategy for a Living Revolution.* San Francisco: W. H. Freeman and Company, 1973. This book, written by a well-known Quaker activist, outlines a blueprint for nonviolent revolution in industrial society. It provides an organizational outline and a philosophy for those searching for intellectually sound alternatives to politics as usual.

44. Ophuls, William. "Prologue to a Political Theory of the Steady-State." Ph.D. dissertation, Yale University, 1973. It is extremely unusual to find such completeness, innovation, and readability in a doctoral dissertation. Ophuls has accomplished a tremendous task in meshing environmental concerns with issues in political theory. Must reading for political science students and others interested in further reading in this field.

45. Ross, Donald. *A Public Citizen's Action Manual.* New York: Grossman, 1973. This "how to do it" manual for the concerned citizen contains vital organizational information for projects ranging from consumer protection to investigations of government agencies.

46. Tugwell, Rexford. *Model for a New Constitution.* Palo Alto, Calif.: James E. Freel and Associates, 1970. This short book contains Tugwell's model constitution, which has been undergoing continued revision at the Center for the Study of Democratic Institutions. It is offered as a possible replacement for the aged original document that no longer seems suited to the critical issues of the day.

47. Wheeler, Harvey. *The Politics of Revolution.* Berkeley, Calif.: The Glendessary Press, 1971. Wheeler attempts to recast revolutionary thinking in light of recent scientific and environmental developments. This is a lucid and well-written book and one of the few to deal with the inadequacies of present methods of decision making in the United States.

Chapter 6

48. Barrett, Marvin, ed. *The Politics of Broadcasting.* New York: Thomas Y. Crowell, 1973. The most recent of a series of surveys on political developments in broadcast journalism, this collection contains both essays and documents dealing with the health of broadcast media.

49. Bronfenbrenner, Urie. *Two Worlds of Childhood: U.S. and U.S.S.R.* New York: Russell Sage Foundation, 1970. This comparative study of Soviet and American education pays special attention to the development of social consciousness. It contains many interesting observations about methods of instilling concern for the collective among young children, but the paucity of data requires that Bronfenbrenner's conclusions be treated with caution.

50. Cirino, Robert. *Don't Blame the People.* Los Angeles: Diversity Press, 1971. A documented and critical account of bias and distortion in the mass media. Cirino claims that the most serious biases result not from deliberate distortion but from the omission of newsworthy stories that might damage the dominant social paradigm.

51. Epstein, Edward. *News From Nowhere.* New York: Random House, 1973. An excellent exposition of the factors that condition the picture of the world presented on network news.

52. Johnson, Nicholas. *How to Talk Back to your Television Set.* Boston: Little, Brown, 1970. An angry book by a former FCC commissioner—a serious attack against private ownership in the television industry.

53. Skornia, Harry. *Television and Society.* New York: McGraw-Hill, 1965. A somewhat dated but fact-filled study of television and its management. Includes a chapter suggesting many useful changes in the television industry.

Chapter 7

54. Barnet, Richard. *Intervention and Revolution.* New York: David McKay, 1969. Outlines American intervention in the affairs of other countries and the role played by the United States government in ensuring a favorable climate for American business in developing countries.

55. Barnet, Richard. *Roots of War.* New York: Atheneum, 1972. This is a more general and theoretical treatment of the domestic roots of America's foreign interventions.

56. Bhagwati, Jagdish. *Economics and World Order.* New York: Macmillan, 1972. This is an excellent collection of essays by an international cast of scholars that focuses on the implications of present economic patterns for future international stability. It is especially useful in documenting the future of the gap between the rich nations and the poor nations.

57. Brown, Lester. *World without Borders.* New York: Random House, 1972. A highly recommended account of many dimensions of the planetary ecological crisis. Includes suggestions for dealing with them. In our view, Brown is overly sanguine about the role to be played by multinational corporations.

58. Ehrlich, Paul, and Harriman, Richard. *How to Be A Survivor: A Plan to Save*

Spaceship Earth. New York: Ballantine Books, 1971. Gives additional perspective on the relationships between the overdeveloped and the underdeveloped countries.

59. Falk, Richard. *This Endangered Planet.* New York: Random House, 1971. An introduction to the international aspects of the environmental crisis and its potential impact on the future of world order. Falk goes beyond analysis of problems and suggests methods of establishing a new international system capable of increasing stability and justice.

60. Greene, Felix. *The Enemy.* New York: Random House, 1971.

61. Julien, Claude. *America's Empire.* New York: Random House, 1971. Both this book and the preceding one are unabashedly polemical texts that offer a radical perspective on United States imperialism. They should be read with caution, but they do contain a number of interesting observations and a great deal of relevant information (as well as some rather dubious "facts").

62. Myrdal, Gunnar. *The Challenge of World Poverty: A World Poverty Program in Outline.* New York: Pantheon, 1970. Based on his classic three-volume *Asian Drama,* this is "must" reading for those interested in problems of economic development and the gap between rich nations and poor nations.

63. Schiller, Herbert. *Mass Communications and American Empire.* New York: Augustus M. Kelley, 1970. The best of a very small selection of books dealing with the international mass media empire controlled by industrial nations and the impact of that empire on the revolution of rising expectations.

64. Sprout, Harold, and Sprout, Margaret. *Toward a Politics of the Planet Earth.* New York: Van Nostrand Reinhold, 1971. The only available book on international relations written from an environmental perspective.

65. Vernon, Raymond. *Sovereignty at Bay.* New York: Basic Books, 1971. This balanced study of the multinational corporation concludes that the multinational corporation is certainly able to add to global productivity but that the benefits of such production are unevenly distributed. The book is an excellent treatment of many important issues raised by the rapid development of multinational corporations.

Chapter 8

66. Burch, William. *Daydreams and Nightmares.* New York: Harper and Row, 1971. One of an extremely limited number of sociological treatments of America's socioenvironmental problems.

67. Goldsmith, Edward, et al. *Blueprint for Survival.* Boston: Houghton Mifflin, 1972. One of the first attempts at global planning by the editors of the outstanding environmental magazine, *The Ecologist.*

68. Illich, Ivan. *Tools for Conviviality.* New York: Harper and Row, 1973. An argument that industrial man has become a slave to machines. Illich suggests de-developing society and establishing "conviviality," which he defines as creative and autonomous intercourse among people.

69. Jencks, Christopher, et al. *Inequality: A Reassessment of the Effect of Family and Schooling in America.* New York: Basic Books, 1972. A widely acclaimed study of inequality in American society and of the difficulties to be faced in attempting to equalize opportunity. An invaluable source of data for those interested in equality-of-opportunity issues and in questions of intergenerational social mobility.

70. Linder, Staffan. *The Harried Leisure Class.* New York: Columbia University Press, 1970. An inquiry into the shortage of time in our consumption-oriented society. It questions whether a high industrial growth rate, leading to material affluence, has led people to ignore the loss of other aspects of affluence, including leisure time.

71. Pirages, Dennis. *Seeing Beyond: Personal, Social, and Political Alternatives.* Reading, Mass.: Addison-Wesley, 1971. A collection of articles that suggest ways of advancing beyond the contemporary social paradigm and establishing alternative life styles without violent revolution.

72. Slater, Philip. *The Pursuit of Loneliness.* Boston: Beacon Press, 1970. An extremely readable and cogent critique of the dominant social paradigm spawned by industrial society.

Notes

Chapter 1

Page 1:   A basic source for the material in this chapter is Paul R. Ehrlich and Anne H. Ehrlich (5), *Population, Resources, Environment: Issues in Human Ecology* (San Francisco: W. H. Freeman and Company, 1972). Most of the points made here are expanded on in that volume; the bibliographies at the end of each of its chapters provide documentation. *Where specific references are not given in this chapter, check this source.*

Page 2:   Information on the scale of human impact on the environment can be found in the Study of Critical Environmental Problems (SCEP) (13), *Man's Impact on the Global Environment* (Cambridge, Mass.: MIT Press, 1972).

Further explanation of these basic ecological ideas can be found in E. J. Kormondy, *Concepts of Ecology* (Englewood Cliffs, N.J.: Prentice-Hall, 1969); C. J. Krebs, *Ecology* (New York: Harper and Row, 1972); and E. P. Odum, *Fundamentals of Ecology*, 3rd ed. (Philadelphia: Saunders, 1972). A more advanced treatment of ecology, including some of its most modern aspects and its interrelations with genetics, can be found in R. Ricklefs, *Ecology* (Newton, Mass.: Chiron Press, 1973).

Page 4: A more detailed treatment of the relationship between population growth, new technologies, and environmental deterioration can be found in Paul R. Ehrlich and John P. Holdren, "The Impact of Population Growth," *Science* 171:1212–1217 (March 26, 1971), and *idem*, "One-Dimensional Ecology," *Science and Public Affairs: The Bulletin of the Atomic Scientists* 28:16–27 (May, 1972).

Page 5: For more detail about the impact of preagricultural man on ecological systems, see Carl O. Sauer, "The Agency of Man on Earth," and O. C. Stewart, "Fire as the First Great Force Employed by Man," both in W. L. Thomas, Jr., *Man's Role in Changing the Face of the Earth* (Chicago: Univ. of Chicago Press, 1956). See also Paul S. Martin, "Prehistoric Overkill," in P. S. Martin and H. E. Wright, Jr., *Pleistocene Extinctions: The Search for a Cause* (New Haven, Conn.: Yale Univ. Press, 1967). Martin's view that man has been a major cause of the extinction of animals has been disputed, but at the moment this explanation seems to be the most cogent one.

Information on the past ecocatastrophe in the Tigris and Euphrates valleys may be found in Thorkeld Jacobsen and Robert M. Adams, "Salt and Silt in Ancient Mesopotamian Agriculture," *Science* 128:1251–1258 (November 21, 1958).

Page 6: For the story of the Irish Potato Famine, see G. L. Carefoot and E. R. Sprott, *Famine on the Wind* (New York: Rand McNally, 1967).

Page 7: For more information on the dangers of loss of genetic variability, see Graham Chedd, "Hidden Peril of the Green Revolution," *New Scientist* (October 22, 1970); and O. H. Frankel, W. K. Agble, J. B. Harlon, and E. Bennett, "Genetic Dangers in the Green Revolution," *Ceres* (FAO): 2(5) (September–October, 1964).

A relatively optimistic view of the green revolution is stated in L. R. Brown, *Seeds of Change: The Green Revolution and Development in the 1970s* (New York: Praeger, 1970). For a fine up-to-date review of the situation by Brown, see "Population and Affluence: Growing Pressures on World Food Resources," *Population Bulletin* 29(2) (1973). A more pessimistic view is stated by W. C. Paddock in "How Green is the Green Revolution?," *BioScience* 20:892–902 (1970). Recent events indicate that the pessimistic view of the green revolution was, unfortunately, correct. For instance, in mid-1973 the Philippine Islands, home of "miracle rice," were essentially out of rice—just four years after the Philippine government boasted that the green revolution would make the Philippines self-sufficient for rice, thus obviating the need for population control. The Philippine population grew approximately 12 percent during those four years.

Ecological problems of farming tropical rainforest areas are well covered by D. Janzen in "The Unexploited Tropics," *Bull. Ecological Soc. America* (September, 1970); and M. McNeil, "Lateritic Soils," *Scientific American* (November, 1964), reprinted in P. R. Ehrlich, J. P. Holdren, and R. W. Holm, eds., *Man and the Ecosphere* (San Francisco: W. H. Freeman and Company, 1971). These works outline the general problem. The dubious prospects for Brazil's recent attempt to open the Amazon Basin to agriculture are made clear in B. J. Meggers, "Some Problems of Cultural Adaptation in Amazonia, with Emphasis on the Pre-European Period," and H. Sioli, "Recent Human Activities in the Brazilian Amazon Region and Their Ecological Effects," both in B. J. Meggers, E. S. Ayensu, and W. D. Duckworth, *Tropical Forest Ecosystems in Africa and South America: A Comparative Review* (Washington, D.C.: Smithsonian Institution Press, 1973). Another example of past ecocatastrophe is described by Jeremy A. Sabloff's "The Collapse of Classic Maya Civilization," in J. Harte and R. H. Socolow, eds., *Patient Earth* (New York: Holt, Rinehart and Winston, 1971).

Page 8: The source of the Odum quote is his fascinating book, *Environment, Power, and Society* (New York: Wiley, 1971), p. 115.

Page 9: Known recoverable reserves in the Alaska field are 8–9 billion barrels (bbl), and estimated recoverable reserves are 45 billion barrels. United States consumption in 1973 was approximately 16.5 million barrels/day, with an annual growth rate of 4.2–4.3 percent (doubling time approximately 16.5 years). Thus, annual consumption is now some 6 billion barrels, and projected annual consumption in the year 2006 is approximately 24 billion barrels. The source of these statistics is the National Petroleum Council Report, *U.S. Energy Outlook to 1985.*

Page 10: It is conceivable that life expectancy in the United States may well turn a corner and decrease during the next decade. In California, a state that is often an indicator of future trends for the rest of the country, the death rate declined for the century preceding the 1960s. Since that time the death rate for young people aged 15–40 has been increasing. There were 1.2 deaths per thousand people in this age bracket in the late 1950s and 1.5 deaths per thousand people in the early 1970s. These State Health Department figures were reported in the *San Francisco Chronicle* of June 27, 1973.

Page 11:   Over the years many Japanese have been poisoned by mercury wastes dumped into Minimata Bay by the Chisso Corporation. The effects of the mercury became known as minimata disease, and not until the late 1960s was the link between the poisoning and the dumping of mercury discovered. The approximate figure of "hundreds" given in the text refers only to the most serious cases. Ken Otani and Jun Ui, writing in J. Ui, ed., *Polluted Japan* (Tokyo: Jishu-Koza, 1972), estimate that "Perhaps more than 10,000 inhabitants received more or less irreversible damage from the activities of Chisso..." (p. 16). This book is an excellent source of information about the ecocatastrophes that have occurred in the world's most polluted country. It may be obtained for a small fee from Jun Ui, c/o Jishu-Koza, Department of Urban Engineering, University of Tokyo, Bunkyo-ku, Tokyo, Japan 113.

Page 12:   The Leopold quote is from *A Sand County Almanac, with Essays on Conservation from Round River*, paperback edition (New York: Ballantine Books, 1970), p. 190. Everyone interested in saving the Earth should read this beautiful, poetic book. Some sample quotes are as follows. On materialism: "Nothing could be more salutary at this stage than a little healthy contempt for a plethora of material blessings" (p. xix); on economists: "Only economists mistake physical opulence for riches" (p. 177); on being an ecologist: "One of the penalties of an ecological education is that one lives alone in a world of wounds. Much of the damage inflicted on land is quite invisible to laymen. An ecologist must either harden his shell and make believe that the consequences of science are none of his business, or he must be the doctor who sees the marks of death in a community that believes itself well and does not want to be told otherwise" (p. 197).

An excellent discussion of the process of exponential growth and its impact on the world in the future is presented in Meadows *et al.* (11).

Page 14: The statistics on birth rates in Latin America are taken from the 1972 *World Population Data Sheet* of the Population Reference Bureau.

Population growth rates for the rest of the world are taken from the *United Nations Statistical Yearbook 1972* (New York: The United Nations, 1973).

Page 15: Lack of sufficient calories is *undernutrition*. *Malnutrition* refers to the lack of one or more essential nutrients, most commonly protein.

The Berelson quotation is from the *1970 Annual Report* of the Population Council. For a detailed account of the momentum of world population growth, see T. Frejka, *The Future of Population Growth* (New York: Wiley, 1973).

Page 16: The vehicle mileage figures represent composite estimates. The most precise, most recent estimates of both freight and passenger mileage are found in G. A. Lincoln, "Energy Conservation," *Science* (April 13, 1973). Lincoln's estimates of mileages are as follows: airplanes, 21–22 passenger miles per gallon; automobiles, 32 passenger miles per gallon; cross-country trains, 80 passenger miles per gallon; commuter trains, 100 passenger miles per gallon; buses, 125 passenger miles per gallon; and two-deck suburban trains, 200 passenger miles per gallon.

Page 17: Data on steel consumption are from the *United Nations Statistical Yearbook* for the relevant year.

Page 18: A more detailed account of the way population growth, increased affluence, and faulty technology interact to cause environmental deterioration can be found in Chapter 7 of Paul R. Ehrlich, Anne H. Ehrlich, and John P. Holdren (6), *Human Ecology: Problems and Solutions* (San Francisco: W. H. Freeman and Company, 1973).

A discussion of the contributions of LDC agriculture to climatic change can be found in R. A. Bryson and W. M. Wendland, "Climatic Effects of Atmospheric Pollution," a paper presented at the American Association for the Advancement of Science meeting, Dallas, 1968.

Page 19: The first Borgstrom quotation comes from Population Reference Bureau, *PRB Selection* No. 31 (January, 1970). The quote "one billion . . .

starvation" is also from Borgstrom, "The World Food Crisis," *Futures* (June 1969), pp. 339–355.

The estimates of Dumont and Rosier are from their book, *The Hungry Future* (New York: Praeger, 1969), pp. 34–35.

Page 20:   The figures for clearing and preparing farm land are taken from Meadows *et al.* (11), pp. 46–54.

Page 21:   The source for Table 1.1 is Food and Agriculture Organization of the United Nations, *Monthly Bulletin of Agricultural Economics and Statistics* (January, 1971).

Page 22:   *Time* magazine of November 8, 1948, contains many other classics of uninformed technological optimism.

An account of the plight of the Philippines is found in J. T. Hopkins, "Philippines Threatened by Serious Shortage of Rice," *Foreign Agriculture* 11(33) (August 13, 1973). See also "World Food Situation: Pessimism Comes Back into Vogue," *Science* (August 17, 1973).

Page 23:   Figures dealing with water requirements are taken from Ehrlich and Ehrlich (5), pp. 76–77, and sources cited therein.

Page 24:   Figures on world fishery production are taken from *The State of Food and Agriculture 1972* (New York: Food and Agriculture Organization of the United Nations, 1973).

Estimates of future yields can be found in Ehrlich and Ehrlich (5), pp. 125–134, and references cited therein. See also D. L. Alverson, A. R. Longhurst, and J. A. Gulland, "How Much Food from the Sea?," *Science* 168:503–505 (April 24, 1970) and John Ryther's reply, which follows.

For data on the decline of anchoveta fishing, see Paul Ferree, "Peru Again Bans Anchovy Fishing, Fishmeal Supplies Tighten," *Foreign Agriculture* 11(32) (August 6, 1973).

Page 25:   Figures from the National Oceanic and Atmospheric Administration were reported by the Associated Press (February 13, 1973).

Page 26: The source for Table 1.2 and statistics on growth in mineral consumption is Meadows *et al.* (11), Chapter 2. Similar figures have been published in "A Blueprint for Survival," *The Ecologist* (January, 1972).

Page 27: It is important to remember that the most critical "increasing costs" here are often *environmental costs.* For instance, the major constraint on the amount of certain minerals that can be made available may well be the amount of energy that can be used for extraction and processing without causing climatic disaster (see p. 32 and note to p. 32).

In 1971 there were 371 oil wells drilled below 15,000 feet, worldwide. In that same year 14,966 oil and gas wells were drilled in the United States. Of these, 10,538 were dry. See *World Oil* (February, 1972).

It should also be mentioned that optimistic plans for coal gasification have run into a snag because the process requires considerable quantities of water, which also is in short supply. See "NAS: Water Scarcity May Limit Use of Western Coal," *Science* (August 10, 1973).

The data on increases in resource costs come from Meadows *et al.* (11), Chapter 2. See also the figures in Earl Cook, "Resource Limits to Growth," paper presented to convention of National Association of Manufacturers, New Orleans (November 16, 1972).

Page 28: Although the Arab-Israeli crises have temporarily slowed the Nixon natural gas negotiations, the deal may very well be culminated in the next few years. The logistics problems inherent in handling the natural gas will be tremendous. The gas must be transported 1,500 miles across Siberia in 56-inch-diameter pipes. A second proposed line will be 2,500 miles long. The cost of these pipelines is estimated to be in excess of $11 billion. The gas must be cooled, liquefied, and then transferred to one of twenty tankers. The total cost of the tankers is likely to be in the neighborhood of $4 billion. The ecological and other hazards of this form of transportation are just beginning to be investigated and may well prove to be extremely difficult to guard against. The figures mentioned here were published in the *San Francisco Chronicle* (November 12, 1972).

Those interested in the energy crisis can obtain a general background from J. P. Holdren's excellent discussion in Holdren and Herrera, *Energy* (New York: Sierra Club Books, 1972). A more detailed discussion of the technology and hazards of nuclear power can be found in D. R. Inglis' fine book, *Nuclear Energy: Its Physics and Its Social Challenge* (Reading, Mass.: Addison-Wesley, 1973).

Page 30: In 1973 there was a dramatic shift in the weight of opinion in the scientific community toward the point of view that the risks of using fission reactors as power sources are simply unacceptable.

Los Angeles was given a foretaste of what a nuclear reactor disaster might be like on September 18, 1973, when a toxic sulphur solution escaped from a storage tank and was borne aloft by winds. The fumes drifted more than forty miles, but fortunately the toxic material did not drift close enough to the ground to kill any human beings.

More details on radiation spills at Hanford, Washington, may be found in "Radiation Spill at Hanford: The Anatomy of an Accident," *Science* (August 24, 1973).

Page 31: The AEC record in handling plutonium is documented in Holdren and Herrera (8), p. 106.

Page 32: Man may already have helped unleash lethal regional disturbances of climate. In a recent paper, "Climatic Modification by Air Pollution, II: The Sahelian Effect" (Univ. of Wisconsin, Report 9), meteorologist Reid Bryson hypothesizes that two of mankind's major polluting activities, the injection of carbon dioxide and particulate matter into the atmosphere, interact to lessen the dependability of the monsoons in Africa and southern Asia. If he is correct, more than one billion human lives are in jeopardy. This article is reprinted in *The Ecologist* (October, 1973.

Physicist Amory B. Lovins has recently completed a more detailed study of the global heat balance that supersedes Holdren's preliminary estimate. His results, soon to be published in *Science and Public Affairs: Bulletin of Atomic Scientists*, show that serious climatic disturbance will occur much sooner than indicated in the earlier approximation. As has so often been true in the past, a more refined knowledge of the environmental problem indicates that it is more, not less, serious than was previously thought.

Page 34: The statement by President Nixon's energy adviser was made at a news conference in early 1973 and was reported in *Newsweek* (January 22,

1973). It is only fair to point out that events deteriorated so rapidly in 1973 that by autumn of that year the Nixon administration was indeed asking people to use less heat in their homes. It should also be mentioned that, during this same period, President Nixon reportedly gave up his habit of sitting in front of a roaring fire while his air conditioners were running.

The Chase Manhattan figure was reported from Brussels by the United Press (March 30, 1973).

Page 36:   The quotation from B. F. Skinner comes from (17), Chapter 1.

Page 38:   Malthus' original work, *An Essay on the Principle of Population as It Affects the Future Improvement of Society with Remarks on the Speculations of Mr. Godwin, M. Condorcet and Other Writers*, was published anonymously in 1798.

Chapter 2

Page 40:   This chapter was written when Russell Train was a member of the Council on Environmental Quality. Since that time, of course, he has been appointed to head the Environmental Protection Agency.

The literature on Soviet environmental problems is steadily growing. Among the more important recent works are: Marshall Goldman, *The Spoils of Progress: Environmental Pollution in the Soviet Union* (Cambridge, Mass.: MIT Press, 1972), and Philip Pryde, *Conservation in the Soviet Union* (Cambridge, Mass.: Cambridge University Press, 1972).

The decision against the Chisso Corporation was reached on March 20, 1973. In September, 1971, the Showa Denko Company was found liable on a similar charge; in July, 1972, six petrochemical firms were fined for air pollution; and in August, 1972, Mitsui Mining and Smelting Company was ordered to pay one-half million dollars for careless dumping of cadmium waste. These payments are, of course, pathetically small in relation to the damage done.

Page 41:   Of course, the lowering of fertility to slightly below replacement level should be done not merely to hasten the arrival of ZPG but to move eventually to negative population growth (NPG). NPG would, ideally, mean a long period during which the death rate would be slightly higher than the birth rate, and population size would gradually be lowered to a more readily sustained level.

Page 43: The idea of dominant paradigms guiding the direction of scientific research was developed by Thomas Kuhn (16). The idea of dominant social paradigms is further developed in Dennis Pirages, "The Unbalanced Revolution," in Nicholas Steneck, ed., *Science and Society* (Ann Arbor: Univ. of Michigan Press, 1974).

Page 44: Cross-national differences in political attitudes and "political cultures" are documented in Gabriel Almond and Sidney Verba, *The Civic Culture* (Princeton, N.J.: Princeton Univ. Press, 1963).

Page 45: B. F. Skinner (17) makes a strong case for a technology of behavior in Chapter 1.

Garrett Hardin (15) discusses the role of supporting ethical theories as guides and justifications for behavior on pp. 83–85.

Page 47: Documentation of the decline of the Mayan civilization is found in Jeremy Sabloff, "The Collapse of Classic Maya Civilization," in J. Harte and R. H. Socolow, eds., *Patient Earth* (New York: Holt, Rinehart and Winston, 1971).

Regarding Mesopotamians, see note to p. 5.

Page 48: Herbert Marcuse's conception of one-dimensional people living in a one-dimensional society is spelled out in philosophical detail in his *One-Dimensional Man* (Boston: Beacon Press, 1971). See also Jerome Frank, "Galloping Technology, A New Social Disease," *Journal of Social Issues*, No. 4 (1966).

Page 51: Additional effects of the New York strike are outlined in *Newsweek* (June 21, 1971).

Page 53: Society is largely defenseless against persons who have so much individual power that they can wreak social havoc. Statistics reveal that only 10 percent of terrorist bombers in the early 1970s was actually caught by law officials.

Page 54: The unbalanced nature of the industrial revolution and the social lag phenomenon are discussed in more detail in Dennis Pirages, "Behavioral Technology and Institutional Transformation," in Harvey Wheeler, ed., *Beyond the Punitive Society* (San Francisco: W. H. Freeman and Company, 1973).

B. F. Skinner (17) discusses the cult of freedom and dignity in Chapters 2 and 3.

Thomas Schelling's important article, "On the Ecology of Micromotives," is found in *The Public Interest* (Fall, 1971).

For more detail on social traps, see John Platt, "Social Traps," *The American Psychologist* (1973, in press).

Page 55: The ideas concerning the tragedy of the commons were originally outlined in Garrett Hardin, "The Tragedy of the Commons," *Science* 162:1243–1248 (December 13, 1968).

Page 57: The two Japanese imports that were claimed to meet the standards were the Honda and the Mazda.

Page 61: Festinger's theory is outlined in detail in Leon Festinger, *A Theory of Cognitive Dissonance* (New York: Row, Peterson and Company, 1957).

Page 62: The $100 billion clean-up bill was suggested by the Council on Environmental Quality in a report released in August, 1971. President Nixon's remarks were made in response to this report. See *Newsweek* (August 16, 1971).

Chapter 3

Page 69: It has been claimed, with much justification, that economic growth was largely responsible for the failure of Karl Marx's dire predictions of class conflict. Industrial growth permitted the owners of the "means of production" effectively to "buy off" the working class by sharing the growing material abundance.

Page 70:   Wallich's comments can be found in *Newsweek* (January 24, 1972), p. 60. Brzezinski's remarks can be found in *Newsweek* (March 27, 1972), p. 54.

Page 73:   The performance of Schlage Lock Company in the second quarter of 1973 is a small but meaningful example of how increased crime and fear lead to increased GNP. This company, which specializes in locks and other types of antiburglar devices, reported second-quarter earnings up 46 percent with a 16 percent increase in sales. Not only does this increase in sales denote an unhealthy contribution to GNP, but the very high profit margins seem to indicate that demand for these devices is high enough that lock companies need not worry about consumer reaction to increased prices. The Schlage figures for the first and second quarters of 1973 were published in the *San Francisco Chronicle* (August 7, 1973).

Page 74:   Gray market conditions in the steel industry and tremendous increases in the demand for paper were reported in *Business Week* (June 2, 1973). Since that time, conditions in the paper industry have steadily worsened as paper mills have shut down rather than comply with new antipollution regulations. It is expected that by early 1974, many types of paper will simply be unavailable.

Page 76:   Although the thought will probably be of little comfort to most Americans, inflation seems to be a characteristic of all industrial and industrializing societies, and many other countries have experienced more serious inflation than has the United States. In late 1972 prices were rising at an annual rate of 12 percent in Great Britain, 10 percent in Italy, and 9 percent in France and Germany. These and similar figures for other countries can be found in the *San Francisco Chronicle* (January 7, 1973) and in *Business Conditions Digest* (Washington, D.C.: Department of Commerce, various months).

Page 77:   Inflation and unemployment statistics are taken from *Business Conditions Digest* (Washington, D.C.: Department of Commerce, various months).

Page 78: Although early in 1973 the petroleum industry had not been substantially affected by government regulations, by late 1973 governmental pressures had been brought to bear on petroleum prices. In November, however, the industry was being allowed to pass along price increases originating "at the well;" but there was no formula to guarantee that excess profits were not being made at the point of origin. Aside from price increases, the petroleum industry was making larger profits by reducing services in a noncompetitive situation. Many service stations began to charge for road maps or discontinued their sale altogether. In July, 1973, three major oil producers (Gulf, Mobil, and BP) lowered the octanes of their gasoline "to conserve fuel" but did not lower prices and made no effort to reimburse consumers. Spokesmen for Gulf and Mobil announced that they were opposed to posting octane ratings on pumps because these ratings vary slightly from time to time. Major petroleum manufacturers have profited handsomely from the fuel shortages. *Business Week* reported that the petroleum industry as a whole showed a 52 percent increase in earnings in the second quarter of 1973 compared with the second quarter of 1972. See "The Profits Boom Rolls On," *Business Week* (August 11, 1973).

Page 79: During the next two years, Japan's economic growth rate is expected to decline to approximately 8 percent. This figure could drop much lower if Middle Eastern nations withhold petroleum from the Japanese. See "World Economies: Strong Growth Rates Tempered by Inflation," *Business Week* (July 28, 1973).

Although he would not necessarily agree with all the points made in this chapter, Irving Friedman presents an excellent treatment of the evils of inflation, in terms that are easy to understand, in *Inflation* (New York: Houghton-Mifflin, 1973).

Page 80: The source for Table 3.1 and for the figures for the discomfort index is *Business Conditions Digest* (Washington, D.C.: Department of Commerce, various months).

Page 82: The source for the statistics on mergers is *The Statistical Abstract of the United States 1972*, p. 481.

A full listing of ITT holdings would require several pages. Suffice it to say that ITT acquired fifty companies over the last ten years, including Avis Rent-A-Car, Hamilton Management, Aetna Finance, the Sheraton Corporation, and Continental Baking. In five years ITT doubled both its sales and its assets. Further details can be found in Barber (19), pp. 42–43.

Page 83: An excellent portrait of how corporate mergers benefit executives is provided by Robert Heilbroner *et al.* (23), Chapter 6.

A more complete treatment of the environmental problems caused by outmoded production techniques in the steel industry can be found in Sheldon Novick, "Steel: The Obsolete Industry," *Environment* (November, 1973).

Page 84: Strip-mining figures are taken from the *1973 World Almanac*, p. 491.

Page 85: These and other figures on executive compensation during a supposed year of economic restraint are from "Executive Compensation: Who Got Most in '72," *Business Week* (May 5, 1973).

Page 89: This particular Friedman argument was made in an article entitled, "The Social Responsibility of Business is to Increase Its Profits," *The New York Times Magazine* (September 13, 1970). He has, of course, made similar arguments elsewhere.

Page 90: The decline of individual stock ownership is documented in Richard Barber (19), p.55.

The Sears Roebuck stock situation is also documented in Richard Barber (19), pp. 30–32.

Page 91: The reach of Morgan Guaranty Trust is graphically displayed in Richard Barber (19), pp. 66–67. Other figures on the scope of the banking elite's power are found in *op. cit.*, pp. 64–66.

The ten largest financial institutions in order of total assets (in billions of dollars) are:

Morgan Guaranty Trust	27.2
Bankers Trust	19.9
Prudential Insurance	18.3

First National City Bank	17.2
United States Trust Company of New York	17.0
Metropolitan Life	16.5
Manufacturer's Hanover Trust	10.9
Mellon National Bank and Trust	10.5
Investor's Diversified Services	9.7
Chase Manhattan Bank	9.2

These figures and the figures on volume of stock traded by institutions are taken from "Are the Institutions Wrecking Wall Street?," *Business Week* (June 2, 1973).

The average yields on stocks are taken from *Newsweek* (December 20, 1972). See also "The Perils of P/E," *Business Week* (May 5, 1973), for more detail on the problems caused by very high price-earnings ratios in the present stock market.

Page 92: The figures on sources of investment capital are taken from Richard Barber (19), Chapter 4.

The $1 trillion energy figure is an estimate by the Chase Manhattan Bank (see p. 34 and notes for that page).

Page 93: In all fairness it should be mentioned that many banks adopted a dual interest rate structure during the credit crunch of 1973, whereby home buyers were able to obtain loans at a slightly lower figure than were industrial customers.

Page 95: The Nixon approach to the energy crisis, as announced in November, 1973, offers yet another example of failure to use long-term planning and equitable methods to deal with resource scarcity. The President encouraged people to turn their home thermostats down six degrees and suggested that the nation's highway speed limits be lowered to 50 mph. For some reason, gas rationing was not instituted then, even though it will almost certainly be necessary in the future. One would also have thought that the time was long past for legislation drastically limiting the horsepower of American automobile engines (perhaps to a maximum of 100 hp), but this and many other obvious ways of cutting the wastage of energy in the United States were not suggested. In fact, it appeared that the "political" approach to the energy crisis was to pretend that the situation could be ameliorated by a few short-term minor adjustments in demand combined with a medium-term attempt at greatly increasing supply (the latter at heavy cost to the environment).

Page 96: A detailed treatment of planning problems in Czechoslovakia and other centralized economies can be found in Dennis C. Pirages, "Resources, Technology, and Foreign Policy Behavior: The Czech Experience," in James Kuhlman, ed., *Comparative Eastern European Foreign Policy* (New York: Praeger, forthcoming), and Dennis Pirages, *Modernization and Political Tension Management: A Socialist Society in Perspective* (New York: Praeger, 1972), Chapter 4.

Page 99: The concept of progressive taxation based on size was suggested by Bernard Rapoport (personal communication).

Page 103: The problem of excess profits on increasingly scarce goods has recently been demonstrated by industries that find themselves in situations where demand exceeds supply. In the second quarter of 1973, for example, the paper industry's production fell short of demand, and the industry reported profits that were 69 percent higher than those earned in the same quarter in 1972. This profit was made on a mere 17 percent increase in sales. In addition, profits in the building materials industry increased 66 percent; in metals and mining, 56 percent; in oil, 52 percent; and in steel, 49 percent. Among individual oil companies, which supposedly were having a difficult time coping with price controls, Standard of Ohio showed a 110 percent increase in profits, and Gulf showed an 82 percent increase. (These figures are from "The Profits Boom Rolls On," *Business Week* (August 11, 1973).

Page 106: In Yugoslavia, consumer protection is taken seriously. The eighty-man market inspection force in Belgrade is equipped with squad cars and a twenty-four-hour-a-day switchboard to monitor complaints. The force has the power to impose small on-the-spot fines, and more serious cases are taken to court. The squad answers from fifty to sixty calls each day (reported by United Press International in the *San Francisco Chronicle*, September 3, 1972).

Page 107: Herman Daly's essay on moral growth, "The Steady-State Economy: Toward a Political Economy of Biophysical Equilibrium and Moral Growth," is found in (20), Chapter 7.

Page 108: The RAND report is by R. D. Doctor *et al.*, "California's Electric Quandary. Slowing the Growth Rate" (Santa Monica, Calif.: RAND Corporation, 1972).

The extensive report by the federal government is "The Potential for Energy Conservation" (Washington, D.C.: Office of Emergency Preparedness, 1972).

The results of the Environmental Protection Agency's tests demonstrated that automobile mileage increases very sharply as the size of engines decreases. The Datsun 1200 produced the best mileage during these tests—28.7 miles to the gallon. The best American-made car in this respect was the Chrysler Cricket sedan, which got 23.2 miles to the gallon. American-made cars dominated the other end of the mileage distribution, however, and nearly one-third of all cars got less than ten miles to a gallon of gasoline. Whether the Environmental Protection Agency will now attempt to come to terms with the fuel crisis by setting efficiency standards for new models remains to be seen.

Page 109: The Daly quotation is taken from (20), p. 14.

Page 110: For more detail on the "hydrogen economy," see D. P. Gregory, D. Y. C. Ng, and G. M. Long, "The Hydrogen Economy," in J. O. Bockris, ed., *Electrochemistry of Cleaner Environments* (New York: Plenum, 1972), and "The Hydrogen Economy," *Scientific American* (January, 1973).

Page 111: For further discussion of depletion quotas, see Herman Daly, "The Steady-State Economy: Toward A Political Economy of Biophysical Equilibrium and Moral Growth," in Daly (20) and references cited therein.

While this chapter was being written and revised, the Nixon administration shifted its energy posture, first denying the existence of an energy crisis, then emphasizing the energy "challenge," and finally emphasizing the energy "crisis." Also, by November, 1973, the President had lengthened the period necessary to make the United States self-sufficient in energy production to ten years. This only serves to highlight the lack of federal government planning on these matters and the frequent failure of politicians to admit that such problems exist. This situation is discussed in detail in Chapter 4.

Page 114: The Daly quotation comes from (20), p. 162.

The natural resource units allocation plan is found in Walter Westman and Roger Gifford, "Environmental Impact: Controlling the Overall Level," *Science* (August 31, 1973).

Chapter 4

Page 116: Politics as "the authoritative allocation of values" is only one of many definitions that have been offered over the years, but it seems to be one of the more sensible and accepted ones. For further explanation, see David Easton, *A Framework for Political Analysis* (Englewood Cliffs, N.J.: Prentice-Hall, 1965).

Page 119: Schelling's ideas are found in Thomas Schelling, "On the Ecology of Micromotives," *The Public Interest* (Fall, 1971).

Page 120: The statements by the student who preferred nuclear holocaust and those academics who felt that mankind should be wiped out were made in recent university meetings and seminars attended by the authors of the present book.

Page 123: The early giveaway programs in land and mineral rights are discussed in some detail in Walter A. Rosenbaum, *The Politics of Environmental Concern* (New York: Praeger, 1973), pp. 10–12. Rosenbaum points out that 180 million acres of land were given to railroad interests in the nineteenth century. This area is larger than France, England, Scotland, and Wales combined. He also reports that many states sold land rich in minerals and abundant in forest land for as little as ten cents an acre. Entrepreneurs, of course, had little trouble turning a profit at those prices. Somehow the origins of those big corporate fortunes are ignored in today's political dialogue about regulation of mineral production. One might think that a government that has given these rights also has the right to take them away.

The composition of the delegation to the Constitutional Convention in 1787 is documented in Thomas Dye and Harmon Zeigler, *The Irony of*

Democracy (Belmont, Calif.: Wadsworth, 1970), pp. 30–34. Page 34 contains an excellent table that categorizes the delegates.

Page 124: For a more detailed treatment of the "politics of muddling through," see Charles Lindbloom, "The Science of Muddling Through," *Public Administration Review* (Spring, 1959).

Page 125: For more details on the congressional committee system and the environment, see Richard A. Cooley and Geoffrey Wandesforde-Smith, *Congress and the Environment* (Seattle: Univ. of Washington Press, 1970).

Page 126: Dahl's efficiency principle is discussed in (42), Section I, p. 126. The Michels quotation comes from Roberto Michels, *Political Parties* (Glencoe, Ill: The Free Press of Glencoe, 1949).

Page 127: The dominance of a small number of families in both the official and unofficial political arenas is documented in G. William Domhoff (30); see especially Chapters 3–5.

Page 128: Lowi's indictment of interest-group liberalism is found in (35); see especially Chapter 10.

Page 129: Obviously, as the energy crisis deepens, the Nixon administration will be forced to take more serious measures. Although the federal government's lethargy in preparing for the crisis is remarkable, such reluctance to take decisive action is only to be expected from politicians who are interested primarily in reelection.

Page 130: The Agnew article, "Division May Be the Price of Progress," was originally printed in *The New York Times* (July 11, 1970). Although Agnew has now been discredited, there is little sign that this philosophy has also been discredited.

Page 132: The report of the Council on Environmental Quality was originally issued without the three chapters. They were later released in response to public questioning of the reasons why they had been withheld. The official excuse was that they had not been prepared in time for distribution.

Page 133:   The literacy figures are taken from David Dempsey, "The Right to Read," *Saturday Review* (April 17, 1971).

Page 134:   The public opinion survey listing politics as nineteenth out of twenty occupations in terms of honesty was carried out by Julian B. Rotter and Donald K. Stein in 1972 and was reported in the *San Francisco Chronicle* (August 20, 1972). Used-car salesmen ranked twentieth, while physicians, clergymen, dentists, judges, and psychologists ranked at the top. That government itself is losing the trust of the people is the conclusion of a study of public opinion undertaken by Arthur Miller. In 1964 only 20 percent of Americans polled distrusted their government. By 1970 the figure had risen to 39 percent. This was reported in the *San Francisco Chronicle* (October 12, 1972). The post-Watergate figures will undoubtedly be higher.

Milgram's experiment is explained in Stanley Milgram, "Behavioral Study of Obedience," *The Journal of Abnormal and Social Psychology*, No. 4 (1963).

Page 135:   Cases of child abuse are documented in *Newsweek* (July 24, 1972).

Page 137:   Lasswell's ideas are expanded in his *World Politics and Personal Insecurity* (New York: The Free Press, 1950).

Page 139:   The campaign expense figures on this page were taken from various wire service stories. At this writing, government agencies have not completed the final tally of reported campaign spending for the 1972 election. It is certain, however, that the reported total will only be a portion of what was actually spent. The most detailed treatment of campaign spending is found in Delmer Dunn (31). The 1968 spending figures are taken from a Citizen's Research Foundation report published in the *San Francisco Chronicle* (June 20, 1971).

Page 141:   These and other contributions for favors are documented in Jack Anderson's syndicated column (June 19, 1973). One executive, Richard Mellon Scaife, reportedly contributed $1 million in the form of 330 separate checks to the Nixon campaign to avoid gift taxes. See the *San Francisco Chronicle* (October 25, 1972).

In addition to these ambassadors, others who purchased offices include Anthony Marshall, New York Research executive, $25,000, Malagasy Republic; John Pritzlaff, Jr., Arizona legislator, $23,000, Malta; Kingdon Gould, Jr., business executive, $22,000, Luxembourg; and J. William Middendorf II, stockbroker, $15,000, the Netherlands. From Associated Press news story appearing in the *San Francisco Chronicle* (June 20, 1971).

Page 142: The anti-Humphrey commercial and other 1968 media tricks and strategies are reported in Joe McGinniss (37).

Page 143: The statistics on composition of the House and Senate are taken from *The Statistical Abstract of the United States 1972.*

The social and economic backgrounds of United States congressmen have been studied by Donald Matthews, *U.S. Senators and Their World* (Chapel Hill, N.C.: Univ. of North Carolina Press, 1960). See also Lewis Anthony Dexter, *The Sociology and Politics of Congress* (Chicago: Rand McNally, 1969).

Page 144: The Dirksen quotation was reported in an article by Stewart Alsop, *Newsweek* (April 6, 1970).

Page 145: The source for Table 4.1 is the *Congressional Directory, 92nd Congress* (Washington, D.C.: Government Printing Office, 1972).

Page 146: For example, see the Nixon speech given on September 3, 1972, reported by the press one day later. In his speech, Nixon attacked George McGovern as a man who would challenge our (Nixon's?) values and weaken the work ethic.

Page 149: The image-tending theatrical presidency is discussed in Thomas E. Cronin, "On the Presidency as Pressagentry," Dialogue Discussion Paper of the Center for the Study of Democratic Institutions (November 9, 1972).

Page 150: The Kleindienst statement was made before a joint session of three Senate subcommittees, April 10, 1973.

The Cronin quotation comes from Thomas Cronin, "The Swelling of the Presidency," *Saturday Review of the Society* (February, 1973).

Page 151: The Henning statement was reported in the *San Francisco Chronicle* (March 8, 1973).

Page 152: Statistics on the size of the military establishment and its propaganda activities are taken from Adam Yarmolinsky (39), Chapters 2–7 and 13.

Page 154: The *Fail Safe* and *Green Berets* incidents are reported in Yarmolinsky (39), p. 201.

Page 155: Sources for Table 4.2 are: *Congressional Record* (March 24, 1969, p. S3074), and Seymour Melman, *Pentagon Capitalism* (New York: McGraw-Hill, 1970, pp. 77–78).

Page 158: Details on the nuclear plane fiasco can be found in Herbert York, *Race to Oblivion* (New York: Simon and Schuster, 1970).

Page 159: The Cheyenne helicopter project was officially scrapped in 1972. Additional cost figures can be found in the *San Francisco Chronicle* (September 3, 1972).

Page 160: The assault ship figures and other arms figures on this page are taken from *Newsweek* (May 1, 1972). Falsification of technological data is reported in an excellent case history included in Heilbroner *et al.*, (23), Chapter 1.

Chapter 5

Page 164: Dahl's three criteria for authority are outlined in detail in Robert Dahl (42), Section 1.

The Hardin quotation comes from Garrett Hardin (15), p. 186.

Page 169: The Gallup Poll taken in the summer of 1973 also revealed that 74 percent of those polled believed that state laws should be passed requiring disclosure of campaign contributions of more than $100. As would be expected, only 44 percent of the Republicans thought public financing of campaigns would be a good idea, whereas 64 percent of the Democrats thought so.

Page 170:   The Vesco contribution, in the form of $100 bills contained in a black attaché case, was turned over to Maurice Stans, President Nixon's finance chairman, on April 10, 1972. In addition, the Nixon campaign committee directly violated federal law in soliciting campaign contributions from corporations, including $55,000 from American Airlines, $40,000 from Goodyear Tire and Rubber Company, and $100,000 each from the Phillips and Gulf Oil companies. Each corporation, especially Phillips and Gulf Oil, had important reasons for retaining the favor of government officials. It has also been reported that the Nixon fund raisers applied a quota system of 1 percent of personal worth or 1 percent of a company's sales in deciding how much should be contributed to the Nixon cause (*San Francisco Chronicle*, July 9, 1973).

Page 171:   The *Los Angeles Times* survey was taken in the summer of 1973; its findings were published in the *San Francisco Chronicle* (June 22, 1973) and in the *Los Angeles Times* (June 21, 1973).

The Common Cause figures come from *Operation Open Up the System* (Washington, D.C.: Common Cause, 1972), p. 27.

Page 172:   Common Cause figures come from *ibid.*, p. 28.

More detail on Tugwell's concept of the "Watchkeeper" can be found in Rexford Tugwell (46), pp. 63–64.

Page 174:   Tugwell's conception of the planning branch is outlined in Rexford Tugwell (46), pp. 52–56.

Perhaps the projection methods used in the fifty-year plan could be similar to those developed by the Educational Policy Research Center of Stanford Research Institute. The group uses the concept of alternative futures in constructing futures "trees" to pinpoint critical decision-making points in America's future. See *Projecting Whole-Body Future Patterns: The Field Anomaly Relaxation Method* (Menlo Park, Calif.: Educational Research Center, 1971).

Page 177:   Information on Holling's work is from a personal communication with him.

Page 180:   The figures on closed committee meetings come from *Operation Open Up the System* (Washington, D.C.: Common Cause, 1972), pp. 11–14.

Page 181:   The cost estimate for keeping secret documents in order was made by the General Accounting Office in 1972. Other government officials familiar with the system of classification have commented that these figures are much too low. See "The Cost of U.S. Secret-Keeping," *San Francisco Chronicle* (January 24, 1972).

Page 182:   It is difficult to claim that there is freedom of the press in the United States as long as newsmen are jailed for refusing to divulge sources of confidential information. In 1972, for example, newsman Peter Bridge was jailed for twenty-two days for refusing to answer grand jury questions about the sources used for a story he wrote. Strong laws must be passed to keep such inquisitions from becoming standard practice. In addition, the Nixon administration attacks on the media have been extremely unhealthy for a democracy. The media have repeatedly been attacked for publishing inaccurate and distorted information, when, in reality, the record shows that it has been the Nixon administration that has most often released distorted information or engaged in outright falsehoods. In an infamous attack on the media in his October 26, 1973, news conference, President Nixon claimed that press reports about him had been "outrageous, vicious, distorted . . . frantic, hysterical" (*Newsweek*, November 5, 1973), but neither he nor his office offered a single documented case to support the claim.

Chapter 6

Page 189:   The pioneering work in attitude change under social pressure was written by Solomon E. Asch. See his "Opinions and Social Pressure," reprinted in Elliott Aronson, ed., *The Social Animal* (San Francisco: W. H. Freeman and Company, 1973), and references cited therein.

An example of the media's refusal to handle sensitive issues was provided by the failure of all three networks to *sell* one hour of prime time to the Population Commission in 1972. The Commission had offered to buy one hour of time to present its findings to the American people, but all the networks refused to sell the time because the issue was too controversial.

The average yearly costs of operating a television station are $650,000, according to Clay Whitehead. This figure is mentioned in his speech, included in Appendix II of Barrett (48). See also Chapter 4 of the same source.

Page 190: The literacy statistics come from *Statistical Abstract of the United States, 1971.*

The California State Board of Education spent a great deal of time and taxpayers' money in 1972 and 1973 debating the issue of teaching the Biblical version of Creation in public schools. They finally decided that, despite scientific evidence to the contrary, the Biblical version of Creation should receive "equal time" with the theory of evolution in the state's schools.

This quotation comes from Ivan Illich, *Deschooling Society* (New York: Harper and Row, 1972), p. 113. This book is highly recommended reading on education from a third-world perspective.

Page 192: The fact that Soviet children display these character traits should not be taken to mean that adults have yet been so affected. Changing these patterns of behavior will require an effort that spans many generations.

The Bronfenbrenner quotation comes from (49), p. 156.

Page 194: The idea of executive sabbaticals is becoming a topic acceptable for discussion in the American business world as both executives and corporations come to realize its potential value. See, for example, "A Sabbatical for the Executive," *The New York Times* (September 23, 1973).

Page 195: In 1973 a panel of the now defunct President's Science Advisory Committee published a report suggesting the need to involve college students with people in other age categories. The report also suggested other radical measures, such as educational vouchers, to achieve a complete restructuring of educational opportunities. The report is entitled, *Youth: Transition to Adulthood,* and is available from the Government Printing Office.

Page 197: The memoranda and comments were published in *Science* (July 20, 1973).

Page 200: This statistic and others are found in Barrett (48), Chapter 1.

Page 201:   The description of the United Nations debate appears in Fred W. Friendly, *Due to Circumstances beyond Our Control* (New York: Random House, 1967), p. 165.

The Whitehead quotations are taken from a speech delivered to the International Radio and Television Society, New York City, October 6, 1971. Speaking before a Senate committee in February, 1972, Whitehead went so far as to question whether public affairs and news commentary should even be carried on public television.

Page 202:   The "popcorn" quotation comes from Friendly, *op. cit.*, p. 274.

When specials are aired during prime time, all the competing programs show increases in ratings, which then linger on during following weeks. For this reason, networks are hesitant to air specials, even though they usually attract large but specialized audiences. See Barrett (48), pp. 8–11. The size of network news audiences has remained fairly constant over the last few years and will undoubtedly show an increase for 1973 as a result of the Watergate Affair.

In 1972 Congress appropriated $155 million for public television, to be spent over two years. President Nixon vetoed the bill and agreed to spend only $45 million for one year. The Corporation for Public Broadcasting, dominated by Nixon appointees, suddenly became very interested in the political content of public affairs programs shown on public television.

Page 203:   The Cirino quotation is taken from (50), p. 2.

A further example of direct station censorship came to light in August, 1973, when 184 CBS affiliates refused to show an antiwar play offered by that network. In the same month a smaller number of stations, including those owned by Catholic and Mormon interests, refused to air the "Maude" show because it dealt with the subject of abortion.

The Vanocur article appeared in *Esquire* (January, 1972).

Page 204:   For information concerning the absence of British government interference in the BBC, see Richard Rose, *Politics in England* (Boston: Little, Brown, 1968), p. 177.

Page 205:   Ideally, commercials could be removed from television altogether. It is symptomatic of the commercialization of industrial society that television was originally conceived as an advertising media. Little thought has been given to alternate paths for media development, including the elimination of commercials.

The Federal Trade Commission has recently taken steps to limit advertising directed at children. For example, bans have been placed on the use of premiums and on the use of characters, live or animated, to encourage children to buy or to ask their parents for items. It would be much more sensible to do away with kiddy advertising altogether, but nearly one-half billion dollars annually is invested in it.

Page 207:   Many of the points made here are elaborated in Carl Kaysen, "Government and Scientific Responsibility," *The Public Interest* (Summer, 1971); J. D. Caroll, "Participatory Technology," *Science* (February 19, 1971); and M. S. Baram, "Social Control of Science and Technology," *Science* (May 7, 1971). See also Dennis Pirages, "The Unbalanced Revolution," in Nicholas Steneck, ed., *Science and Society* (Ann Arbor: Univ. of Michigan Press, 1974); Michael Baram, "Technology Assessment and Social Control," *Science* (May 4, 1973); and Martin Brown, ed., *The Social Responsibility of the Scientist* (New York: The Free Press, 1971).

Page 209:   Another example of the extent to which professional societies look after their own interests is offered by the Massachusetts Medical Society, which moved to censure John Knowles in June, 1972, because he made a statement that 30 to 40 percent of American doctors are making a killing in their practice of medicine. This was reported in the *San Francisco Chronicle* (June 5, 1972).

Page 210:   The President of the National Academy of Sciences is Philip Handler, a biochemist who at one time was a director of a drug company. The quality of his thought on ecological matters can be gleaned from his statement (*Science* 171:148), "The predicted death or blinding by parathion of dozens of Americans last summer must rest on the consciences of every car owner whose bumper sticker urged a total ban on DDT." It is a pity that Handler's apparent ignorance of ecology made it impossible for him to evaluate pesticide risks not associated with acute toxicity.

The ecologist from Cornell was La Mont C. Cole, who, in addition to making fine contributions to the technical literature on ecology, has been a pioneer in educating the public on the environment. See, for instance, his article, "The Ecosphere," *Scientific American* (April, 1958), reprinted in

Paul R. Ehrlich, John P. Holdren, and Richard W. Holm, *Man and the Ecosphere* (San Francisco: W. H. Freeman and Company, 1971).

Lewontin's statement can be found in "Why I Resigned from the National Academy of Sciences," *Science for the People* (September, 1971).

Page 211: The definition of participatory technology comes from J. D. Carroll, "Participatory Technology," *Science* (February 19, 1971).

Page 213: For additional information on technology assessment, see *Technology: Processes of Assessment and Choice* (Washington, D.C.: Report of the National Academy of Sciences, July, 1969), and *A Study of Technology Assessment* (Washington, D.C.: Report of the House Committee on Public Engineering Policy, July, 1969).

See Meadows (11) concerning references to *The Limits to Growth*.

An adversary type of science is suggested in Dean Abrahamson and Donald Geesaman, "Forensic Science: A Proposal," *Science and Public Affairs* (March, 1973).

Page 215: These themes are covered in more detail in Dennis Pirages, "Behavioral Technology and Institutional Transformation," in Harvey Wheeler, ed., *Beyond the Punitive Society* (San Francisco: W. H. Freeman and Company, 1973).

Chapter 7

Page 216: In the late eighteenth and early nineteenth centuries, when the United States was being run by Bostonians and Virginia planters, the American people had a relatively cosmopolitan outlook. There was to be a hiatus of approximately a century before the international outlook of men like Jefferson and Franklin reappeared.

Page 217: An excellent source for such dependency statistics is Nazli Choucri, "Population, Resources, Technology: Political Implications of the Environment Crisis," *International Organization* (Spring, 1972). These figures are taken from Appendix C.

Comparative Soviet-American resource statistics can be found in Raymond

Ewell, "U.S. Will Lag U.S.S.R. in Raw Materials," *Chemical and Engineering News* (August 24, 1970).

Page 221: Statistics on military expenditures are taken from *World Military Expenditures 1971* (Washington, D.C.: United States Arms Control and Disarmament Agency, 1972). Different sources list spending as being as much as $1 billion or $2 billion less. By 1973 military spending had declined slightly.

The United Nations statistics are taken from *Economic and Social Consequences of the Arms Race and of Military Expenditures* (New York: The United Nations, 1972).

These prices for procuring and operating weapons were published in the *San Francisco Chronicle* (September 3, 1972). The price tag for the new battle tank was outlined in the *San Francisco Chronicle* (July 5, 1973). Other figures for weapons procurement are from "Soaring Defense Costs . . . Blame It on the System," *The New York Times* (April 1, 1973).

Page 222: These world military expenditure figures are taken from *Economic and Social Consequences of the Arms Race and Military Expenditures* (New York: The United Nations, 1972). They differ slightly from the figures of the United States Arms Control and Disarmament Agency and from those given in Falk (59). In computing its figures, the United Nations makes no effort to hold prices constant, and therefore its figures are somewhat distorted by the effects of inflation.

The literature on neo-imperialism is voluminous. Perhaps the best way to become acquainted with it is to begin with Greene (60) and Julien (61), always keeping in mind their biases.

The Fulbright speech was given before the Senate on May 21, 1973.

Page 223: The gross national product figures in the middle of this page are taken from Angelos Angelopoulos, *The Third World and the Rich Countries: Prospects for the Year 2000* (New York: Praeger, 1972).

Figures at the bottom of the page were taken from Angelopoulos and Bhagwati (56), Chapters 1 and 2.

Page 224: Statistics on LDC contribution to global GNP are found in Angelopoulos, *op cit.*, pp. 20–25.

Agriculture and foreign aid figures on this page are taken from *United Nations Statistical Yearbook 1970* (New York: The United Nations, 1971).

Page 225: During 1973 the world oil situation steadily worsened. In March, OPEC members called for higher prices to compensate for the devaluation of the dollar. In April, Saudi Arabia linked production increases to a change in United States foreign policy. By October, the Arab-Israeli war had led Arab nations to cut back their oil exports, and Saudi Arabia stopped exporting oil to the United States. Later in the same month Venezuela increased the tax on exported oil by 56 percent.

The Associated Press reported on May 27, 1973, that the United States was preparing to sell Saudi Arabia and Kuwait $1 billion worth of weapons. In the early 1970s Iran received more than $2 billion worth of American arms.

Pages 226–227: Basic data for Table 7.1 have been derived from *World Energy Supplies 1961–70*, Series J, No. 15 (New York: The United Nations, 1973).

Page 228: More information on Western Europe's energy problems may be found in Walter Levy, "Oil Power," *Foreign Affairs* (July, 1971). See also Dennis Pirages, "Global Resources and the Future of Europe," in James Kuhlman and Louis Mensonides, eds., *The Future of European Integration* (1974, in press).

Page 229: Figure 7.1 is taken from Daniel Luten, "The Economic Geography of Energy," *Scientific American* (September, 1971).

Page 230: Alternatives to the never-to-be-developed theme are spelled out in greater detail in Paul R. Ehrlich and Richard L. Harriman, *How to Be a Survivor* (New York: Ballantine Books, 1971).

Data on one-crop economies are from Thomas Weisskopf, "Capitalism, Underdevelopment and the Future of the Poor Countries," in Bhagwati (56). Data on the LDCs' diminishing share of world trade are from Angelos Angelopoulos, *The Third World and the Rich Countries: Prospects for the Year 2000* (New York: Praeger, 1972), pp. 75–79.

Page 231: The flow of world protein is discussed in Borgstrom (2), p. 321.

Statistics on consumption of commodities in the Netherlands are taken from Paul R. Ehrlich and John P. Holdren, "Impact of Population Growth," *Science* 171:1212–1217 (March 26, 1971). Statistics on energy consumption are taken from *World Energy Supplies 1960–69*, Series J, No. 14 (New York: The United Nations, 1972).

United States consumption figures are found in Nazli Choucri, "Population, Resources, Technology: Political Implications of the Environment Crisis," *International Organization* (Spring, 1972).

Page 232: More information on the impact of an industrialized China may be found in Dennis Pirages and Paul Ehrlich, "If All Chinese Had Wheels," *The New York Times* (March 16, 1972). All figures in this article were derived from United Nations sources.

Page 233: These "catch-up" figures are taken from Ehrlich and Ehrlich (5), pp. 72–73.

History has a way of moving quicker than expected. The press reported in October, 1973, that a NATO minister had warned the Arab countries that cutting off petroleum supplies would be tantamount to an act of aggression.

Page 234: This debt repayment figure is taken from Angelos Angelopoulos, *op cit.*, pp. 119–121. From a different perspective, Thomas Weisskopf claims that total debt servicing and investment income payments total more than one-quarter of export earnings in the seven more dependent LDCs. See Thomas Weisskopf, "Capitalism, Underdevelopment, and the Poor Countries," in Bhagwati (56).

Page 235: This quotation is taken from Barnet (55), p. 152.

Page 236: Aid and equipment sales figures are taken from Greene (60), p. 128.

The quotation concerning overseas commodity sales is taken from James O'Conner, "The Meaning of Economic Imperialism," in K. T. Fann and Donald Hodges, eds., *Readings in U.S. Imperialism* (Boston: Porter Sargent, 1971), p. 48.

The data concerning *Fortune* magazine's top 500 is noted in Richard Barnet (55), p. 147. Raymond Vernon's book (65) is an excellent source for additional data on the multinational corporation.

Figures on United States foreign investment are from Barnet (55), p. 146. See also Weisskopf in Bhagwati (56).

Page 238:   For greater detail on the decline of the whaling industry, see Ehrlich and Ehrlich (5), pp. 125–131. A mathematical treatment of the effects on a common resource of the high discount rates adopted by private firms is given by Colin W. Clark in "The Economics of Overexploitation," *Science* 181:630–634 (August 17, 1973). He uses the whale fisheries as an example.

The question of the effects of contrails on the oceans was brought up by meteorologist Reid Bryson of the University of Wisconsin (personal communication).

Page 240:   The Laird statement was reported in the *San Francisco Chronicle* (December 30, 1972). It is also interesting to note the pride with which President Nixon reported to the press that he had taken a "tough" line with the Soviets in averting a Middle East confrontation. As the President phrased it in October, 1973, he and Mr. Brezhnev "knew each other." Perhaps these two leaders are much more similar in the way they approach the world's problems than those who are interested in enduring peace would like to believe.

Page 245:   The Rajaratnorm quotation is taken from Gunnar Myrdal, *The Challenge of World Poverty: A World Poverty Program in Outline* (New York: Pantheon, 1970), p. 229.

Page 249:   Unfortunately, the mineral industry in the United States is opposed to any treaties limiting freedom to exploit the sea. See "Ocean Technology: Race to Seabed Wealth Disturbs More than Fish," *Science* (May 25, 1973).

Page 251:   For more detail on the Urban Coalition's budgetary suggestions, see Robert Benson and Harold Wolman, eds., *Counterbudget* (New York: Praeger, 1971).

Page 252: The I. F. Stone quotation is taken from *I. F. Stone's Bi-Weekly* (October 4, 1971).

United Nations budget figures are taken from *Time* (December 4, 1972).

Chapter 8

Page 256: A complete and scholarly treatment of the blood market is found in Richard Titmuss, *The Gift Relationship* (New York: Random House, 1971).

Page 257: These walled cities, which resemble medieval castles, are springing up in suburbs throughout the country. A brief rundown of some of the major projects is found in *Newsweek* (September 25, 1972). These projects isolate the wealthy homeowner from the lower classes and minority groups that cannot afford to move into such areas. The guards at the gates guarantee that the poor will not even be able to drive on the streets and thus bother the residents.

Page 258: The story about the San Jose pet hospital was carried by the Associated Press (March 3, 1971).

Information on pet cemeteries is taken from the *San Francisco Chronicle* (January 21, 1973).

Page 259: The public opinion data on future personal and social expectations are taken from Albert Cantril and Charles Roll, *Hopes and Fears of the American People* (New York: Universe Books, 1971), pp. 29–30.

These and other projected future costs of energy can be found in Earl Cook, "Resource Limits to Economic Growth," paper presented to meeting of the National Association of Manufacturers, New Orleans, November 16, 1972.

The Oakland shooting was reported in the *San Francisco Chronicle* (May 27, 1973).

Page 260: The future prices of food represent our estimates, based on the Department of Agriculture's figures for a sixty-five-item basket of food, published in *Newsweek* (April 10, 1972), and the rate of inflation in prices of agricultural commodities for the first nine months of 1973.

Page 261: The 2,000 phone calls were reported in the *San Francisco Chronicle* (February 11, 1973).

In London the practice of exacting ransom for the right to buy property is known as "gazumping." See *Newsweek* (July 31, 1972) for more examples of real estate speculation.

A detailed examination of the private benefits and largesse passed out by the federal government is found in Charles Reich, "The New Property," *Yale Law Journal* (April, 1964).

Details on government giveaways can be found in Stewart Udall, *The Quiet Crisis* (New York: Holt, Rinehart and Winston, 1963), Chapter 5.

Page 262: The Pacific Gas and Electric figures were supplied by that company. The national figures are taken from *The Statistical Abstract of the United States 1972* (Washington, D.C.: Department of Commerce, 1973), p. 354.

Page 265: Costs of fighting crime are taken from *The Statistical Abstract of the United States 1972* (Washington, D.C.: Department of Commerce, 1973), p. 152.

Statistics on victimless crime are derived from figures in *The Statistical Abstract of the United States 1972* (Washington, D.C.: Department of Commerce, 1973), p. 148.

Figures from the California Bureau of Criminal Statistics were published in the *San Francisco Chronicle* (December 6, 1971).

Page 266: Statistics on the smoking of marijuana can be found in *Marijuana: A Signal of Misunderstanding*, First Report of the National Commission on Marijuana and Drug Abuse (Washington, D.C.: Government Printing Office, March, 1972). The report points out that 24 million Americans (including 40 percent of the college population) have tried marijuana and that 8.3 million are regular users.

Page 267: Social Darwinism in American literature is covered in Richard Weiss, *The American Myth of Success* (New York: Basic Books, 1969).

See Skinner (17), Chapter 3, for more perspective on his view of whether individuals deserve credit or blame for their behavior.

Page 268: Figures on the concentration of stock are found in Lundberg (24), Chapters 1–5. Stock ownership by thirteen families is documented on p. 211. It is fair to point out that this reference is dated, but there is no evidence that stock ownership has broadened since the early 1940s.

Page 269: The Nixon statement was contained in the message he made to Congress when vetoing the child-care legislation.

Unemployment and income statistics are from the Department of Commerce. At this writing the most readily available published statistics are for the year 1970. In that year, white family income averaged $10,216 and black family income averaged $6,278. This means that in 1970, black family income was 61.5 percent of white family income, a full 2.5 percent higher than in 1972. See *The Statistical Abstract of the United States 1972*, p. 326. See also Jon Nordheimer, "The Dream 1973: Blacks Move Painfully toward Full Equality," *The New York Times* (August 26, 1973), for additional statistics.

Page 270: The distribution of income figures comes from *The American Distribution of Income: A Structural Problem* (Washington, D.C.: Joint Economic Committee, 1972), p. 7.

Page 271: The problem of computing actual income differences in socialist (communist) societies is a very difficult one. Many more factors must be considered than the ones mentioned here. By far the best attempt to come to terms with this problem is found in P. J. D. Wiles and Stefan Markowski, "Income Distribution under Communism and Capitalism: Some Facts about Poland, the United Kingdom, the U.S.A. and the U.S.S.R.," *Soviet Studies* (January, April, 1971).

The lack of redistribution in the American tax system is discussed in detail in Lester C. Thurow, *The Impact of Taxes on the American Economy* (New York: Praeger, 1971), Chapter 4. See also *The American Distribution of Income: A Structural Problem*, pp. 4–5.

Page 272: Poverty-line figures come from Lee Rainwater, "Economic Inequality and the Credit Income Tax," *Working Papers for a New Society* (Spring, 1973).

Very briefly, a Gini index is a measure of the deviation of a distribution from equality. On a graph, if income were distributed equally across a population, a line drawn at a 45° angle would represent the relationship between the cumulative portion of families and the cumulative portion of income earned. This 45° line is equivalent to an index of .00. As incomes become more unequal, the line curves beneath 45° and the Gini coefficient increases. In practice, most industrialized countries have a Gini coefficient for income that varies between .35 and .50.

The Gini figures are taken from Sanford Rose, "The Truth about Income Inequality in the U.S.," *Fortune* (December, 1972).

The figure for the percentage of the population that receives incomes less than half the median is taken from Lee Rainwater, *op. cit.*

Page 273:   The mean income gap information is taken from *The American Distribution of Income: A Structural Problem, op. cit.*, p. 7.

Figures on "get along" incomes are taken from Lee Rainwater, *op. cit.* The public opinion study from which these figures come was the Boston Social Standards Survey, a study of 600 respondents in the Boston area.

Executive salaries for 1972 can be found in "Executive Compensation: Who Got Most in '72," *Business Week* (May 5, 1973).

Income tax figures for 1969 and 1970 were reported in the *San Francisco Chronicle* (March 29, 1971). They represent Treasury Department statistics originally released by Representative Henry Reuss of Wisconsin, who has been attempting to get legislation passed to close these loopholes. Additional information from the same source was reported in the *San Francisco Chronicle* (March 27, 1972).

Page 274:   The data from Ralph Nader's research group were released through the Washington Post News Service and published in the *San Francisco Chronicle* (August 30, 1972).

Page 275:   The ill-fated Family Assistance Plan (FAP) proposed by the Nixon administration during its first term was essentially a guaranteed income program. Its particular advantage was that it included a built-in incentive to work, thus defusing the objections of conservatives who are sure that guaranteed incomes will lead to dropping out on a massive scale.

The FAP originally was to provide a $1,600 income floor for a family of four, plus food stamps, public housing, Medicaid, and state benefits. The family could earn up to $720 without losing any of its $1,600. For every $2 earned above $720, $1 was subtracted from the $1,600. In this way, people on welfare who worked would be better off than those who did not. Unfortunately, the combined opposition of the conservatives and the Welfare Rights Organization (which apparently failed to understand that recipients would not lose their state benefits), plus election politics, killed the plan. In passing it should be noted that various studies on experimental guaranteed income plans have shown that people generally do not rush to stop working when there is no change in income (according to one study), even when the earned income is reduced by taxes. Those who did quit work usually did so to enroll in job training programs to qualify for better jobs. See James Welsh, "Welfare Reform: Born, Aug. 8, 1969; Died, Oct. 4, 1972," *The New York Times Magazine* (January 7, 1973), and Linda Greenhouse, "Nobody Rushed to Quit Work," *The New York Times* (September 2, 1973), for more information.

More detailed information on the credit tax can be found in Earl Rolph, "A Credit Income Tax," in Theodore Marmor, ed., *Poverty Policy* (Chicago: Aldine, 1971).

Page 276: The discussion on this page parallels that found in Lee Rainwater, *op. cit.*

Many of the points in this section have been expanded in detail in Warren Johnson, "The Guaranteed Income as an Environmental Measure," in Warren Johnson and John Hardesty, eds., *Economic Growth vs. the Environment* (Belmont, Calif.: Wadsworth, 1971).

Page 277: Welfare payment figures are for the year 1970. Additional state figures can be found in "Welfare: The Shame of a Nation," *Newsweek* (February 8, 1971). This article also points out that in Boston one in every five residents is on welfare; in New York, Baltimore, St. Louis, and San Francisco, one in every seven persons is on welfare. It seems that the guaranteed annual income would not represent a very great change in these cities.

Page 279: Conviviality and the convivial society are treated in much greater detail in Illich (68), Chapter 2.

Page 280:   Bruno Bettelheim, in *The Children of the Dream* (New York: Macmillan, 1969), and Larry and Joan Constantine, in *Group Marriage* (New York: Macmillan, 1973), treat the subjects of communal child rearing and new types of extended families in detail and in a scholarly manner.

Acknowledgments

First and foremost we wish to thank Anne H. Ehrlich, who has worked constantly with us on this project and has made contributions too numerous to list. Her help has been invaluable.

Many colleagues have read portions or all of the manuscript and have made numerous helpful suggestions. They, of course, do not necessarily agree with all the points we have made and share no responsibility for any errors. These individuals include:

D. L. Bilderback, Department of History, Fresno State College; Iris Brest, Attorney, Palo Alto, California; Thomas Cronin, Center for the Study of Democratic Institutions, Santa Barbara, California; Herman Daly, Department of Economics, Louisiana State University; Garrett Hardin, Department of Biology, University of California, Santa Barbara; John P. Holdren, Energy and Resources Program, University of California, Berkeley; Johnson C. Montgomery, Attorney, Palo Alto; James Morrison, Department of Political Science, University of Florida; William Ophuls, Department of Political Science, Yale University; Kenneth E. F. Watt, Department of Zoology, University of California, Davis.

The staff of the Falconer Biology Library has helped us immeasurably in locating and organizing the vast literature that is pertinent to today's problems. We also wish to thank Jane Lawson Bavelas, Ann Duffield, and Darryl Wheye, who have typed and proofread patiently the many drafts.

Also, many helpful suggestions were offered by the fellows at the Center for the Study of Democratic Institutions during a discussion of the manuscript. Especially useful were the comments offered by Rexford Tugwell, Harvey Wheeler, and Norton Ginsburg.

Index